WORK
— *AND* —
WELL-
BEING

WORK
—AND—
WELL-BEING

THE OCCUPATIONAL
SOCIAL WORK ADVANTAGE

Paul A. Kurzman
Sheila H. Akabas
Editors

NASW PRESS

National Association of Social Workers
Washington, DC
•
Barbara W. White, PhD, ACSW, *President*
Sheldon R. Goldstein, ACSW, LISW, *Executive Director*

Linda Beebe, Executive Editor
Nancy Winchester, Director of Editorial Services
Fran Pflieger, Senior Editor
Wendy Almeleh, Copy Editor
Robert Elwood, Indexer
Sue Harris, Proofreader

Cover and text designed by Naylor Design, Inc.
Text composed by Marsh & Associates
Type set in Janson and printed on Springhill Opaque
Printed and bound by Boyd Printing Company

Library of Congress Cataloging-in-Publication Data

Work and well-being : the occupational social work advantage / Paul A.
  Kurzman and Sheila H. Akabas, editors.
        p.   cm.
  Includes bibliographical references and index.
  ISBN 0-87101-228-6
  1. Welfare work in industry--United States.   2. Employee
assistance programs--United States.   I. Kurzman, Paul A.
II. Akabas, Sheila H., 1931–
HD7654.W67   1993
331.25--dc20   93-4797
                                                   CIP

Printed in the United States of America

 3

To the memory of our parents
Eleanor Hess Kurzman and Harold Philip Kurzman
and
Lillian Lefrak Epstein and Louis Arnold Epstein
who lovingly taught us the meaning of work

and to our families
Margaret, Katherine, Saïd, and David
and
Aaron, Myles, Sharon, Seth, Meg, Miriam, and David
who continue to support us in our commitment
to workers and work organizations

Contents

PART 4: MANAGEMENT AND POLICY INITIATIVES

Preface

These are times that seem to involve an accelerated rate of change in our environment. Some of those changes are welcome. In comparison with the past 12 years, Americans appear to be turning toward a more benevolent national government that accepts responsibility for meeting the basic needs of some of the more fragile members of our society. American business has followed suit and determined that its greatest asset is its human resources. But it understands that the full worth of that asset depends on maximizing the commitment and productivity of the work force. This understanding causes something of a dilemma for managers. At the same time that they recognize the need for a caring work environment, the world of work is focused on leaner organizational behavior. Often leaner has also meant meaner—fewer benefits, less job security, less opportunity for advancement—in short, less of most of what we have come to count on from the workplace.

Although no one can applaud these new, disconcerting pressures, they hold some promise for professionals who seek to practice occupational social work. This is the message that we have tried to carry throughout this volume. A combination of circumstances and practice developments have made occupational social work an expanding professional arena. We have invited the authors to consider how the prospective changes in the world of work are related to social work practice in their arenas of specialization. Each has illuminated the issues in her or his own way. But for each, the bottom line is services that are responsive to the needs of both individuals and organizational sponsors, whether they are direct counseling, a response to substance abuse, the design of employee assistance programs, the provision of disability management, or any of the other micro- and macrointerventions that are considered in this volume.

The authors of the chapters have been devoted in meeting the requests that the editors have made, and we are grateful to them for their cooperation. It is our hope that the final product compensates for the sequential demands we made on so many of them. Our students have been an ongoing inspiration. The field settings that have participated in their education have participated in ours as well. The many practitioners who have worked at the boundaries of occupational social work have helped train a new generation of social workers in creativity and risk taking in the interests of policy development and service delivery. This book would have little to report were it not for their experimentation. We are deeply grateful, as well, to Executive Editor Linda Beebe, Editorial Services Director Nancy Winchester, and Senior Editor Fran Pflieger of the NASW Press, for their encouragement, support, and patience. They have believed in this volume throughout its long incubation. We also appreciate the skill of Wendy Almeleh in the final editing process.

Paul Kurzman wishes to recognize his debt to his colleagues in the world of work at Hunter College. In particular, he is grateful to Florence Vigilante for her many clinical and organizational insights and for her unwavering commitment to this field of practice. He also mourns the recent loss of his colleague, Rebecca Donovan, whose pioneering research with trade unions and with low-income women, in particular, is a legacy that will long be honored and remembered.

Sheila Akabas wants to acknowledge the special stimulation and support of a team of colleagues who have worked with her at the Columbia University's Center for Social Policy and Practice in the Workplace. Without them, she could not have hoped to have the exciting opportunities she has had to pursue rewarding research and program development ideas. She is particularly grateful for the unique partnership that she has developed with Lauren B. Gates, the center's research director for the past six years and her coauthor on many publications, including Chapter 13.

We have been inspired to develop this volume as a kind of progress report to the initial opportunity provided to us by the Lois and Samuel Silberman Fund over a decade ago to look at the then-incipient rumblings of a new arena for practice. Although we received no direct assistance from the fund for this book, we regard the fund as having been influential in the book's accomplishment, having started us on this road. Occupational social work today is a nationally established field of practice, supported by recognized curricular specializations at many graduate schools of social work around the country. We hope that the many professionals who are interested in this field will find this book useful in support of their courses, field practicums, and post-master's programs of continuing education.

We have both contributed equally to the preparation of this book. Our long professional association has been one of the happy circumstances of life for each of us. Because our earlier volume listed our names in alphabetical order, we have reversed the listing for this one. We both look forward to other opportunities to engage in the collaborative process.

May 1993

Paul A. Kurzman
Sheila H. Akabas

Introduction

Sheila H. Akabas

In 1890 the United States officially declared the frontier closed. Although the population would continue to grow and new settlements would be established, the parameters of the country were set, and from then on, Americans would inhabit this continent from coast to coast. A century later the same could be said for occupational social work. Heralded throughout previous decades as the frontier of social work, occupational social work had, by 1990, won widespread acceptance not only in work settings, but among social agencies of every ilk that identified their mission as reaching clients, influencing systems, or both. The world of work and its auspices—trade unions and employing organizations—have proved fertile ground for nurturing and expanding social work practice. The further growth of occupational social work, a likely trend, will involve more agencies, more professionals, more settings, and more and different interventions, but the relationship of social work to world-of-work issues is well accepted and widespread in its application.

Occupational social work deals with all the practice and policy issues that link social welfare to the world of work—from unemployment to stress on the job, from policies on fringe benefits to efforts to establish an inclusive, balanced work force, and from programs that are designed exclusively for employees at a specific work site to service delivery systems that are based on partnerships between the world of work and community resources to provide facilities for child- and elder care. Many would claim that occupational social work is the only new field of practice in social work since World War II.

The term *occupational social work*, itself, conveys the evolution and settlement of this field of practice. The field covers policies and practice targeted at workers, under the sponsoring auspices of trade unions and employers, that are available at the workplace or in the community, to individuals whose eligibility results from their status as workers or their dependent relationship to employees. Initially, it was called "industrial social work." The word *industrial* partly reflected the primary economic activity of the nation at the time and partly conveyed the prominence of the field in *industry*, that is, in the manufacturing sector that was ruled, largely, by collective bargaining agreements.

The world of work has changed noticeably from those early days, and the word *industrial* no longer can be applied to most workplaces. Today, fewer than 25 percent of all employed persons work in manufacturing, the home of "industrial" workers, and fewer than one worker in six is represented by a trade union (U.S. Bureau of the Census, 1992). The use of the term *occupational* is an attempt to be relevant in the present. It has been adopted here with a nostalgic look back to the editors' earlier works and terminology (Kurzman & Akabas, 1981).

In fact, this volume represents the editors' second foray into this subject matter. A comparison of the two helps clarify the evolution that has occurred. In 1982, *Work, Workers, and Work Organizations: A View from Social Work* (Akabas & Kurzman) conveyed a theoretical picture of the coincidence between social work objectives and professional activity in labor and man-agement settings. It suggested what might be possible if practitioners turned their attention to policy and the delivery of service within the world of work. This volume combines theory with practice and reviews the state of the field. It projects a futurist agenda based on actual experience and research findings. In the interim, some significant features have been identified that character-ize the field. As this book begins, it seems appropriate to consider the history of this evolution; the distinguishing qualities of occupational social work; and what the fit, between it and expected trends in society, suggests about its future path of development.

A Historical Overview

The close connection between work and well-being has been clear to social workers from the outset of the profession. Early charity workers recognized that the families they served were plagued by the lack of jobs or low-paying employment, so that the health and welfare of family members required financial assistance from the community (Popple, 1981). But work provides much more than subsistence. It helps define a person's status, provides satisfaction and a sense of self-worth, is a milieu in which social interactions and friendships develop, offers an activity around which to organize one's time (Perlman, 1982); and, for adolescents, is an important step toward independence (Chestang, 1982; Vailliant, 1978). The many functions that work serves help to reaffirm Sigmund Freud's often-quoted statement that the ability to work is one of the two hallmarks of adulthood (the other being the ability to love).

With work so significant to human development and functioning, it is not surprising that social workers have had a long-term interest in the world of work. For example, Jane Addams, director of Hull-House, an early settlement house, is given credit, historically, for settling a long-term strike in the men's clothing industry by visiting one of the owners of Hart, Schaffner and Marx and pointing out the extreme deprivation experienced by families of the industry's workers (Germain & Hartman, 1980). Bertha Reynolds (1951/1975), a radical social work theorist and the then-revered associate dean of Smith College School of Social Work, directed an extensive social work service for merchant seamen during World War II. Her belief that social work should take place in the natural life space of clients is a guiding principle for occupational social work, and her interpretation of that principle has been an inspiration to social workers since she formulated it.

Despite these early activities, in the mid-1960s, Wilensky and Lebeaux (1965) still considered industrial social work a frontier in continuing need of settlement, noting that social work's relationship to the world of work was erratic, never seeming to have gained a secure foothold. But during the 1960s, social work emerged from a period of introspection to pursue its dual interest in dealing with both person and environment to obtain a better fit (Caplan, Cobb, French, Harrison, & Pinneau, 1976). The world of work presented a natural arena for considering the possibilities of such initiatives. At the same time, the unions' long-standing hostility to social workers abated as more psychologically sophisticated labor leaders identified the many ways in which counseling could assist members to resolve substance abuse and other presenting problems (Perlis, 1977). Furthermore, unions began to look for new means of securing the loyalty of their members, and some decided that the road to such loyalty might be paved with the provision of social services.

Management also developed an interest in providing extensive services to employees. Starting with World War II, when wage increases were barred in an attempt to control inflation and employers created fringe benefits to increase the compensation for their workers, management has been a major provider of health insurance and health care to employees and their families. As part of this development, employers began to view social workers as valued allies in the delivery of mental health services (Wagner, 1967). It is estimated that over 10,000 work organizations have employee assistance programs (EAPs) or their parallel, union-sponsored membership assistance programs (MAPs), with social workers as the prime professional providers of services. In addition, the gurus of management organization began telling Americans that the road to productivity is paved with the concern for the needs of workers (Ouchi, 1981; Peters & Waterman, 1982). Attentiveness has taken the form of programs of information and referral for child care, elder care, and substance abuse; efforts to help workers meet the demands of shift work; and policy initiatives to soften the insecurity of employment in an era of corporate mergers and downsizing. All these activities are part of an appropriate agenda for social work attention. Most recently, work organizations' interest in managing a diverse work force and recognition of the importance of responding to the needs of the most vulnerable workers—single working mothers, those serving in the military, workers responsible for the care of fragile elderly relatives, recovering substance abusers, and workers with disabilities—has increased the arena for social work action in the workplace. Thus, it is not surprising that the representatives of auspices in the world of work redefined social work as a profession that is relevant to their primary interests.

In parallel, social workers recognized that the functional community of work is as appropriate a target as any other functional or geographic community. Some social workers were hired by unions and employers, and much broader channels developed between social agencies and the world of work. Community resources received referrals of clients from occupational social workers. Community agencies began to offer services to work settings—not only EAP contracts, but an array of programs to meet other needs, such as work-focused treatment, stress-management training, counseling for families of cancer patients, and referrals for child- and elder care. Social agencies that are involved in vocational rehabilitation, the employment of youths, community mental health care, and related issues have received financial support and received greater acceptance from corporations and unions. Policy alliances between social work interests and those of labor and management have also been formed. Often, an employer who offers EAP services is likely to support legislation like family leave or funding for local child care services. The policy interests of unions are often even more closely associated with a social work agenda.

Distinguishing Features of Occupational Social Work

Today, 110 million Americans spend the better part of their waking hours in the world of work. They are more diverse by gender, national origin, race, sexual orientation, and any other variable that characterizes a working population than ever before. And the rewards they receive are equally diverse. Some labor for long hours eking out a subsistence little better than that of their ancestors of many generations ago. Others, much fewer, appear to have caught the golden ring, particularly during the heyday of supply-side economics. The specific occupations people choose can determine who their friends are; what neighborhoods they live in; which schools their children attend; and what, if any, health care coverage is available to their dependents (Akabas, 1984, 1990). Perhaps more important, their choice of occupation and the jobs they find may decide whether they will be protected by a union contract and experience a preventive, supportive work environment or one dominated by stressful circumstances and unhealthy experiences (Stellman & Daum, 1973). Numerous studies have shown that reaching people through their work connections increases their ego strength (Strauss, 1951), empowers them to make choices for themselves, and equalizes the roles and responsibilities of professional and client (or, in the case of union-directed MAPs, subordinates the former because the social worker is actually the "employee" of the member–client). For the assertive professional, true organizational change is a potential outcome, making the work environment better for all.

Legislation has assumed a major role in that connection. A steady stream of laws dealing with equal employment opportunities, including Title VII of the Civil Rights Act of 1963, the Age Discrimination in Employment Act of 1967, and the Americans with Disabilities Act of 1990, have influenced the nature of the work force. From the Hughes Act of 1970, which established two occupational alcoholism advisers in each state, to the Drug-free Workplace Act of 1988, federal attention has been focused on the world of work as a site for dealing with substance abuse. Conditions of employment are established, in part, by such laws as the Occupational Safety and Health Act; pensions are protected by the Employment Retirement Income Security Act; and most income-support entitlements resulting from the work connection are provided for in the Social Security Act.

Methods of practice and service delivery systems, themselves, have been influenced by the work connection. Presenting problems in the world of work often are defined in relation to the clients' ability to maintain a work role. It is not surprising, therefore, that attention to functional performance, achieved through planned, short-term intervention, has been a preferred model of care. Peer-group support, mutual aid, and supervisory consultation are modalities that have met the dual demands of good-quality care and cost containment, which are regarded as the criteria for service delivery systems in the workplace or those that are targeted at employees. Prevention and early intervention have been heralded as appropriate and feasible goals for practice with a population that has universal access to services.

Change and the Response

As is apparent throughout this book, the world of work is experiencing significant changes that have already had or promise to have a significant impact on its relationship to occupational social work. These changes include the following:

- competition in a global economy that has made American industry "leaner and meaner" and has resulted in increased unemployment and pressure to reduce benefits and to contain the costs for those who remain

- the increasing diversity of the labor force, which reflects high rates of immigration; proportionately higher birthrates among Americans of color; and economic pressure that, along with their own interest, pulls women into the labor market and may keep older workers in it later in their lives

- technological changes that limit the low-skill jobs available and place a premium on education, training, and retraining during the time a person is in the labor force, increasing the "investment" that employers have in their "knowledge" workers

- skyrocketing health care costs that have exerted financial pressure on all service delivery systems to contain costs, sometimes losing sight of the importance of high-quality care

- severe pressure on the trade union movement from the combination of the extensive reduction of jobs in its customary blue-collar turf, 12 years of pressure from a politically unfriendly administration, the inability to protect benefits in the highly competitive environment, and its lack of responsiveness to the changing composition of the labor force and the nature of work.

Most of these changes increase the challenges faced by occupational social workers. Challenge is not a new experience for occupational social work. The positive tone of this introduction should not conceal the history of ideological struggle that the profession has undergone in accepting the world of work as an appropriate arena for practice or its auspices as appropriate partners for the profession (Akabas, 1983). There is concern that social workers may be co-opted by the mission and goals of their corporate employers (Bakalinsky, 1980). The needs of those in poverty are so compelling that some believe that all the profession's energy should be focused in that direction. Still others question whether the professional image can be changed sufficiently for social workers to exert any real influence in the world of work (Fleming, 1979).

These issues are subjects of debate but have not deterred occupational social workers from pursuing service to individuals, families, groups, systems, and communities in a way that has proved effective, cost beneficial, and promising. If this is a field of practice with more than the average number of challenges, it is also one that offers more than the usual opportunities for influence. The profession of social work, the editors believe, will be shaped measurably by the new ideas, techniques, and outcomes that emerge from occupational social work practice.

References

Akabas, S. H. (1983). Industrial social work: Influencing the system at the workplace. In M. Dinerman (Ed.), *Social work in a turbulent world* (pp. 131–141). Silver Spring, MD: National Association of Social Workers.

Akabas, S. H. (1984, September–October). Workers are parents, too. *Child Welfare, 43,* 387–399.

Akabas, S. H. (1990). Essay: Reconciling the demands of work with the needs of families. *Families in Society, 71,* 366–371.

Akabas, S. H., & Kurzman, P. A. (Eds.). (1982). *Work, workers, and work organizations: A view from social work.* Englewood Cliffs, NJ: Prentice Hall.

Bakalinsky, R. (1980). People vs. profits: Social work in industry. *Social Work, 25,* 471–475.

Caplan, J. D., Cobb, S., French, J. P. R., Harrison, R. V., & Pinneau, S. R. (1976). *Job demands and worker health.* Washington, DC: U.S. Department of Health, Education, & Welfare.

Chestang, L. (1982). Work, personal change and human development. In S. H. Akabas & P. A. Kurzman (Eds.), *Work, workers, and work organizations: A view from social work* (pp. 61–89). Englewood Cliffs, NJ: Prentice Hall.

Fleming, C. W. (1979). Does social work have a future in industry? *Social Work, 24,* 183–185.

Germain, C. B., & Hartman, A. (1980). People and ideas in the history of social work practice. *Social Casework, 61,* 323–331.

Kurzman, P. A., & Akabas, S. H. (1981). Industrial social work as an arena for practice. *Social Work, 26,* 52–60.

Ouchi, W. (1981). *Theory Z: How American business can meet the Japanese challenge.* Reading, MA: Addison-Wesley.

Perlis, L. (1977). The human contract in the organized workplace. *Social Thought, 3,* 29–35.

Perlman, H. H. (1982). The client as worker. In S. H. Akabas & P. A. Kurzman (Eds.), *Work, workers, and work organizations: A view from social work* (pp. 90–116). Englewood Cliffs, NJ: Prentice Hall.

Peters, T. J., & Waterman, R. H., Jr. (1982). *In search of excellence: Lessons from America's best-run companies.* New York: Harper & Row.

Popple, P. R. (1981). Social work practice in business and industry, 1875–1930. *Social Service Review, 55,* 257–268.

Reynolds, B. C. (1975). *Social work and social living.* Washington, DC: National Association of Social Workers. (Original work published 1951)

Stellman, J. M., & Daum, S. M. (1973). *Work is dangerous to your health.* New York: Vintage Books.

Strauss, E. T. (1951). The caseworker deals with employment problems. *Social Casework, 32,* 388–392.

U.S. Bureau of the Census. (1992). *Statistical abstract of the United States, 1992* (112th ed.). Washington, DC: U.S. Government Printing Office.

Vailliant, G. E. (1978). *Adaptation to life.* Boston: Little, Brown.

Wagner, P. (1967). Psychiatry for everyman. *Psychiatry: Journal for the Study of Interpersonal Processes, 30,* 79–90.

Wilensky, H., & Lebeaux, C. (1965). *Industrial society and social welfare.* New York: Free Press.

PART 1

OVERVIEW

Introduction to Part 1

Occupational social work has been poised on the cusp of implementation for several decades. In the first part of this book, the gradual evolution of this field of practice and its subsequent institutionalization in recent years are brought into focus from a policy, practice, and research perspective.

What is different are the *auspices* of this field—trade unions and employing organizations—which are new, uncommon host settings for practice, for they are outside the social services arena and not part of the formal human services tradition. The catchment area becomes the workplace, and the focus is the needs of workers (or members) and the productivity (or fair practices) of work organizations. Labor and management's common agenda is geared toward a precious resource that one calls "their employees" and the other calls "their membership." Part 1 focuses on this terrain, on the symbiotic investment that labor and management share in "the work force," and how the social work profession is playing an increasing role in helping them to achieve many of their common objectives.

In Chapter 1, Michael L. Smith and Gary M. Gould discuss the evolution of this field of practice, making persuasive arguments for its recent growth, stability, and institutionalization. Occupational social work as an applied practice that was previously spoken of merely as "promising" has begun systematically to fulfill that promise. For example, that social work should have more to offer than industrial sociology, occupational nursing, alcoholism counseling, or industrial psychology is not by accident. It is a result of considerable planning, preparation, research, and education—a capital investment by schools of social work and the social work profession. The changing work force and dramatically transformed workplace have also contributed to labor and management's need for what social workers have to offer, which is fortunate serendipity and good timing. Moreover, once employing organizations reconceptualized their notion of investment to include *human* resources (as well as plant and materials), a need for what social work could offer was envisioned and a collaborative working relationship based on mutuality could be established.

In Chapter 2, Paul A. Kurzman writes about the arena in which occupational social workers are most thickly settled and active today. Employee assistance programs (EAPs) have become a natural home for practitioners, and the profession has established leadership in the EAP sphere in the past 10 years. However, many early nonprofessional settlers in this arena have felt that their territory was unjustly invaded, and a struggle between them and occupational social workers over the appropriate EAP ideology and requisite expertise has followed. Kurzman notes that the function of an EAP (and hence the role of the EAP worker) are at the core of the differences in domain that are still very much under debate. Reviewing the rationale for the historical "core technology" approach in detail, he looks at the strengths and limitations of this framework and contrasts it with the emerging interdisciplinary "comprehensive service" model. The current preference for the latter conceptualization of the EAP function is explained by focusing on the common and symbiotic needs of workers and work organizations.

The comprehensive model is proposed not only as a conceptualization, but as a framework for practice that emphasizes a social functioning perspective with which the social work profession is increasingly comfortable and expert. In comparing the paraprofessional core technology model of the 1980s with the comprehensive service design that is coming to maturation and dominance in the 1990s, Kurzman is able to explain the reason for this evolution in Parsonian structural–functional terms. A definition of a comprehensive EAP is offered, a prototypical program is described, and the rapid professionalization of the field is confirmed.

In Chapter 3, Daniel J. Molloy and Paul A. Kurzman take a closer look at the frequently undervalued working relationship between organized labor and social work. In tracing the history of the relationship back to the turn of the 20th century, the authors note patterns of ambivalent interaction that conceptually resemble a Hegelian dialectic, with an emerging potential today for synthesis of organizational action.

Motivated by the notion of an implicit "human contract" (to complement the written collective bargaining contract), progressive leaders in the labor movement have reached out to human service providers, in general, and to social workers, in particular. Through collaboration in both policy-making and practice during the Great Depression, World War II, and the recent decades of deindustrialization, social work has showed its sensitivity to the needs of working people and to the ideology and actions of the labor movement. Social workers (from Jane Addams forward) not only have supported many of the goals of American trade unions, but have organized or joined unions at their own agencies in both the public and voluntary sectors, showing their ideological solidarity with their union brothers and sisters. Most important, social workers increasingly have taken positions as staff members in unions to develop and implement member assistance programs, outreach to retirees, health and safety projects, substance abuse services, and disability management programs.

Models of labor-based social work services are explored in Chapter 3, which notes that a synthesis that supports collaboration between peers and professionals is emerging and preferred. Building on a principle of fellowship that is native to the labor movement, this design recognizes and supports the strength of workers' bonds to one another and yet appreciates labor's need for professional interventions and expertise. An authentic partnership model is emerging that shows great promise for future collaboration in policymaking and practice between the labor movement and the social work profession.

Finally, in Chapter 4, Bradley K. Googins presents an overview of the research experience and potential in this field of practice. Although much of the research in the past has been conducted by sociologists, industrial psychologists, and faculty in departments of industrial and labor relations, Googins notes the evolving interest and involvement of social workers since the 1980s. In this catchment area, to which social workers have increased entrée (as major providers of human services), the potential for research collaboration may be even greater than the profession has recognized to date.

Googins perceives social work's lack of familiarity with the operation and culture of the traditional workplace as a deficit that must be overcome if social workers are to gain wider access to the proprietary world of management and labor. By using their presence in these settings, occupational social workers who want to do research may find that doors are opened to them that were closed when they were outsiders to this world. More broadly, however, they need to identify the vested interests of work organizations in agreeing to their research agenda; only then can they expect a collaboration in which organizational secrets will be shared with respectful and neutral professional strangers.

The expertise and prestige of a university-based social work research team may be attractive to managers, and their respect for social workers who staff their EAPs (and other human resource functions) may bring a useful familiarity with the profession. Similarly, the profession's common ideology with most progressive trade unions and the increasing number of social work programs that provide services to their members may promote social work researchers' entrance to labor's inner sanctum, where sanction for research projects must be given.

As social workers have become more involved with labor and business during the recent decades of occupational social work's expansion, a perception of mutuality has emerged. Social workers have come to understand the function and the folkways of their world, and labor and management have developed an appreciation for who social workers are and what they can do. Puzzled by the prevalence of substance abuse, perplexed by workers' dependent care needs, and challenged by the need to respond to new regulations in the area of affirmative action, work organizations have begun to recognize the relevance of applied research to identify needs and define cost-effective solutions.

Googins presents specific recommendations for gaining access to work organizations, maintaining the research relationship, and promoting the strategic advantages of collaboration. Identifying areas that would promote an effective research partnership, he observes, takes careful planning. The profession's historic identification with the public and nonprofit sectors does not make social workers natural allies with business, and whenever research is conducted, he notes, organizational secrets must be shared. However, the increasing prestige of the social work profession makes occupational social workers more legitimate partners than before, and their successful presence in many of these settings today may provide the leverage for the entry of social work researchers that was not present 20 years ago. It is in the best interests of both labor and management (industry) and of the social work profession to seize this opportunity and to promote a research agenda, he argues, because such an agenda may benefit workers and their families not only now, but in the new century that is forthcoming.

CHAPTER 1

A Profession at the Crossroads

OCCUPATIONAL SOCIAL WORK—PRESENT AND FUTURE

Michael Lane Smith and Gary M. Gould

Work is the scythe of time.
> —Napoleon Bonaparte
> *Memoirs*

John Morgan's MSW diploma hangs on his office wall, along with assorted plaques, certificates, and pictures. John has been a practicing social worker for almost 20 years. During most of that time, John was a social worker with the U.S. Air Force. Later, his practice embraced clinical social work, a considerable amount of administrative duties, and extensive work with chemically dependent clients. His current practice involves a variety of activities, including the provision of clinical assessments, brief psychotherapies, the evaluation of community resources, the referral of clients to services, and follow-up. Success in John's work involves a great deal of coordination among service providers, but it also requires the careful and limited exchange of information between John's agency and the clients' employers. This latter feature may seem unusual for many social workers, but it is a characteristic feature of occupational social work, John's specialty. John works for a major provider of contract employee assistance services and is primarily responsible for providing these services to workers at the workplaces of several Fortune 500 companies. These responsibilities call for sophisticated clinical skills, but they also demand sensitivity to organizational policies and culture. Recently, John has extended his repertoire of knowledge and skills to include formal mediation. He has also had to balance the referral of clients to some helpful community agencies with the realities of cost containment and managed care, which have emerged as elements of his practice environment.

This summary of John Morgan's professional practice reflects a number of dimensions of occupational social work as it is practiced in the United States today. Firmly anchored in the broader social work profession, it draws on both the foundation and specialized knowledge and skills that lie at the heart of social work practice. On the other hand, it is also a field of practice with its own history and traditions, some of which are even now being shaped by the unfolding events of the last decade of the 20th century. It is a field that continues to evolve, a field that offers rich rewards for its participants (clients, practitioners, and host organizations), but a field that makes ambitious demands on them as well. It represents an arena of practice that has been available to social workers for nearly a century, but one that has defied easy description and broad recognition in the profession (Googins & Godfrey, 1985).

Occupational social work has made gigantic strides during the past generation. Students and practitioners who are interested in the field and its opportunities will do well to acquaint themselves with its history, its major issues, and its current challenges. This overview of the field is intended to provide a snapshot of these concerns as they can be understood on the eve of the 21st century.

The chapter begins by offering several definitions of occupational social work and reviewing its history. It then presents a framework for understanding the field and the various models of practice the field embraces. This framework permits the examination of both traditional concerns of practitioners of the field and the identification of some of the major issues that seem likely to shape occupational social work in the decades to come.

Defining Occupational Social Work

Because occupational social work is such a diverse field, it is not surprising that it has been defined in a number of ways. Kurzman (1987, p. 899) defined it as

> programs and services, under the auspices of labor or management, that utilize professional social workers to serve members or employees and the legitimate social welfare needs of the labor or industrial organization. It also includes the use, by a voluntary or proprietary social agency, of trained social workers to provide social welfare services or consultation to a trade union or employing organization under a specific contractual agreement.

Googins and Godfrey (1987, p. 5) characterized occupational social work as "a field of practice in which social workers attend to the human and social needs of the work community by designing and executing appropriate interventions to insure healthier individuals and environments." Akabas and Kurzman (1982, p. 197) described it as "that special area of practice where the *focus* is on the individual in the status of worker, the environment as defined by employing organizations and trade unions, work as the goal of functional performance among client populations, and social policy as a recognition of the interconnection between social welfare and the world of work." De Silva (1988, p. 283) envisioned occupational social work as "the application of social work knowledge and skill in responding to the personal, organizational, and community needs and problems of organizational employees, customers, and relevant publics in their interactions with organizations." Straussner (1990, p. 2) offered the following broad definition: "a specialized field of social work practice which addresses the human and social needs of the work community through a variety of interventions which aim to foster optimal adaptation between individuals and their environments."

Although these definitions vary in their particulars, they contain important common themes that suggest the essence of this form of practice as it has evolved. First, occupational social work involves the application of social work expertise by social work professionals. As such, it is firmly anchored to the social work profession as a whole. Second, the community of work is the prime target and context of the application of the practitioners' art. Occupational social work services are offered through the world of work and on behalf of the various publics that compose this arena. Third, the concerns of occupational social workers embrace but go beyond problematic individual behavior. The individual is not neglected, but neither is the broader social context within which individual behavior takes place. As part of its practice mandate, occupational social work is concerned with organizational and environmental change to foster healthier and more healthful organizations and communities.

History

Excellent brief histories of social services–social work in the workplace have been presented by a number of authors, including Googins and Godfrey (1987), Kurzman (1987), Masi (1982), and Popple (1981). Some of the points they make help to clarify both the meaning of occupational social work and the traditions and variations characteristic of the field.

A relationship between social welfare and industry can be traced to the guilds of the Middle Ages (Kurzman, 1987). Much more recently, the roots of present-day occupational social work can be found in "welfare capitalism" (Brandes, 1976) or the "occupational welfare system" (Titmuss, 1968) through which American businesses and trade unions have addressed the health and social issues of the work force. This "third" welfare system (as distinct from governmental and voluntary human service sectors) originated in the late 19th and early 20th centuries and has expanded exponentially, so it now rivals the government in its array of responses to social welfare needs (Googins & Godfrey, 1987; Kurzman, 1987).

Social workers were introduced into the occupational welfare system as early as 1875 (Googins & Godfrey, 1987; Popple, 1981). During that period of rapid industrialization, the introduction of new populations into the American work force and calls for governmental regulation of industry, business leaders welcomed the contributions of social welfare practitioners. Frequently known as "welfare secretaries," these pioneers of what would evolve as occupational social work generally lacked formal training. By 1920, however, university-educated social workers had moved into the occupational arena in modest numbers (Popple, 1981). The primary clients of these practitioners were the women, children, and immigrant men employed in the industries of the Eastern and Great Lakes states. Casework, group work, and benefits administration were common activities of these welfare secretaries. A second type of activity "anticipated the duties of the modern personnel manager, including training, job assignment, and sometimes even hiring, firing, and determination of salaries" (Popple, 1981, p. 262). In time, the popularity of welfare secretaries as contributors to welfare capitalism waned, partly because of the alienation of laborers, who considered them paternalistic, and partly because of the opposition of labor leaders, who viewed them as anti-union. In addition, the development of a distinct field of personnel administration, a strong clinical focus in social work, and more extensive systems of public and voluntary social services in American communities drained energy from social work practice in the industrial and business workplace (Googins & Godfrey, 1987; Popple, 1981).

World War II ushered in a second period in the development of occupational social work. Once again, new populations of workers (women and minorities of color) found opportunities in business and industry, and social workers were called on to help mediate the adjustments that employers and employees had to make to one another. The major employers of occupational social workers during this era were the aircraft and munitions industries. Significantly, unions representing the shipping industry and merchant seamen also employed social workers on behalf of their members. In fact, the stellar occupational social work program of the war years was a joint management–labor effort of the United Seamen's Service, serving members of the National Maritime Union (Kurzman, 1987; Masi, 1982). In addition, professional social workers who were employed through the American Red Cross provided a form of occupational social work to armed forces personnel and their families in ways that anticipated the development of comprehensive military social work programs following the end of World War II (McNelis, 1987; Smith, 1985). With the defeat of the Axis powers, demobilization, and the demilitarization of much of American industry, occupational social work efforts again waned.

The current enthusiasm for social work in the workplace is a continuation of the resurgence of interest and activity that began in the mid-1960s (Kurzman, 1987), a period during which the world of work experienced yet again the widespread employment of women and minorities, consumer pressure for influence in corporate policy-making, expanded federal regulation of the work site, the increased alienation of workers, and greater attention to quality-of-life issues involving work (Popple, 1981). Especially significant was the passage of the Hughes Act and the creation in 1970 of the National Institute on Alcohol Abuse and Alcoholism, the occupational branch of which stimulated the nationwide development of employee assistance programs, or EAPs (a common vehicle for occupational social work activities) (DiNitto & McNeece, 1990; Francek, 1985; Kamerman & Kahn, 1987). In addition, the Vocational Rehabilitation Act, Occupational Safety and Health Act, Employee Retirement Income Security Act, Age Discrimination in Employment Act, and Title VII of the Civil Rights Act all stimulated industry's concern for the welfare of the work force (Kurzman, 1987). Largely because of these events and the advocacy of social work professionals, it is estimated that more than 8,000 EAPs now exist, including programs in 80 percent of the Fortune 500 companies (Maiden & Hardcastle, 1986).

In addition to employee-member assistance, this period of occupational social work development was characterized by a broader array of foci than before. Employer-sponsored day care for children, organizational development activities, human resource management, outplacement counseling, occupational safety and health, management of corporate philanthropic contributions, services to customers, and a wide variety of other activities now occupy industrial social workers in both labor and management settings (Gould & Smith, 1988; Straussner, 1990). Social work in the workplace is maturing, and as it has matured it has become increasingly complex.

A Framework for Understanding Occupational Social Work

Occupational social work has evolved to produce a level of homogeneity in several distinct practice traditions. In part, these traditions spring from three different populations with which organizations interface—employees, customers, and local communities (de Silva, 1988; de Silva, Biasucci, Keegan, & Wijnberg, 1982; Shank, 1985). This insight led de Silva and his associates to distinguish among the employee assistance, customer assistance, and corporate public-involvement traditions in occupational social work. Straussner

(1990) added two elements to this framework: the "employer/work organization service model" and the "work-related public policy model." Altogether, then, it is useful to conceptualize occupational social work as embracing at least five different models of practice, some better known and more extensively developed than others.

The Employee Assistance Model

Probably the best-known and most rapidly developing model of practice in the world of work is employee assistance or employee counseling (Kurzman, 1987). This form of occupational social work is characterized by policies, procedures, and counseling-oriented services to identify or respond to employees with personal, emotional, or behavioral problems, especially those that interfere with their performance at work (Masi, 1984; Ozawa, 1980; Smith, 1988a; Straussner, 1990). It also can be a vehicle for the proactive advocacy of health-promotion and disease-prevention programs (McClellan, 1985).

An important question related to this model is, Just who (or what) is the social worker's primary client? Bakalinsky (1980, p. 475) argued that there is a "basic incompatibility between the goals and values of industry and those of the profession," which discourages occupational social workers from viewing the individual in need as the primary client. Others have argued that ethical employee assistance requires the practitioner never to forget that the person in need is a primary client and that such practice is achievable (Akabas & Kurzman, 1982; Briar & Vinet, 1985; Googins & Godfrey, 1987; Kurzman, 1988).

Issues of client-centered practice and of confidentiality are less prominent when EAPs are offered through the auspices of a labor union rather than through an employing organization. When labor sponsors this type of service, it is generally referred to as "membership assistance" and is likely to emphasize the provision of material services in addition to clinical assistance (Akabas, 1977; Antoniades & Bellinger, 1983; Kurzman, 1987; Masi, 1982; Molloy & Burmeister, 1990; Tramm, 1985). In addition, with member assistance, there generally is less concern with management's becoming aware of sensitive information and a greater sense of harmony between the union's commitment to protect and serve its members and the member assistance offered under its auspices (Antoniades & Bellinger, 1983).

Regardless of auspices, the employee assistance model relies on a number of traditional roles of social workers, including counselor, mediator, advocate, and broker, in addition to the occasional roles of teacher–trainer or "constructive confrontator" (Straussner, 1990). It is important to note that social workers are not the only providers of employee–member assistance services, although today they are the most frequent (Trice & Beyer, 1982). Occupational social work overlaps with the workplace practice of licensed counselors, psychologists, chemical dependency specialists, and others (Smith, 1988b; Wyers & Kaulukukui, 1984). Indeed, practitioners of employee assistance share an increasingly rich literature, regardless of the type and level of their professional training. This literature is reflected in the number of books, book chapters, journals, and magazines that have been published. Important social work contributions to this literature include books by Akabas and Kurzman (1982), Googins and Godfrey (1987), Gould and Smith (1988), Klarreich, Francek, and Moore (1985), Masi (1982, 1984), and Straussner (1990).

The Employer–Work Organization Service Model

Increasingly in the United States, occupational social work reflects forms of practice in which the primary unit of intervention is the work organization itself, rather than employees or members. Straussner (1990) pointed out that this model is oriented to promoting broad-scale policies and services that are sensitive to the interests or needs of the work force. Even though this model was used more extensively in Europe than in the United States in the past (Googins, 1987; Googins & Godfrey, 1987), many examples of such domestic practice exist. A list of but some of its possibilities includes these:

1. consultation on the establishment of corporate- or union-sponsored day care services for workers' dependents (McCroskey, 1988)

2. the negotiation and design of company benefits packages (Antoniades & Bellinger, 1983; Kamerman & Kahn, 1987; Kurzman & Akabas, 1981)

3. a reexamination of shift-work schedules, with an eye to stressors that affect workers' families (Meadow, 1988)

4. the development of company relocation policies and services (Gaylord & Symons, 1986; Gullotta & Donohue, 1981; McGehee, 1985; Siegel, 1988)

5. the design and operation of equal employment and affirmative action systems (Akabas, Fine, & Yasser, 1982; Wilk, 1988)

6. consultation on the promulgation of informed and just policies related to employees with AIDS or AIDS-related disorders (Finch & Ell, 1988; Ryan, 1986)

7. innovative and forward-thinking retirement, partial-retirement, and preretirement programs (Habib & Gutwill, 1985; Wilks, Rowen, Hosang, & Knoepler, 1988)

8. the promotion of occupational safety and health (Lewis, 1989; Shanker, 1983).

The most common roles of practitioners in this form of occupational social work include the consultant, evaluator–analyst, trainer, program developer (Straussner, 1990), and negotiator.

The Customer-Service Model

Historically, occupational social workers were primarily concerned with members of the work force and their families. De Silva (1988) argued that recognition should be afforded the large population of customers or consumers who need services as a result of their interaction with and dependence on business and industry. He pointed out that "industrial organizations have begun to respond to special needs of customers by developing a wide range of services unique to their businesses" (p. 284). Occupational social work interventions are particularly suited for organizations whose clients, customers, or consumers include vulnerable or at-risk populations (Smith, 1988a). Utility companies, trust departments of banks, and funeral homes are among those that have offered professional social work services to their customers.

Typical services offered through customer assistance programs include the provision of consumer education activities, assistance with paying bills for company services or products, short-term counseling, liaison with systems, and referral (de Silva, 1988). The typical roles of practitioners are counselor, program planner, consultant, and advocate (Straussner, 1990).

Corporate Public-Involvement Model

The corporate public-involvement model embraces practice designed to assist corporations and businesses to make commitments to the economic and social well-being of the communities in which they operate (de Silva et al., 1982). It reflects a recognition of the impact of organizational operations on local tax rates, employment opportunities, housing costs, demands for educational services, police and fire protection, and more, on the lives of people living in these communities (Smith, 1988a).

Historically, one of the most common vehicles through which both business and social workers have attended to these issues has been the United Way (Burke, 1987, 1988), with business providing much of the leadership and incentives during fund drives and social workers providing technical expertise and administering and staffing participating agencies. More recently, social workers have found opportunities to influence or manage corporate contributions to civic and humanitarian concerns (Brilliant & Rice, 1988). They also have provided essential training, supervision, and evaluation to businesses that seek to improve community resources or services through specific improvement projects (Masi, 1982; Smith, 1988a).

Titles for social workers who are active in this model include charitable allocations analyst, urban affairs adviser, corporate social responsibility director, community relations consultant, and community services coordinator. Practitioners' roles include community analyst and planner, budget allocator, program developer, broker, advocate, and negotiator (Straussner, 1990).

The Work-Related Public Policy Model

Straussner (1990, p. 13) defined the work-related public policy model in terms of "formulation, identification, analysis and advocacy for those public or governmental policies, program[s] and services which directly or indirectly affect the world of work." Briar (1987, p. 778), for example, argued that "as a question of fundamental human rights and profound human costs, unemployment is increasingly recognized as a social work issue." There is no question that unemployment frequently entails profound psychological and social costs (Briar, 1983; Keefe, 1984). In fact, unemployment and underemployment are issues for which the interests of society, business, individuals, and the social work profession intersect. It is appropriate for social workers to attempt to influence governmental policy on so vital a topic. Policy planning and analysis, program development, advocacy, coalition building, and networking are some of the skills that such practice requires (Foster & Schore, 1989; Sherraden, 1985).

Changes and Challenges

The preceding discussion reflects the evolution of occupational social work, especially in response to changing societal and work environments. There is considerable reason to believe that more changes are in store. The following list reflects some of the specific and ongoing challenges that occupational social workers are likely to face in the next two decades. Each of these predictions was reported between 1984 and 1989 in at least five newspapers or magazines (including *Forbes, Time, Fortune, McLean's, Omni, Futurist, Newsweek, New Republic, New York Times, Washington Post, Wall Street Journal, Canadian Globe and Mail,* and *Los Angeles Times*):

1. Ninety percent of the information used in the year 2010 will have been unknown before 1990.

2. By 2000, many of the current information and service jobs (as well as those in manufacturing) will be eliminated because of automation and artificial intelligence.

3. The cost of occupational health and safety programs and pressure to expand them will increase significantly.

4. International competition for trade will force U.S. companies to shift manufacturing and marketing strategies, resulting in a streamlined factory process, fewer layers of management, and the greater use of interdisciplinary teams.

5. As the European Community continues to develop a major home market, trade barriers between Europe and the United States will result in many more American businesses establishing footholds overseas. Overseas duty and foreign language skills will be vital to professional advancement.

6. Three of every four married couples in the United States will be involved in dual-career marriages. Child care issues will become even more critical, as will "dependent care" (the care of the young, the elderly, and the ill) in general (see Chapter 9).

7. By 2000, 60 percent of American workers will be age 35 or older.

8. Half of all American workers will opt for "flextime" or "flexplace" by 2000, with a greater proportion of American workers laboring at home or in geographically dispersed satellite work stations.

9. People will change jobs and careers with increasing frequency.

Occupational social workers will encounter a continuum of problems generated by these and other social and economic phenomena.

A Changing, Aging Work Force

The next several decades are expected to provide employment for millions of people who were previously denied the opportunity to work. In the next few years alone, over 8 million persons who are suffering or recovering from physical disabilities, mental retardation, alcoholism, AIDS, and other conditions are expected to enter the work force, thanks to the protection against discrimination afforded them by P.L. 101-336 (the Americans with Disabilities Act) (Tucker, 1990). New industrial technologies will redefine the nature of work in such a way as to reduce the physical demands of many jobs, thereby providing opportunities for older workers to continue to work past the traditional retirement age (Wilks et al., 1988). The proportion of U.S.-born white men, once the bulwark of American business and industry, will continue to decrease in proportion to others in the work force. Women, African Americans, Latinos, and new immigrants will become the mainstay of the workplace; upwards of two-thirds of new entrants to the work force during the 1990s alone are expected to be women. By the 21st century, the sheer number of these "nontraditional" workers will reshape much of corporate life, forcing business leaders to reexamine "the old stereotypes that equate difference with deficiency" (Berry, 1990, p. 69). Unfortunately, many of these new workers, particularly those from disadvantaged backgrounds and those without adequate education or skills, are likely to be assigned to the most menial and unstable jobs. Occupational social workers should be prepared to advocate for these workers to ensure that they receive adequate training and career paths that provide opportunities.

Demographics in the 21st century will exert profound effects on social policies and the dynamics of the workplace. Today, approximately 32 million persons over age 65 are living in the United States—a number greater than the entire population of Canada (U.S. Bureau of the Census, 1992). This population is the fastest-growing demographic segment in American society, and its growth rate is projected to increase as the post–World War II baby boomers continue to age. Within the ranks of elderly Americans, the number and proportion of persons over age 85 are predicted to increase as well (Dychtwald & Flower, 1989). In a society that has traditionally valued youth over maturity, new services, products, and policies are needed. Occupational social workers should find rich opportunities to influence corporate contributions, customer assistance programs, human resource policies and benefits packages, and other factors that relate to corporate and union responses to an aging society.

Dependent Care

Day care and other related services for children, fully or partially sponsored or underwritten by employers, will become an even more pressing issue (Burud, Aschbacher, & McCroskey, 1984; McCroskey, 1984, 1988). Birthrates for 1989 and 1990 suggest that the period of low domestic births following the end of the post–World War II baby-boom generation is over. Because the burden of child care continues to fall mostly on women, a rising U.S. birthrate will mean greater barriers to women's participation in the work force unless society provides accessible child care services. In this regard, accessibility includes the issues of cost, location, and availability.

Occupational social workers can respond to this emerging problem in a number of ways. The profession can provide leadership in clarifying the advantages and disadvantages of the various models of corporate support of child care services. Social workers can help shape benefit packages that address child care issues, especially for single-parent households. Drawing on their knowledge of local resources, social workers can develop communitywide coalitions to push for more child-sensitive services.

Concern for employer-sponsored day care for children will be joined by similar demands for support for the elderly and ill. Consider the demographics of age and gender: Women on the whole live longer than do men.

Of Americans over age 80, there are but 42 men for every 100 women. About three-quarters of all men over age 65 live with a mate; in contrast, approximately three-quarters of all women over age 65 live alone or with their children (Dychtwald & Flower, 1989).

These statistics help to clarify the basis for the "sandwich phenomenon" that many American workers are experiencing. More and more people find that they are responsible for the care of both their children and their elderly parents. Again, responsibility for caregiving falls primarily on women: 90 percent of the care given to older parents is provided by middle-aged women, more and more of whom are also members of the formal work force (Dychtwald & Flower, 1989). As of 1986, the average woman could expect to spend more years providing care to her parents than to her children ("Trading Places," 1990). Therefore, it is imperative that both the government and the private sector participate to a greater degree in helping middle-aged workers care for their parents. It is equally vital that social workers provide leadership in promulgating policies and programs that offer older persons opportunities for growth, productivity, and meaning, remembering that the most appropriate *care* that society can provide for many older individuals is meaningful work.

As the world of work addresses these issues, it can expect to accelerate even more the growth of diversity within its ranks as women (freed from many of the constraints of dependent care) seek employment and as elderly people continue to work through partial retirement programs or postretirement employment.

Managed Care

For at least a decade, health care has been "the largest unmanaged cost in industry" (McClellan, 1985, p. 32). According to Wagman and Schiff (1990, p. 53), "managed mental health care has become an increasingly significant influence in the timely, appropriate and cost-conscious delivery of mental health and substance abuse services." This type of service involves the development and implementation of benefit plans for mental health services, both to control costs and to provide adequate coverage. The challenges of this task are obvious when one remembers that the costs for the treatment of mental illness (or emotional problems) and chemical abuse have increased significantly over the years and that many insurance providers now exclude or severely limit coverage for them. The continued coordination between managed care systems and existing EAPs or membership assistance programs is vital to the success of these forms of treatment (Lightman & Wagman, 1988; Wagman & Schiff, 1990), as is the development of efficient case-monitoring systems. It is especially important not to solve cost-containment problems by eliminating or rejecting programs that provide helping services to people in need.

Chemical Abuse

The effects of chemical abuse and dependence on workers' performance is a historical problem in the areas of occupational social work and EAPs. Despite recent studies suggesting some period-specific reduction in alcohol consumption and drug use for segments of the U.S. population (Carroll, 1993), the significant abuse of mind-altering, mood-altering chemicals in the work force is likely to continue. Consider the following:

1. The constant entry into the work force of young people from age groups that are most commonly associated with both the experimental and recreational use of mind-altering drugs makes a major reduction in chemical abuse in the workplace unlikely.

2. The increasing ethnic and class diversity predicted for the work force in the next decade will pose significant challenges for both employers and practitioners because different cultural groups have different patterns of both drug-taking and help-seeking.

3. Many executives and managers are ignorant of the organizational factors that promote chemical abuse in their work forces. In many workplaces, group and organizational variables contribute to a "culture" of chemical abuse (Fine, Akabas, & Bellinger, 1982).

The future presents some specific challenges for occupational social workers with respect to chemical abuse. Social workers will need to work to achieve a better mix of preventive and curative interventions to address this problem. Drug testing can be discouraged (unless public safety is clearly at stake), but if implemented, it should be done in a manner that does not violate the rights of workers (see National Association of Social Workers, 1990). More content on drugs (including alcohol) should be included in the curricula of schools of social work and continuing education programs to prepare social workers to deal with chemical abuse in the workplace (Smith, DeWeaver, & Hosang, 1990).

Complexity of Ethical Choices

Both the social work profession and the world of work are confronted by complex dilemmas of values, ethics, and paradoxical choices. As social workers become more thoroughly entrenched in the design and provision of services in the workplace, they can expect to face difficult choices when the value systems of social work and those of the labor and business worlds conflict (see Akabas, 1984; Bakalinsky, 1980; Kurzman, 1988; Walden, 1978). Consider the following as illustrative of the issues that occupational social workers are likely to face in the next decade:

1. Social workers will face ethical issues surrounding the increasing diversity of the work force. They will be challenged to develop strategies to promote an ethical distribution of work-related efforts, risks, and benefits unskewed by racism, ageism, homophobia, sexism, or other forms of individual or institutional discrimination.

2. Social workers will encounter inconsistent policies pertaining to confidentiality in the increasingly complex and litigious environment of work. For example, the requirements of many company drug-testing policies to report substance abusers run counter to the protection afforded EAP clients. Should workers' confidentiality be differentially protected because they participate in one system as opposed to another (Kurzman, 1988; Maiden, 1987)? What about "whistle blowers" (Lewis, 1985)? As the public demands greater economy and social responsiveness from government and business, what protections will be afforded those who come forth to reveal organizational waste, mismanagement, or graft?

3. Social workers are primarily accustomed to viewing individuals, families, and groups as clients. Occupational social workers, however, must become sensitive to the ethical issues involved in considering their employing organizations as clients.

4. Social workers should examine their responsibilities and options when working on behalf of companies that manufacture or market products that are toxic to individuals or to the environment.

5. Social workers should be sensitive to the ethical issues that arise when organizations place the interests of employees, customers, or stockholders in opposition to one another. Downsizing—the practice of sharply reducing the size of the work force through layoffs or terminations to protect profits—is just such a problem. Preventive responses to the threat of job loss are called for, not just outplacement services or unemployment compensation after the fact.

Occupational social workers face the challenge of providing leadership in one of the most important arrays of social welfare systems society has to offer—the world of work. However, occupational social work is at a crossroad: Is it to continue its business as usual in the 21st century, or should it systematically prepare to meet future challenges by anticipating them today? It is not clear which path occupational social work will take. However, it is clear that the decisions that are made today will have profound consequences for workers and work organizations in the decades ahead.

References

Akabas, S. H. (1977). Labor: Social policy and human services. In J. Turner (Ed.-in-Chief), *Encyclopedia of social work* (17th ed., Vol. 1, pp. 737–744). Washington, DC: National Association of Social Workers.

Akabas, S. H. (1984). Confidentiality: Values and dilemmas. *Social Work Papers, 18*, 83–91.

Akabas, S. H., Fine, M., & Yasser, R. (1982). Putting secondary prevention to the test: A study of an early intervention strategy with disabled workers. *Journal of Primary Prevention, 3*, 165–187.

Akabas, S. H., & Kurzman, P. A. (1982). The industrial social welfare specialist: What's so special? In S. H. Akabas & P. A. Kurzman (Eds.), *Work, workers, and work organizations: A view from social work* (pp. 197–235). Englewood Cliffs, NJ: Prentice Hall.

Antoniades, R., & Bellinger, S. (1983). Organized worksites: A help or a hindrance in the delivery of social work services in and to the workplace? In R. J. Thomlison (Ed.), *Perspectives on industrial social work practice* (pp. 29–38). Ottawa: Family Service Canada.

Bakalinsky, R. (1980). People vs. profits: Social work in industry. *Social Work, 25*, 471–475.

Berry, P. A. (1990). Application of social work skills to human resource management. In S. L. A. Straussner (Ed.), *Occupational social work today* (pp. 67–76). New York: Haworth Press.

Brandes, S. D. (1976). *American welfare capitalism 1880–1940*. Chicago: University of Chicago Press.

Briar, K. H. (1983). Unemployment: Toward a social work agenda. *Social Work, 28*, 211–216.

Briar, K. H. (1987). Unemployment and underemployment. In A. Minahan (Ed.-in-Chief), *Encyclopedia of social work* (18th ed., Vol. 2, pp. 778–788). Silver Spring, MD: National Association of Social Workers.

Briar, K. H., & Vinet, M. (1985). Ethical questions concerning an EAP: Who is the client? (Company or individual?). In S. H. Klarreich, J. L. Francek, & C. E. Moore (Eds.), *The human resources management handbook: Principles and practice of employee assistance programs* (pp. 342–359). New York: Praeger.

Brilliant, E. L., & Rice, K. A. (1988). Influencing corporate philanthropy. In G. M. Gould & M. L. Smith (Eds.), *Social work in the workplace: Practice and principles* (pp. 299–313). New York: Springer.

Burke, E. M. (1987). Corporate social responsibility. In A. Minahan (Ed.-in-Chief), *Encyclopedia of social work* (18th ed., Vol. 1, pp. 345–351). Silver Spring, MD: National Association of Social Workers.

Burke, E. M. (1988). Corporate community relations. In G. M. Gould & M. L. Smith (Eds.), *Social work in the workplace: Practice and principles* (pp. 314–327). New York: Springer.

Burud, S. L., Aschbacher, P. R., & McCroskey, J. (1984). *Employer-supported child care: Investing in human resources.* Dover, MA: Auburn House.

Carroll, C. R. (1993). *Drugs in modern society* (3rd ed.). Dubuque, IA: Brown & Benchmark.

de Silva, E. G. (1988). Services to customers: Customer assistance programs. In G. M. Gould & M. L. Smith (Eds.), *Social work in the workplace: Practice and principles* (pp. 283–298). New York: Springer.

de Silva, E. G., Biasucci, P. A., Keegan, M., & Wijnberg, D. (1982, March). *Promoting the future of social work education through labor and industry: A three dimensional approach.* Paper presented at the Annual Program Meeting of the Council on Social Work Education, New York.

DiNitto, D. M., & McNeece, C. A. (1990). *Social work: Issues and opportunities in a challenging profession.* Englewood Cliffs, NJ: Prentice Hall.

Dychtwald, K., & Flower, J. (1989). *Age wave.* Los Angeles: Jeremy Tarcher.

Finch, W. A., Jr., & Ell, K. O. (1988). AIDS in the workplace. In G. M. Gould & M. L. Smith (Eds.), *Social work in the workplace: Practice and principles* (pp. 229–244). New York: Springer.

Fine, M., Akabas, S. H., & Bellinger, S. (1982). Cultures of drinking: A workplace perspective. *Social Work, 27,* 436–440.

Foster, B., & Schore, L. (1989). Job loss and the occupational social worker. *Employee Assistance Quarterly, 5*(1), 77–97.

Francek, J. L. (1985). The role of the occupational social worker in EAPs. In S. H. Klarreich, J. L. Francek, & C. E. Moore (Eds.), *The human resources management handbook: Principles and practice of employee assistance programs* (pp. 145–154). New York: Praeger.

Gaylord, M., & Symons, E. (1986). Relocation stress: A definition and need for services. *Employee Assistance Quarterly, 2*(1), 31–36.

Googins, B. (1987). Occupational social work: A developmental perspective. *Employee Assistance Quarterly, 2*(3), 37–54.

Googins, B., & Godfrey, J. (1985). The evolution of occupational social work. *Social Work, 30,* 396–402.

Googins, B., & Godfrey, J. (1987). *Occupational social work.* Englewood Cliffs, NJ: Prentice Hall.

Gould, G. M., & Smith, M. L. (Eds.). (1988). *Social work in the workplace: Practice and principles.* New York: Springer.

Gullotta, T. P., & Donohue, K. C. (1981). Corporate families: Implications for preventive intervention. *Social Casework, 62,* 109–114.

Habib, M., & Gutwill, S. (1985). The union setting: Working with retirees. *Journal of Gerontological Social Work, 8*, 247–255.

Kamerman, S. B., & Kahn, A. J. (1987). *The responsive workplace: Employers and a changing labor force.* New York: Columbia University Press.

Keefe, T. (1984). The stresses of unemployment. *Social Work, 29*, 264–268.

Klarreich, S. H., Francek, J. L., & Moore, C. E. (Eds.). (1985). *The human resources management handbook: Principles and practice of employee assistance programs.* New York: Praeger.

Kurzman, P. A. (1987). Industrial social work (occupational social work). In A. Minahan (Ed.-in-Chief), *Encyclopedia of social work* (18th ed., Vol. 1, pp. 899–910). Silver Spring, MD: National Association of Social Workers.

Kurzman, P. A. (1988). The ethical base for social work in the workplace. In G. M. Gould & M. L. Smith (Eds.), *Social work in the workplace: Practice and principles* (pp. 16–27). New York: Springer.

Kurzman, P. A., & Akabas, S. H. (1981). Industrial social work as an arena for practice. *Social Work, 26*, 52–60.

Lewis, B. M. (1989). Social workers' role in promoting health and safety. *Employee Assistance Quarterly, 5*(1), 99–118.

Lewis, H. (1985). The whistleblower and the whistleblowing profession. *Child and Adolescent Social Work Journal, 2*(1), 3–12.

Lightman, R., & Wagman, J. (1988). Working proposal for the EAP role in a managed care system. *The Almacan, 18*(5), 18–21.

Maiden, R. P. (1987). Ethical issues in occupational social work: Implications for practice. *Journal of Independent Social Work, 1*(4), 31–40.

Maiden, R. P., & Hardcastle, D. A. (1986). Social work education: Professionalizing EAPs. *EAP Digest, 7*(1), 63–66.

Masi, D. (1982). *Human services in industry.* Lexington, MA: D. C. Heath.

Masi, D. (1984). *Designing employee assistance programs.* New York: American Management Association.

McClellan, K. (1985). The changing nature of EAP practice: EAPs have a bright future. *Personnel Administrator, 30*(8), 29–37.

McCroskey, J. (1984). In the wake of the subtle revolution—Opportunities and challenges in child care. *Social Work Papers, 18*, 57–64.

McCroskey, J. (1988). Employer supported child care. In G. M. Gould & M. L. Smith (Eds.), *Social work in the workplace: Practice and principles* (pp. 170–184). New York: Springer.

McGehee, L. J. (1985). Executives, families, and the trauma of relocation. In S. H. Klarreich, J. L. Francek, & C. E. Moore (Eds.), *The human resources management handbook: Principles and practice of employee assistance programs* (pp. 281–290). New York: Praeger.

McNelis, P. J. (1987). Military social work. In A. Minahan (Ed.-in-Chief), *Encyclopedia of social work* (18th ed., Vol. 2, pp. 155–161). Silver Spring, MD: National Association of Social Workers.

Meadow, D. (1988). Managing shift work problems. In G. M. Gould & M. L. Smith (Eds.), *Social work in the workplace: Practice and principles* (pp. 152–169). New York: Springer.

Molloy, D., & Burmeister, L. (1990). Social workers in union-based programs. In S. L. A. Straussner (Ed.), *Occupational social work today* (pp. 37–51). New York: Haworth Press.

National Association of Social Workers. (1990). *Drug testing in the workplace.* Silver Spring, MD: Author.

Ozawa, M. N. (1980). Development of social services in industry: Why and how? *Social Work, 25,* 464–470.

Popple, P. R. (1981). Social work practice in business and industry: 1875–1930. *Social Service Review, 55,* 257–269.

Ryan, C. (1986). *AIDS in the workplace.* Fullerton, CA: DaSak Associates.

Shank, B. (1985). Considering a career in occupational social work? *EAP Digest, 5*(5), 54–62.

Shanker, R. (1983). Occupational disease, workers' compensation and the social work advocate. *Social Work, 28,* 24–27.

Sherraden, M. W. (1985). Chronic unemployment: A social work perspective. *Social Work, 30,* 403–408.

Siegel, D. I. (1988). Relocation counseling and services. In G. M. Gould & M. L. Smith (Eds.), *Social work in the workplace: Practice and principles* (pp. 109–122). New York: Springer.

Smith, M. L. (1985). Social work in the military: An occupational social work perspective. *Social Work Papers, 19,* 46–55.

Smith, M. L. (1988a). Social work in the workplace: An overview. In G. M. Gould & M. L. Smith (Eds.), *Social work in the workplace: Practice and principles* (pp. 3–15). New York: Springer.

Smith, M. L. (1988b). With a view to the future. In G. M. Gould & M. L. Smith (Eds.), *Social work in the workplace: Practice and principles* (pp. 343–348). New York: Springer.

Smith, M. L., DeWeaver, K. L., & Hosang, M. (1990, March). *Alcohol and drug abuse: Denial in social work education?* Paper presented at the Annual Program Meeting of the Council on Social Work Education, Reno.

Straussner, S. L. A. (1990). Occupational social work today: An overview. In S. L. A. Straussner (Ed.), *Occupational social work today* (pp. 1–17). New York: Haworth Press.

Titmuss, R. M. (1968). *Commitment to welfare.* New York: Pantheon Books.

Trading places. (1990, July 16). *Newsweek,* p. 49.

Tramm, M. L. (1985). Union-based programs. In S. H. Klarreich, J. L. Francek, & C. E. Moore (Eds.), *The human resources management handbook: Principles and practice of employee assistance programs* (pp. 95–101). New York: Praeger.

Trice, H. M., & Beyer, J. M. (1982). Job-based alcoholism programs: Motivating problem drinkers to rehabilitation. In E. M. Pattison & E. Kaufman (Eds.),

The encyclopedic handbook of alcoholism (pp. 954–978). New York: Gardner Press.

Tucker, B. P. (1990). The Americans with Disabilities Act: An overview. *University of Illinois Law Review, 1989,* 923–939.

U.S. Bureau of the Census. (1992). *Statistical abstract of the United States, 1992* (112th ed.). Washington, DC: U.S. Government Printing Office.

Wagman, J. B., & Schiff, J. (1990). Managed mental health care for employees: Roles for social workers. In S. L. A. Straussner (Ed.), *Occupational social work today* (pp. 53–66). New York: Haworth Press.

Walden, T. (1978). Industrial social work: A conflict in definitions. *NASW News, 23*(5), 3.

Wilk, R. J. (1988). Assisting in affirmative action and equal employment opportunity. In G. M. Gould & M. L. Smith (Eds.), *Social work in the workplace: Practice and principles* (pp. 213–228). New York: Springer.

Wilks, C. S., Rowen, R. B., Hosang, M., & Knoepler, S. (1988). Human resource issues and aging. In G. M. Gould & M. L. Smith (Eds.), *Social work in the workplace: Practice and principles* (pp. 200–212). New York: Springer.

Wyers, N. L., & Kaulukukui, M. (1984). Social services in the workplace: Rhetoric vs. reality. *Social Work, 29,* 167–172.

CHAPTER 2

Employee Assistance Programs

TOWARD A COMPREHENSIVE SERVICE MODEL

Paul A. Kurzman

> Work . . . is about a search, too, for daily meaning as
> well as daily bread, for recognition as well as cash, for
> astonishment rather than torpor; in short, for a sort of
> life rather than a Monday thru Friday sort of dying.
> Perhaps immortality too is part of the quest.
> —Studs Terkel
> *Working*

An irony of the 1990s is that the presence of employee assistance programs may be taken for granted by many in labor, industry, and the service professions. (The term *employee assistance program* is used in this chapter to refer as well to labor-sponsored programs, which generally are termed member assistance programs.) However, they formally began in significant number only 20 years ago in an early form known as occupational alcoholism programs. Starting with the Hughes Act of 1970 and the organization of the Occupational Alcoholism Branch at the National Institute on Alcohol Abuse and Alcoholism (NIAAA), a new concern about the need for *workplace* intervention programs provided the ideological impetus (and subsequent funding) of work-site programs to detect, confront, and refer alcoholic employees. To provide a site for service for other troubled workers and to remove some of the stigma of the alcoholism label, these programs were soon renamed employee assistance programs (EAPs) (see DiNitto & McNeece, 1990, Chap. 13; Kurzman, 1987; McClellan & Miller, 1988; McGowan, 1984). Although the staffs and services of these early EAPs made successful intervention with nonalcoholic troubled workers problematic, small in-house EAPs continued to serve as best they could those who were referred to them, primarily by supervisors, when these personnel were able to document serious and persistent performance problems among supervisees.

By the late 1970s, an increasing number of professional health and mental health providers had become active in the employee assistance field, staffing programs in corporate, governmental, and trade union settings. Professional social workers were becoming involved, and the first conference of industrial (occupational) social work educators and practitioners was held in New York in 1978 (Akabas, Kurzman, & Kolben, 1979). The scope of services began to expand well beyond alcoholism and the addictions to include personal and emotional problems that could, or already were, affecting employees' job performance and use of benefits. Not only had the range of interventions expanded, but the conceptualization of services had become more sophisticated as well (Kurzman & Akabas, 1981).

This chapter describes the evolution of the modern EAP, noting the struggles for definition and domain. It explains why the field emerged at this time, provides a rationale for its current development, and makes predictions for its future as we approach the year 2000. The chapter discusses the contending conceptualizations of the field, along with the implications of several extant models for occupational social work education and practice. It shows that preprofessional approaches, which made an early contribution to the field, have limitations that could be overcome by a professional mental health services model. The chapter demonstrates why social work's unique person-in-environment practice conceptualization gave the profession a clear advantage in the field among the several mental health disciplines. Social work clearly is the "major player" in the EAP arena, and this chapter explains why.

Boundaries of the Terrain

In 1985, Roman and Blum published an article entitled, "The Core Technology of Employee Assistance Programs," supported, in part, by a grant from the NIAAA. They proposed to define what constituted the component roles and functions of EAP providers, which they termed "the core technology of employee assistance programs," to wit:

- identification of employees' behavioral problems on the basis of their job performance
- consultation to supervisors, managers, and shop stewards
- appropriate use of "constructive confrontation" as leverage when employees are referred
- micro- and macro linkages with external counseling, treatment, and other community resources

- the centrality of employees' alcohol problems as the focus of programs with the most significant promise for producing recovery and genuine cost savings for the work organization (Roman & Blum, 1985, pp. 16–17).

Roman and Blum made clear that the principal evidence of the success of EAPs would be the treatment of alcohol problems. This focus and "core technology" soon were adopted by the trade association for EAP specialists (then known as the Association of Labor-Management Administrators and Consultants on Alcoholism, ALMACA, and later renamed the Employee Assistance Professionals Association, EAPA) and became the basis for its certification and credentialing programs. With EAPA's support, Roman and Blum (1988, p. 19) reaffirmed their core technology principles three years later, stating emphatically that "based on our research, we view the EAP as a Personnel/Human Resource Management (P/HRM) tool which has considerable potential for reducing uncertainty in the general management of employees. . . . EAPs are a part of the performance-management and control activity in an organization's P/HRM system . . . and contribute to the attainment of an organization's goals." They urged that EAPs should continue to focus on alcohol and drug abuse as the clearest and most direct contribution to the managerial goal of cost-effectiveness.

Although no one who has worked in or with an EAP would deny the significance of substance abuse as a workplace (indeed, a societal) issue, few today would make as ingenuous a claim as Roman and Blum made in 1985 and reaffirmed three years later. The workplace has changed, as was noted in the Introduction, and issues of concern to employers, employees, and trade unions reflect these changes. As a direct result, there has evolved during the past decade a preferred EAP model that seems to meet the needs of all the parties better. Experts and authors have referred to this preferred model in different terms: Richard Hellan (cited in *Employee Assistance Programs*, 1987, p. 21) spoke of a *full-service system;* McClellan and Miller (1988, p. 39) used the term "health intervention EAPs"; Holosko and Feit (1988, p. 282) conceptualized a "new wave, third generation EAP"; Masi (1984) identified the "comprehensive EAP program"; Vigilante (1988, p. 89) suggested the "full family service model"; Nathan (1984, p. 390) emphasized the emerging "broad-spectrum EAP"; Erfurt, Foote, and Heinrich (1990) preferred the term *mega-brush programs;* and Googins (1991b, p. 17) saw EAPs emerging as "family assistance programs." In their own fashion, each author has suggested that modern EAPs will not be successful unless the early "core technology" model is supplanted by a conceptualization that reflects not only the nature of the modern workplace, but the legitimate vested interests of the *several parties* involved: employers, employees, unions, and third-party payers.

Concern has been raised by EAPA leaders, however, that comprehensive EAPs will ignore alcoholism and effectively abandon alcoholics. They insist that the defense structure of alcoholics rarely permits self-referral and that only the threat of job jeopardy and supervisors' referrals, followed by constructive confrontation, will ensure that alcoholics are identified and served. Systematic field research, however, does not seem to support this claim. In a study in the Midwest, for example, Cunningham (1989, 1990b, pp. 38–39) found that the EAPs surveyed were reporting high self-referral rates for all types of presenting problems, including chemical dependence and codependence. A Texas study found that self- and peer referral accounted for nearly four times the number of alcoholics served by the EAP as did supervisors' referrals (Martin, Heckel, Goodrick, Schreiber, & Young, 1985, p. 31). On the basis of many years of experience staffing an in-house EAP program, MacDonald et al. (1987) argued forcefully that a primary focus on mandatory referrals is truly outdated. Moreover, Foote and Erfurt (1981, p. 231), early proponents of the core technology–alcoholism focus, forthrightly noted the outcome of their own research field studies: "Programs dealing with a variety of employee problems do not necessarily reduce services to alcoholics. . . . it is concluded that comprehensive EAPs are generally no less effective than alcohol-focused programs at reaching alcoholic employees."

In addition, experts on alcoholism have stated that because it is a progressive disease, alcoholism often takes 10 to 15 years before it reaches its middle stages, when it affects job performance (Googins, 1991b; Masi, 1979; Sonnenstuhl & Trice, 1986). "Measurable job impairment in alcoholism usually occurs only after an increased tolerance for the drug alcohol has been developed, changes in behavior are manifested and tardiness and absenteeism have become problems" (McClellan, 1985, p. 32). Because deteriorating job performance is generally a middle or a late sign of alcoholism (rather than an early sign), Shain and Groeneveld (1980, p. 14) noted that with the core technology model, the whole concept of secondary prevention through an EAP may become meaningless. A worker probably would be seriously and chronically ill before intervention and services via the workplace would begin. Particularly with alcoholics, by this point much lasting (and usually irreversible) physical damage (cirrhosis, pancreatitis, and cerebellar degeneration) will have occurred, and there may well be a breakdown of lifelong friendships, peer relationships, and family ties—many of which may be hard to recapture, even upon recovery. Therefore, employers have come to realize that such a tertiary model of intervention should not be the primary focus of their EAPs.

In addition, although studies have shown that alcoholism-focused core technology programs may reach unskilled and semiskilled workers, who are closely supervised, such programs are usually far less successful in reaching skilled clerical, professional, and managerial employees, who now constitute the clear majority of the U.S. labor force. Such classes of employees function under less hierarchical conditions or have secretaries and assistants to cover for them (Googins & Godfrey, 1987; McClellan, 1985).

As noted, core technology-focused EAPs typically employ an alcoholism counselor (often a recovering alcoholic), who provides counseling, confrontation, and referral to outside treatment programs but offers few prevention services. These EAPs are largely perceived by workers and supervisors alike as having a primary mission—getting documented alcoholics into detoxification, rehabilitation, and aftercare. Modern EAPs that emphasize positive changes in employees' life-styles, however, which Nathan (1984) studied, ironically seem to offer more effective alcoholism prevention programs. These programs lack the stigma associated with "alcoholism and addiction" and often are successful in attracting troubled workers (and codependent family members) because their services are perceived as nonjudgmental. An added advantage, Nathan stated, is that the organizational commitment of employers and unions to such broad-spectrum EAPs generally is much greater:

> Many managers have concluded that traditional employee assistance programs, those that focus only on alcoholism detection, referral, and treatment, may not be as effective as programs that extend their purview to a broader range of problems, including familial, vocational and financial, interpersonal, behavioral, and psychological/psychiatric ones. Often, this realization comes when the manager observes that many of the alcohol problems that come to his or her attention are either caused or exacerbated by problems from emotional, behavioral, or familial areas. Yet the traditional EAP counselor is rarely equipped to offer broad-spectrum counseling. (Nathan, 1984, p. 390)

Given both the human and financial advantages inherent in prevention, Nathan concluded that comprehensive EAPs are clearly a preferred model today. "Primary prevention of addictive problems," McClellan (1985, p. 34) added "is far more cost-effective than the secondary prevention and treatment that most EAPs have practiced."

Moreover, the reality is that workers with personal and emotional problems are *not* simply "the worried well." Mental health disorders are pervasive in our society and usually have no relation to the substance abuse of an individual or family member. A federally supported six-year national study of 20,000 people (cited in McClellan, 1985, p. 30) showed that 18.7 percent of American adults suffered from at least one mental health disorder during an average six-month period. In their 1986–87 national study of 182 randomly selected EAP practitioners, McClellan and Miller (1988) noted that the overwhelming number of practitioners and programs had begun to shift their focus to respond to this reality. More than half were providing diagnosis, not just assessment; ongoing counseling, as well as referrals; and health and wellness education, in addition to treatment. The nature of the EAPs' services had broadened and deepened in response to the demand from the workplace and employers' needs. McClellan and Miller concluded that neither the core technology nor EAPA's credentialing program adequately reflected the emerging scope of EAP activities. Furthermore, they observed that 17 percent of the responding EAPs, which reportedly offered mental health services, still did not have the skilled staff necessary to provide these services legally. With a touch of irony, Cunningham further documented the trend. In her study of programs in the Chicago area, she noted that many EAP staff "were distinctly uncomfortable about acknowledging that short-term counseling is as common a part of their practice as it is, commenting, for example, 'Well, you know we don't do any treatment here,' after having just detailed sensitive, perceptive and effective interventions with clients that are clearly examples of sophisticated clinical treatment" (Cunningham, 1989, p. 16).

Alcoholism, of course, is not the only problem in the workplace; indeed, as was just noted, it may no longer even be the dominant problem (Cocozzelli & Hudson, 1989; Dickman & Challenger, 1988). Stress, disability, work–family dilemmas, developmental disorders, dependent care, mental illness, and the addictions (broadly defined) appear to be the principal issues to which EAPs must respond today. Such presenting problems require EAP staff to be able to make complex differential diagnoses and to be trained in making sophisticated clinical and organizational assessments even if ongoing services are provided mainly through referral. Staff must be comfortable with a proactive, preventive, problem-solving mode of intervention with a wide variety of systemic issues and personal problems (Cunningham, 1990a). Therefore, the answer, when possible, has been to form an interdisciplinary EAP team with a qualified mental health professional (generally a social worker) at the helm (Bickerton, 1987, p. 14; Molloy, 1986). State licensure and graduate-level professional credentials have also become significant legal and risk-management requisites for employers, as several authors have noted (Kurzman, 1991; Masi & Montgomery, 1987; Nye, 1986; Nye, 1990, Ch. 8; O'Hair, 1987).

Professionalization

In 1987, EAPA established standards for receiving the designation Certified Employee Assistance Professional (CEAP). Applicants for CEAP are required to have three years of EAP experience and to pass a written examination. Although it is a sign of the further maturation of the field of practice, many believe that the use of the term *professional* is open to debate. The classic

contemporary hallmark of professional status in the Western world—
successful completion of a nationally accredited university course of professional study and a minimum standard of education (usually at the graduate
level)—*are not* requirements for the CEAP credential; one need not even be
a high school graduate to become a CEAP. Furthermore, there is no
nationally standardized curriculum that a CEAP must pursue to qualify for
"professional" status (Kurzman, 1992). By a process of somewhat magical
incrementalism, what Roman and Blum (1985, p. 19) referred to accurately
(in 1985) as the "EAP specialist" became (in 1987) the "EAP professional"
(Delaney, 1988). In an unsigned 1986 editorial ("On Defending Our EAP
Turf," p. 5), the leaders of EAPA (then ALMACA) were able to state simply:
"Through ALMACA's certification program, qualified EAP professionals
will soon have our CEAP designation beside their names. It will denote the
attainment of a professional status that ACSW, PhD, MBA, CAC and others
do not." However, this author agrees with Sonnenstuhl and Trice (1986, p.
56) that to become recognized as professionals, EAP practitioners "must first
lay claim to specialized knowledge and skills and then convince management, labor, employees, other occupations and the state that they actually
possess such knowledge and skills. Unfortunately, the tested body of knowledge about EAPs remains too small to claim the basis for a new occupation,
let alone profession."

Despite EAPA's preferences and predictions, professional social workers
with graduate MSW and or DSW degrees and eligibility for state licensure are
emerging today as the predominant EAP providers (Madonia, cited in *Employee
Assistance Programs*, 1987, p. 82; Tanner, 1991). Their training in both the
clinical and organizational dimensions of practice, education in independently
accredited graduate degree programs, and full qualification for certification or
licensure in all 50 states has helped to position social workers to assume this
leadership function. Like most other health and mental health practitioners,
social workers have had to overcome a paucity of exposure in their graduate
training to labor and management settings and to substance abuse and the
addictions. However, social workers with graduate degrees with a specialization
in the policy and practice of industrial–occupational social work will have
preparation today that includes these two important arenas of education for
EAP practice (Akabas & Kurzman, 1982, Chap. 9; Maiden & Hardcastle, 1986).

Program Models

Over time, the differences in educational preparation and evolving EAP
models have mirrored the perception of need by the major parties who share
a legitimate self-interest: management, labor, workers, and health-care

payers (providers). Table 1 contrasts the variables of the two most prominent models of contemporary EAPs.

As one can see, the comprehensive service paradigm focuses away from the medical model (emphasizing workers' health versus pathology) toward a social functioning perspective that underscores the need to identify and harness workers' strengths. Furthermore, health is reconceptualized, not just as the absence of disease, but as workers' functioning to their potential in the central arenas of life, such as love and work. The comprehensive model suggests that all people (including workers) have problems coping all the time with an environment that provides too few resources and a world that makes too many demands. Thus, it is the "healthy" worker who seeks help and the wholesome workplace that provides it without stigma. The help is likely to be for a personal problem (not for an illness or a disease) that is affecting the worker's ability to function. Hence, the comprehensive EAP should be able to find affordable day care for a worker's young children, elder care for a worker's aging parents, and special education services for a worker's dyslexic adolescent son or daughter. As a locus of information, advocacy, and human service expertise, the EAP becomes an oasis from which an anxious worker can drink. Core technology EAPs may not attract such workers, legitimate such presenting problems, or develop the program expertise to perform these functions well. Moreover, the focus on alcoholism in such EAPs sends a message to those who have problems but do not drink or abuse drugs that somehow *this* is what employers are really interested in (and will devote their resources to serve) and, even worse, that personal, situational, family, and environmental problems are not as important or will be dealt with by staff who do not have professional expertise in mental health.

Moreover, the idea that EAP staff do not need clinical skills because they usually refer workers to private practitioners or community agencies may be more a wish than a reality. For example, Cunningham's (1990b) Chicago-area study found that whereas salaried professional and managerial workers often had these options because they had good fringe-benefit packages or could afford to pay for such services, many wage workers had few or no benefits for outpatient or HMO mental health and substance abuse treatment. The EAPs' function of "assessment and referral" meant in reality that these workers would not be professionally served because the model "presumed" benefits that did not exist. These workers often were left to solve their problems themselves or to seek natural helpers, such as bartenders, beauticians, or clergy who might not have the time, mandate, or expertise to solve the problem.

As was noted earlier, although the core technology model has a history of success in reaching out to and serving middle- and later-stage alcoholics who work under close supervision in manufacturing settings, it may not be well

Table 1
Two EAP Models: Core Technology versus Comprehensive Service

VARIABLE	CORE TECHNOLOGY	COMPREHENSIVE SERVICE
Design	Management tool	A benefit for workers
Orientation	Alcohol and drug abuse	Personal problems that may affect ability to function productively
Principle	A workplace disciplinary alternative	A workplace social utility
Function	Supervisory training and intervention with workers	Supervisory training, intervention with workers, workplace health, education, wellness, and prevention
Focus	Current job performance	Present and potential capacity to function
Objective	To enhance employees' productivity	To preserve precious human and fiscal resources
Concept	New personnel prerogative for employers	New resource and entitlement for workers
Intervention	Constructive confrontation	Differential biopsychosocial assessment and intervention
Services	Prescribed and proscribed by the Roman–Blum (1985) model	Evolving to meet the changing needs of workers and work organizations
Scope	Assessment and referral	Assessment, referral, prevention, and short-term treatment
Intake	Primarily by supervisors' referrals	Referral by supervisors, self, and peers
Clients	Workers	Workers, families, and their communities
Prevention	Tertiary	Primary and secondary
Staffing	CEAPs with CAC counseling credentials	Interdisciplinary team, led by licensed health or mental health professional
Perspective	A health versus pathology perspective; goal: to discipline or to heal (cure)	An ecological-life perspective; goal: to enhance social functioning
Commitment	To provide prescribed services	To provide prescribed services and to promote social change

suited to the variety and complexity of today's presenting problems or organizationally to today's work environment. It is best suited to a factory pattern of production, which is on the wane. As Peter Drucker (cited in Googins, 1991c, p. 44) predicted, by the year 2000, manufacturing jobs will constitute less than 10 percent of employment, and assembly-line jobs *already* constitute less than 2 percent of employment in this country. The increasingly blurred boundary between supervisor and supervisee, as Zuboff (1988) and Peters and Waterman (1984) noted, makes "control" models much more difficult to implement. One of the most fundamental shifts in the American workplace today, according to Naisbitt and Aburdene (1985, p. 297), "is the movement away from the authoritarian hierarchy—where everyone has a superior and everyone has an inferior—to new lateral structures, lattices, networks, and small teams where people manage themselves." As McClellan (1985, p. 32) pointed out, constructive confrontation of the troubled worker in denial (which is the methodological centerpiece of the core technology model), "works best when supervisors are dealing with subordinates, there are clear lines of authority, and there are job descriptions with specific and measurable work performance criteria." These conditions do not exist for most professional, technical, and clerical workers and rarely exist in small businesses, which are the predominant employers in the United States today. Hence, a dispersed work force, performing with greater autonomy, makes the premises and precepts of the core technology less realistic.

The comprehensive service EAP model, underscoring not only supervisors' referral of workers in denial, but the appropriateness of self- and peer referrals, is a conceptually different program. It is an entitlement; a new occupational benefit; an expert, interdisciplinary resource that is available to workers and their families by dint of their affiliation with the workplace. In Kahn's (1973) terms, such EAPs are not stigmatized case services, but social utilities, located in the workplace. Therefore, the author now risks the following definition of the comprehensive service EAP model:

> Comprehensive EAPs are free and confidential workplace entitlements that are voluntarily sponsored by employers or trade unions or jointly by both. In-house (internal) and contract (external) EAPs respond to the human service needs of workers and their families and to the corresponding agendas of the work organization. Under the overall direction of professional health or mental health staff, such EAPs address comprehensive current and prospective biopsychosocial programs of education, prevention, assessment, treatment, case management, and referral.

Comprehensive Family Services

In many ways, the evolution of EAPs, from their original occupational alcoholism format, to "broad-brush" programs, and now increasingly to a comprehensive service arrangement, reflects the changing workplace and its emerging needs. Today, for example, the hallmark of an organizationally successful EAP is that it can attract significant self- and peer referrals. If an EAP is labeled (or is even informally known) only as a place to which workers are dispatched by supervisors, it will not be successful in providing a comprehensive service program. As Googins (1989, p. 10) noted, "If supervisors have the perception that the program over at medical is for drunks, then that is how they will use it." In such a case, the EAP will quickly lose its sense of mission, and the program will be consigned to a residual model of service, focused on "picking up the pieces" rather than on providing an institutional model oriented toward maintaining a physically, structurally, and emotionally healthy workplace. The advantage of the comprehensive design is the equal focus on cause and effect, prevention and treatment, and self-help and mutual aid, as well as professional intervention.

The core technology model, with its focus on workers and their supervisors, is easier to apply when the family and the workplace are conceptualized as separate domains (Roman, 1989). "The factory or office here comes to be seen as a complete, closed autonomous system," Titmuss (1963, p. 111) observed, "pursuing its own goals and developing its own values and norms of behavior regardless of the outside world." Such a closed systems model, however, does not fit well in the real world as we know it today. Therefore, it is surprising that Roman was willing to say, in 1991 (p. 20): "This leads me to a major assertion regarding the employee assistance program–work/family interface. These issues should *not* be accepted as an employee assistance program responsibility."

But Googins (1991c, p. 8) correctly noted that "the work system cannot exist unless it draws on the family system for its labor pool." Reciprocally, healthy families generally cannot be maintained without the income and occupational social welfare (fringe) benefits generated by their adult members. And yet, "there has been remarkably little attempt to link the two, that is, to locate problems in the work–family intersection, to determine the extent to which one system contributes to the health or illness possibilities of the other, or to discover what variations in each system make it most vulnerable to problems from the other" (Kanter, 1977, p. 81). Looking at work and family through separate lenses, as though they were two distinct worlds, is a contemporary myth that must be dispelled (Kurzman, 1988b, p. 68). An EAP that cannot embrace this fact of the 1990s is risking marginality, if not irrelevance.

As Googins (1991b, p. 17) noted in EAPA's own journal, "From many perspectives, the EAP is not only well-situated within the corporate structure, it is also ideologically and programmatically compatible with the work/

family movement. . . . EAPs have realized for some time now that family issues constitute the majority of their caseload, or at least the highest percentage of cases." Indeed two-career families, single-parent families, and unmarried working couples living together constitute more than 90 percent of today's labor force (Sekaran, 1986, p. 95). Any EAP that is unaware of this modern workplace reality or is unwilling to respond to its demands will soon lose the support and sanction of labor and management.

At Burlington Industries, with 35,000 employees at 65 sites, for example, the EAP was initiated to respond to substance abuse problems affecting productivity, using a supervisory referral model. However, the personnel director was surprised to discover that other issues were having an impact on employees' job performance. "Initially, what came out of the EAP right away," he noted, "were a great number of problems that dealt with family situations—financial, emotional problems, conflicts in the family—more so than substance abuse. Obviously, we needed to concentrate on the total scene" (Walters, 1988, p. 103). This business survey concluded that "EAPs still deal with alcoholism and other substance abuse; some get into problems such as gambling, compulsive spending or eating disorders. However, almost all find that increasingly it is mental health problems—stress, depression, grief, anxiety, phobias, as well as marriage, family and aging-parent issues—that bring staff members to the EAP" (Walters, 1988, p. 102). Located on the dividing line at which employee and family roles become theoretically distinct, but practically overlapping, comprehensive EAPs are in a perfect position to assist families and employers to identify and resolve work and family issues (Googins & Burden, 1987).

Cost Containment

The motivation for implementing EAPs is *not* a charitable or humanistic concern of businesses in this country. Nor is it solely a strategy of modern management to help workers function effectively in the context of a more autonomous, lateral, and participatory workplace. The reason that labor's and industry's commitment is so strong is, in part, pure dollars and cents (Donovan, 1984). Scarce health care dollars must be managed well, so they can be contained, on the one hand, and used more effectively, on the other (see Chapter 7). Health care is costing Americans more than $2 billion a day, far more than the total cost of the country's national defense. Total health spending has grown from less than 6 percent of the gross national product three decades ago to more than 14 percent today, and it is projected to reach 18 percent by the year 2000 (Pear, 1991). Contrary to popular opinion, employers, individuals, and private insurers (*not* the state or federal government) pick up the majority of this cost, which has *doubled* in the past five years. In 1990, the cost represented 26 percent of the average employer's net earnings (Pear, 1991, p. A-14). Although many companies have offered employees an option to join a health maintenance organization (HMO), Freudenheim (1991, p. D-1) found that only one-third of surveyed workers chose to join one. Furthermore, HMOs and discount networks have made only a small dent in the overall increases in spending for medical care in recent years and offer few mental health services.

Although the institution of a comprehensive service EAP is no panacea, it is increasingly likely to be one element in a multiphased approach to employers' containment of health care costs. Despite some opinion to the contrary, it is untrue that a core technology EAP will be more valued by labor and management because it is the only model whose cost-effectiveness can be measured. Business and labor leaders are much too sophisticated to accept this line of argument. They know that anxious and depressed workers—not just alcoholics—are making tremendous use of health benefits, that those who smoke, are overweight, or cannot manage stress well are at a high risk of health and mental health problems (Erfurt & Foote, 1990; Jenkins, 1988; Renner, 1987). Employers know, too, that they will pay for emotional problems and psychiatric disorders (even when the mental health benefit is limited or capped) because such employees, for the purposes of eligibility and reimbursement, will be covered under codes for legitimate physical (conversion) symptoms, just as alcoholics frequently are covered and reimbursed under codes for pancreatitis and cirrhosis when an alcoholism benefit does not exist. Managers realize that anxious and overwhelmed working mothers are applying for expensive disability coverage during times of crisis; that men who are depressed by the sadness of divorce are having more accidents, which result in increased premiums for workers' compensation; and that middle-aged daughters at work, who are caught without support in caring both for their young children and their aging parents, show higher rates of tardiness and absenteeism and may ultimately be discharged, under conditions that entitle them to six or more months of costly unemployment insurance.

Aware of these realities even 14 years ago, leaders of labor and management made the following observation at a Wingspread Conference on Human Service Needs in the Workplace:

> For an assistance program to yield its greatest potential, it must intervene in a greater scope of cases than only those where workers' personal problems have grown to interfere with their work performance. The scope must comprise cases where workers generally manage satisfactorily at their job but nonetheless suffer temporarily from personal or emotional problems. . . . Intervention is more cost effective when it is undertaken early than when it is applied after

their problems have spilled over into the workplace. (Meeting Human Service, 1980, p. 8)

From a cost-benefit perspective, waiting for a worker's performance to decline—whether from alcoholism, family problems, or mental illness—to the point at which he or she is in job jeopardy and hence is likely to warrant mandatory referral is much too costly to the employer. Instead, as McClellan (1985, p. 34) observed, "If EAPs are to avoid being part of the problem of rising health care costs, they must actively become part of the solution. They must re-evaluate their emphasis on waiting for supervisory referrals for problems that have already progressed to the point where they are adversely affecting job performance. They must proactively advocate health promotion and disease prevention programs." The die is cast.

Social Change

Roman (1991, p. 20) wrote that "Employee Assistance workers are expert at changing individuals' behavior, but altering environments is not in their kit bag." Such a proposition, if accepted, would pose a problem for social workers who are committed to both social services and social change. The issue tends to be moot in most labor and management settings, however, because the needs of the employing organization generally govern the outcome of this debate. Hence, what employee assistance workers are expert at is far less important than what labor and industry (who employ them) determine they need. Staff who can see the big picture—who can conceptualize the nature of long-range institutional requisites and can help the work organization to position its human resource functions wisely in a competitive world—will be the valued EAP workers. Experience has shown that this is what most work organizations want, even though they may not set such an explicit contract at the beginning.

For the social work profession, this is an old and honored issue, embracing Richmond's (1917) focus on the tension between "retail" and "wholesale," Schwartz's (1969) discussion of "private troubles" and "public issues," Wilensky and Lebeaux's (1965) concern with the "residual" and "institutional," and the Milford Conference's (*Social Case Work*, 1929/1974) attention to "cause" as well as "function." Inseparable from this discussion is the issue of social control and whether occupational social workers' professional use of self will be exclusively in the service of the individual or of the employing organization (Briar & Vinet, 1985). A fundamental question that social workers in these settings ask is this: Whose agent are we? (Kurzman, 1987). It is suggested that the profession's dual commitment to service (private troubles) and to change (public issues) implies that social workers must embrace and balance both functions.

As Walsh (1982, p. 514) noted, "while EAPs that are oriented principally toward organizational effectiveness or productivity continue to administer emotional first-aid to employees they scoop out of the rapids, they should also move upstream in search of explanations for why so many tumble in." Such an *institutional* perspective is valuable to a work organization because it addresses the possibility of prevention, which generally leads to a far less costly human resources solution. However, raising such "public issues" has risks. For example, if an EAP director concludes that a senior manager is sexually harassing employees (many of whom have come to the EAP as victims for help), a residual response alone would be insufficient—even unethical. Nevertheless, intervention "upstream" to deal with the cause may bring on a period of systemic disequilibrium when the problem is reconceptualized as being the result of a "troubled manager" or "troubled workplace," *not* a troubled employee. If the occupational social worker is not willing or able to define the problem properly, there may be a displacement of goals, whereby EAP practitioners (as some critics have noted) could become as much agents of social control as providers of social services (Bakalinsky, 1980; Walden, 1978). "To run an effective EAP," two experienced corporate program directors observed, "the social worker must make the EAP compatible with the environment without sacrificing professional values" (McCarthy & Steck, 1989, p. 23). Otherwise, Googins (1991a, p. 54) noted, the EAP can get "cöopted in very subtle ways to support unhealthy work environments and strategies that do not contribute to the overall well-being of employees and their families." In short, the EAP "kit bag" must be large enough and the commitment clear enough for occupational social workers to embrace both the delivery of professional human services and the promotion of progressive social change (Kurzman, 1988a).

Conclusion

Sixteen years ago, Roman lamented a change he observed in the preferred EAP model. Occupational programs, he wrote, are showing a "decreasing emphasis throughout the country on employee *alcoholism* programs, and the employee *assistance* model, with its broad implications for comprehensive mental health programs, is coming to dominate the scene" (Roman, 1977, p. 9). Roman (and his colleagues in sociology and industrial relations) have ingenuously argued that this shift has occurred not because work organizations prefer the comprehensive model, but because mental health providers have been successful in selling labor and management what they do not want! However, anyone who has worked with corporate and labor leaders would know that they are beholden to their own shareholders for appointment, or members for reelection, not to psychologists or to social workers. Union and corporate leaders generally are shrewd managers who know how to protect their individual and organizational self-interest. In this realm, they are indeed tough negotiators, who guard their legitimate vested interests as cost-effectively as they can. Therefore, anyone who thinks that businesses are adopting the comprehensive service model not because they need it, but because social workers are such good salespersons is inexperienced with respect to decision making in industry. That is apparently why Erfurt and Foote (1977, p. 3) concluded 16 years ago that "there is general agreement . . . that occupational programs should be of the *comprehensive* type, rather than focus on specific types of employee problems."

The shifts and changes noted here are not occurring in the context of a static environment, however. The major changes in society that are taking place are being reflected in the workplace. These demographic, economic, and ecological factors, more than anything else, have shaped modern EAPs and have had an impact on—and perhaps even have resolved—conflicting opinions about the role, services, and domain of EAPs in the year 2000. The comprehensive service EAP model is replacing the core technology design not because professionals prefer it. The comprehensive model is being adopted because it better meets the legitimate vested interests of labor and management for a stable and productive work force on which they *both* depend.

References

Akabas, S. H., & Kurzman, P. A. (Eds.). (1982). *Work, workers and work organizations: A view from social work.* Englewood Cliffs, NJ: Prentice Hall.

Akabas, S. H., Kurzman, P. A., & Kolben, N. S. (Eds.). (1979). *Labor and industrial settings: Sites for social work practice.* New York: Columbia University, Hunter College, & Council on Social Work Education.

Bakalinsky, R. (1980). People vs. profits: Social work in industry. *Social Work, 25,* 471–475.

Bickerton, D. (1987). NIDA sponsors workplace problems meeting. *The Almacan, 17*(5), 12–15.

Briar, K. H., & Vinet, M. (1985). Ethical questions concerning an EAP: Who is the client? In S. H. Klarreich, J. L. Francek, & E. C. Moore (Eds.), *The human resources management handbook* (pp. 342–359). New York: Praeger.

Cocozzelli, C., & Hudson, C. G. (1989). Recent advances in alcoholism diagnosis and treatment assessment research: Implications for practice. *Social Service Review, 63,* 533–552.

Cunningham, G. (1989). *Clinical practices in EAPs: Preliminary research report.* Unpublished manuscript, Loyola University School of Social Work, Chicago.

Cunningham, G. (1990a). Short-term counseling. *Employee Assistance Quarterly*, *10*(4), 21–25.

Cunningham, G. (1990b). Social work and EAPs: Emerging issues. *Social Thought*, *16*(1), 34–40.

Delaney, T. J. (1988). From the executive director. *The Almacan*, *18*(10), 4–5.

Dickman, F., & Challenger, B. R. (1988). Employee assistance programs: Future perspectives. In F. Dickman, B. R. Challenger, W. G. Emener, & W. S. Hutchison (Eds.), *Employee assistance programs* (Chap. 40). Springfield, IL: Charles C Thomas.

DiNitto, D. M., & McNeece, C. A. (1990). Business, industry and the social work profession. In D. M. DiNitto & C. A. McNeece, *Social work: Issues and opportunities* (pp. 261–293). Englewood Cliffs, NJ: Prentice Hall.

Donovan, R. (1984). The dollars and "sense" of human services at the workplace: A review of cost-effectiveness research. *Social Work Papers*, *18*(1), 65–73.

Employee assistance programs: Benefits, prospects and problems. (1987). Washington, DC: Bureau of National Affairs.

Erfurt, J. C., & Foote, A. (1977). *Occupational employee assistance programs for substance abuse and mental health problems.* Ann Arbor: University of Michigan Press.

Erfurt, J. C., & Foote, A. (1990). A healthy alliance: Ford Motor and the UAW endorse a wellness program through their EAP. *Employee Assistance*, *2*(6), 41–44.

Erfurt, J. C., Foote, A., & Heinrich, M. A. (1990). *The core technology of megabrush: Employee assistance and wellness programs combined.* Ann Arbor: Institute of Labor and Industrial Relations, University of Michigan.

Foote, A., & Erfurt, J. C. (1981). Effectiveness of comprehensive EAPs at reaching alcoholics. *Journal of Drug Issues*, *2*, 217–232.

Freudenheim, M. (1991, January 29). Health care: A growing burden. *New York Times*, pp. D1, D9.

Googins, B. K. (1989). Looking in the mirror. *Employee Assistance*, *1*(9), 10–18.

Googins, B. K. (1991a). Challenges for the EAP of the 1990s. *Employee Assistance*, *4*(3), 54–56.

Googins, B. K. (1991b). EAPs and the workplace response. *EAPA Exchange*, *21*(6), 14–18.

Googins, B. K. (1991c). *Work/family conflicts: Private lives, public responses.* Westport, CT: Auburn House.

Googins, B. K., & Burden, D. (1987). Vulnerability of working parents: Balancing work and home roles. *Social Work*, *32*, 295–300.

Googins, B. K., & Godfrey, J. (1987). *Occupational social work.* Englewood Cliffs, NJ: Prentice Hall.

Holosko, M. J., & Feit, M. D. (1988). Onward and upward. *Employee Assistance Quarterly*, *3*(4), 281–283.

Jenkins, J. L. (1988). Health enhancement programs. In G. M. Gould & M. L. Smith (Eds.), *Social work in the workplace* (pp. 125–151). New York: Springer.

Kahn, A. J. (1973). *Social policy and social services.* New York: Random House.

Kanter, R. M. (1977). *Work and family in the United States.* New York: Russell Sage Foundation.

Kurzman, P. A. (1987). Industrial/occupational social work. In A. Minahan (Ed.-in-Chief), *Encyclopedia of social work* (18th ed., Vol. 2, pp. 899–910). Silver Spring, MD: National Association of Social Workers.

Kurzman, P. A. (1988a). The ethical base for social work in the workplace. In G. M. Gould & M. L. Smith (Eds.), *Social work in the workplace* (pp. 17–27). New York: Springer.

Kurzman, P. A. (1988b). Work and family: Some major dilemmas. In C. S. Chilman, F. M. Cox, & E. W. Nunnally (Eds.), *Economic and employment problems: Families in trouble* (pp. 67–83). Newbury Park, CA: Sage Publications.

Kurzman, P. A. (1991). Managing risk in the workplace. In R. L. Edwards & J. A. Yankey (Eds.), *Skills in effective human services management* (pp. 267–280). Silver Spring, MD: National Association of Social Workers.

Kurzman, P. A. (1992). Employee assistance program staffing: Past, present and future. *Employee Assistance Quarterly, 8*(2), 79–88.

Kurzman, P. A., & Akabas, S. H. (1981). Industrial social work as an arena for practice. *Social Work, 26,* 52–60.

MacDonald, G., Trudeau, A., Day, M., Edgeworth, T., Hicks, B., Roznowsky, S., Kotyk, V., & Ladd J. (1987). Mandatory referrals: Are they worth it? *EAP Digest, 7*(6), 46–54.

Maiden, P. R., & Hardcastle, D. A. (1986). Social work education: Professionalizing EAPs. *EAP Digest, 7*(1), 63–66.

Martin, D. W., Heckel, V. M., Goodrick, G. K., Schreiber, M. M., & Young, V. L. (1985). The relationship between referral types, work performance and employee problems. *Employee Assistance Quarterly, 1*(2), 25–33.

Masi, D. A. (1979). Combating alcoholism in the workplace. *Health and Social Work, 4*(4), 41–59.

Masi, D. A. (1984). *Designing employee assistance programs.* New York: AMACOM.

Masi, D., & Montgomery, P. (1987). Future directions for EAPs. *The Almacan, 17*(3), 20–21.

McCarthy, D. E., & Steck, S. B. (1989). Social work in private industry: Assessing the corporate culture. *Employee Assistance Quarterly, 5*(1), 19–35.

McClellan, K. (1985). The changing nature of EAP practice. *Personnel Administrator, 30*(8), 29–37.

McClellan, K., & Miller, R. E. (1988). EAPs in transition: Purpose and scope of services. *Employee Assistance Quarterly, 3*(4), 25–41.

McGowan, B. G. (1984). *Trends in employee counseling programs.* New York: Pergamon Press.

Meeting human service needs in the workplace: A role for social work. (1980). New York: Columbia University, Hunter College, & Council on Social Work Education.

Molloy, D. J. (1986). *Planning and implementing a worker-based and participating model for EAPs.* Unpublished DSW dissertation, City University of New York Graduate Center.

Naisbitt, J., & Aburdene, P. (1985). *Re-inventing the corporation: Transforming your job and your company for the new information society.* New York: Warner Books.

Nathan, P. E. (1984). Alcoholism prevention in the workplace. In P. M. Miller & T. D. Nirenberg (Eds.), *Prevention of alcohol abuse* (pp. 387–405). New York: Plenum.

Nye, S. G. (1986). As EAPs come of age as clinical care providers: What doth the law require? *Employee Assistance Quarterly, 2*(1), 99–101.

Nye, S. G. (1990). *Employee assistance law answer book.* New York: Panel Publishers.

O'Hair, J. R. (1987). Looking into the future of employee assistance. *The Almacan, 7*(3), 22–24.

On defending our EAP turf. (1986). *The Almacan, 16*(11), 5.

Pear, R. (1991, April 17). Darman forecasts dire health costs. *New York Times,* p. A-14.

Peters, T. J., & Waterman, R. H. (1984). *In search of excellence.* New York: Warner Books.

Renner, J. F. (1987). Wellness programs: An investment in cost containment. *EAP Digest, 7*(3), 49–53.

Richmond, M. E. (1917). *Social diagnosis.* New York: Russell Sage Foundation.

Roman, P. M. (1977). *Dimensions of current research in occupational alcoholism.* Unpublished manuscript, Tulane University, New Orleans.

Roman, P. M. (1989). EAPs have been the last stop for unwanted duties. *Employee Assistance, 2*(4), 8–9.

Roman, P. M. (1991). The quagmire of work-family conflicts. *Employee Assistance, 3*(9), 19–21.

Roman, P. M., & Blum, T. C. (1985). The core technology of employee assistance programs. *The Almacan, 15*(3), 8–19.

Roman, P. M., & Blum, T. C. (1988). The core technology of EAPs: A reaffirmation. *The Almacan, 18*(8), 17–22.

Schwartz, W. (1969). Private troubles and public issues: One social work job or two? *Social welfare forum, 1969* (pp. 22–43). New York: Columbia University Press.

Sekaran, U. (1986). *Dual career families.* San Francisco: Jossey-Bass.

Shain, M., & Groeneveld, J. (1980). *Employee assistance programs: Philosophy, theory and practice.* Lexington, MA: Lexington Books.

Social case work: Generic and specific—A report of the Milford Conference (1974). Washington, DC: National Association of Social Workers. (Original work published 1929)

Sonnenstuhl, W. J., & Trice, H. M. (1986). *Strategies for EAPs: The crucial balance.* Ithaca, NY: ILR Press.

Tanner, R. M. (1991). Social work: The profession of choice for EAPs. *Employee Assistance Quarterly, 6*(3), 71–84.

Titmuss, R. M. (1963). *Essays on the welfare state* (2nd ed.). Boston: Beacon Press.

Vigilante, F. W. (1988). The interactive relationship between work life and family life. In C. S. Chilman, F. M. Cox, & E. W. Nunnally (Eds.), *Economic and employment problems: Families in trouble* (pp. 85–101). Newbury Park, CA: Sage Publications.

Walden, T. (1978). Industrial social work: A conflict in definitions. *NASW News, 23*(5), 3, 9.

Walsh, D. C. (1982). Employee assistance programs. *Milbank Memorial Fund Quarterly/Health and Society, 60*(3), 492–517.

Walters, B. R. (1988, February). A mentally healthy work force: EAPs can help managers and employees. *Piedmont Airlines Magazine*, pp. 101–103.

Wilensky, H. L., & Lebeaux, C. N. (1965). *Industrial society and social welfare.* New York: Free Press.

Zuboff, S. (1988). *In the age of the smart machine: The future of work and power.* New York: Basic Books.

CHAPTER 3

Practice with Unions

COLLABORATING TOWARD AN EMPOWERMENT MODEL

Daniel J. Molloy and Paul A. Kurzman

> You can't eat for eight hours a day nor drink for eight hours a
> day nor make love for eight hours a day—all you can do for
> eight hours is work. Which is the reason why man makes
> himself and everybody else so miserable and unhappy.
> —William Faulkner
> *Writers at Work*

The occupational social work literature tends to see the workplace through the lens of the employing organization, viewing employers as the innovators of programs and the providers of services to employees and their families. As an extension of the occupational social welfare benefit system that Titmuss (1968) proposed, these non-legislatively mandated benefits and services are seen as the employer's grant of new entitlements to the work force as a managerial initiative. However, there is a second lens through which occupational programs should be viewed, especially for the almost 16 percent of the American labor force that is represented by a trade union.

This chapter defines and describes the human services provided by unions to their members. Placed in a historical perspective, the programs may have evolved only in the past 50 years; however, the antecedents of the emerging partnership between the labor movement and the social work profession date back to the Industrial Revolution and the turn of the 20th century. This review of the major human service programs under the auspices of labor unions explores the unfolding models, noting the similarities (and differences) to programs under the aegis of employers. The discussion concludes with a projection of future trends, based on forces in the world of work that are already in motion.

Historical Context

The relationship between social work and organized labor in the United States has been ambivalent, reflecting great fluctuations and changes over time. At the turn of the 20th century, social workers were seen as Lady Bountifuls, giving charity to working people, rather than fighting for social justice in the workplace. The assistance they gave to poor immigrant workers and their families came with large doses of advice and moral judgment. Also central to social work's stance was opposition to labor's central weapon, the strike, and a consistent refusal to side with a labor union's fierce enmity toward strikebreakers and "scabs." During the rampantly pro-business decade of the 1920s, social workers often were lured by industry to serve as "welfare secretaries," helping workers with personal and economic problems, but always as agents of the employers. Moreover, it was not lost on the union movement that the corporations that were most likely to hire welfare secretaries were most solidly anti-union in policy and practice (Akabas & Kurzman, 1982).

In the 1930s, social work moved into the public sector because the voluntary agencies (supported largely by corporate dollars) could no longer fulfill the human and social needs of Americans during the Great Depression. No longer tied to private agencies (financed by welfare capitalism in the first two decades of the century), social workers moved toward a closer relationship with the growing labor movement. With a new, public base of financial support and a growing conviction that individual intervention had to give way to collective action and to systemic social change, the emerging social work profession found itself ideologically closer to organized labor. Prominent social workers, such as Jane Addams, supported the garment workers in building their unions; Harry Hopkins sided with workers at every turn, seeing them (not the corporations) as America's heroes; and Harry Lurie led the National Conference on Social Welfare to support Roosevelt's New Deal, as well as the right of workers to organize and bargain collectively with their employers.

Prominent social work educators and practitioners, such as Grace Marcus, Mary Simkhovitch, Inabel Lindsay, and Wayne McMillen, began to support union activities openly and actively. Progressive social work journals, such as *Social Work Today* and *Survey Graphic*, published articles that were fiercely supportive of the growing trade union movement. Most important, social workers themselves were joining labor unions or organizing their own locals when none were present in the voluntary sector (Karger, 1989). Although today professional social workers belong to diverse unions, the majority are members of the American Federation of State, County and Municipal

Employees (AFSCME), the Service Employees International Union (SEIU), the Communications Workers of America (CWA), and the Drug, Hospital and Health Care Employees Union (Alexander, 1987).

In addition, occupational social workers have provided direct services to members of labor unions and their families under union auspices since 1943. The pioneer social work service to merchant seamen who were members of the National Maritime Union was the first major commitment of the profession to a trade union as an employer and a service provider. Reynolds's landmark work as project director of this four-year member assistance program (MAP) set the stage for future collaborative ventures (Reynolds, 1951/1975). Notable among the programs that followed were the achievements of the social work research, rehabilitation, and service project led by Weiner and Akabas at the Amalgamated Clothing Workers of America from 1964 to 1968 and the development in 1971 of ongoing MAP and legal assistance programs at District Council 37 of the AFSCME (Cook & Terruso, 1983; Weiner, Akabas, & Sommer, 1973).

Although today's relationship is a mutually beneficial one, the inherently fragile nature of the link between organized labor and the social work profession cannot be ignored (Straussner & Phillips, 1988). Social workers work in corporate settings more frequently than in labor unions, and the interests and ideology of many social workers are still often more toward the provision of social services than toward the creation of progressive social change (Karger, 1988).

The Labor Setting

Today, most of the more than 200 independent and autonomous unions in the United States belong to a national federation called the American Federation of Labor and Congress of Industrial Organizations (AFL-CIO). Technically international in scope (in that some unions have members in Mexico and Canada as well), the national union structure generally is organized into locals and district councils. Electing its own officers, each union local largely determines its policies and forges its own destiny through the work of its staff in the day-by-day relationship with the employers for whom its members work. In addition, central labor councils are often formed in major cities, so that the many union locals can have a collective influence on public policy and receive training and services for their staffs (representatives and business agents) and volunteers (shop stewards and union counselors), which a central body can best provide. The AFL-CIO central office does considerable research, economic analysis, and lobbying in Washington, DC, on behalf of its member unions, and the AFL-CIO's Committee on Political Education, Department of Education, and Department of Community Services support the several international member unions, state labor councils, and the union locals. All the international unions and many of the locals and district councils manage semiautonomous health and welfare (pension and benefit) funds for their members. These funds frequently provide the auspices and financial support for occupational social work services to union members.

A notable difference between most employing organizations and trade unions is the locus of power. In industry, power ultimately is held by investors and shareholders—"absentee owners," in Veblen's (1938) term. Hence, corporations are controlled from the top. Chief executive officers can be hired or replaced by the vote of the board of directors, reflecting the shareholders' wishes. Trade union leaders, however, are elected "from below" by the collective vote of dues-paying members. Conceptually, labor unions are "member-owned" organizations, whose leaders depend on the relative satisfaction of the members they represent to gain and hold office. The difference in the locus of power in these two organizations has implications, as will be shown, for the evolution of mental health, rehabilitation, and social services in the workplace.

Rationale for Services

The landmark social work service programs at the National Maritime Union, the Amalgamated Clothing Workers of America, and District Council 37 (AFSCME) have already been mentioned. As successful as each program may indeed have proved to be, what also is notable is the path they cut for similar programs, starting primarily in the 1970s. Not only did social work pioneers show skeptical observers that it could be done, they put forward a conceptualization of why their experiments had been successful. As Akabas (1977, p. 743) observed:

> When the benefits of labor organization are available to all workers, either through collective bargaining or through employers' unilateral efforts to avoid organization, some new enticement must be offered to achieve union membership growth and loyalty.

Having won as many financial gains in wages and benefits as they could, the unions now needed to create new services to maintain the loyalty of their members and leaders. Although wages and working conditions would always remain the central labor agenda, there was a perceived need for both "bread *and* roses" (Meltzer, 1967). Members were not looking for charity, but, in Samuel Gompers's term, for "advocates" who would help them achieve a greater measure of social justice (Mandel, 1963).

In this spirit, unions in major industrial centers, with a historically strong and progressive labor tradition, have been the most responsive to occupational social work programs. In Detroit, New York, Philadelphia, San Francisco, and Seattle, unions have expressed interest and begun programs to serve both active and retired members. A partial list of labor unions that employ professional social workers today in such programs includes the Amalgamated Clothing and Textile Workers Union; AFSCME; United Automobile Workers Union; International Ladies' Garment Workers' Union (ILGWU); National Maritime Union; Oil, Chemical and Atomic Workers Union; American Federation of Musicians; Sheet Metal Workers Union; Drug, Hospital and Health Care Employees Union; SEIU; and the International Brotherhood of Teamsters.

In addition to maintaining the loyalty of members to their leaders, labor-based occupational social work programs have proved helpful to union staff in protecting members' jobs. Before such programs were instituted, a union grievance worker often felt helpless at an arbitration hearing against management's detailed documentation of a troubled member's repeated absenteeism, lateness, drinking, or declining job performance. However, when a trained social worker on the staff of the union's MAP can attest to the presence of a health or mental health problem, and make a professional commitment to oversee appropriate individual or group treatment, management's arguments for immediate dismissal may be tempered by the union's guarantee to provide or supervise the necessary care. When a labor leader institutes such an occupational program that helps to protect a member's job, loyalty is likely to follow.

Range of Services

In keeping with the themes of protecting members' jobs and providing an additional membership benefit, labor-sponsored programs have blended advocacy with the provision of services. Recognizing the complexity of managing as an individual or, more commonly, as a family, union-based occupational social work programs have focused on linking members to hard-to-find entitlements, providing short-term on-site personal social services, and removing the stigma associated with accepting help. Hard-to-find entitlements include the many government-sponsored benefits to which working (and retired) people may be entitled but of which they may be unaware or unable to negotiate on their own. Personal services include, in Kamerman and Kahn's (1976) terms, both public and private social utilities and individual and family case services. Negotiating the fragmented and often transient public and voluntary community service arrangements is a skill that social workers have that is of great value to a membership organization. Going well beyond information and referral, professional staff usually have the capacity to form firm links with public benefit programs and voluntary service providers. Equally important, occupational social workers have the expertise to provide specialized and emergency services in-house, including individual and group counseling for substance abuse, disability management, and mental health care (Akabas, Kurzman, & Kolben, 1979).

The range of services that labor-based social workers provide is impressive by any measure. Given the centrality of alcohol and drug abuse, many occupational social workers either have credentials (or their equivalent) as alcoholism counselors or supervise certified substance abuse counselors who have this specialized expertise. The social workers provide constructive confrontation to members in denial, a differential chemical-dependence assessment (using CAGE and MAST questionnaires), referral (if appropriate) for detoxification, links to 12-step programs, ongoing supervision of rehabilitation services and aftercare, job protection while the member is in treatment or on disability, and preparation for reentry to the workplace (Molloy et al., 1980). They bring expert knowledge of the member's fringe-benefit package, the union's collective bargaining agreement, and provisions of the Americans with Disabilities Act of 1990.

Earning too much to qualify for Medicaid-covered services, but too little to pay for services in the marketplace, working people often find themselves without mental health care when they need it. Therefore, the provision of clinical social work intervention for members with recurring personal and emotional problems is a treasured service. Free, confidential, and on-site—and offered by labor-sensitive, licensed mental health providers—such individual and group services would be prohibitively costly for many union members, even if they could find them in the community (Akabas & Kurzman, 1982).

Labor-sponsored mental health care has grown to become an important social work service, in part from the discoveries of Weiner and Akabas in their landmark study from 1964 to 1968 in the unionized garment industry. Weiner and Akabas found that union members could be maintained at work, despite serious mental illness, provided that appropriate professional mental health and rehabilitation services were available. They also demonstrated that a working population would use this service if the professional staff could focus intervention on real-world "here-and-now" issues and through short-term models of service (Weiner et al., 1973). Today, the delivery of task-centered "brief-treatment" mental health care, as discussed in Chapter 11, is a central component of most union-based occupational social work programs (Epstein, 1992).

In a similar vein, social workers have begun to play a significant role in the arenas of occupational safety and health and disability management. The organization of sectors of the industrial work force into labor unions led to specific collective bargaining provisions in the area of safety and health before federal regulations (Straussner & Phillips, 1988). Working with labor–management teams as sponsors and employer or union medical departments as referral agents, occupational social workers have provided these services. The passage of the federal Occupational Safety and Health Act in 1970 gave labor a statutory framework on which the enforcement of standards could be based (through the regulatory functions of the Occupational Safety and Health Administration in the U.S. Department of Labor) and collaborative research could be conducted (through scientific investigations of the National Institute of Occupational Safety and Health in the U.S. Department of Health and Human Services). Union advocacy has been a significant impetus for ensuring that a reluctant federal government maintains these minimum standards and conducts the research it is authorized to oversee on behalf of working people. As numerous observers have noted, social work's presence here has made a difference (Balgopal & Nofz, 1989; Lewis, 1989; Lewis & Mama, 1987; Needleman, 1986; Shanker, 1983).

Similar initiatives have been taken to serve disabled carpenters and electricians under the auspices of the AFL-CIO's Human Resources Development Institute. Helping members with short-term disabilities maintain their connection to the labor force and providing a placement program for those who may have dropped out have been major achievements of the AFL-CIO program. Moreover, in collaboration with union health and security plans, Columbia University School of Social Work's Center for Social Policy and Practice in the Workplace has demonstrated that a labor union's welfare and benefit program may be one of the best places for early access to newly disabled workers (Krauskopf & Akabas, 1988). A pilot social work project, in collaboration with the largest trade union in New York City, showed that the profession's ecological, person-in-situation, early intervention, and systems sensitive foci fit well with the philosophy of the union and the pragmatic needs of its newly disabled members (Akabas, Fine, & Yasser, 1982). Indeed, a partnership in the arena of disability management between social work and labor may hold a key to members' successful return to work following the onset of a disability (Akabas, 1986; Akabas, Gates, & Galvin, 1992; see also Chapter 13).

Opportunities to serve retired workers and to sponsor preretirement planning workshops for members in mid- and late career have also been fertile ground for labor-based services. The union leadership has a stake in its senior and retired members because they often built the union, supported its leaders, and may continue to vote when they retire. These members may also be organized as an active force on behalf of the union's political and social welfare agenda. Group work and community development skills have proved successful in preparing older members for the emotional and financial changes that usually accompany retirement. Retired members tend to be grateful for their union's continued and skillful expression of caring and often return the favor in loyalty and volunteer services (Habib & Gutwill, 1985; Kiezer & Habib, 1980; Monk, 1990; Safford, 1988; True & Wineman, 1989; Wineman, 1990). Among the trade unions that employ occupational social workers to deliver such retiree and preretiree services are District 65, United Auto Workers; District Council 37, AFSCME; Local 237, International Brotherhood of Teamsters; ILGWU; National Maritime Union; and the Amalgamated Clothing and Textile Workers of America.

Social workers' presence in union settings extends to other labor initiatives as well. Included in any list would be the profession's role in programs for displaced workers (Foster & Schore, 1989); child care in the workplace by the SEIU and the Amalgamated Clothing and Textile Workers (McCroskey, 1984); safe-homes projects for battered working women (Cook & Terruso, 1983); and legal services for members, including closed-panel programs under the AFL-CIO's Union Privilege Legal Services Program and prepaid programs of Teamsters Local 237, SEIU's Local 32BJ, and the District Council 37 (AFSCME) Municipal Employees' Legal Services Plan (Menashe & Tronolone, 1982; Molloy & Burmeister, 1989; National Resource Center, n.d.).

Models of Service

Two forms of services for workers and their families have been occurring in union settings over at least the past 20 years. On the one hand, much of the help that workers have been giving to fellow workers, formally and informally, for as long as the labor movement has been in existence has been organized and formalized in recent years. On the other hand, occupational social workers, with professional expertise, have also come to be service providers in many of the progressive union settings just discussed. All too often, however, they have passed each other in the corridors of labor.

The achievements of occupational social workers, as noted, have been built on the creative conceptualizations and documented achievements of professional pioneers at such settings as the National Maritime Union and the Amalgamated Clothing Workers Union. Social work's commitment to advocacy for clients and progressive social change has made it a natural ally of labor in pursuit of the goals of social justice. Unions look to social workers to cultivate an advocacy capacity for their members within the social service system—a system to which they pay taxes, as wage earners, and to which they make generous United Way contributions, through voluntary deductions from their paychecks.

In addition to sharing many values in common, social work's increasing respect for union members' capacity to cope with difficult personal and organizational dilemmas fortuitously came at a time when many social workers were beginning to embrace a more cause-and-effect social functioning practice perspective (Donovan, Kurzman, & Rotman, in press). Social workers came to see that people's needs represent problems in living, rather than personality disturbances. Thus, help could be matched to the problem as the worker defined it (Germain, 1973), and the service could be provided at the "crossroads of life," rather than at a social agency uptown (Meyer, 1976; Reynolds, 1951/1975). The emphasis would not be on workers' pathology, but on their strengths (see Chapter 17).

At the same time, AFL-CIO leaders were promoting the idea of "a human contract," to complement and supplement formal contractual provisions of the collective bargaining agreement. This social contract called for a joint labor-management-social work partnership in building services in the workplace to meet the needs of the labor force. As it was then enunciated by Perlis (1977, pp. 31–32), director of the AFL-CIO's Community Service Department,

> the human contract . . . should concern itself with those personal and family problems which are not covered by the union contract. . . . professionals, equipped with special expertise, can help both management and labor . . . focus attention on the needs of the individual. . . . What every joint union-management committee needs . . . is a professional trained in industrial social work.

However, although Perlis opted for professional helpers to administer and deliver services to workers, this preference has by no means been universal in the labor movement. A large number of labor unions have urged that a peer-outreach model be promoted as an alternative. Whereas the motivation for this latter model may be partly pragmatic (peer counselors are volunteers, not salaried staff), part of the preference is inherent in the ideology of the labor movement. Historically, union "brothers" and "sisters" have helped each other in time of need in the spirit of fellowship and solidarity. Peer outreach and counseling is a logical extension of this principle and is syntonic with the very essence of union folkways and culture (Allen, Chapin, Keller, & Hill, 1979; Antoniades 1984).

The ideology of the union peer-counseling movement is that peers can best identify each other's needs and can best assist each other. Professionals, who are not from the ranks, may not have the members' trust or the occupational acumen to provide meaningful help (Winick, 1982). Hence, the AFL-CIO Community Service Department (and its local committees) regularly sponsor eight- to 10-session evening courses for union volunteers who want to prepare to become peer counselors for labor agencies and labor councils. The sessions focus on recognizing troubled workers, gaining their trust, identifying community services, making an appropriate referral, and ensuring that the members' jobs are properly protected while they receive help. Up to 5,000 union members a year have been trained in such programs (Miller & Metz, 1991).

Peer outreach and counseling programs have been successful in many union settings. Pilots, teachers, flight attendants, garment workers, locomotive engineers, and merchant seamen have used this model effectively under the auspices of their specific unions, reporting wide acceptance of the model by both labor and management and high levels of utilization. The model has worked particularly well in reaching out to members who are dealing with alcohol and drug abuse problems, in that the peer-support and mutual aid principles intersect in the use of 12-step helping programs (Antoniades & Bellinger, 1983; Gardner, 1988; Molloy et al., 1980; Reynolds, 1963/1991; Silverman, Simon, & Woodrow, 1991).

Indeed, mutual aid is a preferred theme in most of the labor movement, which has long approached "outside experts" with some degree of caution. Just as important, research on the effectiveness of peer intervention has been encouraging, leading one observer to conclude that, "peer intervention is an understudied area holding enormous promise for occupational programming" in the future (Molloy, 1989, p. 336). Such findings may account, in part, for why professional MAPs are not more widespread today in labor settings.

Conclusion

The future of the labor movement may depend on the services it can offer present and prospective members. Just as important as wages and benefits, unions will need to offer access to those social and psychological supports that money cannot buy. As one labor economist (Holusha, 1990, p. 12) stated, "Unions will have to become more social service organizations if they are to have much of a future." Workers desperately need the sense of stability and community that unions can provide. The organizations that have traditionally provided advocacy, understanding, fellowship, and links to entitlements (such as schools, churches, political clubs, and community centers) appear to be markedly less effective in doing so today. Workers need to be served and empowered, and services at the workplace may be best positioned to fill this gap and to achieve these objectives.

Peer-service programs do not seem to be incompatible with occupational social work service models. In fact, Molloy's (1986) study of building peer counseling and outreach committees at the National Maritime Union suggested that the linkage of peers with professionals tends to create a partnership between natural and formal helpers, facilitating and enriching the work of both. In this spirit, social workers and other human service providers in the many union settings in New York, for example, have come together for program and planning purposes under the AFL-CIO's New York Central Labor Council as the Human Services Providers Advisory Committee. In addition, several schools of social work (notably Hunter College and Columbia University) have promoted the training of graduate social work students specifically for labor settings, and faculty in these schools have served as consultants in developing new MAPs, as well as legal services, disability management, and retiree outreach programs. In the spirit of Perlis's human contract, these and other schools of social work have insisted on viewing organized labor as a key partner in occupational social work research, policy, and practice (Kurzman, 1987). As testimony to modest success, the ILGWU and AFSCME benefit plans in New York City, for example, *each* now employ more professional social workers than are currently employed in *any* corporate-sponsored setting in the country.

A reality is that social work and the labor movement share many goals and much ideology and they need one another. As Wagner (1991, p. 477) noted:

> In an era of plant closings, deindustrialization, declining per capita incomes, and persistent unemployment, social workers and labor union leaders and members should be natural allies. Working people make up the majority of social work's clientele, and despite the numerical decline of union membership, trade unions remain the only vehicle of representation that exists among working people.

As more social workers themselves have joined unions, more have come to understand the importance of the collectivity and the appropriateness of this environment as a setting for advocacy and service. Labor unions, buffeted by downsizing, deregulation, leveraged buyouts, and a spreading "contingency work force," need what social workers can provide to their members. As AFL-CIO leaders have noted, "There is a race to assist members in solving their 'off the job' problems and the prize is loyalty. Organized labor cannot afford to lose this one" (*The Community*, 1978, p. 16).

The social work profession in general and occupational social workers in particular are in quest of settings that will permit the pursuit of the dual goals of delivering high-quality social services and promoting progressive social change. Those opportunities are available at the workplace, and democratic trade unions are compatible auspices for their quest. The increasing understanding of and support for peer, self-help, and mutual aid program modalities make it more likely today than in the past that the peer and professional models can work side by side. Indeed, one works more effectively, it would appear, with the support of the other.

In addition, social agencies need to develop stronger ties with unions in their communities if they wish to receive referrals and support from the unions at the local United Ways of which they are members. Trade unions are major purchasers of health and welfare services, and unresponsive agencies must be willing to deal with the unions' power to affect their contracts, intake, and funding. For example, because workers' payroll deductions represented 60 percent of the more than $3 billion raised by the United Way in 1991, organized labor has come to recognize that it has great clout in the social welfare sector (personal communication with Nancy Smith, United Way of America, 1992). "Agencies that impose unreasonable barriers to workers through long waiting lists, inconvenient days and hours, inaccessible offices, and inflexible styles of service now must begin to face the prospect of resistance from trade unions" (Kurzman & Akabas, 1981, p. 58).

What the social work profession and the labor movement need to do is to understand and articulate the mutuality of their goals better. Such an articulation could lead to having labor leaders on social agency boards and the development of collaborative service arrangements. To do so, the profession and the labor movement will need to make manifest the still-latent symbiosis between labor and social work as they come to appreciate the potential for synthesis that is present. Only then can they harness the dynamic tension that continues to exist between organized labor and social work on behalf of the needs of working people and the American workplace in the year 2000.

References

Akabas, S. H. (1977). Labor, social policy and human services. In J. Turner (Ed.-in-Chief), *Encyclopedia of social work* (17th ed., Vol. 1, pp. 737–744). Washington, DC: National Association of Social Workers.

Akabas, S. H. (1986). Disability management: A longstanding trade union mission with some new initiatives. *Journal of Applied Rehabilitation Counseling, 17*(3), 33–37.

Akabas, S. H., Fine, M., & Yasser, R. (1982). Putting secondary prevention to the test: A study of an early intervention strategy with disabled workers. *Journal of Primary Prevention, 2*, 165–187.

Akabas, S. H., Gates, L. B., & Galvin, D. E. (1992). *Disability management.* New York: AMACOM.

Akabas, S. H., & Kurzman, P. A. (Eds.). (1982). *Work, workers, and work organizations: A view from social work.* Englewood Cliffs, NJ: Prentice Hall.

Akabas, S. H., Kurzman, P. A., & Kolben, N. S. (Eds.). (1979). *Labor and industrial settings: Sites for social work practice.* New York: Columbia University, Hunter College, and Council on Social Work Education.

Alexander, L. B. (1987). Unions: Social work. In A. Minahan (Ed.-in-Chief), *Encyclopedia of social work* (18th ed., Vol. 2, pp. 793–800). Silver Spring, MD: National Association of Social Workers.

Allen, K., Chapin, I., Keller, S., & Hill, D. (1979). *Volunteers from the workplace.* Washington, DC: National Center for Voluntary Action.

Antoniades, R. (1984). Social work in a trade union setting: A network of volunteers and professionals in self-help groups. *Social Work Papers, 18*(1), 47–56.

Antoniades, R., & Bellinger, S. (1983). Organized worksites: A help or a hindrance in the delivery of social work services in and to the workplace? In R. J. Thomlison (Ed.), *Perspectives on industrial social work practice* (pp. 29–38). Ottawa: Family Service Canada.

Balgopal, P. R., & Nofz, M. P. (1989). Injured workers: From statutory compensation to holistic social work services. *Journal of Sociology and Social Welfare, 15*(1), 147–164.

The Community. (1978, September). (AFL-CIO Community Service Department), pp. 15–18.

Cook, P., & Terruso, R. (1983). An industrial social service delivery system at the crossroads: The case of District Council 37 (AFSCME). In R. J. Thomlison, (Ed.), *Perspectives on industrial social work practice* (pp. 111–122). Ottawa: Family Service Canada.

Donovan, R., Kurzman, P. A., & Rotman, C. (in press). Improving the lives of home care workers: A partnership of social work and labor. *Social Work.*

Epstein, L. (1992). *Brief treatment and a new look at the task-centered approach.* New York: Macmillan.

Foster, B., & Schore, L. (1989). Job loss and the occupational social worker. *Employee Assistance Quarterly, 5*(1), 77–97.

Gardner, C. C. (1988). Promoting EAPs and MAPs through the NY State AFL-CIO network. *The Almacan, 18*(11), 42–45.

Germain, C. B. (1973). An ecological perspective in casework practice. *Social Casework, 54,* 323–330.

Habib, M., & Gutwill, S. (1985). The union setting: Working with retirees. *Journal of Gerontological Social Work, 8,* 247–255.

Holusha, J. (1990, August 19). Unions are expanding their role to survive in the 90's. *New York Times,* p. 12.

Kamerman, S. B., & Kahn, A. J. (1976). *Social services in the United States: Policies and programs.* Philadelphia: Temple University Press.

Karger, H. J. (1988). *Social workers and labor unions.* Westport, CT: Greenwood Press.

Karger, H. J. (1989). The common and conflicting goals of labor and social work. *Administration in Social Work, 13*(1), 1–17.

Kiezer, J., & Habib, M. (1980). Working in a labor union to reach retirees. *Social Casework, 61,* 180–183.

Krauskopf, M. S., & Akabas, S. H. (1988). Children with disabilities: A family-workplace partnership in problem resolution. *Social Work Papers, 21*(1), 28–35.

Kurzman, P. A. (1987). Industrial/occupational social work. In A. Minahan (Ed.-in-Chief), *Encyclopedia of social work* (18th ed., Vol. 1, pp. 899–910). Silver Spring, MD: National Association of Social Workers.

Kurzman, P. A., & Akabas, S. H. (1981). Industrial social work as an arena for practice. *Social Work, 26,* 52–60.

Lewis, B. (1989). Social workers' role in promoting health and safety. *Employee Assistance Quarterly, 5*(1), 99–118.

Lewis, B. M., & Mama, R. (1987). The cost of filing workers' compensation and unmet need in the work-injured/diseased population. *Social Work Papers, 20*(1), 30–45.

Mandel, B. (1963). *Samuel Gompers: A biography.* Yellow Springs, OH: Antioch Press.

McCroskey, J. (1984). In the wake of the subtle revolution: Opportunities and challenges in child care. *Social Work Papers, 18*(1), 57–64.

Meltzer, M. (1967). *Bread and roses: The struggle of American labor.* New York: Alfred A. Knopf.

Menashe, S., & Tronolone, J. (1982). Social and legal service coverage. *Practice Digest, 5*(2), 24–26.

Meyer, C. (1976). *Social work practice: The changing landscape* (2nd ed.). New York: Free Press.

Miller, R. E., & Metz, G. J. (1991). Union counseling as peer assistance. *Employee Assistance Quarterly, 6*(4), 1–21.

Molloy, D. J. (1986). *Planning and implementing a worker-based and participating model for EAPs.* Unpublished doctoral dissertation, City University of New York Graduate Center.

Molloy, D. J. (1989). Peer intervention: An exploratory study. *Journal of Drug Issues, 19,* 319–336.

Molloy, D. J., Barron, J., Farkas, R., Guastella, C., Mulligan, K., & Zeidel, A. (1980). A union alcoholism program working with many employees. *NCA Labor-Management Alcoholism Journal, 9,* 234–245.

Molloy, D. J., & Burmeister, L. (1989). Social workers in union based programs. *Employee Assistance Quarterly, 5*(1), 37–51.

Monk, A. (1990). Pre-retirement planning programs. In A. Monk (Ed.), *Handbook of gerontological services* (2nd ed., pp. 400–419). New York: Columbia University Press.

National Resource Center for Consumers of Legal Services. (n.d.). *Legal services and the labor movement*. Washington, DC: Author.

Needleman, C. (1986). *Testimony on the High Risk Occupational Disease Notification and Prevention Act of 1985* (Joint hearings of the House Committee on Education and Labor, pp. 240–258). Washington, DC: U.S. Government Printing Office.

Perlis, L. (1977). The human contract in the organized workplace. *Social Thought, 3*(1), 29–35.

Reynolds, B. C. (1975). *Social work and social living*. Washington, DC: National Association of Social Workers. (Original work published 1951)

Reynolds, B. C. (1991). *An uncharted journey*. Silver Spring, MD: NASW Press. (Original work published 1963)

Safford, F. (1988). The value of gerontology for occupational social work. *Social Work, 33*, 42–45.

Shanker, R. (1983). Occupational disease, workers' compensation and the social worker advocate. *Social Work, 28*, 24–27.

Silverman, B., Simon, B., & Woodrow, R. (1991). Workers in job jeopardy. In A. Gitterman (Ed.), *Handbook of social work practice with vulnerable populations* (pp. 710–748). New York: Columbia University Press.

Straussner, S. L. A., & Phillips, N. K. (1988). The relationship between social work and labor unions: A history of strife and cooperation. *Journal of Sociology and Social Work, 15*, 105–118.

Titmuss, R. M. (1968). *Commitment to welfare*. New York: Pantheon Books.

True, N. B., & Wineman, J. (1989). Caregiving and retirement planning: A new partnership. *Compensation and Benefits Management, 5*, 283–286.

Veblen, T. (1938). *Absentee ownership and business ownership in recent times*. New York: B. W. Buebsch.

Wagner, D. (1991). Reviving the action research model: Combining case and cause with dislocated workers. *Social Work, 36*, 477–482.

Weiner, H. J., Akabas, S. H., & Sommer, J. J. (1973). *Mental health care in the world of work*. New York: Association Press.

Wineman, J. (1990). Services to older and retired workers. In A. Monk (Ed.), *Handbook of gerontological services* (2nd ed., pp. 377–399). New York: Columbia University Press.

Winick, C. (1982). *A labor approach to dealing with alcohol problems at the work place*. New York: Central Labor Rehabilitation Council of New York.

CHAPTER 4

Work-Site Research

CHALLENGES AND OPPORTUNITIES FOR SOCIAL WORK

Bradley K. Googins

> The principal measure of progress toward equality will
> be that of employment. It is the primary source of
> individual or group identity. In the United States, what
> you do is what you are: to do nothing is to be nothing;
> to do little is to be little. The equations are implacable
> and blunt, and ruthlessly public.
>
> —Daniel P. Moynihan
> *Ghetto Unemployment and Underemployment*

The growth of occupational social work has been nothing short of phenomenal. Over the past two decades, this new arena of practice has created new roles for social workers in an environment that had been closed off to social work. Previously, prevailing ideologies held that individual and family problems were primarily the responsibility of the employee and perhaps of the government and the nonprofit sector in situations when family supports failed. Until recently, the very notion of sanctioning workplace interventions, such as those provided by occupational social workers, violated the deeply held principles of the corporate and trade union cultures.

Equally instructive in understanding this growth is an examination of the literature of this period, which outlines the landscape of occupational social work in great detail. A half-dozen books describe the new skills and the knowledge base that helped to develop a proliferation of occupational work settings, practice approaches, and models and reveal a rich and exciting arena filled with promise (Akabas & Kurzman, 1982; Feinstein & Brown, 1982; Googins & Godfrey, 1987; Gould & Smith, 1988; Masi, 1982; Straussner, 1990). As occurs in many new endeavors, however, practice outstripped knowledge building and the development of models. Thus, occupational social workers have broken through their own frontiers and settled in new workplace territories far faster than traditional theories and knowledge building could guide them. The uniqueness of these newly encountered work environments has presented a number of challenges to the traditional body of social work theory and knowledge. Consequently, over the past two decades, occupational social work has begun to build a body of research to accompany the explosion of practice.

The good news for social work is the promise that awaits occupational social work research. There are almost limitless opportunities for such research because the workplace has now become a widely accepted arena for practice, legitimating research efforts. The current challenge is to exploit the range of opportunities that cover a wide variety of issues: wellness; unions' efforts to develop new service models; populations in need, such as older workers; workers with disabilities; workers who are single parents; AIDS and employment; women's issues; work–family stress; the prevention and treatment of drug and alcohol abuse; and corporate community relations. And the list continues to grow as the workplace undergoes a dramatic transformation in this last decade of the 20th century, much of it related to the recognized need to maximize human capital and to create healthy and productive organizations.

From yet another perspective, the news is particularly good for social work. The revolution in the workplace is occurring along dimensions that are compatible with social work: the development of human potential; the encouragement of empowerment and employee participation; and the growing sense of corporate responsibility to employees, their families, and their communities. As social work and work organizations become more familiar with each other, they will develop a mutuality of interests that will await the further creativity and enthusiasm of the profession in exploring this new frontier from a scientific perspective.

Background

Social workers have already conducted a number of breakthrough studies. Their entrance into the workplace began in a substantive fashion in the 1970s, in part through the involvement of schools of social work in the union movement in New York and with alcoholism programs in Boston. Early pioneers, such as Sheila H. Akabas, Paul A. Kurzman, Dale Masi, and Hyman Weiner, broke dramatically new theoretical and practice ground in a profession that had traditionally aligned its mission with populations who were largely poor, alienated, and disenfranchised with the American economic system.

During the decades of the 1970s and 1980s, the field of occupational social work discovered and legitimated attention to new populations—workers, their families, and retirees—and communities, that is the functional community of work, heretofore ignored and unserved by the social work profession.

Briar (1983), for example, examined the impact of layoffs and social work interventions. De Silva's (1988) conceptualization of a customer assistance program refocused and broadened the traditional concept of the client in workplace practice. Burke's (1988) work on corporate community relations brought traditional community organizing and social work understanding of community systems to corporations as business increasingly appreciates the need to strengthen its role as a corporate citizen. Antoniades and Bellinger's (1983) work on unions and organized workplaces pointed to another population for whom social workers can find a rich practice arena, as did the victim-assistance model of Roy-Brisbois (1983). All these studies deal with the breadth and richness underlying occupational social work.

These initiatives established the fact that this new practice arena, the workplace, involved with the cultural and structural realities of work organizations, was well suited to a systems viewpoint and a unique person-in-environment model. Practice in the workplace proved hospitable to social work theory that is embedded in a conceptualization in which individuals and environments are viewed within an interactional framework. The conceptualization of employees and organizations as clients brings an ideal practice framework to the workplace (Googins & Davidson, in press; Weiner, Akabas, & Sommer, 1973).

Within the past decade, two trends have been evident: research on practice issues in a variety of work settings and research related to social work's new and evident interest in workplace issues that may occur in the workplace or elsewhere. Examples of both trends abound. For example, doctoral dissertations at both the Hunter College and Columbia University schools of social work have presented research on such practice issues as the need for dependent care, in-house versus contractual employee assistance programs (EAPs), the impact on employment opportunities of an employee's disclosure of his or her sexual orientation in the workplace, and differences in the nature of practice of management-sponsored EAPs and labor-based member assistance programs. Dissertations on workplace-related issues have included studies of the needs of low-income women workers of color, collaborative peer–professional intervention in labor settings, the preference for increments in fringe benefits or for wages among nurses, and the impact of union support on adjustment to divorce among African American women.

The "license" that the delivery of services in the workplace has given to social work to pursue its interest in the workplace is also apparent in more extensive studies, many of which are reflected in the content of articles in this volume. With the passage of the Americans with Disabilities Act, the issue of employment for workers with disabilities has become a prime interest in many work sites. Disability management in the workplace is defined by the long-term research agenda carried out by the Center for Social Policy and Practice in the Workplace at Columbia University and summarized by Sheila H. Akabas and Lauren B. Gates in Chapter 13. Understanding the role and significance of fringe benefits as a third, or occupational, welfare system (after the public and voluntary systems) has been promoted by the studies of that system reported by Lawrence S. Root in Chapter 6. Stress in the workplace has been clarified in its origins and meaning by research done by Lee Schore and Jerry Atkin at the Center for Working Life in Oakland, California, and reported in Chapter 17. Attention to dependent care and to structural means for dealing with the needs related to the issue, derives from the research of social workers at the University of Southern California and is reported by Jacqueline McCroskey and Andrew Scharlach in Chapter 9.

But updating the social work knowledge base through research certainly is not the exclusive province of contributors to this volume. Shanker (1983) and Lewis (1989) explored the occupational health of workers and the need for social work advocacy. Feldman (1980) clarified the impact of cancer on the ability to maintain a work role in early explorations with a population of employed patients. Kamerman and Kahn (1987) added significantly to the understanding of the formulation of policy through their survey of the nature of employers' responsiveness to the needs of employees' families. Coudroglou (1979) explored retirement opportunities and dilemmas. Donovan, Jaffe, and Pirie (1987) used qualitative and quantitative research methods to clarify the role of the union in meeting the needs of workers in the health care industry. Although the list could go on, the totality is not large, leading to the impression more of opportunity than of output.

Much of occupational social work practice in its formative years took place in EAPs. A body of EAP research emerged, much of it related to and developed by social workers. A small but persistent band of EAP researchers, primarily from the social sciences, some of them social workers, emerged in the early stages of the employee assistance field, who provided a conceptual framework and developed a research base for both EAPs and occupational social work (Trice & Roman, 1972). The use of EAP databases for research and evaluation, along with several dozen funded research projects, began to build a profession-ally credible research base that provides external legitimacy and a solid founda-tion for the EAP field. Social work researchers were active in this area, bringing new practice models (Masi, 1982) to supervisory roles (Googins & Kurtz, 1980) and focusing on issues from labor settings (Akabas, 1977).

The sense of exploration and adventure that marked the early stages of occupational social work set the stage for launching a broader research agenda. Numerous evaluation and outcome issues were raised, and new arenas for research were identified (Cohen & McGowan, 1982). The movement from alcoholism to a broad-based employee assistance model, for example, was triggered, in large part, by findings of evaluation research that employees who needed assistance often had problems that were separate from alcoholism. Although the roots of the EAP field held strongly to the alcoholism model, the increasing presence of social work, with its systemic, biopsychosocial attention to a considerably broadened range of problems, in effect forced practice to be more responsive and inclusive.

As practice was experiencing a transformation, research followed suit. In contrast to the more traditional research sites of the hospital or the community-based social service agency, the workplace was a territory in which social workers had not previously tread and, at least initially, one in which they were not particularly comfortable on political and ideological grounds. The work environment became a challenge for a number of reasons. External researchers, such as those in social work, generally are held suspect in corporate and labor settings, if for no other reason than that their motivation for conducting research initially may not coincide with the mission and perceived best interests of the organization. For a social worker to gain sanction from a workplace to conduct research on single parents, for example, is a greater stretch than for the same researcher to conduct the same study in a hospital, where human services are a traditional part of the research agenda. The unfamiliarity with social work in the workplace created a set of barriers for those attempting to conduct research. However, the pioneering practice, along with early research and changing agendas in the workplace itself, has gone a long way toward reducing those barriers and opening up opportunities for occupational social work researchers today.

Challenges and Opportunities for Research

One of the ancillary benefits of a new field and environment, such as occupational social work and the workplace, is that it creates a set of opportunities through research to gain a better understanding of the issues present in other environments. The workplace of the 1990s has suddenly become a hotbed for family- or community-based issues: affirmative action, women's rights, cultural diversity, work-life balance, drug and alcohol abuse, and so on. As the boundaries between workplaces and external communities continue to dissolve, individual, family, and social problems are being recognized in the plant or office, as well as at home and in the community.

A large transformation of the American workplace is being fueled by changing demographics, rising expectations by employees for responsiveness by employers, global competition, and a quest for quality, to mention the more prominent issues. In the midst of these changes, personal and family problems, as well as the litany of social ills confronted by the larger society, are now legitimate concerns of the workplace. The recognition of the spillover of social, community, and family problems into the labor and management arenas is raising a set of concerns, all of which are subjects for the occupational social work agenda. What began with a series of exploratory research questions on alcoholism continues to expand into many other areas. To illustrate, two issues are briefly examined next: substance abuse and work–family or work–life balance.

Substance Abuse

EAPs were probably the single greatest factor in opening up the workplace to occupational social workers. What began as an isolated program in a few unions and companies has grown to the status of a specialization with certification, publications, a professional association, and widespread presence in corporate America. Because the roots of this movement were anchored in the alcoholism field, much of the early research focused on questions of recovery and cost-benefit (Alander & Campbell, 1975; Burton, Eggum, & Keller, 1981). As the practice model expanded and the field developed, a whole set of new questions arose that explored aspects of this intervention: for example, the impact of the corporate culture, the value and impact of coercion in the workplace to address substance abuse (Heyman, 1976), and the role of supervisors in the intervention process (Googins & Kurtz, 1980).

A substantial body of literature has developed, focusing on this much broader range of research along the spectrum of EAP practice roles. The process of identifying, documenting, and confronting alcoholism through performance mechanisms has not only been well described, but its efficacy has been evaluated in a number of research studies. That base has provided some interesting insights into the initial programmatic initiatives that are referred to as "workplace substance abuse programs" and has served as a template of sorts for other research in occupational social work. This early literature, primarily descriptions of programs, evolved into a substantially more sophisticated and scientifically grounded body of research that lends credibility to the power and impact of EAPs. Management information systems (MISs) have been structured to track and evaluate EAP practice. They provide a database for the support of studies that will offer answers to these questions and feedback to nurture the increasing responsibilities of practice in the workplace.

Therefore, this new base is giving birth to another generation of research studies that consider newly evolving questions such as these:

- What is the impact of drug testing as a supplemental strategy for dealing with the corporate substance abuse problem?
- What populations at risk for problems with drugs and alcohol can be identified through epidemiological studies?
- Which aspects of the corporate culture work to promote alcoholic behavior, and which act to prevent it?
- What constitutes an effective clinical model for EAP practice that will ensure optimal assessment, referral, and follow-up?
- What are the family dynamics involved in substance abuse in the workplace, and what strategies are effective for involving the family?
- What are the dynamics of work groups in promoting or preventing problem drinking?
- What roles do supervisors and co-workers play in the treatment of substance abuse?
- What factors predict effective outcomes?
- Can prevention activities reduce the incidence of substance abuse in the workplace, and which strategies are more effective than others?

The employee assistance field is staffed primarily by social workers, whose potential for ensuring an even stronger and more professional practice role in the workplace is aided considerably by the increased level and quality of research. The creation of the newly formed Office for Treatment Improvement in the National Institute of Alcohol Abuse and Alcoholism suggests that the field itself is recognizing the need for such research. My colleagues and I, to use one example, are examining the role of social supports in alcoholism treatment. In addition, we have launched a study of assessment practices for substance abuse and are testing a traditional assessment approach with motivational interviewing. It is this type of research that awaits the skills and expertise of social workers in the EAP field.

Work–Family and Work–Life Programs

A second window of opportunity for occupational social work research lies in the area of work-family. In the late 1980s a number of corporations began to acknowledge the plight of working parents by developing programs, including assistance with dependent care; flexible schedules, such as compressed workweeks; job sharing; and telecommunication. Pressed by labor shortages in some markets, these employers began to link the changing demographic profile of their employees (higher percentages of working mothers, single parents, and those caring for elders) with the need to attract and retain workers in what has been forecast as a serious shortage of skilled labor by the year 2000 (Johnston, 1987).

Work–family programs in corporations are in a stage of development that is similar to the stage that EAPs went through in the mid-1970s. In the 1980s employers initially were reluctant to open the door to family issues, just as they hesitated to deal with alcoholism in the 1970s. However, as a few corporate leaders paved the way through widely publicized efforts to establish family-friendly programs and benefits for their employees, other companies have begun to feel the pressure because of the continuous benchmarking that occurs among employers, along with rising expectations among employees that their employers will be as responsive to their needs as will others. These forces have led other corporations to establish substantial corporate policies, benefits, and program activities for supporting families and work–life issues. Viewed from a practice perspective, the work–family arena offers a rich practice agenda for occupational social workers, one that draws directly on their interests and expertise. It links occupational social work with the most traditional interests of the profession.

It is not surprising that these work–family initiatives have stimulated research in this area that is necessary for their further development. Areas such as work–family have been off-limits to most researchers, primarily because researchers have not had access to the inner sanctums of unions and corporations. My initial research on work–family stress, for example, was one of the first corporate-based studies (Googins, 1991), just as Weiner et al.'s (1973) was one of the first in a union setting. However, the accelerated growth of this field promises to build on earlier studies by exploring a number of other stimulating work–family issues:

- strategies for minimizing work–family stress
- factors that link family benefits to gains in productivity
- the impact of dependent care responsibilities on work life and productivity
- the identification of populations at risk through epidemiological studies in the workplace
- understanding work–family dynamics in relation to specific populations (for example, single parents, latchkey children, and relocated families)
- evaluating labor–management–community partnerships for supporting working families.

To examine these issues, a number of studies should be conducted, drawing on data from surveys of the workplace and EAP management information systems (MISs) that many employers and trade unions have instituted to understand the work force and its dependent care needs.

Barriers to Research in the Workplace

Many social scientists have observed that the frustrations of working in corporate and labor settings are enough to redirect their energies to more hospitable environments. Organizations that are closed, closely controlled, jealously guarded about their products and other proprietary rights, naturally suspicious of outsiders, and driven by bottom-line results do not at first blush provide a welcome climate for social researchers. Although barriers to research exist in any applied setting, it is important to understand the unique aspects of the workplace that dictate procedures and approaches to research. Two areas are basic: gaining access and maintaining the research relationship.

Gaining Access

Given the xenophobic attitudes toward external researchers, gaining access to the workplace to conduct research is a challenge for researchers. At the 1985 conference, The Business of Doing Worksite Research, it was noted that although many talk about the theory of gaining access to the workplace, in practice, projects and proposals often fall far short of the theory and founder at the closed gates of a worksite.

From one perspective, C. P. Snow's (1964) clash of two cultures offers a useful analogy from which to understand some of these difficulties. Workplaces are primarily action-oriented organizations that are tied to the production of a product or the delivery of a service. Those who occupy this arena live in a world where the immediate and pragmatic are most likely to influence decisions and to dictate behavior. This environment is in stark contrast to the world of the social researcher, whose academic training and base of operations are grounded in a more reflective philosophical posture— searching for knowledge and theory building and developing a knowledge base on which a more refined and well-thought-out future can emerge.

The act of conducting social research in the workplace brings together these two institutions that have had little previous contact. Critical issues, such as who controls the research, what organizational secrets will be shared, and what will be done with the findings, are paramount to labor and management in developing a contract with a researcher. The researcher needs to understand the parties' concern about protecting their self-interests. Because of their natural suspicion, the researcher will need to develop a strategy to overcome resistance and to build the requisite trust. Because social workers have been grounded in relationship building, the transfer of these skills to the research arena is not difficult and gives the social work researcher a distinct advantage over other social scientists.

A number of other factors account for barriers to access, each of which requires a specific strategy to overcome the attendant resistance.

Fear of uncovering negative findings

A frequently unspoken fear in considering proposed research is the potential that findings will reflect unfavorably on the sponsoring organization, resulting in dire consequences for the manager or work group who championed the project. Upper-level managers may exhibit greater creativity and risk-taking behavior when new, innovative projects are concerned. However, even when organizational leaders are in favor of the social research project, middle managers must be involved; otherwise they may have the power to prevent the project by frustrating its implementation.

Raising employees' expectations

One of the most frequently cited concerns related to occupationally based social research, particularly research that involves surveys of employees or members, is the potential negative consequences of raising expectations about the outcome of the research. Managers often perceive survey research as being tantamount to promising the resolution of problems, which, in turn, serves to increase expectations. This concern becomes even more acute in times of economic distress, when downsizing and poor market conditions tend to inhibit innovation.

Conflicts with existing labor–management relationships

The tenuous and often contentious labor-management relationship found in many settings may result in the project becoming an innocent victim of organizational politics. Employee–employer relationships are a critical dimension of any work force, whether workers are represented by organized labor or through less formal arrangements. The slightest possibility that the proposed research findings will be used to buttress labor's positions or bargaining power, for example, may be enough to scare management from endorsing and adopting such research. In one company, the labor relations department objected to a section of a dependent care survey that examined ways in which employees provided for child care on the grounds that the unions would use these data to strengthen their bargaining position during future contract negotiations.

Concerns over the legal consequences of participation

Corporations traditionally are not risk takers, largely because of the importance they attribute to their corporate image and the need to avoid negative consequences of corporate behavior. Thus, any proposed research will be reviewed by the legal and public relations departments to determine its impact on and potential consequences for the employer's name and public image and to ensure that confidentiality is safeguarded. Even the issue of who "owns" the data could become a potential bone of contention.

The amount of front-end work required to gain access may inhibit potential researchers. Nevertheless, it is important for those who are thinking of working in this environment to be aware of these barriers to access and to develop strategies that anticipate and respond to contingencies in the workplace that govern such research.

Maintaining a Research Relationship

Maintaining the research relationship draws on another set of strategies and skills. The process closely parallels the program development stages of the early days of occupational social work in which social workers also faced an alien environment and underwent a series of trial-by-error relationship-building processes. The purpose of this section is to mitigate such problems and to identify skills and knowledge that are relevant to the research function.

In research conducted outside controlled laboratory conditions, the relationship between the researcher and the environment is a critical variable. In carrying out research in a hospital, for example, it is essential for administrators, as well as the medical staff, to have some degree of buy-in to the research because their cooperation is often necessary not only for the recruitment of subjects, but for ensuring control over and rigor in the design. In health settings, such as hospitals, this relationship is possible not only because of the tradition of research, but because of the perceived mutuality between the human service mission of the organization and the goals of the research.

The relationship between the researcher and those in the work setting is tied directly to the perceived usefulness of and vested interests in the research. As the research design is implemented, it is critical to find mechanisms to ensure that those who are responsible for obtaining access for the researcher are kept in full communication, put into the feedback loop, and provided with ongoing benefits and rewards for their roles, especially in work sites in which familiarity with social research is not strong and the symbiosis is more difficult to explicate. The problem may be mitigated in sites where social workers have gained an effective foothold in the delivery of services because they have already identified the mutuality of interest by accepting social workers as service providers and thus may be better prepared to accept them as social researchers and to affirm their research agenda.

Relationship building to ensure that the project will be completed recognizes the fundamental importance of process and political decision making in the organization. Hence, researchers should develop long-term relation-ships with particular work organizations because the start-up costs of gaining access and establishing relationships can be amortized over time. In a similar vein, the ability to have secured and conducted research in one setting builds a reputation that can be transferred to other settings that are more likely to trust researchers with a track record. Creating an institutional base for research through ongoing relationships with several work sites cuts down on the initial phase and allows for the more productive use of a researcher's time and skills.

Strategic Advantages

The presence of barriers to conducting research in the workplace can be overcome by a set of strategic advantages that occupational social work researchers bring to the workplace.

Person-in-environment framework
The distinct systems approach of social work, which reflects both the ideological and the practice stance of the profession, is a valuable research perspective for work-site research. Unlike many other social science disci-plines, social work is grounded in an ecological approach. Good social work research reflects its systems approach, capturing the interaction between individuals and their environments and developing a better understanding of how problems and issues have an impact on the individual and the environ-ment. This holistic perspective, rather than focusing on a narrow correlate that may be of greater interest to other researchers, places social work research closer to the main interests of gatekeepers at the workplace.

Practice base
Unlike other researchers, social workers operate from a practice base. Because social work programs are a significant presence in the workplace, the practice itself is a rich lode for identifying research issues. As occupational social workers interact daily with employees and the corporate or labor environment, they are on top of the current issues that percolate throughout the system. Because they are boundary spanners, they usually have a systemwide perspective that allows them to have a broader outlook and a wider base from which to view the issues and the setting than may be available to outsiders. In their expert institutional roles of counselors, consultants, trainers, and program planners, social workers are in an ideal position to identify and monitor patterns and trends that may become the topics of research.

Likewise, the practice base offers an opportunity for the researcher to gain access to and trust from the system through partnership with the practitioner.

Although the occupational social work practitioner and social work researcher may have different skills, their ability to collaborate on joint projects recognizes the mutuality of their interests. Linking practice to research takes advantage of the presence of a practice base and the need for practitioners to be better informed through research as they identify the "cause" in function (Lewis, 1976). Furthermore, the fact that social work programs have taken root in the occupational sphere has increased the degree of legitimacy of and comfort with such activities. At the same time, there is increased pressure to measure the outcomes of programs better and to link the contribution of programs to overall organizational goals. Consequently, evaluation and research that focus on outcomes will have a great deal more receptivity at this stage.

Where do the opportunities lie? This question can be addressed from two perspectives: arenas for social work research and strategies for maximizing social work research.

Arenas for Social Work Research

In the nearly two decades of social service in the workplace, the boundaries of the practice arena have consistently broadened and the number of substantive areas have increased considerably.

AIDS

Although research on this major health issue is being conducted in the community, little has been done in the workplace. A great deal of social research could be conducted within the confines of a workplace, including attitudes and behaviors of managers, supervisors, and co-workers; the effects of group norms; and the effectiveness of AIDS-prevention education. The type and effectiveness of workplace accommodations, as required by the Americans with Disabilities Act, can be studied in relation to AIDS and other chronic diseases and health problems.

Mental health

Mental health is a broad term for a variety of issues, from particular emotional problems to help-seeking behavior. Although this area represents the majority of cases of EAPs, it has virtually no research base. The lack of a research base is partly the result of the stance of the National Institute of Mental Health (NIMH), which does not now consider the workplace an arena of interest. Although NIMH supported some pioneering research by Columbia University's Center for Social Policy and Practice in the Workplace, the Labor Mental Health Institute in California, and other research centers more than a decade ago, it has all but abandoned its sponsorship of such efforts to explore the psychosocial correlates of behavior in favor of research on the biological determinants. Consequently, only a few researchers have continued to examine the workplace as a site or the significance of work to the well-being of workers. Perhaps the Clinton administration, with its interest in jobs and employment, will return to the agenda of mental health in the workplace and offer wider opportunities for study.

Prevention

The discovery of the potential for the community to prevent family and public health problems and alcohol and drug abuse presents an opportunity to test models, strategies, and prevention programs at the workplace. Although the workplace is an ideal site to introduce prevention, primarily because it contains relatively well functioning individuals and is a stable and enduring environment, research at the work site has been limited. This area is particularly well suited to social work, which has developed its practice base on a broad range of preventive strategies. Because social work has been at the forefront of many of these issues in communities outside the workplace, the opening up of a new practice arena in work settings would create a number of promising avenues for social work practice and research. For example, in Minneapolis, a group of EAPs have worked together to address family violence from the workplace. Because the incidence of family violence is increasing and much of it takes place in the households of people who work, social workers have a unique opportunity to use the workplace as both a point of intervention and a setting for prevention and education. From a research perspective, such activities would open up opportunities to gather basic data on incidence and prevalence, to test models of prevention and outreach, to gather data that will lead to a better understanding of the precipitating incidents, and to record successful antidotes to domestic violence.

Women's issues

The entrance of women into the workplace in large numbers also suggests a number of areas for research, including work–family stress, career issues (loosening the "sticky floor" and breaking the "glass walls and ceilings"), and sexual harassment. Social work practitioners and researchers can form a partnership to develop data and practice models that are both preventive and educational and that will go a long way toward supporting the needs of women members–employees, and employers' need for skilled women workers.

Behavior of supervisors

Not much is known about what types of supervisory training are effective and which preventive efforts are useful in creating a more sensitive workplace. The close connection many have made between productivity and a responsive climate in the workplace make the latter a contemporary and appropriate area of interest for social work research.

Single parenting

Likewise, social work can consider specific populations, such as single parents, most of whom are women. Although the majority of women who are single parents work and up to a quarter of many workplaces consist of single parents, there has been little research on this population. The workplace acts as both a significant support system for these parents and a potential arena for problems in balancing the demands of work and home. The area for research is rich on both fronts. My colleagues at Boston University and I, for example, are in the midst of a three-year demonstration–research project that is testing out research strategies by which EAPs can respond to the needs of parents whose children are home alone after school. This so-called latchkey problem is of great concern to parents, particularly single parents, and the workplace can begin to understand better the strategies that are being used, the extent to which employees' productivity is influenced by insufficient support, and the impact of such situations on both employees and children.

Case management

A final set of opportunities exists in the very structures in which occupational social workers are currently operating. The EAPs that are staffed by social workers contain an incredible database that has not been fully tapped. MISs are becoming more common and more sophisticated with the movement toward managed health care. Through the systemic use of MISs, occupational social workers will have powerful data on patterns and trends that can support their suggestions for new directions in program development and new populations to be addressed in corporations. The "case to cause" tradition of social work offers an exciting opportunity for occupational social work.

Social work could develop effective studies along the lines of evaluation research. So many new programs have been introduced that there is a great need to conduct evaluative studies to assess their impact and effectiveness. Treatment, education, training of supervisors, child and elder care, the prevention of relapses, and aftercare are all work-based programs with merit, but the outcomes of these programs have not been well documented by systematic evaluations or comparative analyses of the differential input of their service components.

On another level, client-matching research (in which specific characteristics of clients are linked to appropriate forms of treatment) has been widely called for as an improvement over the current broad findings of research on treatment, especially in the field of drug and alcohol abuse, where the vast majority of the researchers do not have a clinical background and thus have avoided such a research model. The advent of the Office for Treatment

Improvement within the National Institute of Alcohol Abuse and Alcoholism, along with the recognition that this type of research is much needed, again gives social work a great opportunity to address a new range of issues.

By carving out fields, such as evaluation research and client outcome research, social work can leave basic research to other social scientists while concentrating on program areas that are consonant with the interests, strengths, and backgrounds of the profession. This approach is consistent with the traditional knowledge-building process of social work that uses concepts and theories from social science to build its own models and theories.

Conclusion

Social work's discovery of the workplace, along with the subsequent explosion of programs, services, and activities, marks a significant development for the profession. Although social work has not yet fully capitalized on the research opportunities, individual social workers now constitute the single largest professional group providing human services in the workplace.

The creation of a research base is both a necessity and a challenge. Without a strong research component to support its practice, occupational social work will have to rely on practice wisdom, accumulated experience, and untested assumptions—a dubious position and strategy for any profession to follow.

On the other hand, the promises of research have never been greater. The opening up of the workplace to EAPs, union social services, work–family initiatives, wellness programs, and a broad range of other initiatives has not only created a new environment for delivering services but has broken long-standing barriers to the development of a research agenda. Building on past achievements, social work can create a new era in occupational social work research.

References

Akabas, S. H. (1977). Labor: Social policy and human services. In J. Turner (Ed.-in-Chief), *Encyclopedia of social work* (17th ed., Vol. 1, pp. 737–744). Washington, DC: National Association of Social Workers.

Akabas, S. H., & Kurzman, P. A. (1982). *Work, workers, and work organizations.* Englewood Cliffs, NJ: Prentice Hall.

Alander, R., & Campbell, T. (1975). An evaluative study of an alcohol and drug recovery program: A case study of the Oldsmobile Experience. *Human Resource Management, 14*(1), 14–18.

Antoniades, R., & Bellinger, S. (1983). Organized worksites: A help or a hindrance in the delivery of social services in and to the workplace? In R. J. Thomlison (Ed.), *Perspectives on industrial social work practice* (pp. 29–38). Ottawa: Family Service Canada.

Briar, K. H. (1983). Lay-offs and social work intervention. *Urban and Social Change Review, 16,* 9–14.

Burke, E. M. (1988). Corporate community relations. In G. Gould & M. Smith (Eds.), *Social work in the workplace* (pp. 314–327). New York: Springer.

Burton, W., Eggum, P., & Keller, P. (1981). High cost employees in an occupational alcoholism program: A preliminary report. *Journal of Occupational Medicine, 23,* 259–262.

Cohen, J., & McGowan, B. G. (1982). What do you do? An inquiry into the potential of work-related research. In S. H. Akabas & P. A. Kurzman (Eds.), *Work, workers, and work organizations: A view from social work* (pp. 117–146). Englewood Cliffs, NJ: Prentice Hall.

Coudroglou, A. (Ed.). (1979). *Retirement: Opportunity or dilemma?* Tempe: Arizona State University Press.

de Silva, E. G. (1988). Services to customers: Customer assistance programs. In G. Gould & M. Smith (Eds.), *Social work in the workplace* (pp. 283–298). New York: Springer.

Donovan, R., Jaffe, N., & Pirie, V. M. (1987). Unemployment among low-income women: An exploratory study. *Social Work, 32,* 301–305.

Feinstein, B. B., & Brown, E. G. (1982). *The new partnership: Human services, business and industry.* Cambridge, MA: Schenkman.

Feldman, F. (1980). *Work and cancer health history: A study of blue collar workers.* Los Angeles: Division of the Cancer Society.

Googins, B. (1991). *Work/family stress: Private lives—Public responses.* Greenwich, CT: Auburn House Press.

Googins, B., & Davidson, B. (in press). The organization as client. *Social Work.*

Googins, B., & Godfrey, J. (1987). *Occupational social work.* Englewood Cliffs, NJ: Prentice Hall.

Googins, B., & Kurtz, N. (1980). Factors inhibiting supervisor referrals to occupational alcoholism intervention programs. *Journal of Studies on Alcohol, 4,* 1196–1208.

Gould, G. M., & Smith, M. L. (Eds.). (1988). *Social work in the workplace.* New York: Springer.

Heyman, M. (1976). Referral to alcoholism programs in industry: Coercion to confrontation and choice. *Journal of Studies on Alcohol, 37,* 900–907.

Johnston, W. B. (1987). *Workforce 2000: Work and workers for the twenty-first century.* Indianapolis, IN: Hudson Institute.

Kamerman, S., & Kahn, A. (1987). *The responsive workplace.* New York: Columbia University Press.

Lewis, B. M. (1989). Social workers' role in promoting occupational health and safety. *Employee Assistance Quarterly, 5*(1), 99–118.

Lewis, H. (1976). The cause in function. *Journal of the Otto Rank Association, 2,* 18–25.

Masi, D. (1982). *Human services in industry.* Lexington, MA: D. C. Heath.

Roy-Brisbois, M. (1983). Victim assistance: An example of meeting the work-related needs of employees. In R. J. Thomlison (Ed.), *Perspectives on industrial social work practice* (pp. 123–132). Ottawa: Family Service Canada.

Shanker, R. (1983). Occupational disease, workers' compensation and the social work advocate. *Social Work, 28,* 24–27.

Snow, C. P. (1964). *The two cultures: A second look* (2nd ed.). Cambridge, MA: Cambridge University Press.

Straussner, S. L. A. (Ed.). (1990). *Occupational social work today.* New York: Haworth Press.

Trice, H. M., & Roman, P. M. (1972). *Spirits and demons at work: Alcohol and other drugs on the job.* Ithaca: Cornell University School of Industrial and Labor Relations.

Weiner, H. J., Akabas, S. H., & Sommer, J. J. (1973). *Mental health care in the world of work.* New York: Association Press.

PART 2

THE CONTEXT OF PRACTICE

Introduction to Part 2

For social work in the workplace, the Dickensian claim, "It was the worst of times, it was the best of times," truly seems applicable. In the Introduction to this book, the editors have indicated the passage of occupational social work from a frontier status to that of a permanent settlement (the best of times). But it is the nature of the profession, whether targeted to the workplace and workers or to any other environment, to be deeply enmeshed in the society of which it is a part. As we approach the end of this century and look forward, there is much concern about the future. Change is pervasive, and its direction is not encouraging. There is evidence that environmental misdeeds have placed our planet at risk, that the inability to accept diversity is destroying political entities, and that religious differences may yet erupt into a "holy war." Equally disconcerting is the evidence that economic growth is slowed worldwide, increasing the need to maximize the outcome of all investments. Social services will be held to the same test as will all other expenditures in this era of lean and mean organizational structure (the worst of times). In this context, professional practice in the workplace may offer one of the few arenas of potential growth for social work because the issues on which it focuses have a direct influence on the well-being of organizations and the productive return on investments.

Consider the chapters in this section. In Chapter 5, Sheila H. Akabas and Beth Grube Farrell review the possibilities offered by prevention initiatives in the workplace. Prevention, as they point out, is often talked about, but rarely receives attention in practice. On a societal level, it has been hard to prove the effectiveness of prevention. In the face of immediate problems that command remediation, it has been hard for prevention to be considered a priority. But in the circumscribed functional community of work, more convincing evidence can be gathered of the cost-effectiveness of a prevention strategy. And among a target population that is able to function at work, the promise of prevention seems more achievable.

The array of possibilities that the authors detail provides an appetizing menu—health promotion and wellness programs that have a proved positive cost-benefit ratio, substance abuse awareness efforts that reduce the incidence of abusive behavior, support systems for those responsible for child care and elder care that allow the caregivers to balance the demands on their time and focus, educational initiatives that are concerned with sensitivity to diversity that reduce the racism and sexism levels in many workplaces, and trauma counseling that predicts and mitigates the negative impact of unexpected violence experienced at work. These and many other activities suggest the creative possibilities presented in work settings. The authors contend that, although the initial focus of prevention may be on improving the lives of individual workers, ultimately the success of prevention efforts may open the door to organizational change that will improve the quality of the environment in which these individuals work and live.

In Chapter 6, the significant role of the employment sector in providing a social welfare base for American society is elucidated by Lawrence S. Root. Root contends that employee benefits represent the unique and increasing role of the workplace as a source of social insurance and social services. Root identifies benefits as an historical development that expresses the mixed motivation of altruism, albeit paternalistic in origin, and control, noting the power of a "management tool" that is "the right thing to do."

The role of employment as the source of social welfare is relatively recent. Benefits began during World War II as a means of controlling the inflation that would certainly have resulted were direct wage payments to increase. After the war, the Supreme Court decided that benefits, as remuneration, are appropriate content for collective bargaining. This ruling stimulated the unions' assumption of a major role in determining the availability of this rich source of support for social well-being. The author notes that "national benefit patterns were largely determined by union efforts, even though only a minority of the work force was actually represented by unions."

However, employer-provided benefits have a downside, as Root indicates, because they are "a distribution of insurance that parallels the differentials in wage and salary" and thereby serve to "create 'enclaves' of protection" that result in inequity and inequality. Furthermore, the "greater use of part-time or temporary workers may be another unintended impact of employee benefit costs." These issues tell us that planners in the private sector and the systems they create have an important impact on social and economic public policies and thus are worthy of serious study.

In Chapter 7, Adrienne Asch and Patricia Abelson examine yet another initiative for which the workplace is destined to provide leadership, namely, managed care of the delivery of mental health services. The entire nation is struggling with the problem of how to provide high-quality care to the population at an affordable cost. The world of work, as the primary provider of health insurance, has been faced with unremitting increases in the cost of all health benefits—costs that have far exceeded the inflationary rate of the consumer price index. As this country's taste for health care has become more sophisticated and as the stresses of modern society have become more damaging, the demand for mental health benefits has mushroomed, causing the cost of that portion of the benefit package to increase even beyond the excessive inflationary rate of the total health care package.

A whole industry has developed around managing the cost of mental health care. As Asch and Abelson note, it is characterized by a high degree of accountability and control. According to the authors, treatment is priced, planned, coordinated, and delivered in a manner that is designed to ensure quality and to contain costs. These initiatives provide many opportunities. Staffing the managed care organization offers an opportunity for social workers, trained to think in a systems approach to problems and familiar with the wealth of community resources, to screen and refer clients and then to review the clients' progress and the need for further treatment. At the same time, social workers are preferred professional providers under a managed care system. Social work's person-in-environment approach, compared to the approaches of models of other mental health professions, often leads to interventions that are most appropriate for assuring the continued functional capacity of its clients. Such an outcome is greatly valued by an employing organization or trade union that is focused on maintaining the continued employability of its employees/members. Although the authors recognize the often-stated criticism that under managed care the variety and flexibility of the services can be limited to those that will achieve adequate care for the majority, not necessarily maximum care for anyone, they argue that the sponsors' interest in having a productive work force constrains solutions to care that ignore assurances of high quality.

The influence of a significant demographic change on social work practice in the workplace, namely, increasing diversity in the ethnicity, cultural backgrounds, and races of employees, is the subject of Chapter 8, by Muriel Gray and Frederica Barrow. The authors point out that "the professional social work concern of promoting maximum social functioning of the individual and the workplace's need for a worker who is functioning optimally are now in tandem." They conclude that effective practice requires knowledge of and the ability to respond to the differences among workers.

According to Gray and Barrow, the twofold goal for occupational social workers is to help diverse workers succeed in the workplace and help managers create an environment that affirms differences among employees. The authors believe that social workers' location in the workplace provides abundant opportunities on the institutional, program, and individual levels to achieve these outcomes. By providing consultation and serving on appropriate organizational task forces, occupational social workers can influence the institutional agenda.

Furthermore, the EAP can be structured and provide services in a way that accounts for the specific nature of organizational diversity. The key, Gray and Barrow suggest, is to have the recognition of diversity permeate all aspects of design of programs and the delivery of services—from recruiting staff to measuring the program's accomplishments—by evaluating whether the staff and the populations served reflect the diversity of the pool of employees. Finally, on the individual level, they point out that if, as competent professionals, occupational social workers are faithful to the profession's mandate to "start where the client is," they need to be sensitive to where the client is in relation to the multicultural, racial, and ethnic groups they seek to serve.

Not demographic change, but the changing interconnection between public policy and the world of work is the issue of Chapter 9, written by Jacquelyn McCroskey and Andrew Scharlach. Based on a concept that to be successful, employers need to support employees and their families throughout the life cycle, the chapter focuses on employees' need for assistance with child care and elder care responsibilities. Dramatic demographic changes, including the proportion of mothers in the work force and the increasing ratio of elderly persons to those of working age, have added dependent care to the responsibilities of many employees. Thus, child care and elder care become workplace problems when employees' need to care for dependent family members interferes with their ability to fulfill the requirements of their jobs.

As the authors observe, social workers in workplace settings need to be familiar with local service systems if they hope to counsel those who have to utilize the "complex system of child care and elder care services that is difficult to understand and even more difficult to gain access to." In addition, often on the basis of social workers' recommendations, many workplaces have provided cafeteria benefit plans, flexible work schedules, before-tax dependent care accounts, and actual financial assistance. In the end, however, the authors acknowledge that an appropriate and adequate response to the significant changes in demographics and responsibilities that today's labor pool face cannot depend solely on the business sector. They advocate for public–private partnerships and legislative initiatives, understanding, as do all the authors of chapters in Part 2, that public and private policies are reciprocal in their influence and their ultimate power over the development of social service programs in the workplace.

In all these chapters, the vital message seems to be that occupational social workers are faced with great challenges and an equally great potential influence. Their strength rests in their professional model of person-in-environment, a biopsychosocial approach that honors individual differences and the development of programs that integrate the contribution of the public and private sectors. If they work within that paradigm, they will make a significant contribution to empowering workers, employers, and trade unions to achieve a productive, cost-effective workplace and a society that meets human needs; in short, they will fulfill their professional agenda.

CHAPTER 5

Prevention

AN ORGANIZING CONCEPT FOR WORKPLACE SERVICES

Sheila H. Akabas and Beth Grube Farrell

Being out of work he was out of temper with the world
and society.
—Thomas Hardy
The Mayor of Casterbridge

Little studied and rarely promoted as a strategy in social work, prevention is
an intervention of great potential (Bloom, 1987a). Taken literally, prevention means keeping something from happening, but in the context of a social
work intervention, it means much more than that. If you assume that you
want to prevent something because it is an undesirable state, for instance,
physical or mental ill health, prevention takes on a passive character. In
actuality, it is an activist strategy that seeks not only to prevent the negative
outcome from occurring, but to protect the present state of functioning and
to promote a better future through improved well-being (Bloom, 1987b).

A formal definition of prevention, offered in the *Social Work Dictionary*
(Barker, 1991, p. 180), identifies "actions taken by social workers and others
to minimize and eliminate those social, psychological, or other conditions
known to cause or contribute to physical and emotional illness and sometimes socioeconomic problems. Prevention includes establishing those
conditions in society that enhance the opportunities for individuals, families
and communities to achieve positive fulfillment." When this definition is
considered in relation to the world of work, the relevance of prevention is
immediately apparent. In few sites can social workers more successfully
identify the "conditions known to cause or contribute to . . . illness." Karasak
(cited in Wegman, 1992), for example, successfully demonstrated that jobs
with high responsibility and inadequate levels of authority are connected

with significantly higher rates of cardiovascular disease than may be randomly expected. Stellman and Daum (1973) wrote an entire book about how *Work is Dangerous to Your Health*. There are few sites where social workers can more effectively "establish conditions . . . to achieve positive fulfillment" than in the workplace. Freud (1930/1962) noted that the two hallmarks of adult functioning are the ability to love and the ability to work, and Maslow (1970) was only one of a long line of social scientists who have understood that self-actualization through one's production is the ultimate achievement of a fulfilled person.

This chapter contends that the world of work is the ideal place for primary prevention activities (Akabas, 1987; Akabas & Kurzman, 1982). It starts by reviewing the history of prevention and identifying the components of primary prevention that distinguish it from secondary and tertiary prevention and then explores the rationale for and the many facets of prevention efforts in the world of work. Following a cataloging of opportunities, it ends with cautions that should be observed by those who seek to "improve" the private lives of working people.

Historical Overview

The roots of prevention are firmly planted in public health efforts to use the tools of epidemiology to overcome the problem of infectious disease (Wegman, 1992). Early efforts sought to break the pattern of disease, even if its cause was not understood. For example, Dr. John Snow, an epidemiologist, did not know the cause of cholera, but when he determined, in 1849, that his London patients with cholera were all drawing water from the same pump, he was able to end the epidemic by removing the pump handle. It was not until many years later that scientists determined that the cause of cholera is bacteria in water, which, when ingested, can cause often fatal dehydration. Interpreting the public health model, Bloom (1979) suggested the sequential steps of (1) identifying an event that appears to have negative consequences, (2) developing hypotheses about how those consequences can be reduced, and (3) implementing prevention programs that fit the hypotheses. The extension of this paradigm to emotional illness is obvious. One does not need to know the cause of low self-esteem to understand that a supportive work environment in which a person achieves unexpected success can have a significant remedial power over his or her self-image.

Wittman (1977, p. 1050) stated that the "goals of preventive social work have their origins in the profession itself." Certainly, social workers' dedication to the person-in-environment fit is instrumental in the achievement of prevention. Research and practice experience have identified the coincidence between supportive social policy and the well-being and developmental growth of persons who may be considered to belong to at-risk populations. This coincidence has provided the rationale for the profession's advocacy on behalf of community development and political action. A body of conceptual writings has helped clarify the meaning of prevention for social workers. Caplan (1964) made a major contribution in this regard by offering definitions for categorizing prevention efforts. Under his schema, reducing the incidence of mental illness is classified as primary prevention. Limiting, by treatment, the duration of disorders once they occur is categorized as secondary prevention. Finally, circumscribing, by rehabilitation, the impairment that results from the disorder is defined as tertiary prevention (Forgays, 1983).

Distinguishing the levels of prevention makes it more feasible to structure primary prevention efforts. Cowan (1982) built on this beginning to provide an explicit, taut definition of primary prevention as an effort that meets a trilogy of criteria. For him it is primary prevention only if it is group or mass directed (not individually oriented), if it is targeted at groups before significant impairment occurs, and if it is based on knowledge that it will work to improve health or prevent maladaptation. The last criterion suggests the importance of evaluating primary prevention practice, rather than jawboning its value. But such criteria need not deter the interested party. Albee (1983) presented a workable framework that is still the formula for designing prevention programs. In defining the occurrence of mental illness, he balanced difficult life circumstances with available strengths and resources as follows:

$$\frac{\text{Incidence of}}{\text{psychopathology}} = \frac{\text{organic factors} + \text{stress} + \text{exploitation}}{\text{coping skills} + \text{self-esteem} + \text{social support}}$$

For Albee, reducing the numerator factors results in lowering the incidence of illness. Consider the ways in which these factors can be decreased. If health conditions are improved, organic factors are minimized, from birth abnormalities that could be eliminated with proper maternal nutrition and prenatal care to stroke and its accompanying brain damage through the prescription of proper medication. In the workplace, the prevention of accidents can meet this condition. Stress can obviously be reduced by limiting environmental and self-imposed circumstances that evoke it. Brenner (1973), for example, proved that, throughout the world, unemployment is accompanied, in a lagged relationship, by suicide, homicide, and admissions to mental hospitals (see also Gullotta, 1983). Workplaces that provide stable employment and in which employees can have faith in the management have a head start of minimizing stressful experiences at work. For individuals, reducing self-blame for not achieving the American dream of unbounded financial success, or what Lerner (1980) called "surplus powerlessness," proves helpful in placing boundaries around stressful experiences. Exploitation, including sexism, racism, and ageism, concerns the specific ways in which society treats groups or, as Ivins (1992, p. 63) expounded with regard to sexual harassment: "A boss who hits on his employees, an executive who hits on his secretary, a professor who hits on his students, a doctor or psychiatrist who hits on his patients—that's not lusty pursuit in a game of love played by both sexes: That's abuse of authority, that's preying on the weak, and it is morally repellent." Its termination would also contribute to mental health!

So, too, would increasing the power of the denominator factors in Albee's formulation reduce mental illness. If people expand their repertoire of psychosocial competence by increasing their ability to deal with others and to handle crises, they are less likely to become ill and more likely to have, or gain, a sense of self-esteem. Workers who learn the skill of conflict resolution function more effectively with peers, supervisors, and supervisees, achieving a sense of personal competence and self-mastery. In addition, the availability of others to provide various kinds of support—emotional, informational, instrumental, and appraisal—strengthens the ability to face life events without damage to oneself (Gottlieb, 1987). By combining the concepts of Caplan, Cowan, and Albee, one now has a workable definition of primary prevention as those specific, research-documented activities that minimize organic, stress, and exploitation factors and maximize competence, self-esteem, and support not only to prevent maladaptation, but to protect and promote the well-being of groups who are at risk but who are not yet damaged by their circumstances.

Rationale for Interest by the World of Work

The next step is to understand why such activity should be of interest to parties in the world of work. Employers are interested in reducing the incidence of mental illness, including substance abuse (and physical illness, although this issue will not be discussed here) for economic, political, and social reasons. These reasons range from the need to have a favorable public image in order to recruit the best pool of employees to the legal responsibility to create a workplace climate that is free of discrimination. They include the management of global competition, which has proved to be accomplished most produc-tively and, therefore, effectively by valuing workers (Ouchi, 1981; Peters & Waterman, 1982) as well as the necessity to contain health care costs in a world in which Lee Iacocca identified Blue Cross/Blue Shield as Chrysler's largest supplier, by dollars paid. As Schinnar, Rothbard, and Hadley (1992) observed, "prevention is an alternative to treatment or supply of mental health care; it is intended to reduce the demand for service delivery by either promoting early treatment of symptoms or by alleviating social and environmental stressors that may exacerbate mental symptoms."

Unions have similar interests because, if health care costs are not contained, not enough money is available for them to bargain to enhance the breadth of their members' benefits packages. Furthermore, in this era of attacks on the power of unions, it is harder and harder for unions to carry out their primary function, identified by Mills (1948) as "the ability to organize discontent and sit on it." When wage increases are elusive at best, the service route is an important means of retaining the members' loyalty. Many prevention initiatives carry a service ingredient (Reynolds, 1975). Others deal with the climate of the workplace; for example, the stability of jobs and employees' participation in decision making are basic protections expected from effective unions.

In the past several decades, social workers, particularly those in the world of work, have shown increased interest in prevention as research has confirmed the gains that can occur from moving the profession "upstream" from its focus on individuals with problems to a focus on the potential for social policies and service delivery systems that can protect and promote the well-being of at-risk groups (Siefert, Jayaratne, & Martin, 1992). There is an allegorical story of a fisherman who, while rescuing people floating downstream who are in danger of drowning, accumulates a crowd about him, admiring his heroic feats. When he suddenly starts walking away, viewers express horror that he would consider deserting a spot where he is saving people. He replies, "I am going upstream to see where they are throwing them in!" Upstream is clearly the world of work, where many individuals may be at risk, but as long as they are able to keep their jobs, they are viewed as functioning effectively.

There are many other reasons why occupational social workers have an interest in primary prevention. The population is universal, including those who fit Cowan's criteria; that is, there are many in the world of work who are at risk of depression or substance abuse but who are not yet depressed or abusers. In addition, it is easy for the potential beneficiaries to use the services because they are destigmatized—a sort of "help-without-hassle" kind of delivery system—so it is possible to receive professional help without asking for it. Furthermore, the sponsoring parties, labor and management, are likely to be responsive to those who advocate for primary prevention services in the functional community of work, unlike advocacy in the general community, which is usually rejected on the basis of inadequate resources and unconvincing cost-benefit arguments.

Primary Prevention Programs in the World of Work

With the three relevant parties—labor, management, and the social work profession—in agreement about the goals and potential of primary prevention, it would seem that work-sited programs would be spreading rapidly. In fact, that is the situation. Many of the chapters in this book, such as the ones on substance abuse, child and elder care, stress management, women in high-risk jobs, and EAPs, are filled with examples of such programs. However, many untapped, organizationally focused opportunities remain. The rest of this chapter deals with a few of these opportunities, namely managing the diverse work force, developing health-promotion programs, organizing self-help support groups, and orchestrating change in the system. Each meets the definition of and criteria established for primary prevention. Each is within the grasp of a social worker with experience and skill in the world of work. The authors believe that these initiatives represent a level of activity to which occupational social workers have gained access by virtue of an intensive decade of delivering direct services.

According to Gullotta (1987), there are five prime strategies in prevention: education, intervention in systems, the promotion of competence, collaboration–consultation, and natural caregiving–social supports. The aim of these technologies of primary prevention, used individually and in concert, is to increase an individual's coping resources (Albee's denominator) and mitigate the environment's noxious impact (Albee's numerator) so that the host (individual) will be better able to cope.

Managing the Diverse Work Force

In many work settings, management has made a conscious effort to fulfill the requirements of laws that govern affirmative action and nondiscrimination. Managers who are involved in these activities often express their concern, viewing the glass-ceiling effect as inevitable, that although women and minorities are recruited and trained, they do not exhibit the skills needed to reach the top. Women and people of color, however, often complain that their differences are not valued, that the only route to success is assimilation, and that such a route is a denial of self and therefore unacceptable. In this process, many members of the affirmatively recruited groups begin to feel inadequate and unsuccessful, lose their sense of self-esteem, doubt their coping skills, and experience isolation and stress.

Prevention begins when someone identifies the need for change and mobilizes support for that change. One of the authors (Akabas) provided consultation to a large corporation that was concerned about the exit rate of professional women and people of color who had been recruited at great cost only to leave within a brief period. A series of interviews and focus-group sessions with both the target population and the managers uncovered the typical situation just described. Although the managers thought they were developing all employees equally, they gave the best assignments, the superior training, and the greatest understanding to those with whom they felt most comfortable, usually white men. The managers did not understand the potential advantage that their expensively recruited diverse employees could provide for them and rejected any behavior or appearance of the newcomers that did not fit the corporation's long-standing mold. They had no appreciation of the symbolic meaning of many of their procedures and expectations to persons who were different from them. The managers' investment in recruiting women and people of color and their concern about legal requirements, however, bolstered their commitment to work on the issues that were uncovered.

After the needs assessment, the team of social workers provided consultation and educational presentations to the managers that improved their understanding of human behavior, both their own and the recruits'. Attention was directed to the organization's operation. Managers were encouraged, for example, to identify the various assignments that had brought them to the top and to mirror those assignments for the newcomers. This change in the system provided actual training opportunities for both the women and people of color that carried a message of trust and succeeded in promoting competence. Over a period of years, the primary prevention initiative reversed the previous situation. Instead of everyone experiencing undue stress and the exiters leaving with a reduced self-image, turnover was reduced; many managers had modified their behavior; and, as Gullotta (1987) suggested, all parties increased their understanding of themselves and their environments.

In the process, some unintended gains accrued to the corporation. Like Xerox, Digital, and Corning, all of whom are well-known for their celebration of diversity in their work forces (Akabas & Gates, 1993), the company began to find recruitment easier and, therefore, less costly. It received positive publicity in publications, and its diverse staff were invited to make numerous presentations at conferences, giving consumers the opportunity to view the corporation favorably. When global sales opportunities developed, the company had appropriate personnel to assign. Furthermore, encouraged by research that has suggested that problem-solving groups are more effective when their membership is diverse, the company looks forward to even more positive outcomes in the future.

Developing Health-Promotion Programs

Despite the large health care bill paid through the world of work, it is estimated that less than 2 percent of the total amount spent for health care is devoted to keeping people healthy (Cohen, 1985). Many have suggested that the most efficient way to contain health care costs is to shift from a philosophy of curing disease to one of preventing illness and promoting health (National Institute for Occupational Safety and Health, 1990). Such programs can emphasize reducing the susceptibility of individuals to disease, as well as improving the environment for achieving health. Strategies include education to alter both social values and behavior—to introduce a healthful lifestyle—as well as ongoing support and reinforcement for that change through social support groups and attention to the environment, including such changes in the system as office policies on no smoking, supplying healthy foods in snack vending machines, and even offering exercise facilities on-site.

There is a growing feeling that although social workers may lack the specific information needed for promoting health, their knowledge of human behavior, skills in motivating people, and understanding of organizations are the essential ingredients in the effective promotion of health (Anderson & Stark, 1988; Doherty, 1988; Gebhardt & Crump, 1990). Others can be hired to provide specialty content, but the basic elements of a successful program—which include developing goals and objectives, introducing the program, taking account of the organizational culture, developing a long-term evaluation strategy, and recruiting participants—constitute tasks within a competent social worker's range of skills.

Often, it is the recruitment of participants that proves the most challenging (Bailey, 1990; Bushbin & Campbell, 1990). Targeting subgroups who are considered to be at risk, allowing employees to participate in the design of programs, ensuring confidentiality, and encouraging the involvement of family members have had positive effects on participation. As in all other areas of service delivery, it is important that participation be voluntary and that the management be honest about its goals, which usually include ultimate cost saving (Polakoff & O'Rourke, 1990). A long-term commitment is crucial because it generally takes four to five years to demonstrate savings (Mitchell, 1990). The promotion of health certainly strengthens the host, but in more than physical ways. Feeling healthy often is accompanied by feeling competent, experiencing minimal stress, and having a positive self-image. Positive feedback (appraisal support), as well as informational and emotional support, usually characterize health-promotion programs, combining to achieve the primary prevention goals of promoting the mental health and well-being of participants and often reduced absenteeism and improved productivity that benefit employers (Jones, Bly, & Richardson, 1990; Polakoff & O'Rourke, 1990).

Organizing Self-help and Social Support

Research continues to mount on the value of social support in a variety of situations. There is an indication that our immune systems function better, our mental health is enhanced, and our life expectancy is lengthened when we feel that we have social support. What appears to distinguish whether depression follows unemployment among men is their perceived level of support (Figueira-McDonough, 1978). Among work groups, noticeable improvements in productivity have been correlated with group cohesion. Caplan (quoted in Weiss, 1976, p. 177) was one of the first to identify the significance of social support systems, which he defined as "an enduring pattern of continuous or intermittent ties that play a significant part in maintaining the psychological and physical integrity of the individual over time."

Unions are an important example of self-help groups in work settings. They seek to determine the conditions of employment and protect all their members, including the weakest, from stress and exploitation. The concept of "in unity there is strength" on which unions are based is a long-standing expression of the recent idea of empowerment (Swift & Levin, 1987), a process that Katz and Hermalin (1986, p. 171) suggested facilitates a person's feelings of power or mastery over predictable and unforeseen stresses and trauma. Although social workers have no mandate to organize unions in workplaces where they are delivering services, neither should they become involved in undermining the unions' power. Social workers who are employed by unions find extensive, rich opportunities for delivering primary prevention interventions by using all the strategies of prevention listed earlier.

But there are many groups that can be organized in the workplace to provide opportunities for self-help or social support, even without the presence of a union (Liem & Liem, 1979). Consider, as one corporation did, a number of newly divorced middle managers who are likely to feel lonely; with a reduced sense of self, they probably are suffering from reduced productivity. An in-house EAP social worker organized a support group to facilitate their exchange of vital information, for example, where to live or how to spend recreational time; offer each other emotional support, such as someone with whom to have dinner; provide appraisal when they appear to be sinking into depression; and share instrumental aid, including an exchange of baby-sitting services (Akabas, 1982).

Imagine a group of young pregnant workers, unsettled about whether to return to work after giving birth. Their indecisiveness was causing stress, casting self-doubt on their ability to parent, and generally reducing their sense of competence. Educational intervention by a social worker who was called in from a local community mental health center provided an excellent example of a primary prevention approach. Convening and linking this group and providing counseling offered some basis for answers. The support of a group struggling with similar ambiguities reduced the self-blame that was interfering with a feeling of individual mastery. Furthermore, problem solving on this issue helped the organization plan its likely labor supply more efficiently. Such problem-solving groups will be even more significant now that President Clinton has signed the Family Leave Act.

At Travelers Insurance Company, the social workers became aware that elder-care responsibilities were interfering with some employees' ability to function productively. An ongoing support group for those who are caregivers to the elderly has maintained workers on the job while enhancing their sense of competence in the difficult task of juggling work and family demands. In addition, networking opportunities have been used effectively to achieve the aims of managing diversity. As the earlier discussion suggested, feelings of isolation often lead to the failure of new recruits in the workplace. Some corporations have understood this problem and have encouraged (or at least allowed) social workers to develop caucuses that lend support, link employees with the greater whole, and help them anticipate problems, thereby enhancing their capacity to cope. Such groups have also taken on advocacy roles, which help the members overcome persistent and pervasive inequalities (Swift & Levin, 1987). Social workers can contribute to affirmative action by evolving primary prevention strategies.

Orchestrating Organizational Change

Work plays so significant a role in people's lives that a work connection is probably essential to mental health for most adults. Workplaces can be benevolent, benign, or destructive in relation to individual well-being (Bezold, Carlson, & Peck, 1986; Special Task Force, 1973). Though the literature is replete with research findings about the link between economic success and organizational concern for people, American employers, for the most part, continue to be hierarchically organized and authoritarian in their operation. Social workers often sense the environmental quality of an organization as a result of their interactions with employees. Such information provides an ideal base for attempting organizational change.

Some years ago, this chapter's first author coauthored a book that suggested that trying to temper the climate of an organization was beyond the mandate of the social worker in the workplace (Weiner, Akabas, & Sommer, 1973). She wishes to withdraw that evaluation and state emphatically that such action is the responsibility of any social worker who observes organizational dysfunction that is having a negative impact on workers and their mental health. The obligation comes not only from responsibility to the individual so affected, but from the profession's mandate to help fit the environment to the individual and from the organizational role assigned to a social worker.

It is probable that the social worker in an employing organization introduces subdominant values to that organization (Patti, 1982). But those values are often the basis for the unique contribution that social workers can make to the business culture. The creative use of those values to focus on humanistic needs, question organizational norms, and establish strategies for changing the system can help the culture identify new ways of handling issues that will prevent mental illness, protect functional capacity, and promote well-being (Allen, 1986), thereby realizing the full potential of primary prevention.

Borrowing heavily from Kurt Lewin's concept of force-field analysis, Brager and Holloway (1978) and Resnick and Patti (1980) offered a model for effecting organizational change that is available to professionals with little organizational power. The model is applicable to circumstances as varied as unsafe working conditions (organic factors), inappropriate alloca-tions of authority and responsibility (stress-producing factors), or insidious evidence of systematic discrimination (exploitation factors). The model involves an initial assessment that describes the problem and identifies a goal; a preinitiation stage during which organizational support is developed (often by increasing the visibility of the problem or building up the credibility of the change agent); initiating the change, which may require enlisting a more powerful spokesperson to carry the advocacy role; and, finally, implement-ing the change and linking it structurally to the organization.

Behind the effort is an organizational analysis that identifies and evaluates the contending forces that will promote or resist the change being sought. Properly analyzed, planned, and managed, an organizational change can empower and promote the competence of the primary target population (those who are most at risk from the identified problem) while improving the quality of organizationwide interactions, reducing friction and competitive infighting, and accomplishing lasting cultural change (Allen, 1986).

Social Work Agencies as Employers

The strategies discussed here are but the tip of the iceberg in relation to the potential of primary prevention in the workplace. The authors do not claim that prevention is missing from the daily practice of many occupational social workers in a great variety of settings. What they do believe, however, is that it is too often a process that occurs by chance, rather than by plan, and misses the strength of the identification, attainment, and measurement of goals. Occupational social workers do not build sufficiently from one effort to the other in a systematic process that saves lives and dollars. In short, they miss the full potential of their interventions.

Sites that are most in need of a primary prevention focus, perhaps, are social agencies, the workplaces of most social workers. In their commitment to clients, these agencies often neglect the needs and rights of their employ-ees (Akabas, 1990; Farley, 1991). Although advocacy is a key professional skill, and one that is often performed well in the interests of clients, social workers have not been effective in empowering themselves. Concerns about burnout, the symptom of those who feel powerless and lack self-esteem, are expressed frequently by social workers and other helping professionals (University of Michigan, 1990).

If one considers just the four arenas of primary prevention dealt with in this chapter, it is possible to discern many opportunities for primary prevention initiatives. The effective management of diversity may include the development of family-sensitive policies that are responsive to the demanding family-work strains experienced by social workers, largely a female labor force that includes many single-parent heads of households. Education in personal health care can be as significant a portion of staff development and training as the conveyance of knowledge and skill involved in the performance of tasks on which most efforts concentrate today. Support groups that help workers deal with issues of death and dying and other traumata that professionals experience daily would minimize the stresses that cause depression and anxiety among social workers. Quality circles that maximize the participation of employees, including circles that empower support staff, would represent a substantial organizational change for most social agencies. The important consideration is that in seeking to improve the workplace, we social workers take care to include our own.

Cautions in the Search for Primary Prevention

Primary prevention is essentially an attempt to modify the social environ-ment and redistribute power in the interest of promoting positive outcomes. But it is important to recognize its limitations as well as its potential. As occupational social workers seek to improve employees' life-styles and the environment of the workplace through primary prevention, their programs can become excessively intrusive, serving as a means of social control rather than empowerment (Conrad & Walsh, 1992; Henifin & Hubbard, 1983).

Examples include EAPs (and drug testing), as well as health-promotion efforts to which employers may become so committed that they punish those who "don't play."

In addition, not all the strategies are tried and true. Although proof of effectiveness was suggested earlier as an important criterion for initiating any primary prevention plan, many efforts lack such credentials. For example MacDuffie, (1988, p. 15) noted, "It is now widely acknowledged that quality circles are of little use unless they are linked to broader changes in decision making, authority and job design." The need to evaluate programs and provide feedback so that practitioners are informed about what works—and what seems logically as if it would work but does not—is a vital but often-missing element in any prevention effort.

It will come as no surprise to the reader that although primary prevention sounds wonderful, its supporters are a modest crew. Primary prevention is hard to measure; its goal of preventing something from happening makes it difficult to assess whether something might have happened without the initiative. As a result, in the battle for resources, attention focuses on existing problems, rather than on illusive at-risk groups who may or may not develop a given problem (Albee, 1983). Mental illness has so many causes that its etiology is difficult to specify. Lacking knowledge of its causes, it is difficult to be sure that any particular intervention will pay off. As Freyman, (1981, p. 669) noted,

> The ideal result of preventive measures is, in a clinical sense *zero*: the complete absence of disease. To an activist by nature and education, prevention is dull. It lacks the excitement and satisfaction of discovering pathology and working for a cure. This is reinforced by our custom (in the U.S.) of paying only for performance of a measurable act and placing no dollar value on preventive services rendered to individuals.

One of the special qualities of the workplace is that it is a bounded community in which measurement is more feasible than in most settings. The logic behind primary prevention is its parallel to the interests of the workplace's sponsors. The measures for evaluation are there—reduced absenteeism, tardiness, turnover, health care costs, and the like. All the occupational social worker has to do is to find the problem, hypothesize a solution, and then measure its outcome. Therein lie many major questions and great potential.

References

Akabas, S. H. (1982). The world of work: A site for mental health promotion. In F. D. Perlmutter, (Ed.), *Mental health promotion and primary prevention* (pp. 33–44). San Francisco: Jossey-Bass.

Akabas, S. H. (1987). Mighty oaks: The potential of prevention in the workplace. In J. Hermalin & J. A. Morell (Eds.), *Prevention planning in mental health* (pp. 191–226). Beverly Hills, CA: Sage Publications.

Akabas, S. H. (1990). Reconciling the demands of work with the needs of families. *Family in Society 71*, 366–371.

Akabas, S. H., & Gates, L. B. (1993). Managing workforce diversity. In J. Klein & J. Miller (Eds.), *The American edge.* New York: McGraw-Hill.

Akabas, S. H., & Kurzman, P. A. (1982). The industrial social welfare specialist: What's so special? In S. H. Akabas and P. A. Kurzman (Eds.), *Work, workers, and work organizations: A view from social work* (pp. 197–235). Englewood Cliffs, NJ: Prentice Hall.

Albee, G. W. (1983). Psychopathology, prevention and the just society. *Journal of Primary Prevention 4*(1), 5–42.

Allen, J. (1986). Achieving primary prevention program objectives through culture change systems. *Journal of Primary Prevention 7*(2), 91–107.

Anderson, C., & Stark, C. (1988). Psychosocial problems of job relocation: Preventive roles in industry. *Social Work, 33,* 38–41.

Bailey, N. C. (1990). Wellness programs that work. *Business and Health 8*(11), 28–40.

Barker, R. L. (1991). *The social work dictionary* (2nd ed.). Silver Spring, MD: National Association of Social Workers.

Bezold, C., Carlson, R. J., & Peck, J. C. (1986). *The future of work and health.* Dover, MA: Auburn House.

Bloom, B. L. (1979). Prevention of mental disorders: Recent advances in theory and practice. *Community Mental Health Journal, 15,* 179–191.

Bloom, M. (1987a). Prevention. In A. Minahan (Ed.-in-Chief), *Encyclopedia of social work* (18th ed., Vol. 2, pp. 303–315). Silver Spring, MD: National Association of Social Workers.

Bloom, M. (1987b). Toward a technology in primary prevention: Educational strategies and tactics. *Journal of Primary Prevention, 8*(1–2), 25–48.

Brager, G., & Holloway, S. (1978). *Changing human service organizations.* New York: Free Press.

Brenner, M. H. (1973). *Mental illness and the economy.* Cambridge, MA: Harvard University Press.

Bushbin, J. W., & Campbell, D. P. (1990). Employee wellness programs: A strategy for increasing participation. *Journal of Health Care Marketing, 10*(4) 22–30.

Caplan, G. (1964). *Principles of preventive psychiatry.* New York: Basic Books.

Cohen, W. S. (1985). Health promotion in the workplace. *American Psychologist, 40,* 213–216.

Conrad, P., & Walsh, D. C. (1992). The new corporate health ethic: Lifestyle and the social control of work. *International Journal of Health Services, 22*(1), 89–111.

Cowan, E. L. (1982). Primary prevention research: Barriers, needs and opportunities. *Journal of Primary Prevention, 2,* 131–137.

Doherty, K. (1988). Health returns. *Healthy Companies, 1*(3), 22–27.

Farley, J. E. (1991). Responses of mental health professionals to lay-offs. *Hospital and Community Psychiatry, 42*, 624–627.

Figueira-McDonough, J. (1978). Mental health among unemployed Detroiters. *Social Service Review, 52*, 383–399.

Forgays, D. G. (1983). Primary prevention: Up the revolution! *Journal of Primary Prevention, 4*(1), 41–53.

Freud, S. (1962). *Civilization and its discontents.* New York: W. W. Norton. (Original work published 1930)

Freyman, J. G. (1981). The origins of disease orientation in American medical education. *Preventive Medicine, 10*, 663–673.

Gebhardt, D. L., & Crump, C. E. (1990). Employee fitness and wellness programs in the workplace. *American Psychologist, 45*, 161–171.

Gottlieb, B. H. (1987). Using social support to protect and promote health. *Journal of Primary Prevention, 8*(1–2), 49–71.

Gullotta, T. P. (1983). Comment: Unemployment and mental health. *Journal of Primary Prevention, 4*(1), 3–4.

Gullotta, T. P. (1987). Prevention's technology. *Journal of Primary Prevention, 8*(1–2), 4–25.

Henifin, M. S., & Hubbard, R. (1983, November–December). Genetic screening in the workplace. *GeneWATCH*, pp. 5–9.

Ivins, M. (1992). *Molly Ivins can't say that, can she?* New York: Vintage Books.

Jones, R. C., Bly, J. L., & Richardson, J. E. (1990). Study of a worksite health promotion program and absenteeism. *Journal of Occupational Medicine, 32*, 95–99.

Katz, A. H., & Hermalin, J. (1986). Self-help and prevention. In J. Hermalin & J. A. Morell (Eds.), *Prevention planning in mental health* (pp. 151–190). Beverly Hills, CA: Sage Publications.

Lerner, M. (1980). Stress at the workplace: The approach of the Institute for Labor and Mental Health. *Catalyst, 2*, 75–82.

Liem, G. R., & Liem, J. H. (1979). Social support and stress: Some general issues and their application to the problem of unemployment. In L. A. Ferman & J. P. Gordus (Eds.), *Mental health and the economy* (pp. 347–377). Kalamazoo, MI: W. E. UpJohn Institute for Employment Research.

MacDuffie, J. P. (1988). The Japanese auto transplants: Challenges to conventional wisdom. *ILR Report, 26*(1), 12–18.

Maslow, A. H. (1970). *Motivation and personality* (2nd ed.). New York: Harper & Row.

Mills, C. W. (1948). *The new men of power: America's labor leaders.* New York: Harcourt, Brace.

Mitchell, J. (1990). EAPs and wellness programs. *Employee Assistance, 2*, 25–27.

National Institute for Occupational Safety and Health, U.S. Department of Health and Human Services. (1990). *Healthy people 2000: Occupational safety and health.* Washington, DC: U.S. Government Printing Office.

Ouchi, W. (1981). *Theory Z: How American business can meet the Japanese challenge.* Reading, MA: Addison-Wesley.

Patti, R. J. (1982). Applying business management strategies in social agencies. In S. H. Akabas & P. A. Kurzman (Eds.), *Work, workers, and work organizations: A view from social work* (pp. 147–175). Englewood Cliffs, NJ: Prentice Hall.

Peters, T. J., & Waterman, R. H., Jr. (1982). *In search of excellence: Lessons from America's best-run companies.* New York: Harper & Row.

Polakoff, P. L., & O'Rourke, P. F. (1990). Healthy worker—Healthy workplace: The productivity connection. *Benefits Quarterly 6*(2), 37–57.

Resnick, H., & Patti, R. (1980). *Change from within.* Philadelphia: Temple University Press.

Reynolds, B. C. (1975). *Social work and social living.* Washington, DC: National Association of Social Workers. (Original work published 1951)

Schinnar, A. P., Rothbard, A. B., & Hadley, T. R. (1992). A prospective management approach to the delivery of public mental health services. *Administration and Policy in Mental Health, 19,* 291–308.

Siefert, K., Jayaratne, S., & Martin, L. D. (1992). Implementing the public health social work forward plan: A research-based prevention curriculum for schools of social work. *Health and Social Work, 17,* 17–27.

Special Task Force to the Secretary of Health, Education, and Welfare. (1973). *Work in America.* Cambridge, MA: MIT Press.

Stellman, J. M., & Daum, S. M. (1973). *Work is dangerous to your health.* New York: Vintage Books.

Swift, C., & Levin, G. (1987). Empowerment: An emerging mental health technology. *Journal of Primary Prevention, 8*(1–2), 71–94.

University of Michigan School of Social Work. (1990). *Prevention training program for social work.* Ann Arbor: Author.

Wegman, D. H. (1992) The potential impact of epidemiology on the prevention of occupational disease. *American Journal of Public Health, 82,* 944–954.

Weiner, H. J., Akabas, S. H., & Sommer, J. (1973). *Mental health care in the world of work.* New York: Association Press.

Weiss, R. S. (1976). The contributions of an organization of single parents to the well-being of its members. In G. Caplan & M. Killilea (Eds.), *Support systems and mutual help* (pp. 177–185). New York: Grune & Stratton.

Wittman, M. (1977). Preventive social work. In J. Turner (Ed.-in-Chief), *Encyclopedia of social work* (17th ed., Vol. 2, pp. 1049–1053). Washington, DC: National Association of Social Workers.

CHAPTER 6

Employee Benefits

THE ROLE OF SOCIAL INSURANCE AND SOCIAL SERVICES

Lawrence S. Root

> A physician once said of work, "It is the open sesame to
> every portal, the great equalizer in the world, the true
> philosopher's stone which transmutes all the base metal
> of humanity into gold."
>
> —Sir William Osler
> *Science and Immortality*

The role of paid employment in the ordering of society is obvious: Paid employment is the principal vehicle for distributing income. Differentials in salaries and wages sculpt the income profile, with social programs operating primarily at the margins. Even in countries with advanced social welfare systems, programs of income redistribution represent a relatively small proportion of individual incomes.

What we *do*, our *work*, dominates our self-definition. The "division of labor" in society is basic to the development of culture, and it constitutes a fundamental organizing principle for all but the most primitive societies. It is not without justification that one's employment is often thought of as the "master role."

Roughly two-thirds of the adult population are in the labor force; that is, they are either employed or looking for work (see Table 1). For men, the "labor force participation rate" is 76.6 percent and represents a decrease over time because fewer older men continue to work. On the other hand, women's labor force participation rate, although not as high as men's, has increased in recent years. The current rate of 57.3 percent has been boosted by the steady increase in the labor force of the number of married women and women with young children.

Table 1
Employment Status of the Population Ages 16 and Older, September 1990

POPULATION	TOTAL	MEN	WOMEN
Civilian population (numbers × 1,000)	188,401	89,830	98,571
Civilian labor force (numbers × 1,000)	124,967	68,369	56,598
Labor force participation rate (percentage)	66.1	76.6	57.3
Employed (numbers × 1,000)	117,898	64,426	53,472
Unemployed (numbers × 1,000)	7,069	3,943	3,126
Unemployment rate (percentage)	5.7	5.8	5.5
Percentage of those "employed" part time (1988 data)			
Voluntarily	14.2	7.9	21.8
For economic reasons[a]	4.5	3.9	5.3

[a]Includes individuals who usually work full-time but are involuntarily working part-time for economic reasons (a slack demand for labor, for example).

SOURCES: Calculated to exclude the armed forces, from Tables 4 and 6 of "Current Labor Statistics" in *Monthly Labor Review* (November 1990), and U.S. Bureau of Labor Statistics (1989), Table 12.

In the United States, the economic role of the workplace extends beyond wages and salaries to the provision of basic social insurance and, to an increasing degree, of other social services. Unions have been the initiators of much of this expansion, and patterns established in the organized sectors have set the standards for other employers. Programs, such as health insurance, which are a centralized governmental responsibility in other industrialized countries, are a part of the employment relationship in the United States. The integration of such programs into the employer-employee relationship has profound implications for the role of government, as well as for the operations of the workplace. Access to jobs has become the key to social insurance protection. Differences in the comprehensiveness of employee benefits amplify the disparity between "good jobs" and "bad jobs."

Employee benefits also influence employers' decisions about the management of the work force. Cost factors are introduced into their calculation, with important implications for scheduling work, hiring, and layoffs.

The impact of workplace benefits extends to the actual provision of the services. Differences in employment opportunities, such as those associated with race and gender, become differences in *access to services*. And controls on the cost of employee benefits often define the parameters of therapeutic interventions, influencing the nature and extent of the treatment that is available.

Social work has traditionally focused on the individual in the social context. For most people, the workplace is a central part of their life experiences and a key determinant of the quality of their lives. Understanding the world of work, therefore, is critical to understanding the situations of individuals and families.

This chapter examines employee benefits as a vehicle for the provision of social insurance and social services. First, it explores the background of work-based programs, observing their growth historically as well as current manifestations. It then considers the overall impact of such services, both on the individuals served and on those who have been left out of this social welfare development. Finally, it discusses the implications and the unintended impact of the employee benefit structure on managerial decisions, collective bargaining, social insurance, and social services.

Background of Benefits

The origins of the current benefits structure can be understood in terms of the evolving relationship between employer and employee, the role of unions, and the labor contract. Although this chapter focuses on the current benefits structure, it is essential to view employee benefits within their broader social context.

Work in preindustrial society involved a range of mutual obligations between the peasant and the lord that largely defined the social order. Workers owed the master labor and loyalty, and the master, in turn, provided access to the land and some measure of security. With the Industrial Revolution came a sea change in work relations: Social obligations were replaced by a more limited exchange relationship based on the selling of one's labor. The shrinking of the agrarian economy and the rise of large-scale production under private ownership brought the "wage relationship" to center stage.

Although the idea of payment for time worked is now the norm in our society, it is a relatively new phenomenon and one that continued to concern social critics as late as the early 1900s (Rodgers, 1978, pp. 30–33ff). The depersonalized aspect of the wage system was decried as "wage slavery" and portrayed as a dehumanization of the work relationship. One indication of the revolutionary aspect of this new relationship was the depiction in literature and art of the destructive aspects of the new economic order, from the social critiques of Charles Dickens and Theodore Dreiser to the indictments of depersonalized labor in early films, including Fritz Lang's *Metropolis* and Charlie Chaplin's *Modern Times*.

Although the new wage system defined a circumscribed role for the employer–employee relationship, one does not have to look far to find examples of employers who went beyond those limits. The motivation for these initiatives was a blend of altruistic (or, perhaps, paternalistic) concern with a desire to exercise greater control over the work force.

The Pullman experience is a well-documented example (Buder, 1967). In the late 1800s, this large maker of railway cars created a model industrial village in what is now south Chicago. Reacting to the poor living conditions of the nearby tenements, the company built its town of Pullman on a careful plan. Drawing on the city-planning principles of the time, it laid out the village with a central square, a marketplace, and a hotel. The housing built for employees was graded by status, with more spacious accommodations designated for the managers.

In addition to planning the physical environment, the designers sought to create a "utopian" social environment by instituting rules of behavior, ranging from a dress code to confining alcohol to the hotel (which was off-limits to the average worker). The main church in Pullman was Protestant. Efforts to obtain space for a Catholic church were resisted for years. When permission was finally given to establish a Catholic church, the church had to be located outside Pullman's official town limits (Buder, 1967).

Thus, the progressive goals of the company were blended with the practical desire to shape the work force. For the planners, this desire meant "Americanizing" the recent immigrants and discouraging Old World associations, which were seen as detrimental to an orderly industrial work environment.

Pullman's model industrial village was seen by many as a futuristic expression of welfare capitalism—the humanization of industrial society (for a discussion of "welfare capitalism" and its context, see Brandes, 1976). Special sightseeing trips were arranged during Chicago's 1892 Columbian Exposition. Despite this external recognition, resentment of the social controls existed, and when the company imposed wage cuts in response to a recession (without corresponding cuts in rent), the Pullman workers struck, triggering a national railroad strike that paralyzed the nation and resulted in the imprisonment of its leader, Eugene Debs.

The village of Pullman never recovered from this breakdown in industrial relations. Soon after, it was disbanded as a corporate entity and absorbed into the expanding city of Chicago. It is still discernible as a planned community by its orderly building plan and substantial housing stock.

Although Pullman village was an unusually extensive programmatic effort, there are numerous examples of other programs that combined altruistic with practical motivations. For instance, from its inception, Henry Ford's "sociology department" combined advice and assistance to workers with identifying undesirable workers (eventually giving up the former role) (Collier & Horowitz, 1987).

Medical services were introduced into the workplace following increases in court judgments holding employers liable in industrial accidents. It was also said that physical examinations of employees were used to uncover the "disease of unionism," providing employers with a rationale for dismissing those so infected.

A similar dualism continues to characterize the motivation for developing programs in the workplace. Discussions of the role of businesses in the provision of social services incorporate the language of values and altruism ("It's the right thing to do"), along with practical considerations (attracting and retaining good workers).

Employee benefits continue to be useful management tools for employers. For example, retirement programs (pensions, profit sharing, and the like) are often structured to discourage employees from changing jobs by rewarding long service. Pension accumulations are not usually "vested" until employees have been with a company for at least five years. Bonuses that are built into many retirement packages create "golden handcuffs" that make it costly for employees to leave a company.

Health insurance, as an employee benefit, can also make it more costly for an employee to change jobs. If a worker or dependent is undergoing medical treatment, a change of job (and associated change in health insurance) may threaten his or her continued coverage for that condition. In addition, the possible suspension of health insurance can reduce the likelihood of a strike and add greater weight to disciplinary processes in the workplace.

But for the most part, employee benefits are used as a positive inducement. They attract desired employees and contribute to the definition of what is a good job and what is a good employer.

Employee Benefits

Employee benefits have become an integral part of the social insurance picture. Titmuss (1969) highlighted this fact in his seminal essay identifying "occupational welfare" as one of the three sources of social welfare provisions. Employee benefits create "enclaves" of protection, defining a national social welfare structure in terms of basic governmental programs, supplemented by a wide variety of employee benefit systems (Root, 1982).

Assessing the social insurance role of employee benefits presents methodological challenges because, unlike governmental social insurance programs, employee benefits are not under any central administrative control; individual companies and unions design and implement their own programs.

Benefit packages are developed by employee benefit specialists, such as the major insurance carriers and other benefit consultants, often based on models created through collective bargaining. Because of this decentralization, knowledge of the current structure of benefits comes from surveys and other data-collection efforts.

The Chamber of Commerce of the United States of America annually provides information on overall expenditures for employee benefits (see Table 2). Its 1990 survey included 957 firms that employed over 4 million people. The survey estimated that employee benefits cost an average of $11,527 per employee (37.6 percent of the payroll costs) (Chamber of Commerce, 1990). This overall estimate reflects the full range of noncash personnel costs.

For this discussion, it is useful to separate the broad category of "employee benefits" into its components and concentrate on those that are particularly relevant to social insurance and social services. The pertinent components are these:

1. *insurance benefits:* payments for a variety of types of insurance (for example, health, dental, and life insurance)

2. *income support:* programs to provide income when employees are not able to work (such as pensions, sick pay, and supplements to unemployment insurance)

3. *social services:* a variety of direct services (including employee assistance and day care).

Table 2

Overall Costs of Employee Benefits as a Percentage of Total Payroll Costs

BENEFIT AREA	PERCENTAGE OF PAYROLL
Medically related	9.3
Retirement income	5.1
Life insurance	0.5
Legally mandated benefits	8.7
Pay for time not worked (including vacations)	10.8
Rest periods	2.3
Other (such as educational benefits, day care, and meals)	0.9
Total employee benefits	37.6

Source: Chamber of Commerce (1990).

Insurance Benefits

Of all the workplace programs, health insurance is the most significant in terms of cost and of implications for public policy and the well-being of employees and their families. Health insurance became a part of the nego- tiating agendas of unions in the late 1940s and early 1950s after the political defeat of national health insurance. Wage controls during World War II further channeled inflationary pressures into fringe benefits. After the war, unions took the lead in regularizing the place of benefits in the labor contract, with the Supreme Court ruling that benefits are part of a worker's remuneration and are subject to the rules of collective bargaining.

These initiatives set the pattern for expanded benefits as a part of the wage package. As a result, health care expenditures in the United States, unlike those in other industrialized countries, are dominated by private dollars. National benefit patterns were determined largely by union efforts, even though a minority of the work force was actually represented by unions. Major agreements by the national unions created patterns of coverage that were then packaged by insurers to be "sold" to other employment contexts. In this way, the patterns developed by unions became the vehicle for the diffusion of benefit innovations.

Public and private expenditures for health and medical services from 1975 to 1987 are presented in Figure 1. These expenditures totaled over $490 billion in 1987. As the cost of these services rose, from 8.3 percent of the gross national product in 1975 to 11.1 percent in 1987, the proportion paid by private dollars continued to account for almost 60 percent of the total expenditures (Kerns & Glanz, 1990, Table 2, p. 21).

The key governmental health insurance programs, Medicare (for the aged and disabled) and Medicaid (for the poor), together account for over 70 percent of the public expenditures (42.6 percent and 27.7 percent, respec- tively) (Bixby, 1990, Table 7, p. 26).

Most full-time workers have health insurance through the workplace. According to the U.S. Bureau of Labor Statistics (1990), 92 percent of the employees in medium or large firms (over 100 employees) received health insurance in 1989. Table 3 shows the extent to which full-time workers are covered by all the employee benefits that are normally associated with social insurance.

These health insurance programs cover the full range of medical care, but the specifics of the coverage (copayments, deductibles, limits on coverage, and so forth) reflect a variety of approaches and affect the value of the plan to the participant. For example, virtually all the plans of medium and large firms cover hospital costs, with 80 percent requiring copayment by the participant or imposing limits on the extent of coverage. Some services, such

Figure 1
Health and Medical Expenditures, 1975–1987

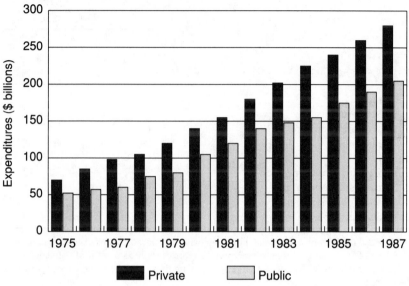

SOURCE: Kerns & Glanz (1989), Table 2.

as vision care and hospice services, are covered only in a minority of plans, whereas for other services, such as for mental health and substance abuse, coverage is virtually universal but *always* subject to special limitations, deductibles, and or co-payments. Such limitations are discussed later in relation to their implications for the provision of social services.

Information about full-time employees in large firms tells only part of the story. Less than half the labor force work in establishments with 100 or more employees (U.S. Bureau of the Census, 1990a, Table 870). If both full-time and part-time employees are considered, 26 percent of the labor force are employed in businesses with fewer than 20 employees, and 29 percent are in establishments with 20 to 99 employees.

Employee benefit coverage is much less common in these smaller firms. As Table 3 shows, 69 percent of the employees in companies with fewer than 100 employees have health insurance.

The lower proportion of coverage in small businesses reflects several factors. First, small businesses are generally less affluent and less stable than are larger ones. Second, the economies of scale in the administration of

Table 3
Employee Benefits Coverage for Full-time Workers

	PERCENTAGE COVERED	
TYPE OF COVERAGE	LARGE AND MEDIUM FIRMS[a]	SMALL FIRMS[a]
Insurance		
Health insurance	92	69
Dental care insurance	66	30
Life insurance	94	64
Income		
Retirement income-pension	81	42
Sickness and accident pay	43	26
Long-term disability pay	45	19
Paid maternity leave	3	2

[a]"Large and medium firms" include those employing 100 or more employees. "Small firms," those with fewer than 100 employees, represent approximately 55 percent of the national employed labor force. The data for large and medium firms are for 1989; the data for small firms are for 1990.

SOURCES: U.S. Bureau of Labor Statistics (1990), Table 1; U.S. Bureau of Labor Statistics (1991), Table 1.

benefits are not realized in small businesses; therefore the smallness of the businesses makes the provision of benefits more difficult. Third, workers in these smaller establishments are less likely to be unionized.

A fourth factor is the higher proportion of the small-business work force that works part-time. The benefit coverage for part-timers is about one-fifth that of full-time employees (Woods, 1989). In small establishments, these differences are even more pronounced. For example, in these firms, only about 6 percent of the part-time employees have health insurance through their jobs, compared to 69 percent of the full-time employees (U.S. Bureau of Labor Statistics, 1991, Table 2).

Dental and life insurance, also shown in Table 3, represent a much smaller expenditure for employers (and a smaller contribution to the overall welfare benefits of workers). However, the incidence of dental insurance has continued to increase in recent years. In 1979, 49 percent of the full-time work force in medium and large establishments had dental coverage; by 1989, 66 percent had it. Life insurance, one of the earliest and most common employee benefits, continues to be widespread. The dominant pattern is a two-tier system; basic coverage is paid entirely by the employer, with optional supplements based on employees' contributions.

Prepaid legal services (legal insurance) are not widely used and have not expanded greatly since their inception. In 1989, only 4 percent of medium and large companies offered such a benefit (Welling, 1987).

Income Support

In addition to insurance programs, income-support programs are an essential source of financial protection provided through employee benefits. The largest of these programs in the workplace are those that provide retirement income: pension, profit-sharing, and related programs.

As Table 3 indicates, 81 percent of the full-time employees in medium and large firms are in jobs with retirement-income programs. Effective participation in pension plans, however, is considerably lower. These plans often require a minimum length of service. In some cases (particularly with early retirement schemes), eligibility is determined by a combination of age and length of service. Many employees whose jobs are covered by pension plans never become eligible for benefits because they leave their jobs, voluntarily or involuntarily, before the minimum period. Taking such eligibility rules into account, it is estimated that only 48 percent of full-time employees and 9 percent of part-time employees participate in retirement income plans (Woods, 1989, Table 4, p. 8).

Legal challenges have been raised by workers against pension plans that are designed to make the eventual receipt of a pension unlikely. One court decision supported such claims by a group of workers on the Alaskan pipeline. Because of the short-term nature of their jobs, the workers were virtually excluded from achieving coverage, through vesting, under their employee-benefit pension plan (see Pollock, 1991, p. B1).

Although private-sector pensions are intended to provide recipients with a reliable source of retirement income, that support can be compromised by subsequent managerial or financial changes. Federal regulatory policies, such as the Employee Retirement Income Security Act (ERISA), provide some protections. Management takeovers and bankruptcies, however, can disrupt existing pension programs. This was the case for thousands of retirees in the steel industry and continues to be a threat for many others. Textile workers in North Carolina, for another example, saw their pensions reduced by 30 percent because of a change in ownership and subsequent bankruptcy proceedings in California (Applebome, 1991, p. 1).

Sickness-and-accident pay and long-term disability are the two other primary income-replacement programs provided through the workplace. These programs cover 43 percent and 45 percent, respectively, of full-time workers in firms with 100 workers or more (and 26 percent and 19 percent in smaller firms). Because most states do not have programs for the temporarily disabled (and these workers would be ineligible for unemployment benefits because they are not "available to work"), sickness-and-accident pay is an important protection for workers. (Workers' compensation also provides support when an accident or illness is work connected. As a legally mandated program, it is not included in this discussion of nonmandatory employee benefits.)

Pregnancy is covered under the sickness-and-accident plans. Special provisions for paid maternity leave are rare, including only a small proportion of workers. Unpaid leave is more common. Before the 1993 passage of federal legislation mandating family leave, 37 percent of employees in medium and large firms and 17 percent in small firms had the option of unpaid leaves. This benefit, however, fails to meet the need for replacement income when employees are not working.

Supplemental unemployment benefits are relatively uncommon. Although they have been institutionalized in the employee benefit systems of some large unionized industries, these benefits during a layoff apply to only 5 percent of the workers in medium and large firms.

Social Services

In addition to their insurance and income-support roles, employee benefits also involve the direct provision of a variety of social services. Employee assistance programs (EAPs) and their union counterpart, membership assistance programs (MAPs), and day care are the most common. Because they are addressed elsewhere in this book, in this chapter, the discussion of them is limited to an overview of their incidence as a part of the overall portrait of the provision of employee benefits.

Day care programs in the workplace run the gamut from advice-referral services to financial assistance to the actual provision of on-site day care. The motivation for providing these programs can be understood in terms of the increasing number of working mothers and related demographic changes in the national labor force (see, for example, U.S. Bureau of the Census, 1990b).

Estimates of the extent of day care services in the workplace vary. In its survey of employee benefits in medium and large firms, the U.S. Bureau of Labor Statistics (1990) found that, in 1989, 5 percent of the work force in these firms were covered by day care benefits, involving either a subsidy from their employers for services or the provision of services. Although this percentage represents a fivefold increase since 1985, day care still is provided for only a small proportion of those working in large firms. In small firms, only 1 percent have some form of child care provision.

Day care counseling, information, and referral services are more wide-spread. Such services are provided by close to one-fifth of the employers with 250 or more employees, but by only a few smaller firms (U.S. Bureau of the Census, 1990a). It should be noted, however, that *informal* policies (such as allowing an employee to take a maternity leave even though there is no explicit policy) may play a much greater role in small firms. These ad hoc arrangements vary widely and provide considerable latitude for discretionary application by employers (Kamerman & Kahn, 1987).

Day care is often conceptualized more broadly to include care for other dependents. Elder care programs, however, are provided to only about 3 percent of the workers in medium and large firms (U.S. Bureau of Labor Statistics, 1990, Table 2, p. 5). The demand for such programs is expected to grow as this country faces the dilemma of an aging work force coping with the demand of caring for elderly parents.

Another manifestation of this demographic change is the growth in long-term care insurance as an employee benefit. Although still not widespread (covering only 3 percent of the workers), it may expand as the need for domiciliary care for the elderly increases (U.S. Bureau of Labor Statistics, 1990).

Estimates of the number of EAPs vary. The U.S. Bureau of Labor Statistics (1990) reported that half the workers in medium and large firms have access to EAPs. Estimates in the business press suggest there may be 5,000 to 8,000 EAPs nationwide (see, for example, Lee, 1988; Lyons, 1987). Special arrangements have been made to provide EAP services to small businesses (Perkins & Reynolds, 1986).

Wellness programs, designed to improve the health of workers (and, consequently, lower health insurance costs) are provided to one-quarter of the workers in medium and large firms. These programs focus on preventive measures (for example, physical examinations, the reduction of cholesterol, the control of high blood pressure, the cessation of smoking, and weight loss).

Educational assistance programs are also a part of the employee benefit picture in larger companies. Tuition support for job-related education is most common (available to 69 percent of those in firms employing 100 or more). Almost one-fifth of these workers can also receive tuition support for education that is not job related (U.S. Bureau of Labor Statistics, 1990, p. 5). A growing concern among employers about employees' "basic skills" is evidenced in the United States and Canada and may influence the vested interest of employers in this country (see, for example, Des Lauriers, 1989; Hargroves, 1989).

Counseling services, specifically targeted to assisting workers with educational planning, are becoming part of the employee benefit structure in some collective bargaining agreements with larger firms. For example, the United

Auto Workers and the three major American automakers are jointly providing educational counseling to workers. The goal of this counseling is to encourage the effective use of educational benefits. It is explicitly targeted to education that is *not* job related. Professionally trained educational counselors are working in auto plants nationally, helping individual workers plan for their continuing education.

Implications of Employee Benefits

Employee benefits have introduced new cost considerations for employers, redefined expectations for the government and the private sector, and created opportunities and financial constraints for service providers. To assess these implications, it is useful to examine each in turn.

Employee Benefits and Managerial Decisions

The expansion of benefits, particularly health insurance, has introduced a cost factor into employment relationships in the United States that does not exist in other countries. Inflation in health care costs has resulted in greater payroll costs for American industry. It is now estimated that health insurance for auto workers adds more to the cost of a new car than does the price of steel.

There is some indication that the rate of increase in medical costs has abated somewhat in recent years. Overall the cost of benefits increased more slowly in the late 1980s (about 3.5 percent per year) than earlier, when the increases were over 10 percent per year (Braden, 1988). Nevertheless, the cost of health care continues to be an important factor in the planning of businesses.

There are several implications of the cost of benefits for managerial decisions. First, benefits are largely a "fixed cost": The cost of a benefit package for a worker does not increase greatly with increases in hours worked. On the other hand, *hiring* a worker does involve a substantial increase in the cost of benefits. Therefore, the existence of benefits creates economic incentives to schedule overtime work for current employees, rather than to hire new workers as the workload increases.

Cost considerations may also exercise additional effects on managerial decisions. Benefits create incentives to avoid hiring workers who appear to be a greater risk for higher medical care expenditures, such as older persons or people with chronic health problems. These considerations may introduce factors into the hiring decision that are unrelated to a person's ability to perform a job.

The structure of the benefit plan can affect other personnel decisions as well. In a lawsuit brought by the United Steelworkers of America, a large national company was found to have orchestrated layoffs and recalls to minimize the number of workers who would be eligible for pensions. The court ordered $415 million in pension payments to compensate workers who had been adversely affected (Ansberry, 1991, p. A3).

The greater use of part-time or temporary workers may be another unintended impact of the cost of employee benefits. The number of part-time workers increased by 20 percent from 1980 to 1987, a time when the overall civilian labor force increased by only 12 percent. During that period, the number of temporary workers more than doubled (although the total number of temporary workers remained small—about 1 percent of the labor force) (Belous, 1989). Employers appear to be turning to such "contingent" workers to have greater flexibility for expanding and contracting their work force, as well as to avoid unionization and the cost of benefits.

Part-time workers now represent almost one-fifth of the labor force (see Table 1). Most of these workers do not have health insurance through their jobs (three-quarters of voluntary part-timers and two-thirds of those who would like to work full-time but cannot find a full-time position) (Williams, 1989). Temporary employees are less often eligible for health insurance.

Employee benefits also affect broader managerial decisions. Health insurance commitments to retirees, for example, may weaken a company's overall fiscal position. Proposals are being considered to alter standard accounting procedures to include such liabilities. They would add large financial liabilities to the balance sheets of many companies and affect their perceived value in the eyes of investors.

Pension assets have also been a factor in large-scale managerial decisions. The rising stock market in the 1970s and 1980s resulted in pension funds with more assets than necessary to cover their current obligations to workers under the terms of their "defined benefit" pensions. Many companies closed down their pension plans, paid out their contractual benefits to workers, and then absorbed the surplus cash. These "pension reversions" were often followed by the replacement of the original pension plans with those that were less costly to employers.

Employee Benefits and Social Insurance

Employee benefits are a major source of income security and social insurance in the United States. As such, they have both supported and undermined the national Social Security program. Employee benefits for many workers provide secure retirements and substantial protection against the high costs of medical care. But the institutionalization of social insurance benefits through the workplace has undercut support for governmental social welfare initiatives, such as national health insurance and improved Social Security benefits. By reducing the aggregate need for governmental programs, they fragment political support for more universal programs (Root, 1985).

Linking social insurance protection to the job also results in a distribution of insurance that parallels the differentials in wage and salary. Lower-paid jobs, often non-union and characterized by instability, are the least likely to provide protection for workers and their dependents. In this way, the benefit structure reinforces the income differences among jobs.

This link between jobs and social insurance protection has immediate and striking effects on disadvantaged minorities and women. Women are more likely to be employed part-time than are men. As a result, they usually are not covered by adequate health insurance and pension programs.

The impact on minorities is just as striking. The exclusion of minorities from protection by employee benefits can be seen most clearly in the statistics on health insurance coverage. Nationally, it is estimated that approximately 33 million people have no health insurance. Among non-Hispanic whites, 68 percent are covered by private health insurance (primarily through employee benefits). The comparable percentages for African Americans and Mexican Americans are 46 percent and 44 percent, respectively.

When one looks at both public and private programs, the gaps in coverage are clear. Ten percent of whites have no health insurance, compared to almost 20 percent of African Americans and 37 percent of Mexican Americans (Trevino, Moyer, Valdez, & Stroup-Benham, 1991). This absence of protection for health care costs is virtually unparalleled among developed nations.

Social Services

Employee benefits have a direct effect on social services, often through the provision of services in the workplace. The indirect effects of employee-benefit health insurance programs on social work practice and services, however, are even more widespread and profound.

Inflation in the cost of health care has been a recurring theme. Mental health services are a part of that concern. Estimates of the proportion of health care expenditures that go to mental health services (including substance abuse treatment) range from just under 10 percent to 30 percent of the total corporate health bill (see, for example, Bailey, 1990; Caldwell, 1990; Prest, 1990). Despite differences in estimates, there is general agreement that the cost of mental health care is growing faster than is the cost of other health care services. One major company estimated that the cost of psychiatric and substance abuse services for its 700,000 employees, retirees, and dependents is increasing 20 percent annually (compared with 10 or 11 percent for medical costs in general) (Gilbert, 1990). This increase in costs has been paralleled by the founding of new facilities. From 1984 to 1988, 652 new freestanding psychiatric and substance abuse facilities were started, increasing the total number of facilities by 46 percent (Lee, 1988).

Although mental health services are included in the coverage of most health insurance plans, a substantial majority of the plans do not cover alcoholism and other substance abuse programs. When covered, these services are usually subject to special limitations that do not apply to other health care services. Table 4 identifies the principal types of limitations of coverage and their incidence in the health insurance plans of medium and large employers.

Table 4
Major Limitations in Coverage for Mental Health and Substance Abuse for Those Covered for Services

	PERCENTAGE OF PARTICIPANTS IN LARGE AND MEDIUM FIRMS[a]					
	MENTAL HEALTH		ALCOHOL ABUSE		OTHER SUBSTANCE ABUSE	
COVERAGE	IN-PATIENT	OUT-PATIENT	IN-PATIENT[b]	OUT-PATIENT	IN-PATIENT[b]	OUT-PATIENT
Not covered	2	5	32	39	36	42
Covered	98	95	68	61	64	58
Same as other illnesses	21	2	9	8	8	7
Separate limitations						
Days per year	38	34	31	20	28	18
Days per "incident"	9	—[c]	12	2	12	2
Days per lifetime	33	31	14	6	13	5
Dollars per year	5	29	6	25	6	24
Dollars per lifetime	33	31	18	18	18	18
Higher copayments	9	56	6	18	6	18
Unlimited copayments	15	41	8	18	8	18

[a]"Large and medium firms" include those employing 100 or more employees. "Small firms," those with fewer than 100 employees, represent approximately 55 percent of the national employed labor force. The data for large and medium firms are for 1989; the data for small firms are for 1990.

[b]Detoxification is often covered with different limitations than are other inpatient hospitalizations.

[c]Less than 0.5 percent.

SOURCE: U.S. Bureau of Labor Statistics (1990), Tables 48, 49, and 50.

For mental health services, the most common limits are on the maximum number of days of inpatient treatment per year and on the number of days of treatment and total expenditures in a lifetime. In addition, higher copayments are frequently required of the client, and often these copayments are not limited by a specified maximum.

Cost control measures, such as the use of health maintenance organizations (HMOs) and other forms of managed care, have become a prominent part of the provision of mental health services. Managed care arrangements can determine the availability of treatment, the modality of service offered, and the duration of treatment. But these management systems may have their own costs in terms of the quality of care. A recent survey of mental health professionals found that 86 percent believed that HMOs and related cost-control measures are detrimental to the quality of care provided. For example, it was estimated that one out of 10 patients needed more time in treatment than was allowed under their health insurance plans (Martinsons, 1988). An emerging development is the creation of specialized "managed mental health" plans. Under this approach, mental health services are provided through a plan that is separate from general health insurance. This model is particularly applicable for large employers, both in the private sector and the government (see, for example, Gilbert, 1990; Schachner, 1990).

These cost-control initiatives create a new set of conditions for social service providers. Although the expansion of employee benefits has enlarged the pool of clients for practitioners, the administration of the benefits will continue to present challenges to both cost- and outcome-effective service delivery.

Future of Benefits

The expansion of employee benefits has fundamentally influenced the structure of social insurance and social services in the United States. Proposals for more universal health insurance, such as President Carter's Better Jobs and Income program and the state-level program in Massachusetts, are typically "fill-in" programs, constructed around the continued existence of widespread coverage of the labor force. More recently, Oregon has taken the initiative to reform its state Medicaid program to cover a larger proportion of low-income people. And the Clinton administration is committed to comprehensive reform of the health care system, to provide universal coverage.

Employee benefits, through tax policy, enjoy implicit governmental subsidies. The exclusion of benefits from taxation as income results in a considerable loss of tax revenue. In 1988, this "tax expenditure" provided a de facto subsidy of almost $25 billion for health insurance and close to $50 billion for pensions. With an ever-growing national deficit, these tax exclusions face mounting opposition (Munnell, 1989).

Governmental financial pressures have also been a factor in the attempt to reduce Medicare costs. For example, changes in governmental rules effectively made employee benefits the first payer for those age 65 who are still employed. Before that change, the employee-benefit health insurance costs for older workers *decreased* at age 65, when Medicare was treated as the primary health insurance and the employee benefit plan was secondary. The change in rules reversed that priority, shifting the bulk of the health insurance costs to the private employee benefit system and hence effectively increasing the cost of employing older people in most companies.

One can anticipate that cost control will continue to motivate decisions regarding employee benefits in both the private sector and in governmental policy-making. In part, governmental cost controls will seek to shift expenditures to the private sector. They may also entail increasing minimum standards for employee benefits or eliminating tax subsidies. Private-sector cost-control efforts will seek to counter this governmental approach as employers attempt to shift some of these costs to the public sector or, more likely, shift greater responsibility for the cost of benefits directly to employees. One example of this latter strategy is the increase in flexible-benefits (or "cafeteria") plans.

Under flexible-benefit plans, the employee has a fixed dollar amount ("flex-dollars") that can be applied to a menu of benefits. One employee may choose a comprehensive health insurance plan, whereas another may increase pension protection or financial assistance for day care. The theoretical advantage to employees is that they can choose benefits according to their own priorities. For example, one person of a married couple may have health insurance that covers the whole family. Under a flexible plan, the other person can choose not to have redundant health insurance, choosing to allocate his or her flex-dollars to some other benefit.

Flexible plans are particularly attractive to employers because they offer a means of controlling liability for inflation in the cost of benefits. Under traditional plans, increases in health insurance, for example, fall on employers. To maintain a plan (even without improving coverage), employers face annual increases in their payroll costs because of inflation in the cost of services. Under a flexible-benefit plan, the employer's liability is limited to the amount of the flex-dollars. For example, if wages and flex-dollars are increased by 4 percent annually, but health insurance costs increase by 12 percent, the difference (between 4 percent and 12 percent) is the responsibility of the employee, rather than of the employer. Health insurance will take up a greater portion of the employee's flex-dollars, perhaps requiring increased contributions by the employee to maintain the coverage.

Flexible-benefit plans also tend to increase the cost of particular benefits because of "adverse selection." When only those who need the coverage sign up for it (for example, eliminating double coverage for health insurance), the cost per participant goes up, adding to the problem of a shortfall in flex-dollars.

Despite these negative factors (and the added administrative costs of flexible-benefit plans), flexible benefits continue to expand. As of 1989, about 9 percent of the employees in medium and large firms had flexible-benefit options (U.S. Bureau of Labor Statistics, 1990, Table 114).

Flexible benefits can offer advantages for some workers, such as dual-earner households with relatively generous benefits. They are much less attractive for others, such as single-earner households, including the large number of working single parents. Their primary appeal for employers is as a cost-control measure.

Flexible benefits represent one approach to workplace programs. The rising importance and cost of employee benefits suggests that these benefits will continue to be an area for change. The directions for these changes will be influenced by the background and experience of those who are enlisted in their solution. Social workers have traditionally considered the workplace a key determinant of the social situation of individuals and families. But the expansion of employee benefits and their impact on society ironically have largely been overlooked by social work education and practice.

Demographic trends will necessitate changes in the workplace. The number of new workers will decrease; more employees will have to balance the responsibilities of their jobs and of care for dependents; an aging work force will have to confront decisions about retirement while facing uncertainties about inflation, the cost of health care, and a longer life expectancy. These issues call for public- and private-sector planners who can look at the social as well as the economic roles of policies and programs. These changes also call for professional practitioners who can provide services to working clients with a clear understanding of the realities of the workplace that they face. This is a challenge for social work as a profession. The profession's response will determine its relevance to individuals, families, and society in the 21st century.

References

Ansberry, C. (1991, January 3). Kiewit unit sets huge payment in pension case. *Wall Street Journal*, p. A3.

Applebome, P. (1991, July 30). Mill town pensioners pay for Wall Street sins. *New York Times*, p. 1.

Bailey, N. C. (1990). Mental health benefits: Breaking through the clouds. *Business and Health, 8*(16), 46–50.

Belous, R. S. (1989). How human resource systems adjust to the shift toward contingent workers. *Monthly Labor Review, 112*(3), 7–12.

Bixby, A. K. (1990). Public social welfare expenditures, fiscal years 1965–1987. *Social Security Bulletin, 2,* 10–26.

Braden, B. R. (1988). Increases in employer costs for employee benefits dampen dramatically. *Monthly Labor Review, 111*(7), 3–7.

Brandes, S. D. (1976). *American welfare capitalism, 1880–1940.* Chicago: University of Chicago Press.

Buder, S. (1967). *Pullman: An experiment in industrial order and community planning, 1880–1930.* New York: Oxford University Press.

Caldwell, B. (1990). Are behavioral benefits out of control? *Employee Benefit Plan Review, 44*(8), 8–9.

Chamber of Commerce of the United States of America. (1990). *Employee benefits.* Washington, DC: Author.

Collier, P., & Horowitz, D. (1987). *The Fords: An American epic.* New York: Summit Books.

Des Lauriers, B. (1989). Functional illiteracy in Canadian business. *Canadian Business Review, 16*(4), 36–39.

Gilbert, E. (1990). IBM launches targeted managed care plan. *National Underwriter, 94*(34), 37, 41.

Hargroves, J. S. (1989, September–October). The basic skills crisis: One bank looks at its training investment. *New England Economic Review,* pp. 58–68.

Kamerman, S. B., & Kahn, A. J. (1987). *The responsive workplace: Employers and a changing labor force.* New York: Columbia University Press.

Kerns, W. L., & Glanz, M. P. (1990). Private social welfare expenditures, 1972–1987. *Social Security Bulletin, 53*(11), 18–26.

Lee, R. (1988). The evolution of managed mental health care. *Compensation and Benefits Management, 5*(1), 61–66.

Lyons, P. V. (1987). EAPs: The only real cure for substance abuse. *Management Review, 76*(3), 38–41.

Martinsons, J. N. (1988). Are HMOs slamming the door on psychiatric treatment? *Hospitals, 62*(5), 50–56.

Munnell, A. H. (1989, July–August). It's time to tax employee benefits. *New England Economic Review,* pp. 49–63.

Perkins, A. W., & Reynolds, D. L. (1986). EAP consortium provides vital job saving services to small employers. *Business and Health, 3*(3), 52–53.

Pollock, E. J. (1991, January 3). Lawsuits could affect pension-plan structure. *Wall Street Journal,* p. B1.

Prest, S. (1990). Controlling mental health costs. *Business Insurance, 24*(16), 24.

Rodgers, D. T. (1978). *The work ethic in industrial America, 1850–1920.* Chicago: University of Chicago Press.

Root, L. S. (1982). *Fringe benefit: Social insurance in the steel industry.* Beverly Hills, CA: Sage.

Root, L. S. (1985). Employee benefits and social welfare: Complement and conflict. *Annals of the American Academy of Political and Social Science, 479,* 101–118.

Schachner, M. (1990). Ohio adopts managed mental health plan. *Business Insurance, 24*(15), 6.

Titmuss, R. M. (1969). *Essays on the welfare state.* Boston: Beacon Press.

Trevino, F. M., Moyer, M. E., Valdez, R. B., & Stroup-Benham, C. A. (1991). Health insurance coverage and utilization of health services by Mexican Americans, Mainland Puerto Ricans, and Cuban Americans. *Journal of the American Medical Association, 265,* 233–237.

U.S. Bureau of the Census. (1990a). *Statistical abstract of the United States, 1990.* Washington, DC: U.S. Government Printing Office.

U.S. Bureau of the Census. (1990b). *Work and family patterns of American women, Current Population Reports* (Series P-23, No. 165). Washington, DC: U.S. Government Printing Office.

U.S. Bureau of Labor Statistics. (1989). *Handbook of labor statistics* (Bulletin No. 2340). Washington, DC: U.S. Government Printing Office.

U.S. Bureau of Labor Statistics. (1990). *Employee benefits in medium and large firms, 1989* (Bulletin No. 2363). Washington, DC: U.S. Government Printing Office.

U.S. Bureau of Labor Statistics. (1991, June 10). BLS reports on its first survey of employee benefits in small private establishments. *News* (press release, USDL 91-260). Washington, DC: Author.

Welling, K. M. (1987, June 8). Lowered expectations: Providers of legal insurance suffer setbacks. *Barron's, 15,* 39–41.

Williams, H. B. (1989). What temporary workers earn: Findings from new BLS survey. *Monthly Labor Review, 112*(3), 3–6.

Woods, J. R. (1989). Pension coverage among private wage and salary workers: Preliminary findings from the 1988 Survey of Employee Benefits. *Social Security Bulletin, 52*(10), 2–19.

CHAPTER 7

Serving Workers through Managed Mental Health Care

THE SOCIAL WORK ROLE

Adrienne Asch and Patricia Abelson

> People and profits are inexorably linked. In an
> information society, human resources are a company's
> competitive edge.
>
> —John Naisbitt and Patricia Aburdene
> *Re-inventing the Corporation*

Stress seems to be ubiquitous throughout all strata of society. People's work lives can be adversely affected by the emotional and practical problems that they carry with them to their jobs. In the past, unions and employers responded in two ways to such facts of life at work: by providing a measure of financial reimbursement for mental health treatment as part of a benefit package and, more recently, by creating on-site social services for members–workers. As worthy and sensible as these responses have been, they no longer are proving adequate. Paying for mental health services through insurance benefits has become extremely costly; work-site services cannot be broad enough to respond to the diverse situations that employees with increasingly varied backgrounds and life circumstances are confronting. Managed care programs represent a creative effort to offer people the range of services they need at a cost that they and their employers can accept. Yet they are surrounded by questions and controversy (Barnes, 1991; Feldman, 1992).

This chapter lays out those issues and considers how they may be resolved in the future. The resolution of these issues is a key concern for those who are interested in social work in the workplace, not only because so much health care is provided through one's attachment to the labor force, but because the overlap between employee assistance programs (EAPs) and managed mental health care (hereinafter called managed care) promises to command significant attention from occupational social workers in the near future (Wenzel, 1988).

Background

It is noteworthy that the earliest managed care initiatives, for example, the Health Insurance Plan (HIP) in New York City, were experimental health maintenance organizations (HMOs) that were designed to provide access to service to those who had previously been outside the health care delivery system or those who were without funds and were, therefore, expected to accept whatever services were available without any control over their quality. This theme has continued to the present, for, as Blum (1992, p. 245) stated, "the increasing presence of managed care in the American market-place is, historically, an extension of social policies that seek to increase the effectiveness of health care services." Of course, only in the past 50 years has it been possible for most employees in this country to count on obtaining any assistance with medical or personal problems from their employers. Today, according to O'Brien (1991), nearly 212 million people (80 percent of Americans) obtain health care through their own or a family's employment benefit plan. Many working people would now acknowledge that the possibility of losing this help with health care (including mental health care) is a significant concern whenever they face changing or losing jobs. However, it is likely that the forced immobility of job holders who are concerned about maintaining this coverage will cease with the introduction of health care reform by the Clinton administration.

The conventional means of providing assistance to employees has been for a firm to arrange health insurance that would reimburse them for a portion of the cost of visits to physicians, hospitalization, and prescription drugs. Beginning in the 1950s, many such plans incorporated reimbursement for the treatment of mental illness, emotional problems, and detoxification from drugs and alcohol when these treatments were performed by licensed professionals, including psychiatrists, psychologists, social workers, and social work agencies.

Until the past two decades, considerable stigma was associated with the admission of having emotional difficulties that required professional help; consequently, relatively few employees used mental health services that were paid for by employers' insurance plans. Thus, these services were like a "free" benefit: Employers could be credited for offering them, but would not be concerned because the utilization of the services was so low that costs were automatically contained. By the 1970s and 1980s, however, many more workers and their families began to seek treatment for emotional problems, interpersonal conflicts, and addiction to self-destructive or illegal drugs that interfered with their lives on and off the job (Wagman & Schiff, 1989).

Whether a symptom or a cause of emotional and interpersonal problems, substance abuse continues to pervade the work force. Some reports have revealed that 16 million workers perform their jobs under the influence of alcohol or other addictive drugs ("Drugs in the Workplace," 1991). Nor is substance abuse the only problem that spurs employers to include mental health coverage in their benefit packages. As is discussed elsewhere in this book, such behavior has a staggering cost at work and at home, making mental health coverage an imperative for employers who wish to have a positive impact on workers and their productivity.

The increased search for help with emotional problems and the need for a broad array of social services to ameliorate them have been attributed to stress from many sources; juggling changing family roles, surviving in an uncertain economy, and managing the tensions created by working in a more diverse work force and in more demanding jobs. Citing a 1991 study of Northwestern National Life Insurance Company, Lee (1991) noted that stress-related disability cases accounted for 13 percent of all disability cases in 1990, up from 6 percent in 1982. The study sampled employees from hundreds of companies and found that the existence of benefits for mental health and substance abuse problems was one factor that reduced stress in an organization.

The rapid growth of EAPs, sponsored by employers, and membership assistance plans (MAPs), sponsored by trade unions, also attests to the recognition by labor and management that workers are people, that most people have problems some of the time, and that the untended problems of one person eventually spill over to become the problems of others around them. As valuable as EAPs and MAPs are, they are not a substitute for a comprehensive mental health benefit plan in many situations. An EAP or MAP cannot provide workers with the specialized services that are required to resolve some problems. Inevitably, the staff must rely on referrals to community resources for many of the difficulties employees–members and their families experience. For other employees–members, the workplace may not be the ideal vehicle for such help. Whether it is realistically necessary, some workers prefer to maintain their privacy by keeping their personal problems far from the scrutiny of any supervisor, personnel officer, or union representative. Companies may prefer that workers not feel imprisoned in an organization to retain their access to medical care or social services.

Nonetheless, the workplace has become a force that can motivate people to seek help and that can assist the individuals and institutions providing it. By pointing out that workers' personal problems are affecting their job performance, supervisors or union representatives can encourage them to face parts of their lives that they may prefer to avoid. By being the source that finances much of the nation's medical care and social services, the workplace can influence the types of services that are provided, as well as their convenience and cost.

As of 1989, 94 percent of the employers who offered any health care coverage included some type of assistance with treating their workers' mental health or substance abuse problems (Weiner & Siegel, 1989). But during the 1980s, employers began to realize that their method of delivering health benefits to workers was proving extremely costly. "As a nation we now spend nearly 700 billion dollars on health care, 12.5 percent of our gross national product" (Croweak, 1991, p. 6). In 1988, 14 percent of the national health expenditures were for mental health and drug abuse (Fields, Lilly, & Sutton-Bell, 1991). A 1991 *New York Times* article (Goleman, 1991) reported that although costs for health care in the nation are increasing across the board, the expenditures on mental health care account for the sharpest rise in health care costs. The article noted that between 1987 and 1988, employers' overall health costs rose 18.6 percent, whereas those for mental health rose 27 percent. According to Weiner and Siegel (1989), the cost of mental health claims can be as much as two-and-one-half times the cost of treating other conditions, even those requiring surgery.

In less than 50 years, employers went from adopting responsibility for the cost of health care in the interest of maintaining a healthy and productive labor force to concern about the rising proportion of their expenditures that were being eaten up by that benefit. And mental health care came in for extreme surveillance because it became the cost leader. Actually, managing the cost and quality of care has been a concern throughout the nation and of employers since the 1970s (O'Brien, 1991). Congress enacted legislation that laid the groundwork for today's philosophy of managed care as long ago as the Social Security Amendments of 1972, which established that hospitals should perform reviews of treatment decisions and hospital admissions concurrently, rather than retrospectively.

The 1973 Health Maintenance Organization Act legitimated the idea that health care organizations could deliver treatment as an alternative to customary fee-for-service plans (Yandrick & Rothermel, 1988). Even with the proliferation of legislation and programs intended to control health care expenditures, however, the nation's health care budget has continued to climb. O'Brien (1991, p. 17) reported that paying for coverage for workers' health and mental health problems accounted for one-third of American companies' total profits and blamed the high cost of this benefit for "weakening the nation's productive capacity." This is a theme that the Clinton forces have found convincing.

The response of employers has increasingly been to replace traditional health insurance benefits with plans that offer workers mental health treatment and social services from approved providers who will be accountable to and monitored by a staff that specializes in reviewing treatment plans and ensuring that they are in accord with employers' benefits and quality criteria that often are viewed as ambiguous and limiting. Termed *managed care*, such programs have two goals: to provide effective treatment and to reduce its cost. Because the people who render the treatment are accountable to the employers through managed care organizations, but are not on the premises or payrolls of the employers, they may be perceived as offering workers more privacy and confidentiality than treatment by internal EAPs. Because the people who hold the treatment providers accountable are often third parties in the service transaction (in addition to the consumers and the providers), they may be perceived as gatekeepers who deny entrance to needed care (Blum, 1992; Langman-Dorwart, Wahl, Singer, & Dorwart, 1992). What is certainly clear about these new arrangements is that they are more complex than were earlier systems for delivering services ("A Brief Look at Managed Care," 1990). Whether they are also more effective is a question that will be considered later in this chapter.

How Managed Care Works

This section describes how managed care works, how it resembles and differs from other employer-financed arrangements for offering assistance, and the typical activities and experience of social workers connected with such programs. The systems for delivering managed care are characterized by a high degree of accountability and control of "health care utilization, quality, and claims, using a variety of cost-containment methods" (Lightman & Wagman, 1988, p. 19). At its best, treatment is priced, planned, coordinated and delivered in a manner that is designed to ensure high quality and to contain costs. In one common model, for example, the employer contracts with the managed care organization to oversee the mental health and substance abuse treatment that the employer will subsidize for its employees. When an employer chooses to use such an organization, the employer usually pays it a fixed sum and expects that it will arrange for treatment that will not exceed the sum the employer has allocated. The managed care organization explains to the employer the range of services it can offer, but, as with any other benefit, an employer may not choose to pay for everything the managed care organization could make available. Thus, the employer exercises some control over costs by selecting the types and amounts of treatment it will cover.

Employees who want to take advantage of the mental health benefit of such an employer must go through the managed care organization. In turn, the organization authorizes the type of service that fits the individual's problem and selects the individual or agency that will provide it. To be effective, the organization must be comprehensive in the variety of treatment it can arrange. It must be conversant with the spectrum of needs and problems that workers and their families could experience and must locate practitioners and community agencies that will provide the appropriate direct service to the person who needs the help. From among all the practitioners and social agencies in a geographic area, the organization refers individuals only to those who meet its standards of professional qualification and experience, agree to provide services for specified fees, and are willing to accept the organization's review of the treatment they are providing.

Employees who are the clients, individual mental health practitioners, and social service agencies all can gain from working with a managed care organization. The employer hires expert professionals to guide its employees through the maze of treatment options. Although the employees are not free to use any physician or clinic in the community, they can be assured that those to whom they are referred have met certain standards of competence. Social agencies and individual practitioners who become connected with such an organization can expect many referrals. They are usually expected to trade off this consistent stream of clients by accepting a reduced fee from the organization, thereby providing one of the bases for cost containment. Because a typical managed care organization handles the mental health and substance abuse treatment for many companies and unions and thus links thousands of clients to the world of mental health and social services, it can monitor and influence the type, flexibility, and quality of services that are provided. By refusing to refer clients to individuals and agencies that will not be responsive to clients' needs as the managed care organization defines them, it can improve practice or merely limit its availability. Thus, managed care is neither good nor bad for clients. Such judgments depend entirely on how the managed care organization uses its influence. When effective it can achieve more appropriate utilization of services, contain costs, and maintain or even improve the quality of care. As Blum (1992, p. 253) claimed, "the addition of third parties to managing and paying for treatment means that people other than the patient and the clinician have a voice, perhaps a controlling one, in the treatment process."

The Job of the Managed Care Staff

To fulfill its role in a positive manner, the managed care organization must be composed of skilled, experienced mental health professionals (managed care representatives), many of whom should be social workers who are trained in a systems approach to problems and are familiar with the wealth of community resources. The organization performs three tasks that profoundly affect the quality of care an individual will ultimately receive. First, the staff locates and screens qualified practitioners and agencies who will provide the actual services. Second, a managed care representative is the link between the troubled worker or family member and the ultimate provider of service. Third, the managed care representative keeps in touch with the practitioner or agency to whom the initial referral was made to review the treatment plan the practitioner designs after seeing the client.

The managed care representative determines whether the practitioner's plan meets professional standards, is likely to resolve the client's difficulties, and falls within the range of services that the client's employer has agreed to subsidize. For treatment that will take more than a few visits or that will involve more than one type of service, the managed care organization reviews the work in progress by staying in touch with the practitioner or the social agency. After receiving approval for an initial arrangement, the practitioner must contact the organization if she or he proposes to modify the plan. Thus, the managed care representative must be skilled at ascertaining the competence of fellow professionals, discovering the problems of troubled clients, and determining whether treatment plans make sense initially and are appropriate in practice. Ultimately it is the managed care representative who determines the type and length of treatment and the goals to be set for the intervention.

Creating and Managing the Network of Providers

Clients bring a wealth of problems to the managed care organization, and without contracts with many different practitioners and agencies, the organization cannot hope to assist in the resolution of these problems. Because substance abuse continues to be the primary problem for many people and to compound the difficulties of others, many practitioners and agencies in the network must be adept at working with people who have problems with substance abuse. Although managed care organizations favor the least intrusive treatment, which is often treatment that keeps clients in their homes and communities, when possible, inpatient detoxification and treatment centers are some of the resources of the typical network.

Clients, of course, may present many other types of problems (including relationship issues, the death or illness of someone they love, financial problems, their children's difficulties in school or with the law, and stress from their jobs) either directly to the managed care organization or to a provider, who must then request authorization from the managed care representative. Managed care organizations respond by including practitioners and agencies that, whatever their orientation, bring a problem-solving strength to their work. Therapists in a usual network of providers may be behavioral, cognitive, or psychodynamic in orientation and are likely to include those who are proficient in individual counseling, couple and family therapy, and group work.

Because most employers and unions who hire managed care organizations are reluctant to pay for long-term, in-depth psychoanalytic treatment, practitioners require a set of skills that are new to many. They must be sufficiently astute and versatile to engage a client, formulate a diagnosis, articulate the goals of short-term treatment, and gain the cooperation of the client and the endorsement of the managed care representative in the devised treatment plan. There is certainly a bias toward short-term care by managed care organizations that some believe means that they "try too hard to find reasons for denying inpatient admissions and reducing lengths of stay" (Feldman, 1992, p. 7). However, most managed care organizations recognize that some long-standing and chronic problems require intensive treatment. A network's organizations include some that offer inpatient, halfway house, partial hospital, day treatment, rehabilitation, and other services. Child guidance clinics; senior citizens centers; and practitioners who specialize in working with survivors of rape, incest, child abuse, or violent crime all are needed. Experts in financial counseling are becoming increasingly important, as are practitioners who conduct groups for people who face job stress, layoffs, or the onset of a physical disability. A managed care organization that is committed to achieving its multiple goals will have the rich network just described. When cost containment becomes uppermost, however, the options may be reduced and the needs overlooked. This is a major problem in HMOs, which, although they may do an excellent job of providing appropriate physical health care, usually overlook or seriously underestimate the need for mental health services.

Inherent in the concept of managed care is the explicit recognition of the tension that always exists between needs and resources. Regardless of the practice setting or the practitioner's idealism, all practice and services are constrained by limits: on the practitioner's time, of the client's availability and life circumstances, and on the institutional and personal resources that exist or that can be marshaled to meet a particular need. The practitioner who works in a managed care program operates within a system in which such often-implicit limits are made explicit. The negotiation that takes place has been identified as an interaction in "constructive tension" (Feldman, 1992). It *should* have a positive effect on the quality of care, but it does not always. The union or employer who has contracted with the managed care provider determines how much money it will allocate to its members' or employees' need for mental health, substance abuse, or social services. In authorizing a service plan for a client, one of the criteria that the managed care program must use is a measure indicating that the cost of the services for one individual will not absorb such a large share of the employer's mental health dollars that others will be deprived of the help they need (Barnes, 1991).

Assessing the Problem and Designing an Intervention

Ideally, in a managed care program, a skilled clinician should speak with a client immediately upon or soon after the client's call to the agency to request help. Typically, this managed care representative makes a preliminary determination of the type of problem the client has and refers the client for a full-scale assessment to a direct service practitioner. Under this scheme, the direct service provider forms the relationship with the client and has the greatest knowledge of what is wrong and what should be done. To determine the necessity of the practitioner's proposed treatment, the managed care representative asks: What can you tell me to convince me that the client has the problem you describe, and why do you think that the treatment you propose will be appropriate? The direct service practitioner and the managed care representative must make judgments about likely outcomes in the face of uncertainty. Although no one can ever guarantee a treatment's outcome, it is not inappropriate for the practitioner who has met with and assessed the client to be asked why he or she believes that a certain treatment should help an individual or a family; it is also reasonable for the practitioner to explain to the managed care representative why shorter, less frequent treatment may be inadequate. Such questions are not necessarily inappropriate in what Winegar (1992) described as a "cottage industry" that lacks clear standards. They may also introduce a level of bureaucracy and inflexibility into an art form.

The Review of Care: A Case Illustration

A computer programmer for a bank calls the managed-care organization with which her bank has a contract, seeking help because of a troubled relationship with her stepson. The managed care representative who speaks with her refers her to a social worker who works with families in short-term treatment and who is particularly knowledgeable about strains in blended families. The managed care representative asks the social worker to provide a diagnosis from the *Diagnostic and Statistical Manual of Mental Disorders*,

Third Edition–Revised (American Psychiatric Association, 1987), commonly known as DSM-III-R, along with a description of the immediate problem and a proposed treatment plan.

After meeting the woman, the social worker submits a proposal to the managed care representative for 10 sessions of family therapy. The review process is a vehicle for validating that the treatment is appropriate to the diagnosis. Midway through the treatment of the woman and her stepson, the social worker concludes that the child's father should be brought into the treatment and will benefit from some individual therapy sessions. Under these circumstances, the social worker must give the managed care representative enough information about the family situation and the content of the treatment to justify a modified treatment plan. Because this conversation must take place *before* the father is seen, he is being discussed without his consent. Violations of confidentiality may occur in such circumstances, which makes it essential that the information shared between practitioner and managed care representative be extremely guarded. One may ask how the dilemma between authorization and violation of confidentiality can be managed in this setting.

Working in managed care compels practitioners to open themselves up to scrutiny and evaluation by the managed care staff. Although some practitioners may consider this requirement an infringement on their professional autonomy, they could see it as no different from bringing their work to a more experienced supervisor. A more important issue is that there is room for argument about what treatment is needed in this or any case. Someone with imagination and commitment to human well-being must decide what treatment is necessary. The choice of treatment cannot be based on an ideology (such as cognitive therapy or behavioral therapy) that favors or is inimical to one or another mode of treatment. The situation does suggest, however, that a thorough assessment and good advocacy skills may be necessary to ensure that the client receives the level of care he or she requires because, in the absence of a convincing argument, the managed care representative may be honor bound to cut costs.

EAPs and Managed Care

The concept of managed care that has been described does not depend on the existence of an EAP. However, some unions and employers have linked their provision of workplace services to the concept of managed care by providing incentives for members to use the panels of providers that their EAPs or MAPs select. Some employers' benefit packages waive copayments and deductibles and reduce out-of-pocket expenses for members who obtain their health and mental health services from the managed care providers with whom the EAPs have a relationship. Other employers insist that they will reimburse treatment costs only for employees who go through their EAPs, and treatment programs must contact the EAPs before beginning work with covered individuals. In this second model, the EAP or MAP itself becomes the principal reviewer of a client's progress and a practitioner's competence, in short, a managed care operator. Such a role may benefit employees who have reason to trust in-house personnel, but because the reviewers and authorizers of treatment are part of the work organization or union, employees and their families may fear breaches of confidentiality and may avoid seeking the services they need. There are situations in which the EAP comes into conflict with the managed care organization that serves the same employer as does the EAP. In some settings, EAPs carry out the managed care function. In others, authorization for care by a referral source can come either from the EAP or from the managed care organization. A major question for the year 2000 is whether managed care will replace EAPs or whether EAPs can remain separate functions (Wenzel, 1988). One expert (Winegar, 1992, p. 184) stated: "It seems likely that as both systems evolve, an increased merging of functions will occur." Others may disagree, but this is certainly an issue for EAPs.

Working within Limits

Among the terms that some professionals use to describe managed care is *limited.* It is true that employers and unions seek shorter, less intense, less costly treatment for their employees–members whenever possible. It is also true that the client needs and is entitled to treatment for a covered disorder. Sometimes an employer's contract with a managed care organization will not include provisions for psychological or neurological testing that may be essential to determine the nature of a young child's problems. The managed care organization must then find creative ways to negotiate the limits of the plan, perhaps by finding a university program that will give a free assessment as training for its students or by negotiating an exception to the no-payment rule by documenting the urgency of such an assessment in the specific instance. Sometimes the stated limits will be dysfunctional for a particular person in a particular situation. Perhaps a plan covers only individual treatment and not marital therapy, or perhaps it does not pay for complex neurological assessments that could determine whether a worker's difficulties stem from a hitherto undiagnosed attention deficit disorder, rather than from an emotional problem.

In the vocabulary of the field, there are cases that fall outside the norm; what is available is insufficient or is the wrong intervention for the client's problem. If the practitioner or social agency can make a convincing argument for longer, more frequent, or extraordinary intervention, the case manager may then authorize services that are not part of the traditional plan. To retain its credibility with the union or employer, the organization must restrict such atypical authorizations to a small fraction of cases, and the outcomes must justify the unusual service. However, if a managed care organization is to accomplish the employer's or the union's goal of having productive workers and to maintain its credibility with providers and consumers of services, it must be given flexibility in how it intervenes in a given situation.

The Social Work Role in Managed Care

Social work training stresses the person-in-environment approach to understanding people's lives (Greene & Ephross, 1991), constantly reminding students and professionals to notice the many overlapping systems in which people function—whether the systems are families, schools, communities, or the workplace. In essence, managed care programs embody the systems orientation of contemporary social work. Regardless of the setting of practice, responsible social work traditionally incorporates attention to an individual's psychological world and his or her physical, interpersonal, and social environments.

Independent of any pressures from payers, the profession recognizes that social workers can often be extremely effective by dealing with circumscribed problems in creative ways. It was social work, after all, that long ago talked about assessing a person in a situation, creating a more adaptive fit of a person to a situation or a situation to a person, through efficacious intervention anywhere, anytime. The ideal is to be both realistic and flexible in the interventions and goals that are espoused on the clients' behalf.

From this vantage point, the types of interventions that are consonant with the managed care mentality are also consonant with excellence in social work practice. Social workers are probably the mental health professionals who are best equipped to pioneer in this field—and they have a special responsibility to do so. It would not serve clients or the providers of services to leave the field to some other profession because services might deteriorate and costs might rise. For example, the clinicians who provide the services to clients through the managed care organization are in an excellent position to discover that certain resources are necessary but are not available through the existing system of community agencies. When those clinicians are social workers, well versed in program development and advocacy, they may use the leverage of their organization, and the unions and employers who count on it, to fight for necessary changes. Sometimes a change will simply be an expansion of rules to handle a problem that is unique to a particular client. At other times, the client's need will stimulate some kind of change in the system.

Managed care representatives and providers working together, for example, have found that inpatient services for persons with alcohol problems may not be the best form of care. Inpatient services remove an employee from the workplace, which may be the most supportive and demanding influence in the person's life. Therefore, separation from the workplace may be contraindicated. Managed care organizations have been known to shift an inpatient benefit to outpatient services that were rarely covered in the benefit contract that was being utilized.

Dilemmas of Managed Care

The workplace fills much of the gap in services posed by the lack of a governmental commitment to provide a variety of help to its citizens. Without subsidies for mental health care, substance abuse treatment, and social services for employees and their dependents (as are provided by employers and unions), many employees would be unable to afford even such help as is now available. Yet because services come through employers who are committed to maintaining a productive work force, but are not necessarily committed to the full self-realization of each individual worker, the variety and flexibility of the services may be limited to those that will achieve adequate care for the majority, not necessarily optimal care for any one person.

Despite this caveat, those who endorse managed care argue that the benefits provided cannot be truly effective for employers unless they are sufficiently flexible and responsive to the needs of individual employees (North, 1992). Employers must be interested in the well-being of the people who work for them, simply to deal with people who can bring requisite skills and attention to their jobs. Too-stringent limits on the types of practitioners; the number of outpatient counseling sessions; and the mix of inpatient, outpatient, and intermediate care services for which an individual is eligible could defeat the purpose of the benefit by failing to provide help that genuinely responds to an individual's difficulties. Furthermore, there are practical implications for managed care and cost containment because experience tells us that untreated mental health problems can later show up somatically in more costly forms of illness or accident. The key, suggested throughout this chapter, is to seek longer-range solutions, rather than to count the immediate investment and seek an equally immediate payoff. Human beings have a way of blossoming over time; they do not behave like robots who respond to the flick of a switch. Most research shows that investment in people is well rewarded, in the loyalty, productivity, availability, and commitment of the labor force.

Nonetheless, not all managed care programs will be benign. As McClellan (1989, p. 77) pointed out, they can "disguise the quality of care," rather than act as a guide to appropriate treatment. Sometimes people will recognize a need for more in-depth help than any system of managed care can provide them. Given the make-the-best-of-it mentality of the culture, psychological problems are still more stigmatized than are physical ones. Employers' benefit plans put more restrictions on mental health services than on those for physical problems, such as diabetes. Professionals, their clients, and employers will continue to wrestle with the issue of whether psychological difficulties should be subject to stringent limits on help that do not exist for other medical conditions. This issue will continue to be important as long as some managed care organizations maintain the inappropriate practices of early practitioners who were so bent on saving money that they sometimes neglected the issue of quality ("Utilization Review," 1990).

Yet another problem is the larger question of whether any union or employer should be subsidizing medical assistance for its members or workers. What happens to the expectation that people will stay in their jobs because they want the jobs—not because they are trapped by the needs of their medical care? Is this practice good for maintaining the best work force? Is it fair to stockholders, who may receive more return on their investments if the employers were not so anxious to provide mental health services to their employees?

Furthermore, even though three-fourths of them are employed, more than 30 million Americans do not have any kind of health insurance (Goleman, 1991). There is good reason to question whether the social work profession should continue to endorse a system in which the government abdicates its responsibility to people and expects employers to shoulder it. Although a beneficent system of managed care can potentially aid clients and yet make a dent in the escalating costs of health and mental health care, it still props up an arrangement in which the government shortchanges its responsibility to its citizens. And if dollars are saved because employees are receiving different or less expensive care, should those dollars be allocated to other benefits for employees, or should the gain be provided to consumers of the product in lower prices or to the shareholders in higher profits? Dilemmas abound as this country "manages" its health care system. Certainly, the Clinton administration will have much to say about these issues, and perhaps the experience with managed care for employees will become significant in decisions about the delivery of health care, including mental health care, to all people in this country.

References

A brief look at managed care. (1990, October). *NASW social work practice update* (pp. 1–13). Silver Spring, MD: National Association of Social Workers.

American Psychiatric Association. (1987). *Diagnostic and statistical manual of mental disorders* (3rd ed., rev.). Washington, DC: Author.

Barnes, P. D. (1991). Managed mental health care: A balancing act. *Administration and Policy in Mental Health, 19*(1), 51–55.

Blum, S. R. (1992). Ethical issues in managed mental health. In S. Feldman (Ed.), *Managed mental health services* (pp. 245–265). Springfield, IL: Charles C Thomas.

Croweak, J. F. (1991). Introduction to Special Issue on Managed Care. *Benefits Quarterly, 7*(4), 6–7.

Drugs in the workplace. (1991, May). *Group Health Incorporated Newsletter, 7*(1), 1–4.

Feldman, S. (1992). Managed mental health services: Ideas and issues. In S. Feldman (Ed.), *Managed mental health services* (pp. 3–26). Springfield, IL: Charles C Thomas.

Fields, J. A., Lilly, F. S., & Sutton-Bell, N. (1991). Health care challenges and opportunities in the 1990s. *Benefits Quarterly, 7*(4), 8–16.

Goleman, D. (1991, October 24). Battle of insurers vs. therapists: Cost control pitted against proper care. *New York Times*, pp. 1, D9.

Greene, R. R., & Ephross, P. H. (Eds.). (1991). *Human behavior theory and social work practice*. New York: Aldine de Gruyter.

Langman-Dorwart, N., Wahl, R. J., Singer, C. J., & Dorwart, R. A. (1992). *Administration and Policy in Mental Health, 19*, 345–353.

Lee, F. C. (1991). Managing mental health care. *Benefits Quarterly, 7*(4), 91–100.

Lightman, R., & Wagman, J. B. (1988). A working proposal for the EAP role in a managed care system. *The Almacan, 18*(5), 18–21.

McClellan, K. (1989, February). What's the bottom line? *Employee Assistance, 1*(7), 75–77.

North, R. D. (1992, January–February). Striking the right balance with EAP-based managed care. *EAP Digest*, pp. 36–39.

O'Brien, R. G. (1991). Managing health care quality can lower costs and generate access. *Benefits Quarterly, 7*(4), 17–22.

"Utilization review": Does it cut costs or imperil patients? (1990, August). *Consumer Reports*, pp. 520–521.

Wagman, J. B., & Schiff, J. (1989). Managed mental health care for employees: Roles for social workers. *Employee Assistance Quarterly, 5*(1), 53–66.

Weiner, R. B., & Siegel, D. (1989). Mental health care issues and strategies. *Benefits Quarterly, 5*(3), 21–31.

Wenzel, L. (1988). The courtship of EAPs and managed care. *The Almacan, 18*(5), 30–32.

Winegar, N. (1992). *Clinician's guide to managed mental health care*. New York: Haworth Press.

Yandrick, R., & Rothermel, S. (1988). For thirty years health care costs have been on a collision course. *The Almacan, 18*(5), 15–17.

CHAPTER 8

Ethnic, Cultural, and Racial Diversity in the Workplace

Muriel Gray and Frederica Barrow

> Work buttons you up.
>
> —Helen Harris Perlman
> *Persona*

Social work in the workplace does not exist in a vacuum. As society changes, so, too, must social work's response. The U.S. Department of Labor (1987) forecast that the U.S. work force will change drastically as a result of changing demographics. African Americans, Asian Americans, Hispanic Americans, women, immigrants, and older white men (U.S. Department of Labor, 1988) will constitute a far more significant portion of the work force than in the past. The changing composition of the work force is a significant reason for the workplace to be receptive to the needs of people, in this case those of different ethnic backgrounds and cultures, if it is to remain competitive in the world economy.

The task of occupational social workers in relation to the more diverse labor force is twofold: to help workers of various ethnic and cultural backgrounds adjust to and succeed in the workplace and to help managers develop the skills needed to create an environment that is receptive to understanding and affirming differences among workers so the skills and talents of a multicultural force can be tapped. Both the workplace and the work force need help in changing and adjusting to each other (Mandell & Kohler-Gray, 1990). This chapter considers some of the needs of both ethnically and culturally diverse workers and of the emerging workplace and suggests social work responses.

The authors recognize that professional skills equip social workers to function in a variety of human resource programs (Berry, 1990). This chapter, however, focuses on practice in employee assistance programs

(EAPs), identifying the skills, knowledge, and roles needed for ethnic and cultural competence to develop effective strategies of intervention at all levels in the workplace.

Observations about workers and the workplace offer a context by which the challenges may be understood. Therefore, the first section reviews the themes, observations, and assumptions about the emerging work force and the emerging workplace to provide a context for the second section, which discusses levels of intervention and specific social work skills that reflect competence in dealing with issues of ethnic and cultural significance.

Attention is centered on EAP strategies for (1) institutional-level intervention, reflected in workplace policies on diversity; (2) diversity-sensitive program interventions, reflected in specific EAP policies and procedures; and (3) individual interventions, reflected in direct EAP services. Although the authors recognize that human beings differ in many ways, the issues discussed in this chapter are restricted to those related to cultural, ethnic, and racial diversity.

General Themes

When one considers the racial, cultural, and ethnic groups that will make up the new work force, certain observations provide a context for understanding and responding to their needs and behavior.

- Because these groups have been denied access to equal opportunities, their economic and social development has been restricted (Almquist, 1979; Braddock & McPortland, 1987; Devore & Schlesinger, 1991).

- These groups have been victimized by societal and institutional practices of racism and other forms of discrimination (Cook, 1987; Feagin, 1987).

- They lack connections to the centers of power in organizations and may have weak links even within their own informal systems (Mandell & Kohler-Gray, 1990).

- They are perceived as having more problems than traditional employees and, therefore, more deficits (Mandell & Kohler-Gray, 1990).

- They have had fewer opportunities than have earlier groups in the workplace to learn to be strategic in resolving life's problems (Cook, 1987).

- They have few economic resources with which to resolve problems (U.S. Department of Labor, 1988, p. 68; Wallace, 1980).

Historically, the workplace has been composed primarily of white workers of various familiar European cultural and ethnic backgrounds. Aspects of culture, such as tradition, beliefs, and values, and aspects of ethnicity, including shared customs, language, and religion, had a uniform base for mutual understanding and acceptance. Unlike the traditional work force, however, the new work force will consist of workers who heretofore have had token and marginal representation in the workplace and thus are not familiar to the workplace. Moreover, it will be a work force of cultural, ethnic, and racial variations. As a result, not only will the workplace face the challenge of being sensitive to diversity in general, it will also need to meet the challenge of *specific* issues that grow out of the workers' many diverse cultural, racial, and ethnic backgrounds.

To satisfy the need for labor to compete in the global economy, the U.S. workplace must empower these previously disenfranchised workers. It must remove barriers and help workers develop strategies to gain meaningful opportunities for employment (U.S. Department of Labor, 1988) that are compatible with the workers' individual identities.

According to Naisbett (1982), all Americans will need to be able to adapt continuously to new trends. For instance, in this information society, workers will have to become skilled enough to use high technology. Naisbett (1990) emphasized that by the year 2000, workers will have to participate in the international economy, free-market socialism, a global life-style, and cultural nationalism. Thus, occupational social workers who provide services to groups of individuals whose opportunities to participate in "mainstream" America have been restricted will face great challenges. These challenges can be met, in part, by assisting workers from diverse backgrounds to understand the forces that are operating on their lives. For example, the assessment of problems with these groups requires attention to both the personal and societal barriers to success that they face.

It will be insufficient to focus on the feelings of the clients to the exclusion of their cognitive needs. These barriers will require intervention on several levels. For instance, clients are likely to need individual education and training, to which the occupational social worker can provide access. On the other hand, because managers of successful workplaces will have to adopt a global life-style and come to understand other cultures (Naisbett, 1990), the occupational social worker will have opportunities to help *them* learn about cultural diversity from their employees.

Considering historical realities, current trends, and future needs, both the workers and managers will have to be educated, trained, and socialized to function in a global economy (Brock, 1988). This socialization will not occur without conflict between workers and their work organizations or among workers. Therefore, the workplace will need mechanisms to manage organizational and individual conflict.

Culture, Race, and Ethnicity

Cultural issues

By definition, culture embodies traditions, ideas, attitudes, beliefs, and values (Atkinson, Morten, & Sue, 1989). Everyone has a cultural heritage, whether she or he is aware of it, and each workplace also has a culture. For individuals to succeed in the workplace, they must be able to mediate between these two basic cultures. The occupational social worker can help workers do so by knowing about and being sensitive to workers' cultural differences and by sharing his or her knowledge of the dynamics of the culture of the workplace.

It is important to include cultural awareness in EAP administrative and clinical practices. There is a fine line, however, between making generalizations about workers' cultural heritage and stereotyping them on the basis of one's perceptions of cultural groups. For instance, Atkinson, Mariyama, and Matsui (1978) found that "minority" clients in a counseling relationship prefer an active, directive counseling style to a nondirective one. Yet other authors (Bell & Evans, 1981) pointed to the need to assess the extent to which a particular client identifies with his or her "traditional" culture. Knowing that most members of Latino cultures depend on their churches for a variety of emotional and social needs may be an important generalization to take into account, but the social worker must also assess the extent to which the individual client identifies with the traditional culture or is acculturated into the mainstream American culture (Atkinson et al., 1989, p. 271). In short, using physical characteristics to determine someone's culture could lead to misunderstandings based on stereotyping.

Racial issues

Race refers to a system of classifying groups of people on the basis of a combination of physical characteristics and genetic origin. Such characteristics may include skin pigmentation, head form, facial features, and hair texture (Atkinson et al., 1989). Race as a biological phenomenon is straightforward and has few social consequences. What this society believes about race and racial differences, however, has profound social, psychological, and economic consequences. This society has a history of institutional practices that have resulted in discrimination and limited opportunities for racial minorities. Real and perceived discrimination are often themes among the problems presented by members of racial minority groups to EAP workers. In most workplaces, the Equal Employment Offices (EEOs) may address formal complaints of discrimination. The EAPs, however, often are where first-level informal complaints and requests for assistance are received. The social worker should be prepared to help an individual document a perceived situation and to identify and express the concern the situation elicits.

Ethnic issues

Ethnicity, according to Atkinson et al. (1989), refers to a shared social and cultural heritage, including customs, language, and religion. It should not be confused with race in that it is possible to be of the same ethnic group but not of the same race. Conversely, there may be various ethnic groups within one race, for example, Caribbean and African American or Vietnamese, Chinese, Korean, and Japanese. Although the value of recognizing and preserving individuals' ethnic-group heritage and customs is often articulated, the acceptance of these differences has not always been realized in day-to-day life. For instance, many workplaces have strict dress codes that are insensitive to such ethnic customs as hair braiding among African American women and the wearing of saris by Indian women or of tribal adornments by Native Americans.

Many issues related to ethnicity may be present in the workplace. They may reflect a tendency to want to create a "melting pot" in which all workers assimilate and adopt the norms and values of the majority culture instead of a workplace that has policies and practices that affirm differences. In the EAP, such affirmation may be reflected in having an ethnically diverse staff and in establishing practices that contribute to the acceptance of differences.

Social Work Theory

Given this diversity and the complexity of the challenges facing the emerging work force and workplace, occupational social workers must adopt a theoretical frame of reference to understand, plan, and develop appropriate interventions. An analysis of the earlier observations suggests that social workers require an understanding of systems and social systems theory and of the socialization process and socialization theory, especially as they relate to the development of workers' roles.

Social systems theory provides a means by which one may gain a clearer perspective of the reciprocal influences among such individual factors as culture, ethnicity, and race and environmental factors, including the workplace. Socialization theories, especially social learning theory, provide an interpretation by which social workers may help workers and the work organization gain a clearer perspective of the reciprocal influences of individual cognitive, emotional, and behavioral influences on the process of adopting a different role and adapting to a new (workplace) culture. Inherent in this process is the concept of mediation between the needs of the individual worker and the needs of the broader culture of the workplace.

These theories suggest that in the process of becoming socialized, both the workplace and its workers give up their separate identities and begin to share aspects of the other's identity. In this sense, the individual takes on aspects of the worker role, and the workplace develops mechanisms that are sensitive to workers. Occupational social workers may mediate between the needs of both the workers and the workplace to help maintain an equitably balanced work environment.

Social Workers' Roles

Occupational social workers use various functional roles, such as consultant, ombudsman, mediator, advocate, clinician, and researcher. To be effective in carrying out these roles with a culturally, ethnically, and racially diverse work force, they need to

- know North, South, and Latin American history and Asian and Asian American history, especially in relation to the world of work—the jobs these groups have performed historically and the particular interests and skills they bring to the workplace
- understand the history of work in the United States, in general, and the history of work with racial, cultural, and ethnic workers, in particular,
- be sensitive to the contemporary workplace and be able to analyze the organizational culture
- understand the workplace as a social system and a socialization agent.

Readings or life experiences that shed light on perspectives of the world of work and its effect on ordinary men and women and their social, political, and economic experiences are helpful. One such book is *Who Built America: Working People and the Nation's Economy, Politics and Society* (Levine et al., 1990).

Levels of Intervention

The EAP must be prepared to address the issues of a diverse work force on the institutional level with the work organization as a whole; on the program level, by structuring the EAP in a way to avoid the perception of engaging in discriminating practices or in being sympathetic to institutional practices that result in discrimination; and on the individual level, by delivering services in a way that workers may develop empowering strategies.

Institutional-Level Interventions

Institutional-level interventions usually deal with policies and plans that lead to the achievement of the organization's mission. It is from this level that the most important organizational values are communicated to the wider public. To create an environment that is hospitable to diversity may require the EAP's advice on workplace interventions that are designed to replace policies and practices that may have been a standard part of the workplace's routine with new ones that reflect diversity (Akabas & Hanson, 1989). In such situations, EAP personnel may have a sense of the organization that allows them to generalize from case to class in relation to dysfunctional policies. Some corporations, such as Digital, Procter and Gamble, and U.S. West, have aggressively institutionalized policies and practices that are designed to define and affirm the importance of diversity in the workplace. For example, U.S. West, a communication company, holds company executives accountable for proposing slates of workers to be considered for promotion that include women and people of color; the executives' raises and bonuses hinge, in part, on the race and gender of the workers they hire and promote.

It is imperative that the occupational social worker provide consultation to influence and support the policies of the organization that focus on and reflect the acceptance of diversity (Thomas, 1990). Such policies must be written and well articulated. A specific policy to address diversity should contain statements about the following:

- the organization's position–philosophy on diversity
- provisions for creating practices that affirm diversity, for example, doing business with companies whose leaders are ethnically and racially diverse
- employee benefits that acknowledge diverse themes and needs, for instance, tuition assistance for career development
- reasonable accommodation for workers that includes provisions for time and resources to meet work-related goals, for example, time and money to take a language course
- diversity-education programs that explain cultural and ethnic customs, values, and traditions
- multicultural sensitivity training for supervisors that includes information on diversity
- a collaborative relationship between management and labor in activities that are designed to affirm diversity
- specific programs and support services to promote employees' development and well-being
- provisions to monitor managers' compliance with the company's philosophies and policies on diversity; for instance, an annual review of the recruitment, promotion, and retention of workers

- the evaluation of services and organizational programs for their relevance to affirming diversity.

To be relevant to a diverse work force, policy development requires participation by representatives of the groups that are involved and of the human resource programs in the organization that deal directly with such issues.

The integration of new workers into the organization may create disequilibrium, and any program that is designed to assist with integration and adjustment may be met with misgivings. Therefore, attention should be given to all responses, formal and informal, to make sure that they communicate fairness and acceptance. The experience at Digital Corporation provides an example of operating procedures that were insensitive to the issues of diversity and shows how small changes improved the environment for all:

> At the end of a sales meeting, the men would go into a bar—and that was where they got real feedback. That's uncomfortable for women. Or sales meetings were held at country clubs, but a lot of minorities don't go to country clubs because they don't feel welcome. A very sharp manager at Digital established some new norms: breakfast meetings at hotels in cities—places that were comfortable for everyone. It had a tremendous impact. (Copeland, 1988, p. 56)

The occupational social worker can assist the workplace not only by providing consultation, but by seizing opportunities to serve on task forces and special projects outside the traditional EAP role. Other important opportunities at the institutional level that can be used for strategic intervention include writing papers for publication or presentation; generating position papers on related topics for the organization; and requesting opportunities to brief officials of the organization on matters of race, culture, and ethnicity.

Program-Level Interventions

A variety of program-level interventions, including training; the design of benefits; and special services, such as child care programs, literacy, and elder care, may each have their roots in an organizational response to diversity. This section discusses how the EAP can be structured, designed, and managed to meet the needs of workers, namely, African Americans, Latinos, and Asian Americans, whose culture, ethnic backgrounds, and races have historically not been valued in the workplace.

The EAP is a human resource strategy designed to assist the organization with personnel-related issues by helping workers with personal concerns (see Chapter 2). The components of the EAP include both administrative and clinical services. All the facets of a comprehensive EAP program that is designed for the groups discussed here must reflect sensitivity to their needs and experiences: access to programs; staffing and qualifications; clinical and program policy; publicity, marketing, and outreach; physical setting; quality assurance; and the selection of resources.

Administrative services

Administrative services that are relevant to diversity include access to programs, staffing, publicity and marketing, the physical plant, the nature of services that are provided, and quality assurance. As with all programs, the EAP's hours of operation need to be those during which workers are available to use it. There should also be enough flexibility that workers have the option of using the program during work time (if policy permits) or during their own time.

Unlike the projected changes in the general labor force, the labor market from which occupational social workers will be selected will continue to be predominantly white because of the underrepresentation of students of color in schools of social work, decreased financial support for education, and the competitive professional environment. In this regard, being a member of an ethnic, racial, or cultural minority does not, in itself, make a social worker effective in working with minority clients (Gray & Lanier, 1985). All other things being equal, however, demographic similarity between the client and the helper contributes to the client's positive perceptions of the helping relationship, as Beutler and Clarkin (1990) pointed out in a study of perceptions of the helping relationship.

To meet the needs of a culturally diverse work force, EAP administrators should participate in the recruitment and screening of applicants, the selection of candidates, and the hiring of staff. In highly stratified organizations, their involvement may not be the accepted practice, but when consideration is given to the workplace's limited experience and poor track record in recruiting, hiring, and retaining workers from diverse backgrounds (Herren, 1989), such an approach is justified.

EAP administrators who do participate in recruitment need to use formal and informal means of seeking social workers from diverse backgrounds by placing advertisements in ethnic community newspapers; notifying community and church leaders; contacting workers in public agencies; informing community social clubs, fraternal organizations, and sororities; and contacting professional organizations that address the needs of minority social workers. Help may be available from the National Association of Black Social Workers, the National Association of Black Alcoholism Counselors, the National Hispanic Social Work Network, and the National Association of Social Workers' Caucus of Asian American and Pacific Islander American Social Workers.

When recruiting from the more traditional labor pool of white professionals, the organization should select those who are open to diversity and are motivated to continue learning about other cultures. The actual job interview can identify applicants with cross-cultural experiences, such as travel; fluency in more than one language; and other ethnic skills, interests, and experiences.

In the EAP's publicity, marketing, and outreach, a multifaceted approach that incorporates symbols and physical representations of all workers is recommended. There also should be a balance in the representation; for instance, the use of posters, paycheck inserts, brochures, and other printed media should depict the racial, cultural, and ethnic affinity of all workers in the workplace.

People generally associate the appearance of an office in which services are delivered with how others perceive them. A neglected and unkempt office used to deliver services to minority clients may be perceived as a message of not caring or as the acceptance of a commonly held negative stereotype and myth about minorities, namely, that poor and or minority people do not care about cleanliness and beauty and that they do not value or take care of possessions. The EAP must guard against projecting an appearance of insensitivity or negative stereotyping in any way, especially when evaluating referral resources, which is an important reason to make site visits.

The services offered by the EAP must reflect the needs and issues of the work force. For instance, many cultural and ethnic groups have been disenfranchised and thus may lack basic workplace-socialization and career-development strategies. Immigrant workers may need to select new career paths or begin work in this country at lower levels than their accustomed positions abroad. Because the mutual adjustment by the workplace and workers may result in tension and conflict, an important component of an EAP program is group conflict resolution, as well as other social group work methods for problem solving. For instance, the EAP may be approached by a supervisor to work with an entire work unit when tension and conflict among workers affect the productivity of the overall unit.

Quality assurance

Quality assurance refers to plans, procedures, and activities that are carried out to review the degree to which a program's objectives are being met. It relies heavily on data collection as a means of reviewing a program's activities. The performance of the program can be measured against a variety of variables. For instance, the extent to which the EAP serves each work group in relation to the group's representation in the work force can be determined to aid in developing outreach strategies. A comparison of the outcome of EAP intervention between clients of the diverse groups and other clients can be reviewed to check the EAP's performance. The sources to which clients are referred require careful analysis with the same criteria that the EAP applies to itself. They should either be responsive to diversity or to the culture, ethnicity, or race of the specific individuals being referred.

The use of data can also influence organizational responses to cultural, racial, and ethnic workers in long-range planning of benefit programs in health and education. For instance, through data from traditional EAP assessments of African American clients, the EAP may recommend the establishment of a blood-pressure-monitoring program in the workplace. Further changes in geography and family structure may also create the need for new social and health supports that may suggest the utilization of religiously sensitive family planning services for Catholic Latinos. The EAP can use its demographic information to help the workplace design programs that will help accommodate those needs.

Individual-Level Interventions

Individual-level interventions include all the face-to-face activities carried out by the social worker with and on behalf of individual workers, groups of workers, or family members. The focus of these interventions is to help maximize the functioning and career development of workers. The profession has a long history of individual-level interventions, but the occupational social worker functions in a context that is somewhat different from that of many other social work colleagues in that he or she has two clients—the work organization and the workers. Conceptually, the EAP mediates between the organization and the individual workers to promote the workers' success on the job. As a result of proper assessments and the skillful selection of resources, the social worker is expected to help resolve the workers' personal or work-related problems.

Social workers have traditionally "started where the client is." In working with people of familiar backgrounds and cultures, this dictum allows the social worker to define problems from a familiar cultural perspective, making the validation of the clients' points of view within his or her own cultural context. Professional practice with people whose experiences have been different from that of the social worker (because of socially, economically, and politically biased responses to ethnicity, race, or culture) requires additional knowledge. Social workers cannot "start where the client is" until they have the skills to determine *where* the client actually is. The anthropological principle of cultural relativity tells us that one culture should not be judged by another's standards (Havilland, 1985).

Multicultural racial or ethnic counseling is most effective when it uses a model that allows the client to help the social worker understand and interpret responses from the client's perspective. Such a model requires the social worker to give up control of the counseling process in favor of a collaborative approach. It is this type of approach that many multicultural counselors and cultural anthropologists have found effective in understanding and interpreting behaviors of people whose experiences have been different from their own. This approach not only suggests a change from the traditional approach, but suggests that more time should be allowed for the assessment phase (Gray & Lanier, 1985).

Selection of and referral to resources

Once the worker's problem or issues have been determined on the basis of standards relevant to the appropriate reference group and culturally sensitive options have been presented, the social worker can begin to match the client to resources that are knowledgeable of and sensitive to issues of diversity. When possible, the ideal match is one that maximizes similarities between the client and the social worker. The use of resources whose staffs are sensitive to cultural, racial, gender, and ethnic issues is the most critical part of this process because, for many EAPs, these resources perform the treatment.

No matter how outstanding a provider's reputation may be, it is important to determine whom she or he has served and the range of interventions she or he is prepared to make on behalf of clients. To determine the extent to which a resource is culturally and ethnically sensitive, it is important to consider several components and to answer the following questions:

1. Does the physical facility reflect aspects of the clients' culture?

2. Are written materials and service personnel "language sensitive"? For instance, consider the debate about the use of *Latino* versus *Hispanic* when referring to people of Latin ancestry or the use of the term *African American* or *black* when referring to blacks born in the United States.

3. Do clinical interventions include a range of traditional and nontraditional options, such as the appropriateness of folk medicines and remedies and conducting conjoint clinical services with ministers, spiritual healers, or yoga trainers?

4. Do clinical modalities allow for the inclusion of "nontraditional" family members as a part of a client's family system?

5. Does the resource demonstrate knowledge of the history of culturally and ethnically diverse cohorts of workers in the workplace?

6. Is the resource located in a neighborhood where the client will feel comfortable?

Crisis intervention
Like other aspects of cross-cultural counseling, people of different cultures define problems differently. In this regard, the perception of what is a crisis also is culturally relative. Similarly, people of various cultural backgrounds may be accustomed to handling situations in different ways. Because a crisis requires an immediate plan of action, the social worker must take care to interpret the presenting problem from a cultural and ethnic perspective before he or she develops the plan of action. For instance, relying on emotional affect as a measure of assessing a person's potential for suicide could result in a different assessment of a client who comes from a culture that considers suicide a noble act than of a client who comes from a culture that considers suicide an act of a disturbed person.

The EAP in a diverse workplace will also have to develop strategies for managing interpersonal and intergroup conflict, even though such strategies may not be a component of traditional EAP direct services. The EAP may be the mechanism by which conflict within work units may be resolved. Social workers have experience mediating and managing conflicts, but occupational social workers primarily have used these skills on behalf of individual workers. Now EAP social workers can introduce the concept of group work to the world of work and help groups resolve their conflictual situations.

Conclusion

Social workers in the workplace are in a special position to help the workplace develop interventions that are needed to create an environment that is receptive to a multicultural work force and to help workers of various ethnic and cultural backgrounds succeed in the workplace. To be effective, these interventions must be directed toward institutional policies and practices that affirm diversity—at the EAP level, by developing, restructuring, and broadening the scope of EAP practice and at the individual level, by delivering services in a way that helps workers to feel empowered. Therefore, occupational social workers may have opportunities to broaden their practice base from primarily micro-level interventions to include more macro approaches that are specifically designed to help the workplace respond to its ethnically, culturally, and racially diverse workers.

References

Akabas, S. H., & Hanson, M. (1989). Organizational implications of drug abuse programming: Making the organization work for you. *Drug abuse curriculum for employee assistance program professionals.* Washington, DC: U.S. Department of Health & Human Services.

Almquist, E. M. (1979). *Minorities, gender and work.* Lexington, MA: Lexington Books.

Atkinson, D., Morten, G., & Sue, D. (1989). *Counseling American minorities.* Dubuque, IA: William C. Brown.

Atkinson, D., Mariyama, M., & Matsui, S. (1978). The effects of counselor race and counseling approach on Asian Americans' perceptions of counselor credibility and utility. *Journal of Counseling Psychology, 25,* 76–83.

Bell, P., & Evans, J. (1981). *Counseling black clients: Alcohol use and abuse in black America.* Center City, MN: Hazelden Press.

Berry, P. (1990). Application of social work skills to human resource management. In S. L. A. Straussner (Ed.), *Occupational social work today* (pp. 67–75). New York: Haworth Press.

Beutler, L., & Clarkin, J. (1990). *Systematic treatment selection: Toward targeted therapeutic interventions.* New York: Brunner/Mazel.

Brock, W. (1988, February). Workforce 2000 agenda recognizes lifelong need to improve skills. *Monthly Labor Review, 3*(2), 54–56.

Braddock, J., & McPortland, J. (1987). How minorities continue to be excluded from equal employment opportunity: Research on labor market and institutional barriers. *Journal of Social Issues, 43*(1), 5–39.

Cook, S. (1987). Behavior-change implications of low involvement in an issue. *Journal of Social Issues, 43*(1), 105–112.

Copeland, L. (1988, June). Making the most of cultural differences at the workplace. *Personnel,* 52–56.

Devore, W., & Schlesinger, E. (1991). *Ethnic-sensitive social work practice.* New York: Macmillan.

Feagin, J. (1987). Changing black Americans to fit a racist system. *Journal of Social Issues, 43*(1), 85–89.

Googins, B., & Godfrey, J. (1987). *Occupational social work.* Englewood Cliffs, NJ: Prentice Hall.

Gray, M., & Lanier, D. (1985). Designing employee assistance programs to meet the needs of black clients. In F. Brisbane & M. Womble (Eds.), *The treatment of black alcoholics* (pp. 85–96). New York: Haworth Press.

Havilland, W. (1985). *Anthropology.* New York: Holt, Rinehart & Winston.

Herren, L. (1989, June). The new game of HR: Playing to win. *Personnel,* 19–22.

Levine, B., Brier, D., Countryman, E., Fennel, D., & Rediker, M. (1989). *Who built America: Working people and the nation's economy, politics, culture and society.* New York: Pantheon Press.

Mandell, B., & Kohler-Gray, S. (1990, March). Management development that values diversity. *Personnel, 67,* 41–47.

Naisbett, J. (1982). *Megatrends.* New York: Avon Books.

Naisbett, J. (1990). *Megatrends 2000.* New York: Avon Books.

Thomas, R., Jr. (1990, March–April). From affirmative action to affirming diversity. *Harvard Business Review, 68*, 107–117.

U.S. Department of Labor. (1987). *Workforce 2000.* Washington, DC: U.S. Government Printing Office.

U.S. Department of Labor. (1988). *Opportunity 2000.* Washington, DC: U.S. Government Printing Office.

Wallace, P. (1980). *Black women in the labor force.* Cambridge, MA: MIT Press.

CHAPTER 9

Family and Work

TRENDS AND PROSPECTS FOR DEPENDENT CARE

Jacquelyn McCroskey and Andrew Scharlach

> One sees the human significance of work—not merely as
> a means of biological survival—but also as the giver of
> self and the transcender of self, as the center for human
> identity and human evolution.
>
> —Betty Friedan
> *The Feminine Mystique*

More and more American businesses are expressing interest in investing in
public education to prepare children to enter the work force; employment
training programs, to help workers acquire new skills; and human resource
programs, to keep workers functioning well on the job. Business journals
feature articles on partnerships to restructure education and to get children
on the path to productivity; business leaders support philanthropic programs
to invest in poor communities; and eminent business organizations, such as
the Committee for Economic Development (1990), suggest a "life cycle
approach to a competitive work force" that encourages policymakers to
support programs that make better use of limited human resources. These
initiatives provide exciting new opportunities for occupational social workers to help businesses understand complex community service systems,
initiate employer-supported programs, and collaborate with public and
private leaders to improve public policies. This chapter discusses the challenges and opportunities for occupational social workers to help businesses
maximize their investments in families by improving care for dependent
children and elderly family members.

Increasing Need for Dependent Care

Today's employees are faced with greater responsibilities for the care of dependent family members than ever before, primarily because of social and demographic changes that have brought more women into the work force at a time of increased rates of divorce, teenage pregnancy, and geographic separation from kin. As of 1988, 72 percent of women ages 25 to 54 were in the civilian labor force, compared to only 34 percent in 1948 and only 20 percent in 1900 (Committee for Economic Development, 1990; Foster, Siegel, & Jacobs, 1988). By the year 2000, it is projected that more than 80 percent of women ages 25 to 64 will be working (Green & Epstein, 1988).

These increases in the female labor force have had a profound and largely uncharted impact on all aspects of family life. But perhaps the most troubling changes have been in the care of family members who are unable to care for themselves—those who are dependent by virtue of their age or health. As a result of women's increased participation in the labor force, for example, more than 26 million children under age 15 have working mothers; approximately 17 million have mothers who work full-time. In 1993, 60 percent of the women who had preschool-age children were in the labor force (Center for the Study of Social Policy, 1993). If this trend continues, it is estimated that by 1995 more than three-fourths of school-age children and two-thirds of preschool children will have mothers in the work force (Hofferth & Phillips, 1987; U.S. House of Representatives, 1988).

Patterns of care for children have also changed dramatically. In 1958, only 18 percent of married mothers with children under age 6 were employed; of those who were employed, more than half arranged care in their own homes with relatives, about a quarter arranged care in relatives' homes, and less than 5 percent used organized child care centers. By the late 1980s, half the mothers with children under age 6 were working, and only one-quarter of their children were cared for at home; 40 percent were cared for in the homes of others, and 30 percent were in organized child care centers (Hofferth & Phillips, 1987).

However, women continue to bear the majority of family responsibilities: 49 percent of married employed mothers reported having full responsibility for household chores, compared with only 4 percent of married employed fathers (Burden & Googins, 1987). When their children are ill, moreover, female employees are six times as likely as are their male counterparts to stay home to provide care (Burden & Googins, 1987). Women are also more likely than are men to provide intensive care to elderly relatives and to rearrange their work schedules to do so (Stone, Cafferata, & Sangl, 1987).

At the same time, employees' responsibilities for elderly family members are increasing dramatically, largely in response to the increasing number of elderly persons who need care. There are approximately 31 million persons aged 65 and older in the United States, up from only 3 million in 1900. By the year 2030 this figure is projected to grow to about 66 million elderly persons, or 21 percent of the American population (American Association of Retired Persons, AARP, 1991). The fastest growing segment of American society is the 85 and older age group, almost half of whom require assistance with day-to-day activities (U.S. Senate, 1985–86).

Of particular importance is the dramatic increase in the ratio of elderly persons to those of working age, from seven elderly persons per 100 persons ages 18 to 64 in 1900 to 19 per 100 in 1985. The Senate Special Committee on Aging (1985–86) predicted that by the year 2010 there will be 22 elderly persons per 100 working-age persons, and by 2050 there will be 38 per 100. Approximately 43 percent of women and 69 percent of men with disabled parents and spouses work full-time (Stone & Kemper, 1989). At least 9 percent of all Americans employed 30 or more hours per week have a disabled elderly spouse or parent (Stone & Kemper, 1989), with some companies reporting prevalence rates as high as 28 percent (Travelers Companies, 1985). Employees caring for a disabled elderly person provide an average of six to 10.2 hours per week of assistance, with 8 percent spending 35 hours or more per week helping an elderly person, nearly the equivalent of a second full-time job (Travelers Companies, 1985). More than a third of these caregiving employees are responsible for the care of two or more elderly persons (Scharlach & Boyd, 1989).

Approximately 3 percent of women in the work force have children under age 15, as well as a disabled parent (Stone & Kemper, 1989). The number of years with such simultaneous responsibilities for elderly parents and dependent children has increased 150 percent since 1800 and is expected to continue to increase as more working women delay childbearing into their 30s and 40s (Watkins, Menken, & Bongaarts, 1987).

As the number of employees who care for older adults and or children has increased, the workplace has been directly affected. Tardiness, excessive absenteeism, unscheduled time off, telephone calls home, and lost concentration because of the concern for dependent relatives can reduce productivity and affect an employee's well-being (Kola & Dunkle, 1988).

Studies of the impact of child care on parents' work behavior underscore the stress and strain associated with locating and maintaining adequate child care. Such stress affects parents' health and work performance (Anastas, Gibeau, & Larson, 1990; Burden & Googins, 1987; Crouter, 1984; Emlen & Koren, 1984; Galinsky, 1988). When child care arrangements are inadequate or undependable, employers suffer from decreased productivity, parents suffer from stress, and children may suffer from the consequences of inadequate supervision. The lack of affordable and dependable child care is a primary barrier to mothers' participation in the labor force. Among mothers in families with incomes of less than $15,000 per year, 36 percent would look for work if child care were available at a reasonable cost (U.S. House of Representatives, 1988).

Among employees caring for elderly relatives, 80 percent report emotional strain, 61 percent report physical strain, and 55 percent report financial strain as a result of their caregiving responsibilities. Thirty-seven percent visit friends less often, 33 percent go out to dinner less often, and 50 percent report less time for themselves (Scharlach & Boyd, 1989). Persons caring for disabled elderly persons also experience elevated levels of anxiety, depression, and ill health (George & Gwyther, 1986; Rabins, Mace, & Lucas, 1982).

A study by Brody, Kleban, Johnsen, Hoffman, and Schoonover (1987) indicated that substantial proportions of working women reported that caring for their parents had made them miss work (58 percent), caused work interruptions (47 percent), made them lose pay (18 percent), robbed them of the energy to do their work well (15 percent), and made them wish they did not work (17 percent). Employees who care for dependent elderly relatives or children have a greater number of family-related absences and are more likely to take time off during the workday to take care of family responsibilities than are noncaregiving employees (Scharlach, Lowe, & Schneider, 1990).

The added responsibilities associated with dependent care can also take a professional toll on employees. Such employees may have to miss opportunities for career advancement, restrict travel for their jobs, turn down promotions, or forgo valuable overtime or training. They are apt to deplete sick leave and vacation time to provide care. A study by Transamerica Life Companies, for example, found that 42 percent of caregiving employees gave up their own vacation time to provide care for elderly relatives (Scharlach & Boyd, 1989). A 1982 national survey of givers of long-term care found that 12 percent of adult daughters and 5 percent of sons caring for elderly parents had quit their jobs because of the demands of caregiving (Stone et al., 1987).

Caring for both a child and an impaired elderly relative can be doubly difficult. Stress and worry about family finances are reported by 70 percent of the women who care for both children and dependent adults, compared with 64 percent of the women who care only for children and 59 percent who care only for adults (Emlen, Koren, & Louise, 1988). Difficulty finding adequate child care is reported by 55 percent of the mothers who also care for dependent adults, but by 48 percent of the mothers who do not. Similarly, difficulty finding adequate adult care is reported by 73 percent of the women who also care for children, but by 66 percent of those who do not.

Public Policy on Dependent Care

As a background for devising effective employer-supported dependent care services, it is important to understand the public policy context of care for children and the elderly. Primary responsibility for this care continues to be assumed by family members, neighbors, and friends, who turn to formal community-based child care and elder care providers only when necessary. In fact, families and other unpaid helpers provide up to 85 percent of the care received by disabled older persons in the United States (Kane & Kane, 1987). And, only about 30 percent of young children are cared for in organized group care settings; the majority of child care is provided in the children's homes (23 percent) or in other families' homes (43 percent) (Bianchi, 1990).

Although federal dollars pay for only a small proportion of dependent care, public policy at the federal level sets the context for a complex and multifaceted system of community-based child- and elder care services. Federal responsibility for such services was first established in the 1935 Social Security Act, but has been augmented only occasionally since then as a result of well-organized and generally hard-fought campaigns by advocates and concerned citizens. Whereas the 1980s were characterized by cutbacks in federal spending and responsibility for dependent care, 1990 marked an important milestone in the ongoing effort to increase federal support for dependent care.

In 1990, Congress finally passed the first comprehensive child care package since the 1942 Lanham Act. This package included four major components: (1) the Child Care and Development Block Grant (originally referred to as the Act for Better Child Care), to subsidize child care for low-income parents and to improve the quality of child care; (2) child care amendments to the Title IV-A Social Security Act to help families avoid dependence on welfare; (3) the expansion of the Earned Income Tax Credit for low-income families; and (4) the expansion of the federal Head Start program.

This landmark legislation was especially important because it came after many years of failure to establish a federal role in child care. In 1970, success in the long battle to establish the Comprehensive Child Development Act was reversed at the last minute in a veto by President Nixon; the president vetoed the bipartisan bill because he thought that a national system of comprehensive child development centers would "communalize" the family. In like manner, a family leave bill, defeated under President Bush, who thought it weighed too heavily on employers, was passed by Congress and signed by President Clinton in 1993 as a sign that the new administration values families and supports workers' rights to carry out their family obligations.

The service delivery systems for community-based child care and elder care services are complex and multifaceted. Formal child care services include paid care for children in their own homes, in the homes of family day care providers, and in child care centers, nursery schools, or afterschool programs. Formal elder care services include home health care, visiting

nurses, adult day health care, respite care, and residential care. Persons using
these child care and elder care services may pay the full cost of services, or
their payments may be augmented by governmental, charitable, or employers' subsidies. The legislative, regulatory, and funding systems that guide
services include federal, state, and local governments, as well as not-for-
profit, proprietary, religious, civic, and community organizations. The
result is somewhat different in each community, but every city has a complex
system of child- and elder care services that generally is difficult for families
to understand and even more difficult for them to gain access to.

Community-Based Services

Child care
The federal government funds and administers all Head Start services
(which are contracted locally but supervised from regional federal offices),
provides block-grant child care funds to states, oversees Internal Revenue
Service tax deductions for child care, and supervises child care provisions in
federal job training and welfare programs. Each state administers and
regulates government-subsidized child care, licenses child care facilities, and
develops its own state-sponsored child care initiatives.

Elder care
The federal government's role in assisting older persons and their families
includes primarily the coverage of hospital, physicians', and nursing home
expenses, through Medicare and Medicaid (Titles XVIII and XIX of the
Social Security Act, respectively). The Older Americans Act (OAA), a much
more modest program, provides support for nutritional services, transpor-
tation, limited non-medical home care, and other essential social services.
OAA services are administered through a network of state and local agencies.
In addition, the Social Services Block Grant (Title XX of the Social Security
Act) has helped to fund in-home supportive services in some states.

The Roles of Employers and Unions
Although the number of employer-supported child care programs grew
from 600 in 1982 to 4,000 by 1989, these programs still represented only a
small fraction of the 6 million employers in the United States, or even of the
44,000 employers with more than 100 employees (Friedman, 1986, 1990). A
similar pattern is seen with regard to elder care. As of 1987, employer-
supported elder care programs were offered by only 2 to 3 percent of all
employers, although another 15 percent were considering doing so (Creedon,
1987). Among major corporations, 32 percent were offering programs or
benefits that were likely to be of assistance to employees with elder care
responsibilities or concerns. Some labor unions also have been active in

promoting employer-supported child and elder care services, although there are many fewer union- than employer-supported programs (True & Wineman, 1989).

Although support from employers and unions for child care and elder care is extremely important, it is unrealistic to believe that such support will meet the entire need for dependent care by itself. Nor should it. However, employers and unions can be important contributors to the resolution of dependent care problems by working in partnership with other community groups to define and resolve local problems, advocate for increased child care and elder care resources at all levels, and develop creative integrative solutions to these complex and far-reaching problems. Occupational social workers have the special training and expertise to help lead the way in these efforts.

Dependent Care Initiatives

This section describes some exemplary child care and elder care programs that have been designed to assist employees who have dependent care responsibilities or concerns. These dependent care programs fall into six major categories: informational programs, resource-and-referral programs, counseling and supportive services, financial assistance, direct caregiving services, and flexible personnel policies. Further information on each of these programs is readily available from published resource materials (see, for example, AARP, 1987; Burud, Aschbacher, & McCroskey, 1984; Burud & Ransom, 1990; Fernandez, 1986; Scharlach, Sobel, & Roberts, 1991; Wagner, Creedon, Sasala, & Neal, 1989).

Informational Programs

Many companies provide a variety of informational programs, including parent-education seminars, brown-bag discussion groups, caregiver fairs, newsletters, videos, and other materials on child care and elder care. These programs, often developed by occupational social workers, are among the most inexpensive and least complicated dependent care efforts. Moreover, they often are a first step that helps employers assess the need for other services while demonstrating concern for employees who must balance work and family needs.

Although the difficulties of working parents have received a great deal of attention during the past decade, the conflicts experienced by employees who are caring for elderly dependents have only recently received public attention. Therefore, informational programs on elder care are especially important because they encourage employees to share their problems and concerns; identify community resources; and provide specific information on dependent needs, resources, and financing. For example, Travelers

Companies (1985) initiated a comprehensive informational program for its caregiving employees, including caregiving fairs, lunchtime seminars, and videotaped information about providing elder care. AARP (1987) developed a Caregivers in the Workplace Program kit, which includes a variety of informational materials that are useful for social workers who are interested in implementing informational programs for employees with elder care responsibilities or concerns.

Resource-and-Referral Programs

Because it is so difficult to find adequate (let alone, high-quality) child care and elder care at an affordable price in a convenient location, referral services have become essential for families with young children or disabled elderly members. With regard to child care, about 300 community-based resource and referral agencies around the country are funded by governmental and charitable funds. About 1,000 companies support and benefit from these community resources by contracting for enhanced services for their employees; these special services include on-site counseling, access to a child care hot line at the work site, and follow-up to ensure that child care has been found.

Area Agencies on Aging in more than 650 communities offer limited resource-and-referral information on local services for elderly people. However, efforts to provide referrals for elder care services are complicated by the fact that 25 percent of the employees live at a distance from the elderly persons for whom they are caring. Moreover, persons who seek referrals may not know what services are available or which specific services are apt to be helpful in their particular situation. As a result, a growing number of employers contract with social service organizations or private elder care specialists for elder care resource-and-referral services.

The most notable example of a single contractor coordinating both child- and elder care services is the resource-and-referral program created by IBM to serve its employees and retirees nationwide. IBM contracts with Work/Family Directions, a private company whose elder care division is directed by a social worker, for its child care and elder care consultation-and-referral services. IBM's program links employees with existing community resource-and-referral agencies, provides seed money for needed services in communities where they were lacking, and has provided computer equipment to track referral resources. At least 35 other national corporations have followed IBM's lead and now contract for services for their employees from the same network (Friedman, 1990). In addition, the Communications Workers of America, the International Brotherhood of Electrical Workers, and a number of other labor unions have begun to include such resource-and-referral services in their contract negotiations.

Counseling and Support

Counseling and support services for employees with personal or family problems are usually offered through employee assistance programs (EAPs). Unfortunately, many occupational social workers and other professional EAP counselors have had little professional training in the area of child care or elder care. A survey of New York EAP professionals, for example, found that less than one-fourth had ever attended a seminar or training program on elder care (Brice & Alegre, 1989). Because of the technical nature of dependent care, some companies—such as Hallmark and Marriott—contract with specialists to provide resource counseling for elder care problems, and others—such as Transamerica—have developed multifaceted on-site child care support-and-counseling services. In addition, some labor unions routinely provide counseling-and-support services to members with personal or family problems (Molloy & Burmeister, 1989).

Financial Assistance

Although about 50 companies offer partial subsidization for the child care of the parents' choice or access to reduced-price child care programs that they support, most of the 2,000 companies that offer financial assistance do so through flexible benefits plans (Friedman, 1990). Flexible benefits plans give employees access to before-tax wages to support the cost of dependent care, and some also include employers' contributions to augment employees' funds. Dependent Care Assistance Plans (DCAPs), authorized under Section 129 of the Internal Revenue Code, allow companies to set up dependent care accounts with before-tax dollars to be used for dependent care expenses, including both child and elder care.

Dependent care is exorbitant, averaging $2,500 to $3,500 per year for child care in metropolitan areas (Hill-Scott & Shimek, 1989) and $20,000 to $30,000 per year for long-term care for elderly persons. Thus, financial assistance programs are especially important for low-income and single persons. Some employers, such as Polaroid and the Ford Foundation, developed reimbursement programs for employees with low family incomes in the early 1970s (Burud et al., 1984). Some service businesses, such as fast-food companies and hospitals, which have particular difficulty recruiting employees, offer financial assistance to offset part of the cost of child care.

Direct Child Care and Elder Care Services

Although on-site or near-site child care centers are the most familiar form of employer-supported child care, they are not the most common; only 1,000 of the 4,100 employer-supported child care programs identified by the

Conference Board in 1989 were center programs; 50 other employer-supported direct service programs included family day care, care for school-age children, and care for sick children (Friedman, 1990). Unions have sometimes been a potent force in negotiating for child care centers as part of employees' benefit packages.

Employer-supported child care centers have been around for a long time—the first was established during the Civil War—but employer-supported elder care centers are a recent development. In one ground-breaking cooperative project known to the authors, the National Association of Area Agencies on Aging and Wang Laboratories provided services to working caregivers to prevent the premature institutionalization of the employees' elderly dependents. The demonstration project included support for an adult day care center where Wang employees could leave their elderly relatives during work hours.

The potential benefits of employer-supported intergenerational care have been observed in child care centers for the children of employees at nursing homes, such as that established at the Boise Valley (Idaho) Sunset Nursing Home in 1978 (Burud et al., 1984). The Stride Rite Children's Center in Boston, in collaboration with Lesley College and Somerville-Cambridge Elder Services, also established an employer-supported intergenerational child and elder care center to supplement its child care program begun in 1971.

Flexible Personnel Policies

Flexible work schedules and flexible leave policies allow many employees to meet the needs of their dependents without neglecting their job responsibilities. Part-time work has been a desirable option for women with young children or other family responsibilities for many years; however, if part-time jobs do not offer benefits, they may not be viable options for many workers.

Flexible work hours are becoming increasingly prevalent; 50 percent of the large companies surveyed by the Conference Board in 1987 reported that they offer flextime (Christensen, 1987). Surveys show that employees invariably desire opportunities for such flexibility. Moreover, flextime consistently has been found to reduce job turnover and enhance employees' morale (Golembiewski & Proehl, 1980).

Even before the passage of the 1993 Family Leave bill, many companies had flexible-leave policies, which give workers the option to use leave for other personal reasons, such as caregiving. Having personal leave or release time available for emergencies, when child care arrangements fall apart or relatives are ill or for planned visits to physicians, school conferences, or the like, can be helpful to employees with complicated family schedules. Labor unions are playing an increasingly important role in advocating such options in negotiations over new collective bargaining agreements.

Developing Integrative Solutions

Companies use many different administrative options to structure dependent care programs. Some employers may find it most effective to maintain separate child care programs, elder care programs, and EAPs, whereas other employers may want to consider overall dependent care programs that include specialists in both child care and elder care in coordination with EAP services. Although each field clearly requires special knowledge, there also are a number of similarities in the design, management, and evaluation of programs across services, so that combined administration may be a more efficient use of a company's resources.

The Bottom Line: From Whose Point of View?

Although it can be difficult to evaluate the effects of dependent care programs on employees' productivity and their families' well-being, it is obviously important that program managers regularly collect and assess data on programs and costs to document the effects of programs and to justify the costs. Ransom, Aschbacher, and Burud's (1989) study of the benefits of on-site child care centers, for example, demonstrated positive effects and estimated cost savings of $138,000 to $232,000 during the first year of operation for the Union Bank Center in Monterey Park, California; savings were due to reduced absenteeism and turnover, as well as to improved publicity. Positive outcomes were seen in all areas studied—retaining employees; reducing absenteeism, tardiness, and maternity leave time; recruiting new employees; improving morale and work performance; and providing favorable publicity.

Opportunities for Partnerships

Employees' elder care and child care problems result, in large part, from society's failure to provide adequate community support services for families. Therefore, employers alone cannot expect to meet all their employees' dependent care needs. Rather, employers need to collaborate with governmental agencies, community-based service providers, and advocacy groups to identify gaps in local systems of care, to develop new programs, and to enhance employees' access to needed services. Using a systems perspective, social workers can understand the larger service delivery and policy issues that provide a context for employees' dependent care concerns, and they may thus be best able to identify and develop integrative solutions to employees' dependent care problems (Anastas et al., 1990).

Partnerships that link employers with community agencies and organizations can help to ensure the maximum use of scarce service dollars and the maximum benefits for workers and their families. The following are a few examples of creative partnerships for developing integrative solutions:

- In the early 1980s, two California foundations—Levi Strauss and Hewlett-Packard—jointly funded the start-up of the San Juan Bautista Child Development Center's program for the care of sick children whose parents worked in the Silicon Valley area. The City of San Jose also gave a block grant to support the program, which offered a "sick bay" or "get-well room" in a large child care center (Burud et al., 1984).

- In 1988, American Express, Phillip Morris, and J. P. Morgan Bank helped sponsor the Partnership for Eldercare, enabling employees at participating companies to receive information on elder care and consultation services from a local public agency. Similar public-private ventures have been initiated in Los Angeles and a number of other communities, with social workers often taking the lead in developing the partnerships and providing the services.

- In 1989, the Washington Business Group on Health (WBGH) helped develop coalitions on elder care between employers and community agencies in Boston, Hartford, Cleveland, and Mississippi. The project, which included surveys of employees, lunchtime seminars, on-site caregiver fairs, individual consultation, a resource guide, and an Eldercare Guide for Benefit Managers, was supported by grants from the Robert Wood Johnson Foundation and the U.S. Administration on Aging.

Such coalitions or partnerships would be especially valuable for small and medium-sized companies that may not have sufficient caregiving employees to justify company-run programs. And the importance of providing such dependent care programs may actually be greater in smaller companies, where most American workers are employed and where the impact on a few employees who experience caregiving difficulties can be significant.

It is also important for employers to invest directly in the development of needed community services; sometimes the most effective answer to an employer's dependent care problem is to improve the whole community's dependent care services. Without the network of health and social service programs already in place in each community and supported by governmental and charitable funds, for example, employees would have an even greater need for social and health services. In the 1980s, there were a number of innovative corporate attempts to assist communities to develop programs that were specifically designed to meet dependent care needs. For example, IBM created a $25 million Community Resource Development Fund to provide seed money to promote the development of dependent care services in communities that do not have them. AT&T, in its contract negotiations with the Communication Workers of America and the International Brotherhood of Electrical Workers, created a similar fund. Southwestern Bell Telephone Company established an audiovisual program to assist communities to develop elder care programs; heighten awareness about caregiving; and offer practical advice to professionals, community organizations, and employers (Cohen, 1985).

Implications for Occupational Social Work

Businesses' interest in providing dependent care services for individual employees and in improving community social programs (to prepare and sustain a productive work force) has increased greatly during the past decade, paralleling cuts in programs and diminished public resources for social and health services. Employer-supported dependent care programs are becoming an increasingly important piece of the complex system of interrelated services provided in each community by governmental, not-for-profit, and proprietary service providers. Business and community leaders are realizing that they cannot improve the economic bottom line without working together to ensure adequate services for employees who need assistance. Yet, corporate human resource managers and community social service providers often have different goals and seldom have the opportunity to define a common agenda or to develop integrated solutions.

Occupational social workers can play an important role in bridging this gap, often by helping businesses identify leaders in the service delivery system in each community who have the ideas, energy, and know-how to develop innovative local partnerships (Gibeau & Anastas, 1989).

There is also a growing need for occupational social workers who can help design, implement, and evaluate employer-supported dependent care programs, while assisting employers to enhance the community service infrastructure. As more employers realize the need for such services, investigate program options, and establish dependent care programs, this field of practice will present increasing opportunities for occupational social work practice.

Preparation for work in the area of dependent care, however, requires the development of specialized knowledge that is not included in the curricula of most schools of social work. For example, the majority of occupational social workers have little knowledge of the basic disorders of aging, the typical difficulties involved in caring for disabled elderly persons, or the kinds of elder- and child care services available in their communities (Brice & Alegre, 1989). Consequently, schools of social work, especially those with occupational social work sequences, will need to include more content on child- and elder care issues, as well as education for working effectively across traditional disciplinary boundaries. Moreover, social workers who are interested in serving employees with dependent care responsibilities and concerns will continue to require supplemental specialized training.

Conclusion

As this chapter has indicated, child- and elder care issues in a changing work force have many similar implications for occupational social work. Child care and elder care share commonalities with regard to the problems experienced by affected employees; the services needed; and the lack of a coherent, coordinated, family-centered service delivery system. The impact on an employer, moreover, is much the same whether employees are absent or distracted over their concern for young children, disabled elderly relatives, or any other loved ones who require assistance because of their age or disability. Therefore, the coordination and integration of child care and elder care programs, including the development of intergenerational efforts, may be particularly important.

Although neither employers, the government, nor community-based service organizations can meet the challenges alone, collaboration can leverage the power of all to help more families become self-sufficient and productive. Occupational social workers have the opportunity to provide leadership in this movement by virtue of their generic approach to service delivery, their broad range of skills and knowledge, and their orientation to multidisciplinary work. Building programs that help families care for their children and elderly relatives, help employees keep their jobs, and help employers retain a productive work force is an essential and rewarding enterprise that calls for social workers' expertise.

References

American Association of Retired Persons. (1987). *Caregivers in the work place program kit.* Washington, DC: Author.
American Association of Retired Persons. (1991). *A profile of older Americans: 1991.* Washington, DC: Author.

Anastas, J. W., Gibeau, J. L., & Larson, P. J. (1990). Working families and eldercare: A national perspective in an aging America. *Social Work, 35*, 405–411.

Bianchi, S. M. (1990). America's children: Mixed prospects. *Population Bulletin* (Population Reference Bureau), *45*(1), 20–30.

Brice, G. C., & Alegre, M. R. (1989, July–August). Eldercare as an EAP concern. *EAP Digest*, 31–34.

Brody, E. M., Kleban, M. H., Johnsen, P. T., Hoffman, C., & Schoonover, C. B. (1987). Work status and parent care: A comparison of four groups of women. *The Gerontologist, 27*, 201–208.

Burden, D. S., & Googins, B. K. (1987). *Balancing job and home life study.* Boston: Boston University School of Social Work.

Burud, S. L., Aschbacher, P. R., & McCroskey, J. (1984). *Employer supported child care: Investing in human resources* (report of the National Employer Supported Child Care Project). Dover, MA: Auburn House.

Burud, S., & Ransom, C. (1990). *Directory of corporate child care assistance programs.* Pasadena, CA: Burud & Associates.

Center for the Study of Social Policy. (1993). *Kids count data book: Profiles of child well-being.* Washington, DC: Author.

Christensen, K. E. (1987). *Flexible staffing and scheduling.* New York: The Conference Board.

Cohen, E. W. (1985, November–December). Companies help employees cope with aging parents. *EAP Digest.*

Committee for Economic Development. (1990). *An America that works: The life cycle approach to a competitive work force.* New York: Author.

Creedon, M. A. (1987). *Issues for an aging America: Employees and eldercare.* Bridgeport, CT: University of Bridgeport Center for the Study of Aging.

Crouter, A. C. (1984). Spillover from family to work: The neglected side of the work–family interface. *Human Relations, 37*, 425–442.

Emlen, A., & Koren, P. (1984). *Hard to find and difficult to manage: The effects of child care on the workplace.* Portland, OR: Regional Research Institute for Human Services, Portland State University.

Emlen, A. C., Koren, P. E., & Louise, D. (1988). *Child and elder care: Final report of an employee survey at the Sisters of Providence.* Portland, OR: Regional Research Institute for Human Services, Portland State University.

Fernandez, J. P. (1986). *Child care and corporate productivity.* Lexington, MA: Lexington Books.

Foster, C. D., Siegel, M. A., & Jacobs, N. R. (Eds.). (1988). *Women's changing roles.* Wylie, TX: Information Aids.

Friedman, D. (1986). Child care for employees' kids. *Harvard Business Review, 64*, 28–34.

Friedman, D. (1990). Corporate responses to family needs. In D. G. Unger & M. B. Sussman (Eds.), *Families in community settings: Interdisciplinary perspectives* (pp. 77–98). New York: Haworth Press.

Galinsky, E. (1988). *The impact of child care problems on parents on the job and at home.* (Paper prepared for Child Care Action Campaign, New York; available from Family and Work Institute, 330 Seventh Avenue, New York, NY 10001).

George, L. K., & Gwyther, L. P. (1986). Caregiver well-being: A multidimensional examination of family caregivers of demented adults. *The Gerontologist, 26,* 253–260.

Gibeau, J. L., & Anastas, J. W. (1989). Breadwinners and caregivers: Interviews with working women. *Journal of Gerontological Social Work, 14*(1–2), 19–40.

Golembiewski, R. T., & Proehl, C. W. (1980). Public sector application of flexible work hours: A review of available experience. *Public Administration Review, 40,* 72–85.

Green, G. P., & Epstein, R. K. (Eds.). (1988). *Employment and earnings, vol. 35(2).* Washington, DC: U.S. Department of Labor, Bureau of Labor Statistics.

Hill-Scott, K., & Shimek, P. (1989). *Analysis of child care in the private sector.* Los Angeles: Crystal Stairs.

Hofferth, S. L., & Phillips, D. A. (1987). Child care in the United States, 1970 to 1995. *Journal of Marriage and the Family, 49,* 559–571.

Kane, R., & Kane, R. (1987). *Long-term care: Principles, programs and policies.* New York: Springer.

Kola, L., & Dunkle, R. (1988). Eldercare in the workforce. *Social Casework, 69,* 569–574.

Molloy, D., & Burmeister, L. (1989). Social workers in union-based programs. *Employee Assistance Quarterly, 5*(1), 37–51.

Rabins, P., Mace, N., & Lucas, M. J. (1982). The impact of dementia on the family. *Journal of the American Medical Association, 248,* 333–335.

Ransom, C., Aschbacher, P., & Burud, S. (1989). The return in the child-care investment. *Personnel Administrator, 34,* 54–58.

Scharlach, A., & Boyd, S. (1989). Caregiving and employment: Results of an employee survey. *The Gerontologist, 29,* 382–387.

Scharlach, A., Lowe, B., & Schneider, E. (1990). *Elder care and the work force: Blueprint for action.* Lexington, MA: Lexington Books.

Scharlach, A., Sobel, E., & Roberts, R. (1991). Employment and caregiver strain: An integrative model. *The Gerontologist, 31,* 778–787.

Stone, R. S., Cafferata, G. L., & Sangl, J. (1987). Caregivers of the frail elderly: A national profile. *The Gerontologist, 27,* 616–626.

Stone, R. S., & Kemper, P. (1989). Spouses and children of disabled elders: How large a constituency for long-term care reform? *Milbank Quarterly, 67,* 485–506.

Travelers Companies. (1985). *The Travelers employee caregiver survey.* Hartford, CT: Author.

True, N. B., & Wineman, J. (1989). Caregiving and retirement planning: A new partnership. *Compensation and Benefits Management, 5,* 283–286.

U.S. House of Representatives, Select Committee on Children, Youth, and Families. (1988). *Double duty: Caring for children and the elderly.* Washington, DC: U.S. Government Printing Office.

U.S. Senate, Special Committee on Aging, in conjunction with the American Association of Retired Persons, the Federal Council on the Aging, and the Administration on Aging. (1985–86). *Aging America: Trends and projections.* Washington, DC: U.S. Government Printing Office.

Wagner, D., Creedon, M., Sasala, J., & Neal, M. (1989). *Employees and eldercare: Designing effective responses for the workplace.* Bridgeport, CT: University of Bridgeport Center for the Study of Aging.

Watkins, S. C., Menken, J. A., & Bongaarts, J. (1987). Demographic foundations of family change. *American Sociological Review, 52,* 346–358.

PART 3

DIRECT SERVICES

Introduction to Part 3

Occupational social work, like all fields of social work practice, has derived its identity and boundaries primarily from the direct services that practitioners provide. Anchored by its focus (on work) to a population in need (of workers) and ultimately by its unique auspices (work organizations), this practice domain has been defined by the clinical and organizational expertise of the social workers who have come to inhabit its terrain. Analogs can be drawn to other host settings in which social workers practice; however, it can be argued that no other setting requires the practice ingenuity that this one does because others (such as schools and hospitals) share the norms and values of a human service tradition. As the authors of the chapters in Part 3 show, creativity and adaptation become essential skills.

In Chapter 10, Florence Wexler Vigilante presents just such a creative conceptualization for occupational practice. Viewed as a stress–vulnerability–coping matrix, her clinical paradigm fits well into a constructivist framework. The world of work is presented as a social system, with both stress and reward, that meets more of one's needs than wages and benefits alone can fulfill. Work is central to adult identity, for example, and practitioners who serve working people must appreciate this reality. Rational or scientific models of clinical inquiry may miss this fact in their quest for a "correct" intervention. Truth, we are reminded, is influenced less by fact than by perception.

The environment becomes a key variable and the client's "story" provides a metaphor for the client's reality. This is a particularly useful conceptualization for assessment and intervention in work settings, where social life and work life may be blended. How work and family stress affect vulnerability, to which clients marshal their coping devices, tells a lot in the assessment process, if social workers will listen. This analysis provides the framework for a partnership—what others may term a therapeutic alliance—that has strength, durability, and authenticity. Moreover, the occupational social worker's role as both a "therapist" and a "co-worker" provides the context for an ecologically shared experience that is virtually impossible to achieve in traditional settings. Through case illustrations, Vigilante puts this constructivist conceptualization to the test, and the product is a synthesis of theory and practice. She concludes that "work is probably the most important indicator of the level of human functioning . . . understanding work in the helping process calls for a comprehensive, humanistic practice model, sensitive to the dynamics of the workplace and the potential productivity of a highly interactive worker–client engagement using narrative and experiential techniques."

Maria DeOca Corwin follows with a solution-focused counseling model in Chapter 11 that is very much in sync with Vigilante's practice propositions. In the world of work, "time is money." The urgency of a referral to an employee assistance program (EAP) is underscored by a supervisor's statement to an occupational social worker: "I don't care what you do or how you do it, but I want her back at work tomorrow—we've got deadlines to meet and she's essential."

Treatment is expensive, both in paying the provider and in "subsidizing" time away from work, hence ambulatory, time-limited, solution-focused practice approaches are valued. Corwin argues that the brief treatment model she presents is not a clinical compromise or an adaptation to limits imposed by declining resources. Rather, solution-focused treatment is a model of choice in work settings. "Such structured, time-limited interventions have been found to be not only cost-effective," she notes, "but equally as efficient as long-term or open-ended treatment for problems in living." Even single-session therapy has been shown to be effective, as Corwin illustrates in a case example. Focused on clients' strengths and building on a concept of clients' competence, this approach dwells less on the past than on the present.

Pragmatism and parsimony are central tenets of this clinical design. Many of the principles of task-centered treatment, cognitive therapy, and even behavioral techniques are brought to bear in the assessment and intervention process. Time limits are seen as strengthening the worker–client alliance, not as a barrier or a problem. Moreover, enhancing a client's social functioning "in love and in work" is often viewed as an optimal (not just a satisfactory) solution.

This metamodel serves as an excellent introduction to the theory and practice of time-limited work. Although it is potentially appropriate in all settings, this model is uncommonly useful, Corwin notes, when services are provided under the auspices of the world of work, where *time* is the currency of the realm.

In Chapter 12, Meredith Hanson continues the practice focus, but on a specific population: substance abusers. Regardless of the still-popular notion of the alcoholic as a "Bowery bum" or the addict as "street thief," the author reminds us that the majority of alcohol and drug abusers are in the work force. Astonishingly, a national survey found that substance abuse was perceived as the second most serious problem facing industry—behind the national debt. And for employers and unions that were in "organizational denial," mounting costs and the 1988 federal Drug Free Workplace Act pushed them to pay attention to a long-standing problem.

Although he embraces most of the elements of the disease model, Hanson places this conceptualization within a broader biopsychosocial framework that he believes better reflects the contextual complexity of the problem. For example, he notes that although there may be a biological predisposition, the reason why certain workers become alcoholics and others do not requires a more powerful paradigm than the disease model permits.

Through practice illustrations, Hanson proceeds to show how to interview substance-abusing workers, to motivate them to seek help, and to create a treatment alliance. Once such a partnership is formed, triage decisions can be reached, and referral to appropriate clinics, providers, and self-help groups can be made. Often overlooked in the substance abuse literature, Hanson states, is the additional responsibility of the occupational social worker to ensure the smooth reintegration of such recovering workers back into the workplace so they will not relapse. This professional use of self requires a sophisticated systems approach, for which social workers are known, and builds on the person-in-environment focus and ecological perspective that are central components of clinical social work training. A detailed case presentation makes these program and practice issues come alive.

With the enforcement in 1992 of the landmark Americans with Disabilities Act of 1990, nothing could be more timely than Chapter 13, by Sheila H. Akabas and Lauren B. Gates. Spanning age, race, class, gender, and sexual orientation, disability is a common denominator that places a whole sub-population in the world of work at risk because they are disabled or have disabled children.

The authors draw their conclusions and recommendations, in part, from a national survey of 1,000 EAPs and member assistance programs (MAPs). They found little activity taking place in the arena of disability programs or policy initiatives at these key workplace outposts, despite the opportunities. An additional study confirmed, however, that when early identification and intervention were implemented through health and benefit programs in the workplace, such proactive disability management programs saved money and productive lives.

Akabas and Gates outline the process of initiating such a program. Beginning with a needs assessment, a coordinating committee then should be formed to help translate these needs into policies and procedures. Early case finding and outreach will bring in clients whose need for services and advocacy (and subsequent interventions) will be monitored through a case management design. Moving from "case to cause," the authors note that the discovery of collective unmet needs may then argue for accommodations to or changes in work systems—skills that are equally congenial with social workers' expertise.

Disability management can be conceptualized fundamentally as protecting workers' jobs, which is the central function of trade unions. Therefore, Akabas and Gates note that opportunities are present for unions to build these service and advocacy initiatives into their MAPs, and later into the funded benefit provisions of their collective bargaining agreement.

Akabas and Gates conclude that "assuming a responsible role in managing disability in the workplace is compatible with the values of social work and the knowledge and skill bases of the profession. The outcome of such activities will enhance the well-being of individuals, the productivity and profitability of the American workplace, and the contribution of the social work profession to the world of work. It is rare for a profession to be offered such a win-win opportunity."

Cynthia Stuen and Barbara Drahus Worden speak to the needs of another vulnerable population in the world of work—older workers. With the demographic fact that people are living longer comes the life-cycle reality that 65 may no longer be a suitable retirement age, and because pensions and savings are rarely sufficient to support a long period of nonworking (such as in retirement), continued participation in the work force may become more a necessity than an option. Fortuitously, the needs of such aging persons are matched by a growing shortage of skilled and experienced workers, which may create a symbiotic relationship between the needs of employers and older workers. Therefore, Stuen and Worden point up the inexorable fact that employers and trade unions will need to learn how to work with and serve older workers and will look to occupational social workers for guidance on programs and policies in this regard. Like disability and substance abuse, discussed in previous chapters, aging (and hence older workers) is a societal reality from which the workplace is neither protected nor immune.

The authors review the relevant laws, regulations, and entitlements specifically for older workers, putting occupational social work intervention in a policy perspective. They also review the findings of two major national opinion polls by the American Association of Retired Persons that reflect a mix of negative and positive attitudes by employers toward older workers. They conclude that older workers' need for continued employment and employers' need for reliable and mature workers may dictate pragmatic outcomes, even solutions. However, the frequent need to retrain older workers; the double-jeopardy of bias against older women and older persons of color; and the quiet but pervasive ageism, which tends to be even stronger in the workplace than in society at large, have created the need for occupational social workers to initiate innovative programs, policies, and services. Through case examples, Stuen and Worden present some cost-effective solutions that call on the full range and depth of social workers' professional expertise.

Recognizing that continued income is not the only motivation for working, the authors also look at volunteer (unpaid) work as an option for older adults. They conclude (as do many authors in this book) that the clinical or organizational demands here are congruent with an occupational social worker's organizational mandate and professional preparation.

"The goal should be a mutually beneficial environment for the older worker and employer," they note, "in light of the increasing number of and longevity among older adults and the workplace's need for trained, dependable, and flexible workers." They conclude with the conceptualization of a gerontological occupational social work subspecialization, well suited to the emerging needs of both labor and management settings. These social workers would be responsible for responding to issues of elder care among younger workers, as well as preretirement counseling, postretirement services, and retraining programs for the reentry of older workers into the workplace.

Coming full cycle in this section on direct services, Chapter 15, by Jesse J. Harris, takes a close look at the U.S. military as employer and the concept of social workers who practice in the military as being occupational social workers. Harris, who served as the most senior social worker in the American armed forces, notes that the military is an employer not just of armed combatants, but of cooks and clerks, teachers and transport workers. Indeed, the U.S. Department of Defense is one of the largest employing organizations in the country.

Like other employers, the military hires staff to perform its social service functions, including officers in its Medical Service Corps who act like EAP and human resources staff do in civilian settings. Staffing mental health clinics, family and child support centers, alcohol rehabilitation programs, race relations training units, social service departments of military hospitals, correctional facilities, and community advocacy projects, professional social workers in these settings mirror the functions of their civilian counterparts. Such occupational practitioners deal with absenteeism, alcoholism, mental illness, and work–family issues, often complicated by the danger of their clients' work and forced separation from their families.

Placing these current program and policy needs in a historical perspective, Harris underscores the reality of stress and separation as central issues for these workers in uniform and their families. Moreover, with the rapid increase of women in the armed services, new issues have emerged from which these settings had been largely protected in the past, including sexual harassment and child care. In addition, special programs, such as relocation assistance, trauma counseling, consumer awareness, and family support services, have become priorities in these settings.

Harris concludes that social work in the military offers a superb opportunity for occupational practice, often overshadowed by traditional civilian settings, but providing equally good career opportunities. In many ways, he notes, the military subculture is a hospitable environment for the quintessential occupational social work functions that have been outlined in the different chapters of this book.

CHAPTER 10

Work

ITS USE IN ASSESSMENT AND INTERVENTION WITH CLIENTS IN THE WORKPLACE

Florence Wexler Vigilante

Work has a greater effect than any other technique of living in the direction of binding the individual more closely to reality.

—Sigmund Freud
Civilization and Its Discontents

Providing employee assistance in the workplace includes assessment and intervention processes that are well known to social workers in direct practice. As in all social work settings, the processes rest on the application of basic principles, values, and techniques of practice modified by the setting. The work setting offers some interesting challenges for practice that demand adaptations of established practice models.

The employee assistance program (EAP) discussed here is located in a large urban university with institutional supports from within the university and outside community. The practice uses a stress–vulnerability–coping focus within a constructivist framework (Anderson & Goolishian, 1988; Hoffman, 1990; White & Epston, 1990). This perspective is representative of the emergence of new modes of inquiry in the human sciences in response to understanding the increasing complexities of the current human condition. To provide a background for this model, this chapter presents a brief overview of the sociology and the meaning of work. This overview is followed by a review of traditional perspectives of assessment and intervention, the constructivist stress–vulnerability–coping model, and illustrations of this model in the EAP.

Sociology of Work

Work is significant in all aspects of assessment and intervention because it is a key aspect of personal functioning (Akabas & Kurzman, 1982) and a major influence on all family members (Germain, 1991). We often define ourselves and each other in terms of the work we do, the status of that work, and how well we do it. Among our roles as spouse, partner, parent, child, grandparent, community member, volunteer, and friend, none defines our place in the world as does work.

The demographics of the work force are constantly changing. There are more women, more single parents, more people of color and of diverse cultural backgrounds, more gay and lesbian people (some who are "out" and some who are not), and more persons with disabilities. The work environment contains cultural, class, and psychological nuances that may be alternately threatening or supportive to employees. The experiences of the mix of young and old, various ethnic and racial groups, and part-time and full-time employees add to the social experiences of individuals and families. All these experiences may simultaneously stimulate interpersonal and social problems, widely prevalent in modern society, as different personal views and experiences are brought together in pluralistic environments (Kurzman, 1988).

The workplace is a complex social milieu. There are formal and informal structures, rules, and decision-making processes. There are groups (formal and natural), subgroups, cliques, and unions. There is stress of all kinds, not the least of which is the ever-present fear of losing one's job. Between the employer and employee, attitudes and values about authority, the work ethic, how the work is done, use of time, privacy, and rewards and punishment may be compatible or conflictual. Physical and emotional proximity among workers, such as eating lunch or having coffee in groups, recreation during and after work, and the nature of the interactions among employees and with each other's families, create collegial relationships that are part of the norms and values of organizational life. These interactions and relationships may be personal experiences of inclusion or exclusion (Vigilante, 1982).

Meaning of Work

An examination of a person's reactions to assigned work tasks reveals idiosyncratic responses. For example, tasks that have predictable outcomes and organized and repetitive processes may be perceived by one employee as comfortable and contributory and by another, as the epitome of boredom; this second employee may consider unpredictable demands, unpredictable outcomes, and crises to be creative and challenging. Aspects of the setting, such as isolation, the lack of privacy, high expectations of socialization, repeated work crises, and authoritarian demands, may be more comfortable or less comfortable to different employees. Understanding work as it creates stress or support for individual employees and their families is part of a dynamic assessment (Vigilante, 1982).

Stress may be precipitated by unintentional discrimination. For example, heart disease and cancer, both increasingly "normative" conditions, are often responded to sympathetically, but subtle messages about the loss of competence may be delivered simultaneously (Vigilante, 1988); that is, employers and co-workers may make few demands and, in effect, reinforce normal temporary depression and withdrawal. Workers who are HIV-positive experience many stressful dilemmas (Weitz, 1991). If their condition is revealed, they may be ostracized. If it is not revealed, they risk not receiving appropriate benefits, entitlements, and support. In both cases, companions and families of employees with health problems attempt to cope with a range of fears while struggling to adjust to temporary or permanent restrictions on life.

Women experience special stresses in the workplace (Belle, 1982). Still socialized to be dependent, many have difficulty asserting their abilities and entitlements or even claiming credit for their work (Miller, 1991). According to Kaplan (1991), women are at risk of depression when the demands of their jobs require them to be assertive. Stiver (1991) observed that, unlike men, women rarely come into treatment for work problems; typically, they request help with personal relationships, although as their treatment progresses, work issues emerge. Helping women to become aware of work issues encourages their earlier sensitivity to problems.

Perspectives on Assessment and Intervention

Although a traditional part of the social work mission has been the restoration and maintenance of social functioning, it is startling that, until recently, work was referred to in the practice literature only peripherally (see, for example, Hamilton, 1953). The modifications of the workplace profile during the current era of social transition, including a reemphasis on functioning as a goal, have increased the significance of the relevance of work. Current writers, including Germain (1991); Holder and Anderson (1989); and Silverman, Simon, and Woodrow (1991) now discuss the significant effects of work on families, social growth, and job loss. Personality factors, individual adjustment, family interactions, relationships of couples, friendships, and social phenomena (such as class, race, and sexual orientation) have variously occupied the central focus of assessments of behavior. The author's examination of the intake sheets of 15 social service agencies revealed that employment data were limited to two items: the employers' names and the employees' income. Work, a central organizing factor in individual and family life, is usually viewed simplistically as the determinant of economic and social status. The exclusion of the work experience, in its fuller meaning, suggests a vast unused source of data and resources that may be helpful in the intervention process.

Attention can now be turned to assessment and intervention from a work-oriented perspective. Assessment, common to all professional practice, is a dynamic process that continually takes in and discards information in an effort to order the multiplicity of ideas that are necessary to approach an accurate description of a client's situation (Lewis, 1982). Although many theoretical perspectives that social workers use are associated with a variety of treatment models, there continues to be a lack of clarity about the assessment process. Turner (1986) identified 17 theoretical perspectives, and Dorfman (1988) identified 12. Mailick (1991) raised central questions about assessment that include its link to theory, the method of intervention, the psychosocial concept, the agency's function, the client's problem, professional values, and the personal values of the client and the worker, among others.

Richmond (1917) established the principle that assessment requires the collection of quantities of social data that will eventually reveal an objective understanding of behavior. She was undoubtedly influenced by scientific thinking, the dominant mode of inquiry of her time. Following Richmond, whose model of practice may be metaphorically described as sweeping enormous amounts of data across an objective, "scientific" template, many seminal thinkers have developed models of practice, culminating in a widely "eclectic" array of approaches. Each approach, in its way, deals with psychosocial phenomena, usually defined in terms of the interactive process of individuals, groups, and families with their interpersonal and their social-institutional environments (Vigilante, Lodge, Lucton, Kaplan, & Mason, 1981).

Roberts (1990) identified "person in the environment" as the central social work focus. This psychosocial phenomenon permeates a variety of practice models and practice perspectives: the person-in-situation, ecological, life model, functional, crisis, problem-solving, task-centered, social functioning, structural, unitary, family, and social learning models, among others (Bartlett, 1970; Epstein, 1988; Germain & Gitterman, 1980; Goldstein, 1981; Middleman & Goldberg, 1974; Perlman, 1957, 1970; Walters, Carter, Papp, & Silverstein, 1988). The other major principle in practice models is objectivity. Both principles have been and continue to be central to the assessment process. However, whereas the essence of the *psychosocial* phenomenon has persisted with minor changes in interpretation, the principle of *objectivity* has been subject to serious challenges by recent writers (Anderson & Goolishian,

1988; Bateson, 1972, 1979; Bruner, 1986, 1987; Hoffman, 1990; Kelly, 1983). Changes in the value of this principle are evident throughout the various phases of intervention.

Mailick (1991) discussed three major strategies for assessment:

1. Examine the broadest range of social and psychological variables using the principle of salience and the client's perception of need. Scanning a larger field of variables avoids a limited view of the client's situation (Germain & Gitterman, 1980; Mailick & Vigilante, 1987; Monkman & Allen-Meares, 1985).

2. Assume that the complexity of the client's situation requires a protocol for assessment that isolates particular behaviors. The assessment instrument breaks the process up into a series of decisions that will determine the appropriate intervention (Gambrill, 1983; Specht & Specht, 1986; Thomas, 1970).

3. Assume that systematic data gathering and classification cannot accurately reflect the complexities of human functioning. The third strategy consists of the client and worker successively framing and reframing the client's story until coherent and shared meanings are achieved. This strategy provides the perspective of this chapter.

Relevant Epistemological Issues

Constructivism, the intervention modality discussed here, is derived from major conceptual differences regarding the knowledge that informs practice. A brief discussion of these emerging differences follows.

New theoretical approaches to intellectual inquiry in the epistemologies of the human sciences and social work practice reveal a past tradition of a relatively narrow and limited approach to assessment (Hartman, 1990; Polkinghorne, 1983). Efforts to use an objective, "scientific" model of inquiry have tended to force the assessment process into a preconceived structure to fit specific practice models, which may cut off other important sources of information and creative approaches to assessment. The problem has been identified as an enduring effort in the human sciences to emulate the traditional methods of the natural sciences (Coyne, 1985; Homans, 1987; Pieper, 1990; Vigilante et al., 1991; Wallerstein, 1987). According to Toulmin (1990, p. 132):

> Until the 1970s, the history and philosophy of science were written by people with a rationalist outlook, who were interested above all in the *intellectual* aspects of natural science. When non-scientists read ethical or political implications into the results of science, that was (for them) a historical accident that threw no light on the meaning of the results . . . only in the 1980s have

scholars gone far beyond changes in the internal content of the sciences, and asked how the external context influences their choice of problems and patterns of explanation.

From another perspective, particularly relevant for social work, Janik and Toulmin (1973, pp. 228–229) stated earlier: "Subjective truth is communicable only indirectly, through fable, polemics, irony and satire. This is the only way that one can come to 'see the world aright.' The meaning of life was no more an academic question. . . . It was not, and could not, be answered by reason, since it is resolved only by the way in which one lives." Following this course of analysis, Pieper's (1990) heuristic paradigm raised the issue of alternative methods of inquiry for social work.

Constructivism

The new intellectual perspectives on the human sciences have led to *constructivism* as an appropriate theoretical fit for social work practice. Constructivism draws from theories of understanding of the human experience as a social construct, the development of knowledge as a social phenomenon, and communication as dependent on social and culturally derived perceptions (Anderson & Goolishian, 1988; Gergen, 1985; Janik & Toulmin, 1973). Meanings evolve from ongoing interactions between and among people and a flow of continually changing narratives. "The theory bypasses the fixity of the model of biologically based cognition, claiming instead that the development of concepts is a fluid process, socially derived" (Hoffman, 1990, p. 3).

Constructivist theorists believe that perspectives of human experience cannot be objective or quantifiable. Descriptions of experience are creations, rather than discoveries (Bateson, 1979). Reality is not discovered through objectivity, but is arrived at consensually through social discourse, language, and interaction (Berger & Luckman, 1966; Gergen, 1985). The belief that standing apart from the system to describe and manipulate it in a replicable manner is seen as illusionary. "Constructivism is influenced by the current thinking in physics, biology, post modern aesthetics in art and literature and the anthropological use of the narrative. Behaviors can only be mutually defined in reference to their surroundings. We live in a world not of things but of patterns of relationships, of information. Bateson's work changed us from the world of the quantifiable and the objective, which has been the bulwark of science since the 17th century" (Real, 1990, p. 258).

Laird (1989) used the "story" metaphor to depict the effort to make sense of self and other. In a constructivist epistemology, "story" is about the construction of experience. In clinical work (individual or family), the personal narrative, the life story, is usually central, as is how individual narratives fit with the family and the larger sociocultural story. The narrative is an individual's interpretation of the relationship among events over time, a way of constructing a coherent story of his or her life. "Reality" is built on the sense the client can make of his or her life experiences.

The active engagement of both the worker and the client in exploring the client's "story" is the basis of the professional relationship. Listening and engaging nonjudgmentally and respecting the client's contributions as a valid source of information occur in an ongoing dialogue. Laird (1989) suggested that the client's "story" is relevant to every level of individual, family, and group experience and to past, present, and future time. The therapeutic work involves helping the client to explore his or her own narrative while offering alternative realities until shared meanings are achieved. Ongoing discussion produces evolving meanings. This approach challenges traditional methods of taking history, that is, gathering facts separate from their personal and evolving meanings. "Facts" are also perceptions that change over time as their meanings are perceived differently.

Stress–Vulnerability–Coping

Stress-vulnerability-coping provides the focus for the application of constructivist theory in practice. The concept expands in meaning and gains increasing applicability as the profession becomes more sophisticated about unique, complex, interacting human needs and social stressors (Folkman & Lazarus, 1991; Lazarus & Folkman, 1991; Locke & Taylor, 1991). It serves as an organizing instrument for the exploration of the client's story and is compatible with the constructivist view of professional engagement. The use of stress–vulnerability–coping is not limited by an agency's function, the unit of attention, time elements, formulation, or organizational constraints. It is a way of thinking about a broad range of biological, social, cultural, psychological, historical, political, and organizational phenomena without the restraints of overclassification. Although "out of awareness" phenomena seem to link stress–vulnerability–coping to a psychodynamic perspective, this method is not tied to a single clinical approach or theoretical perspective.

Stress is any stimulus—physical, psychological, or environmental—that threatens the client (family, group, or organization) (Coelho, Hamburg, & Adams, 1974; Reiss & Oliveri, 1991; Selye, 1991). But understanding stress alone does not serve to individualize the client and, therefore, it cannot provide the basis for an assessment. Identifying and understanding stress, in conjunction with the person's unique vulnerability and potential ability to cope, enables individualization. Much of the stress people experience is out of their conscious awareness, is not clearly understood, or has been internalized or institutionalized to such an extent that it feels normal. Social pathologies, including institutional racism, sexism, or homophobia, create significant ongoing stress. Experiences, such as poverty, abuse, unemployment, neglect, family alcoholism, disability, inadequate parenting, or community neglect, leave their marks on many levels of personality development and social functioning (Chestang, 1982; Vigilante & Mailick, 1988). Much the same may be said of cohort experiences, for example, those of the Holocaust; certain political and social events; or a health trauma, such as AIDS (Germain, 1991). Negative experiences, although differentially processed, have a negative effect on self-esteem and can retard a person's capacity to cope.

Constructivism and Stress–Vulnerability–Coping

The constructivist perspective assumes a therapeutic partnership in which the client's situation is mutually framed and reframed by the worker and client until coherent meanings are achieved and understood. Dialogue between the worker and the client regarding the client's perceptions of conflictual experiences are discussed within the context of relevant sociocultural phenomena (social class and ethnic, racial, or national background, typified by rituals, myths, other patterns of behavior, and relevant descriptive metaphors). Understanding the client's use of metaphors for personal experience is critical to creating a mutually collaborative dialogue. As the client interacts with the worker, it is assumed that more and more complex and adaptive constructions of reality will occur, leading to more creative adaptations. This formulation focuses on new "ways of knowing" the construction of knowledge about the self, others, and outer reality (Anderson & Goolishian, 1988). In a vigorous sense, "psyche" and "social" are inseparable in this paradigm (Rosen, 1988).

An important task for the worker is to know how to frame questions, using the client's metaphors, to elicit the client's perceptions of his or her experience, and to understand that these perceptions will change over time as more and more complex meanings evolve. Weingarten (1992) discussed "intimate" and "nonintimate" interactions between the client and the worker. Intimate interactions occur when the worker and client cocreate meanings; nonintimate interactions occur when the worker imposes meaning on the client's productions. The cocreation of meaning implies that new meaning evolves, not just that meaning is shared. The mutual exploration of the client's situation is essential to the cocreation of meaning.

The constructivist process is especially applicable to social work in the workplace, where the complications of the dual roles of "therapist" and "coworker" (colleagues in the workplace) can be conflictual for both. The mutual search for shared meanings mitigates the client's feelings of vulnerability in the face of the worker's special "expertise," which may otherwise be experienced as isolating or belittling.

Techniques

In their work with families, Real (1990) and Tomm (1988) have suggested techniques of questioning and questions that are useful in constructivist practice. They view questions as tools that create new meanings and develop new connections. It is the worker's role to help the client transform experience into words and to raise questions that expand understanding for both the client and the worker. Real described five techniques that refer to "the use of self in multiple engagement," and Tomm identified four modes of questions that have different therapeutic intent. The following discussion describes these questions and techniques with modifications for the EAP setting.

Eliciting

In sessions with families, the worker asks for explanations of the presenting problem from all who are present. In sessions with an individual client, the worker elicits the client's perceptions and what the client believes the perceptions of relevant persons may be. This *pursuit of specificity* expands the understanding of the problem or may produce new perspectives. It is the beginning of a process of "thinking about a problem," widening the field of attention and considering alternatives. The case of Jeff may serve as an example:

> Jeff, a unit chief, was seen because of his agitation and highly critical manner with the staff. He believed that these problems were due to his wife's rejection of him. Jeff and Nora were seen jointly. They have an apartment in the city, where they both work, and a vacation house about two hours from the city. Wherever Jeff plans to be on weekends, Nora manages to arrange her schedule to be in the other place. Jeff experiences Nora's behavior as rejection. He alternately forces himself on Nora and becomes severely depressed.
>
> The presenting problem was seen by both as Nora's selfishness, hostility, and rejection of Jeff. Nora believed she was wrong, but could not help herself. Later, Jeff's drinking problem surfaced. Both Jeff and Nora came from families where alcoholism was present, but not seen as a problem. Likewise, Jeff's drinking had not been identified as a problem. It became clear that Jeff managed the workweek with minimum drinking, but was drunk from Friday afternoon through Sunday. Nora's avoidance was a response to Jeff's demanding and verbally abusive behavior. She had not associated his behavior with an alcohol problem. Nora, as her mother and sister before her, was codependent. By denying Jeff's drinking, she enabled it. After several sessions at the EAP, Nora demonstrated an increasing ability to confront Jeff with his behavior when he was drinking. Her confrontations facilitated his beginning efforts to reframe the problem from her rejection to his substance abuse.

Questions to Jeff elicited empathic responses from Nora when she was able to "hear" that Jeff's single response to all questions was fear of abandonment. "Do you think Nora avoids you on weekends?" "What do you think she's doing when she is not with you?" "What is she like with other people?" "What ideas do you have about why she doesn't want to be with you on weekends?" "What about other people; what do they think?" "How do you explain your relationship with Nora to friends and family?" "What are their responses?"

Nora's answers shocked Jeff, as he heard himself described as abusive, frightening, unclean, and uncaring. "Tell me about how you plan your weekends." "How are decisions made about where you spend them and what you do?" "How are meals planned?" "Who shops?" "Take me through 24 hours in detail." "What do you think escalated that argument?" "Would the same argument during the week have turned out differently?" This last question, repeated in different ways, was key in Jeff's gradual recognition of his substance abuse. Reframing the problem provided a new reality and new options for the couple. Instead of running away on weekends, Nora could set conditions for their being together. Jeff needed to begin treatment for his primary problem, alcoholism, and Nora needed help to interrupt her patterns of denial and avoidance. As Jeff began to understand the relationship between his drinking and his agitated behavior at work, his performance improved dramatically (Bepko & Krestan, 1985).

Probing

In this technique, the worker offers new frames of the problem, not as the expert revealing truth, but as a participant in an exploration. The purpose of not using explanations previously offered by the clients is to broaden and deepen the discussion. The guideline is "tolerable difference": The worker's frame must be different enough from preexisting descriptions to be illuminating, but not so discrepant as to be offensive (Real, 1990). In offering new frames and constructions of the problem, the worker can then respond to the client's agreement, corrections, or rejections by questioning the differences. If the clients disagree with the worker's framing, it is useful to ask how they would correct it. Disagreeing with the worker has therapeutic value because it furthers his or her ability to express negative feelings and to talk about problems and to reduce childish expectations of disapproval or expert answers. The case of Pete and Marcia is an illustration.

Pete and Marcia, parents of two children in elementary school and one in junior high school, began their sessions enraged at each other and speaking to each other only when necessary. Marcia complained about Pete's lack of sexual interest in her, her overwhelming work schedule as a professor, and Pete's lack of responsibility for household chores. Pete allowed that it was not possible to sleep with a shrew, and Marcia wept as she described how sexually "repulsive" she felt. Each projected the problem on the other.

Little empathy was evoked from Marcia in discussions about Pete's belief that Marcia's prominent family looked down on him and disapproved of his career in the theater. Likewise, Pete had little feeling about Marcia's problems managing three children and an apartment that was too small for five people, while she struggled to meet criteria for promotion. In fact, Marcia's pattern of absence from her department, except when she had teaching assignments, would clearly interfere with her promotion. Pete and Marcia focused only on their negative marital interactions. There was no yielding to another perspective. In reality, they were excellent and caring parents, admiring of each other's abilities to parent, and unusually supportive of each other's careers.

The new frame was this: As excellent parents and as positive supports to each other's work, they must surely have a good relationship. Could they explain why they "pretended" to hate each other? They responded to this probing and paradoxical frame by becoming curious about the perpetuation of their anger at each other. Marcia and Pete both came from families where belittling, repression, and humiliation were normal child-rearing practices. The prescribed intimacy of a marital relationship carried the threat that these earlier experiences would be recreated. Their anger kept them at a safe distance from each other. The stress and vulnerability that they both experienced was their out-of-awareness response to historical events.

Amplifying

Amplifying yields new material or can redirect the focus. The social worker chooses an idea, affect, theme, or behavior, and his or her concentrated attention to it evokes more response. This technique was productive in the work with Pete and Marcia. As time went on, they were civil to each other. Pete took increasing responsibility for the children and household chores, freeing Marcia to fulfill her obligations at the college. Although their time together as a couple was much more civil, they were still cautiously circling each other. Their reports that they were "getting along" because they were not arguing led the worker to amplify her reaction to their new positive relationship. Tentatively, they began to explore more alternatives for their time together as they became less threatened by their closeness.

Contextualizing

Contextualizing emphasizes the interactive nature of behavior. The focus is on the patterns that connect individuals to each other. For example, if Mother is depressed, exploration may concentrate exclusively on Mother: What precipitated the depression? How debilitating is it? Is Mother eating? Sleeping? Is medication desirable? In contextualizing the problem, the worker and client discuss who is affected by the depression. Does Mother reveal the depression to one person more than to another? Who responds most to the depression? Who responds least? What do they do about it? Who comforts her the most? Who comforts her the least? This technique was used with Janet:

Janet, a supervisor of a large administrative staff, was efficient and valued by her employer. Yet, her staff found her to be rigid, intolerant, and unsympathetic. She came to the EAP for help in managing an unappreciative staff, assuming that she would learn how to control them better. When the social worker could not evoke an empathic response in Janet to the staff's needs or to an exploration of Janet's motivation, she contextualized the problem by asking who would understand Janet's efficiency and who would be critical of it. Further contextualizing questions led Janet to recall her father's relentless criticism of her brothers and her mother. She concluded that it was hard to feel warm toward "tyrants." With great difficulty, Janet began to explore how her expectations of herself and others provided little room for warmth in her relationships. She was surprised to discover that empathy did not subvert efficiency.

Matching

In contrast to probing, in which new perspectives are offered, in matching, the worker does not offer new views, but reflects back what the client has said, using the client's metaphors. The client is free to process what the worker offers, agreeing, disagreeing, or modifying it. "Observing" the situation expressed by another allows the client to perceive it differently. A new perception can break a deadlock in treatment, as occurred with Sally and Josh:

Sally and Josh both work in universities in a large city. Sally reported that Josh precipitated arguments for no reason that she could discern and that they ended up not speaking to each other for days after these conflicts. She wasn't sure what they argued about. Each argument was viewed as unique. It became clear that these arguments occurred when the couple was about to entertain, on holidays, or at any event shared with friends or family.

The social worker reflected back what Sally and Josh said about the arguments, including the specific periods they had identified. With some surprise, Josh was able to discuss a lifetime of feeling excluded, especially on holidays. These feelings were provoked by Sally's preparations to entertain or otherwise plan for holidays and by her attention to her family and friends. The social worker's reflecting back of Josh's discussion allowed him to reframe the problem from anger at Sally to his feelings of exclusion on holidays. Josh realized that his depression on holidays was a long-standing problem and had nothing to do with Sally. As the discussion progressed, Josh was also able to identify the anger he felt toward colleagues when he believed they had excluded him. This new perspective was the beginning of improved relationships at home and at work (Real, 1990).

Therapeutic Questions

Lineal questions have an investigative intent. Who did that? When? If a client's complaint is depression, for example, lineal questions ask, Are you sleeping? Are you on medication? Are you eating?

Circular questions have an exploratory intent and assume that all events are connected in some way. These questions help the client and worker find patterns that connect persons, objects, actions, beliefs, and feelings. Who feels bad when you are depressed? What do they do about it? Who makes you feel better? What does your partner do when you get depressed?

Strategic questions attempt to influence the client or clients in a specific way and communicate a preferred action. A strategic question may be, When you get depressed, why don't you talk to your husband about it instead of involving the children? If your husband is irresponsible about household tasks, why don't you specify the tasks you especially want done? To the husband: Can you see that your wife gets depressed when you withdraw? Strategic questions reveal what the worker believes "ought to be."

Reflexive questions are used to facilitate, to open new possibilities, and to gain new perspectives for the client. Some examples are these: If you were to share with your husband how sad you feel when he withdraws, how would he react? How would you want him to react? If he were angry at you, how would you convince him that you want to know about it so you could do things differently? (Tomm, 1988).

Use of the Model in a University EAP

A professional resource at the work site in the form of an EAP facilitates the understanding of work as a variable in the assessment and service delivery process by illuminating the direct connection between work and individual–family problems. Whereas traditional social work practice has discouraged close social or professional relationships between workers and clients, this principle cannot be strictly adhered to in the EAP. Indeed, it is probably facilitative to the professional process by which both employees (clients) and social workers recognize that they are professional colleagues in other roles.

The EAP that serves as a "laboratory" for this chapter is in a large urban university and serves 2,600 employees and their families or companions. It is an on-site social service program that offers individual, couple, and family counseling; group services; organizational consultation; and prevention and educational programs. Referrals are made only for specific services that are not available on-site, such as hospital care, detoxification for drug and alcohol abuse, and nursing home and psychiatric care.

The EAP is under the direct administrative jurisdiction of the vice president for administration. Its director is a senior member of the faculty of the school of social work. Counseling services are provided by the director; an administrator; and an additional social worker, who also serves as supervisor of the graduate students. Eight members of the social work faculty serve as part-time counselors or consultants. Important parts of the organizational structure are the President's Advisory Committee and the Labor-Management Advisory Committee. These committees provide advice, guidance, and consultation, while serving as an instrument of accountability to the college and the community. The Labor-Management Committee is an especially important interpretive conduit to constituent groups in the college.

The expansion of the staff and program of this EAP, which has been in operation since 1983, has been carefully planned. The categories of problems that are addressed include marital, family, and parent–child problems; children's adjustment to school; substance abuse; individual adjustment; health, especially AIDS; special problems for gay and lesbian families; and work stress. The program has also conducted educational and prevention workshops and provided organizational consultation to a variety of units in the university. Clients include faculty members and members of the administration (professional and nonprofessional), security, maintenance, and secretarial staffs and their families or companions.

A management information system (MIS), designed and maintained by the research consultant, keeps a current profile of the populations using the program. It helps determine the effectiveness of various aspects of the program and pinpoints the unmet needs of special groups. The MIS is also a useful assessment tool. For example, it produces a profile of characteristics of the population by problem, job classification, ethnic–racial distribution, gender, relationship status (married, gay or lesbian, or living together), age, years employed, and number of contacts with the EAP. The system is designed to cross-tabulate for more specific information; it yields only aggregate information to ensure confidentiality.

The EAP has also sponsored group meetings and seminars to address special problems of groups of employees. Sessions on financial and legal planning for aging relatives, special problems of adult children of alcoholics, and co-dependence are among those that have been widely attended. The group sessions have frequently led to extended individual and family contacts. Groups have also been excellent indicators of organizational problems.

A newsletter is distributed to the university community twice a year. An article on dyslexia, for example, encouraged several employees to apply for help to discuss their long histories of settling for jobs that were below their capacities to avoid being labeled "stupid." An article about premenstrual syndrome helped a number of men and women reevaluate the reasons for their stormy personal relationships. Articles on codependence and enabling in substance abuse brought many requests for service. Educational programs have also encouraged employees to ask for help.

When AIDS was declared a national health problem, many employees were at high risk, and many others were terrified. Because this population of employees is ethnically, culturally, racially, and emotionally diverse, misunderstandings are often the source of interpersonal problems, precipitated by such issues as entitlements, expectations about work tasks, appropriate behavior, use of time, and fairness in promotions. A lack of knowledge and socially determined prejudice about AIDS were found to be common. Educating employees about AIDS and about diversity was the intervention of choice. The EAP invited experts at the university to join an EAP task force to help develop educational programs. Eventually, the administration instituted several universitywide task forces.

Special Groups

Experiences with the concerns of special groups in the university community have reinforced the contemporary professional view that disability, gender, sexual orientation, race, and ethnicity require special understanding and techniques of intervention. These techniques have emerged as a part of the constructivist approach discussed earlier. The EAP's work with women is representative of the approach to working with special groups.

Work with women

Women have had a significant impact on the workplace. As Gilligan (1982) pointed out, a woman's sense of self and morality are related to responsibility for and care and inclusion of other people. Miller (1976, p. 53) supported this idea and suggested that "women have traditionally built a sense of self-worth on activities that they can manage to define as taking care of and giving to others." These characteristics have brought a novel form of rational civility to many workplaces. Yet, the workplace creates unusual stress for women, based on their gender status, sometimes in a manner that induces them to assume the styles of the aggressor (Belle, 1991).

On the one hand, women are frequently advised to become more competitive, task oriented, and impersonal; to be less vulnerable; to take more power; and to think more analytically (Stiver, 1991). On the other hand, women themselves frequently equate competitiveness with being aggressive and destructive and may be fearful of being perceived that way. On a deeper level, it may be hard to be empathic and competitive at the same time. To add to the inner conflict, the fear of being called "castrating" and "ball breakers" goes far in subduing women's motivation to claim their talents. Traditionally, women have had "permission" to compete in only one area: with other women—for men. Women's self-doubts, insecurity about their professional demeanor, dread of competition, and fear of success are major obstacles for them in the workplace (Stiver, 1991). Women are socialized early to believe it is safer to be incompetent than to be competent. Many women came to the

EAP over their struggle with the dilemma of competence versus acceptable behavior, as was the case with Enid:

> In her first session, Enid recalled a poem, learned in her early years, that symbolized her current fears:
>
>> I'm sorry that I spelled the word,
>> I hate to go above you,
>> Because, the brown eyes lower fell,
>> Because you see I love you.

A housewife and mother of two children, Enid had always worked. The jobs were part-time and planned around the needs of her family. Soon after she was hired as an adjunct instructor at the university, she discovered that she was an excellent teacher and enjoyed academia. When a rare full-time position became available six months later, she accepted it with the understanding that she would get an advanced degree. Her assignments were teaching and part-time administration. Enid worked for her doctoral degree while she held two major administrative assignments (referred to ironically as the "housekeeping work" of the department), along with full-time teaching and her home and child care responsibilities. These heavy assignments, which were characteristically given to the women in the department, interfered with Enid's opportunity to write and publish. Deeply appreciative of the confidence shown in her ability to do the administrative work and despite responsibilities at home and in the workplace, she worked even harder and earned tenure and promotion. She was not aware that she was being exploited in that she was held to the same criteria for promotion as were the men in the department, although they had few responsibilities other than teaching.

Enid was well liked by her colleagues until it became clear that she was becoming eligible for and interested in assignments that were not of the "housekeeping" variety. Overnight she developed a reputation as a "ball breaker" and was harassed by several younger men in her department. She came to the EAP feeling great stress and was depressed. She asked for help in understanding what she was doing to make people dislike her.

This highly intelligent woman had demonstrated her capacity to cope well with both the typical gender stresses at home and in the academic learning area. She achieved recognition and status at work. It was not until she was exposed to sexual discrimination, both open and subtle, that her coping capacities failed. A new form of self-protection arose ("it's my fault") that damaged her self-esteem and was likely to halt her professional growth.

Enid feared success because she feared it would isolate her. This outcome was being confirmed. When it became clear that she was not going to be satisfied with departmental "housekeeping" tasks, many colleagues were threatened and threatened her in return. Through services, however, she was helped to become openly assertive with the people who were harassing her. She responded, as many women do, when her confidence increased. She became affiliative and helpful to younger women on the faculty and allied herself with women colleagues who were having similar experiences.

Conclusion

Successes and failures at work extend to and permeate life at work and outside work. The importance of work and the dynamics of the workplace have been largely neglected or minimized in most, if not all, models of social work intervention. Interventions have been traditionally and theoretically understood from the ground of an epistemology that assumes both the possibility and the desirability of practitioners' objectivity and minimal involvement with clients. This approach has restricted methods of inquiry and creativity in theory building for the human sciences and the human service professions. Such a restrictive approach is particularly inappropriate for human services offered in the work setting, which is dominated by unusually critical realities and "here and now" challenges to functioning.

Work, which is probably the most important indicator of the level of human functioning, is emphasized by only a few writers in the profession. Understanding work and its meaning throughout individual and family social systems and the use of this understanding in the helping process calls for a comprehensive, humanistic practice model that is sensitive to the dynamics of the workplace and the potential productivity of a highly interactive, dynamic worker–client engagement using narrative and experiential techniques.

The constructivist stress–vulnerability–coping model is recommended as the intervention of choice in the workplace. It is particularly appropriate for EAPs because it is not limited by the function of agencies, the unit of attention, time elements, the formulation of problems, or organizational restraints. In their concern with stress, the components of this model illuminate the effects of social pathologies, such as institutional racism, sexism, homophobia, and ageism, on human adjustment. This model does not delimit the use of current developmental and human behavior theories, and it supports a strong psychosocial perspective. The social structure of the workplace—the physical and emotional proximity of workers, the centrality of work to the human condition, and the collegial relationship between the worker and the client—are particularly compatible with the essential elements of constructivist practice.

References

Akabas, S. H., & Kurzman, P. A. (Eds.). (1982). *Work, workers, and work organizations: A view from social work.* Englewood Cliffs, NJ: Prentice Hall.

Anderson, H., & Goolishian, H. (1988). Human systems as linguistic systems: Preliminary and evolving ideas about the implications for clinical theory. *Family Process, 27,* 371–393.

Bartlett, H. (1970). *The common base of social work practice.* New York: National Association of Social Workers.

Bateson, G. (1972). *Steps to an ecology of the mind.* New York: Ballantine Books.

Bateson, G. (1979). *Mind and nature: A necessary unity.* New York: E. P. Dutton.

Belle, D. (Ed.). (1982). *Lives in stress.* Beverly Hills, CA: Sage Publications.

Belle, D. (1991). Gender differences in the social moderators of stress. In A. Monat & R. Lazarus (Eds.), *Stress and coping: An anthology* (3rd ed., pp. 258–274). New York: Columbia University Press.

Bepko, C., & Krestan, J. (1985). *The responsibility trap.* New York: Free Press.

Berger, P., & Luckman, T. (1966). *The social construction of reality.* Garden City, NY: Doubleday.

Bruner, J. (1986). *Actual minds, possible words.* Cambridge, MA: Harvard University Press.

Bruner, J. (1987). *Acts of meaning.* Cambridge, MA: Harvard University Press.

Chestang, L. (1982). Work, personal change, and human development. In S. H. Akabas & P. A. Kurzman (Eds.), *Work, workers, and work organizations: A view from social work* (pp. 61–89). Englewood Cliffs, NJ: Prentice Hall.

Coelho, G., Hamburg, D., & Adams, J. (Eds.). (1974). *Coping and adaptation.* New York: Basic Books.

Coyne, J. C. (1985). Toward a theory of frames and reframing: The social nature of frames. *Journal of Marital and Family Therapy, 11,* 1–20.

Dorfman, R. A. (1988). *Paradigms of clinical social work.* New York: Brunner/ Mazel.

Epstein, L. (1988). *Helping people, the task centered approach* (2nd ed.). Columbus, OH: Charles E. Merrill.

Folkman, S., & Lazarus, R. (1991). Coping and emotion. In A. Monat & R. Lazarus (Eds.), *Stress and coping: An anthology* (3rd ed., pp. 207–227). New York: Columbia University Press.

Gambrill, E. (1983). *Casework: A competency based approach.* Englewood Cliffs, NJ: Prentice Hall.

Gergen, K. (1985). The constructivist movement in modern psychology. *American Psychologist, 40,* 266–275.

Germain, C. (1991). *Human behavior in the social environment: An ecological view.* New York: Columbia University Press.

Germain, C., & Gitterman, A. (1980). *The life model of social work practice.* New York: Columbia University Press.

Gilligan, C. (1982). *In a different voice: Psychological theory and women's development.* Cambridge, MA: Harvard University Press.

Goldstein, H. (1981). *Social learning and change: A cognitive approach to human services.* New York: Tavistock Publications.

Hamilton, G. (1953). *Theory and practice of social casework* (rev. ed.). New York: Columbia University Press.

Hartman, A. (1990). Many ways of knowing. *Social Casework, 35,* 3–4.

Hoffman, L. (1990). Constructing realities: An art of lenses. *Family Process, 29,* 1–12.

Holder, D., & Anderson, H. (1989). Women, work and the family. In M. McGoldrick, C. Anderson, & F. Walsh (Eds.), *Women in families: A framework for family therapy* (pp. 357–380). New York: W. W. Norton.

Hollis, F., & Woods, M. (1981). *Casework: A psychosocial therapy.* New York: McGraw-Hill.

Homans, G. (1987). Behaviorism and after. In A. Giddens & J. Turner (Eds.), *Social theory today* (pp. 58–81). Stanford, CA: Stanford University Press.

Janik, A., & Toulmin, S. (1973). *Wittgenstein's Vienna.* New York: Simon & Schuster.

Kaplan, A. (1991). The self-in-relation implications for depression in women. In J. V. Jordan, A. G. Kaplan, J. B. Miller, I. P. Stiver, & J. L. Surrey (Eds.), *Women's growth in connection: Writings from the Stone Center* (pp. 206–222). New York: Guilford Press.

Kelly, G. A. (1983). *A theory of personality.* New York: W. W. Norton.

Kurzman, P. A. (1988). Work and the family: Some major dilemmas. In C. Chilman, F. Cox, & E. Nunnally (Eds.), *Employment and economic problems* (pp. 67–84). Beverly Hills, CA: Sage Publications.

Laird, J. (1989). Women and stories: Restorying women's self-construction. In M. McGoldrick, C. Anderson, & F. Walsh (Eds.), *Women in families: A framework for family therapy* (pp. 427–450). New York: W. W. Norton.

Lazarus, R., & Folkman, S. (1991). The concept of coping. In A. Monat & R. Lazarus (Eds.), *Stress and coping: An anthology* (3rd ed., pp. 189–206). New York: Columbia University Press.

Lewis, H. (1982). *The intellectual base of social work practice: Tools for thought in a helping profession.* New York: Haworth Press.

Locke, E., & Taylor, M. S. (1991). Stress, coping and the meaning of work. In A. Monat & R. Lazarus (Eds.), *Stress and coping: An anthology* (3rd ed., pp. 140–157). New York: Columbia University Press.

Mailick, M. (1991). Differential assessment in clinical practice. *Smith College Studies in Social Work, 62,* 3–19.

Mailick, M., & Vigilante, F. W. (1987). Human behavior and the social environment: A sequence providing the theoretical base for teaching assessment. *Journal of Teaching in Social Work, 1*(2), 33–47.

Middleman, R., & Goldberg, G. (1974). *Social service delivery: A structural approach to social work practice.* New York: Columbia University Press.

Miller, J. B. (1976). *Toward a new psychology of women.* Boston: Beacon Press.

Miller, J. B. (1991). Women and power. In J. V. Jordan, A. G. Kaplan, J. B. Miller, I. P. Stiver, & J. L. Surrey (Eds.), *Women's growth in connection: Writings from the Stone Center* (pp. 197–205). New York: Guilford Press.

Monkman, M., & Allen-Meares, P. (1985). The tie framework: A conceptual map for social work assessment. *Arete, 10*(1), 44–49.

Perlman, H. H. (1957). *Social casework: A problem-solving process.* Chicago: University of Chicago Press.

Perlman, H. H. (1970). The problem solving model in social casework. In R. Roberts & R. Nee (Eds.), *Theories of social casework* (pp. 129–180). Chicago: University of Chicago Press.

Pieper, M. H. (1990). The heuristic paradigm: A unifying and comprehensive approach to social work research. *Smith College Studies in Social Work, 60*, 8–34.

Polkinghorne, D. (1983). *Methodology for the human sciences systems of inquiry.* Albany: State University of New York Press.

Real, T. (1990). The therapeutic use of self in constructionist systemic therapy. *Family Process, 29*, 255–272.

Reiss, D., & Oliveri, M. E. (1991). The family's conception of accountability and competence: A new approach to the conceptualization and assessment of family stress. *Family Process, 30*, 193–214.

Richmond, M. (1917). *Social diagnosis.* New York: Russell Sage Foundation.

Roberts, R. (1990). *Lessons from the past: Issues for social work theory.* London: Tavistock-Routledge.

Rosen, H. (1988). The constructivist developmental paradigm. In R. Dorfman (Ed.), *Paradigms of clinical social work* (pp. 317–355). New York: Brunner/ Mazel.

Selye, H. (1991). History and present status of the stress concept. In A. Monat & R. Lazarus (Eds.), *Stress and coping: An anthology* (3rd ed., pp. 21–35). New York: Columbia University Press.

Silverman, B., Simon, B., & Woodrow, R. (1991). Workers in job jeopardy. In A. Gitterman (Ed.), *Handbook of social work practice with vulnerable populations* (pp. 710–748). New York: Columbia University Press.

Specht, H., & Specht, R. (1986). Social work assessment: Route to clienthood: Part 1. *Social Casework, 67*, 525–532.

Stiver, I. (1991). Work inhibitions in women. In J. V. Jordan, A. G. Kaplan, J. B. Miller, I. P. Stiver, & J. L. Surrey (Eds.), *Women's growth in connection: Writings from the Stone Center* (pp. 223–236). New York: Guilford Press.

Thomas, E. (1970). Behavior modification and casework. In R. Roberts & R. Nee (Eds.), *Theories of social casework* (pp. 181–218). Chicago: University of Chicago Press.

Tomm, K. (1988). Interventive interviewing: Part 3. Intending to ask circular, strategic, or reflexive questions. *Family Process, 27*, 1–16.

Toulmin, S. (1990). *Cosmopolis: The hidden agenda of modernity.* New York: Free Press.

Turner, F. (Ed.). (1986). *Social work treatment.* New York: Free Press.

Vigilante, F. W. (1982). Use of work in the assessment process. *Social Casework, 5*, 296–300.

Vigilante, F. W. (1988). The interactive relationship between work and family life: Professional intervention. In C. Chilman, F. Cox, & E. Nunnally (Eds.), *Employment and economic problems* (pp. 85–102). Beverly Hills, CA: Sage Publications.

Vigilante, F. W., & Mailick, M. (1988). Needs-resource evaluation in the assessment process. *Social Work, 30*, 101–104.

Vigilante, J. L., Lodge, R., Lucton, R., Kaplan, S., & Mason, R. (1981, March 4). *Searching for theory—following Hearn*. Invitational paper presented at the Annual Program Meeting, Council on Social Work Education, Louisville, KY.

Wallerstein, I. (1987). World systems analysis. In A. Giddens & J. Turner (Eds.), *Social theory today*. Stanford, CA: Stanford University Press.

Walters, A., Carter, B., Papp, P., & Silverstein, O. (1988). *The invisible web: Gender patterns in family relationships*. New York: Guilford Press.

Weingarten, K. (1992). A consideration of intimate and non-intimate interactions in therapy. *Family Process, 31*, 45–59.

Weitz, R. (1991). Uncertainty and the lives of persons with AIDS. In A. Monat & R. Lazarus (Eds.), *Stress and coping: An anthology* (3rd ed., pp. 352–369). New York: Columbia University Press.

White, M., & Epston, D. (1990). *Narrative means to therapeutic ends*. New York: W. W. Norton.

CHAPTER 11

Solution-Focused Brief Workplace Counseling

Maria DeOca Corwin

> When the ploughman asked Almustafa to speak of work he said, "Always you have been told that work is a source of curse and labor, a misfortune. But I say to you that when you work you fulfill a part of earth's furthest dream, assigned to you when the dream was born; and in keeping yourself with labor you are in truth loving life, and to love life through labor is to be intimate with life's inmost secret."
>
> —Kahlil Gibran
> *The Prophet*

Intervention models in social work practice must be measured against the values, purposes, and goals of the profession in general and against the needs of a field of practice in particular before they can be deemed appropriate. Measured against these criteria, solution-focused brief counseling seems to meet the standard for an appropriate social work intervention model. With its emphasis on problem solving and improving coping capacities through the development of skills and resources for the management of environmental and life demands, it adheres to the social work values of self-determination and respect for the individual and to the profession's goal of enhancing social functioning (Compton & Galaway, 1989). In addition, this intervention model meets the needs of occupational social work for a practice approach that will improve the fit between the individual and the workplace in an efficient and effective manner.

The counseling services offered by employee assistance programs in corporations and member assistance programs in unions are generally time limited, inasmuch as one of the primary goals of these programs is to return the worker to an effective level of functioning as soon as possible (Webb, 1990). Thus, in the assessment–referral model, the client may be seen only for one to three sessions, and in the assessment–treatment model, the client is generally seen for fewer than 15 sessions (Fleisher & Kaplan, 1988). Therefore, to be an effective practitioner, the occupational social worker must have practice knowledge of and be trained in the skills of time-limited work.

This chapter presents a metamodel approach to brief counseling in which the guiding principles of time-limited work are examined. Although practice models differ in the degree to which personal, situational, or transactional factors are the focus of intervention and in technical strategies, there are values and principles that are common to most practice approaches. Thus, intervention strategies are examined from an integrated or eclectic perspective, rather than from a specific practice model. In addition, variations on time-limited work (single-session and crisis intervention work) are also discussed because occupational social workers are frequently called on to provide these services.

Brief counseling is defined here as a planned, time-limited intervention that is typically fewer than 15 sessions. *Crisis intervention work* is usually six to eight weeks in duration, and *single-session work* consists of a single working session with a planned follow-up visit. *Solution-focused counseling* refers to those practice approaches, such as the cognitive–behavioral, task-centered, or problem-solving approaches, in which "well-explicated, well-organized procedures [are] usually carried out step by step and designed to achieve relatively specific goals" (Reid & Hanrahan, 1982, p. 329).

Theoretical Principles

The rationale for using time limits in counseling is founded both on empirical research evidence that time-limited intervention is as effective as is long-term or open-ended treatment (Orlinsky & Howard, 1986; Reid & Hanrahan, 1982) and on the value of parsimony of intervention. It is also founded on the systems-theory principles of equifinality (that different interventions can lead to the same outcome) and the ripple effect (that a change in one area of functioning in an individual can stimulate growth and change in other areas of functioning). Therefore, the attainment of the limited goals typical of brief counseling can lead to a more general improvement in functioning, and this ripple effect can continue even after termination (Budman & Gurman, 1988; Grinnell, Kyte, & Bostwick, 1981).

Another central feature of effective time-limited counseling is that the counselor builds on the client's existing strengths. Therefore, the assessment process includes an evaluation of the client's internal resources and the resources in his or her environment, as well as of the factors that created and maintain the problem. It is assumed that the individual is more inclined to continue to develop in areas in which he or she has achieved competence than in those that are deemed deficient or pathological (Weick, Rapp, Sullivan, & Kisthardt, 1989). This perspective is especially relevant to occupational social work because the client is employed (one index of ego strength) and because this area of functioning is one in which the client is usually motivated to enhance his or her adaptation and performance. Motivation is a good predictor of a positive outcome of treatment, so it makes sense to begin with the client's functioning at work (Gold, 1990).

Furthermore, it is recognized that development occurs throughout the adult life cycle and that significant changes can occur in adulthood. As Grinnell et al. (1981, p. 169) noted, the concept of competence "helps us to view the person as active (rather than reactive or passive) and as possessing an innate capacity for growth and change, for affecting as well as being affected by his environment."

The reciprocal interaction between the individual and his or her environment is another tenet of brief therapy. The client's social environment can either act as a buffer to life's stresses or can be a source of stress (Rutter, 1986). The social context, then, is always taken into consideration in planning an intervention, and the goals are to maximize the client's support systems, reduce interpersonal conflicts, and enhance the client's social functioning. Improving a client's social adjustment, including his or her adjustment to the workplace, may result in improvements in such areas of ego functioning as problem solving, judgment, impulse control, and the accurate perception of reality. Likewise, an improvement in personal functioning contributes to improved social adjustment (Singh, 1982).

The focus of brief counseling is on current functioning. For example, the occupational social worker evaluates the client's work performance for types of behavior that may indicate maladaptive responses to stress from the job, family problems, or financial difficulties. "Such behavior includes late arrival or early departure from work, continual absenteeism, and filing company grievances or other expense-related factors including injury, poor health, medication requirement, hospitalization, and medical leave" (Yamatani, 1988, p. 34). These behaviors are generally the beginning foci in the intervention process.

Although meanings attached to stresses and problems are partly a function of the individual's personal history, this history is explored only to the extent that the client's knowledge of it will help uncover and remove obstacles to change, such as self-defeating attitudes, fears, and negative expectations. Because it is understood that causal explanations of the origins of a problem do not necessarily lead to strategies for change, the focus of brief counseling has shifted from diagnosis and genetic formulations to strategies of intervention that may or may not be independent of the hypothesized origin of the problem (Fischer, 1986; Tolson, 1988). Thus, pragmatism is another guiding principle of brief treatment (Budman & Gurman, 1988).

Finally, the emphasis in time-limited interventions is on improved functioning and a better fit between the person and the environment, rather than on a "cure" or restructuring of the client's character. Therefore, the goals in time-limited work are realistic and attainable, and it is expected that the client may return at some future time when new stresses or an accumulation of stresses have created another state of disequilibrium. However, it is also expected that if a client needs to return, the previous competence-enhancing counseling experience will have enabled him or her to function more effectively in the interim and that the client will quickly be able to make good use of the subsequent counseling contact (Budman & Gurman, 1988; Talmon, 1990). This principle of intermittent, as-needed, brief contact is congruent with the structure and function of workplace counseling programs because accessibility, availability, and flexibility are characteristic dimensions of these programs.

Principles of Intervention

The sine qua non of effective brief counseling is planned intervention. The skill of moving from assessment and definition of the problem to an intervention plan with goals, objectives, and tasks that are clearly linked to the assessment enables the social worker to arrive at the focus that all major models of brief therapy agree is essential for doing time-limited work (Fischer, 1986; Fortune, 1985; Mann, 1981; Reid, 1987; Rosen, Proctor, & Livne, 1985). This focus is the means by which it is possible to make significant changes within a limited time frame. By defining and maintaining a clear focus, the social worker can connect seemingly disparate elements of the client's life and structure each session to achieve the agreed-on goals.

The assessment process involves a rapid but comprehensive evaluation of the needs and resources of the person-in-situation. The evaluation and intervention processes in brief therapy are intertwined from the first session, in contrast to the lengthy evaluation of open-ended treatment that must be completed before any intervention takes place. The determination of a focus and the setting of simple, clear, realistic goals and tasks usually occur in the first session, although the focus and goals may be modified during the ongoing assessment as new data become known or if the small goals are achieved and there is time to set additional goals (Budman & Gurman, 1988). This approach is congruent with the expectation of many workplace clients from diverse cultural and class backgrounds that relief will be forthcoming; these clients also may not find a prolonged search for etiological factors relevant to the solution of their presenting problems.

Assessment tools, such as Vigilante and Mailick's (1988) Development Assessment Wheel, Hartman's (1978) Ecomap, or the rapid assessment instruments found in Hudson's (1982) Clinical Management Package, can help the counselor to gather and organize data quickly from multiple systems (personal, interpersonal, and environmental). Counselors who are located in the work setting and are knowledgeable about "the organization as a system, its communication channels, its personnel policies, and its informal struc-ture" (Fleisher & Kaplan, 1988, p. 40) can use this knowledge to assess the client's situation and to determine goals rapidly.

The assessment process should yield information on the client's most pressing concern and the most promising intervention. In time-limited work, the social worker always pays close attention to what the client defines as the problem, although the worker's definition of the problem may come to include causal or contributing factors that may not be part of the client's understanding of the problem (Tolson, 1988). Because in time-limited work the social worker needs to engage the client quickly in a working alliance, he or she must select goals that the client is motivated to work on; clients are much more likely to be motivated to achieve goals that are meaningful to them (Gold, 1990; Moore-Kirkland, 1981).

To arrive at the most promising intervention plan, the social worker conducts a force-field analysis in which the forces that "might aid or restrain change" are delineated (Fischer, 1986, p. 340). In addition, solutions to problems must correspond with the client's motivation and ability to change and with the client's value and belief system, derived from his or her sociocultural background (Parad & Parad, 1990). One way to determine the aiding and restraining forces is to examine the client's previous attempts to solve the presenting problem, including previous attempts at counseling. Because there is no time to waste on recycling past unsuccessful attempts, the counselor should formulate solutions that are meaningful alternatives to the client's present way of operating. To ensure in the contracting process that the goals selected are mutually defined and attainable, the social worker can find out from the client how the client will know when things are better or what would constitute a satisfactory outcome for him or her (De Shazer et al., 1986).

Determining the foci of intervention requires that the assessment data be analyzed and synthesized and that problems be broken down and priorities established among them according to the foregoing criteria. It also requires the social worker to be able to identify recurrent themes in the client's presentation that may indicate key unresolved issues that are creating or maintaining the client's current state of distress (Strupp & Binder, 1984). Several models can aid the social worker in identifying potential foci for time-limited work. For example, Germain and Gitterman (1980) classified problems in living according to the needs and tasks required by life transition, interpersonal, and environmental demands, and Budman and Gurman (1988) described interpersonal, developmental, and existential events (the I-D-E checklist), such as losses, developmental dyssynchronies, interpersonal conflicts, symptomatic presentations, and personality disorders, as useful foci.

In brief therapy, the social worker is active and directive. In the first session, he or she tests hypotheses about the central issues and causative factors, eliciting the client's feedback on them and on the proposed goals of counseling. Problems are redefined in solvable terms, and the direction of the counseling sessions is clearly stated (De Shazer et al., 1986). In addition, the social worker seeks to provide an immediate benefit to the client, for example, by relieving symptoms, such as depression and anxiety; offering cognitive clarity to a client who is feeling confused and indecisive; offering hope to a demoralized client; or normalizing a client's distress (Budman & Gurman, 1988; Sue & Zane, 1987). This approach rapidly establishes the social worker as trustworthy and credible and increases the client's motivation to continue working to accomplish tasks and to resolve the problems.

Other ways in which the social worker is more active than in long-term work include providing information about resources, teaching new skills, offering more constructive perspectives on the client's problems, giving advice and guidance, asking leading questions to promote the client's self-awareness, and suggesting tasks and "homework" assignments that will give the client the opportunity to try out more constructive behaviors (De Shazer et al., 1986; Singh, 1982). Thus, in the workplace, the counselor may provide clients with information about medical, legal, day care, or home-making services and about benefits available to employees, such as a union's financial assistance program, or he or she may use role-playing or anticipatory guidance techniques to help the client deal with interpersonal conflicts on the job (Parad, 1988). Budman and Gurman (1988) suggested that it is wise for the counselor to approach each session as if it were the only session. Doing so helps keep the sessions focused and moving toward the attainment of goals. In each session, the social worker monitors the client's progress in resolving problems or conflicts.

Although the social worker engages in a high level of activity in time-limited work, he or she also needs to be flexible and responsive to the client's shifts in presentation and concerns. The social worker is directive, structuring, and goal oriented, but also reflective, perceptive, and in tune with the client's true feelings about the relationship and strategies for achieving goals (Singh, 1982). The selection of a focus allows for the efficient use of time, but should never lead to the client acquiescing to the demands of a "domineering professional" (Strupp & Binder, 1984).

Sensitivity to the client's unspoken feelings and concerns is particularly important in workplace counseling, where clients may be involuntary, that is, they may have been referred to the service by supervisors and their jobs may be in jeopardy. Involuntary clients often have negative reactions to being identified as having problems or being forced to seek help and thus may deny that a problem exists or minimize the extent of the problem and its consequences for them. One way of overcoming this initial resistance is for the social worker to try to find a common ground between the referred problem and the client's concerns, while clarifying with the client the negative consequences of not addressing the problem. The social worker may also need to help a client articulate the unspoken fears and anxieties or the negative expectations that he or she may have of counseling or of any relationship, particularly if the client has a history of problems in interpersonal relationships (Moore-Kirkland, 1981; Rooney, 1988).

Once the client is engaged in a positive working relationship with the social worker and the two have agreed on the goals, the social worker must then decide what will be the most effective means for achieving the goals. Effective time-limited work requires that the social worker be comfortable with the flexible use of time, self, and intervention techniques. For example, the length and spacing of the sessions must be a function of the client's needs. Initially, the sessions may have to be longer and more frequent, especially if the client is in a crisis. They then may be gradually tapered off as a way of maximizing the client's opportunity to explore and try out new ways of thinking, feeling, and doing in the real world (Parad & Parad, 1990). Tapering of sessions is also useful with clients who are uncomfortable with the time limits or struggle with dependence in relationships. The occupational social worker may initially encourage a client to take sick leave or a leave of absence during the height of a crisis, but then encourage a timely return to work when symptoms have abated or, for the client who is already on sick leave, recommend an immediate return to work when symptoms of anxiety and depression are being exacerbated by inactivity or isolation.

Within each session and from session to session, the occupational social worker may assume different roles and employ a differential use of self. For example, he or she may inform the client about resources for addressing environmental deficits, advocate on behalf of the client to gain access to those resources, instruct the client in the skills necessary to access entitlements, improve interpersonal relationships or manage the stresses of the job, and provide the understanding and sustaining necessary for the client to become comfortable with these new behaviors. In a crisis, the occupational social worker may have to assume more responsibility for decision making, be more direct in offering encouragement and support, and be more directive in sorting out the tasks that have to be accomplished to begin the process of adjusting to the situation (Tabachnick, 1990).

To maximize the benefits of brief treatment, the occupational social worker needs to enhance existing social supports or assist the client to develop new social networks, such as self-help groups, social groups in the community, churches, peer groups in the workplace, or mutual-aid groups for managing the stresses of unemployment or impending layoffs. In addition to their extended availability to the client, these groups provide an opportunity for the client to test out and solidify skills in social functioning. The emphasis in time-limited therapy on enhancing competence, developing knowledge, and improving social functioning makes the termination process less stressful than in long-term therapy because the client most often has gained an increased sense of mastery and independence (Hepworth & Larsen, 1990).

Case Illustration

Bob, age 34, single, and white, was self-referred after his internist indicated there was nothing more he could do to help Bob with his chronic, debilitating headaches, insomnia, and generalized anxiety. These ailments had resulted in Bob using all his sick leave and vacation time for the days when he was incapacitated by pain or anxiety. Bob had not had a vacation in his 10 years of employment as a claims processor for a state agency. As these conditions were getting worse in spite of his daily use of powerful medications, Bob was becoming fearful that his diminishing level of productivity (or the probability that he would exceed the allotted time off) would cause him to lose his job.

Bob dated the onset of his symptoms to the period of his hospitalization for bipolar disorder. Following the breakup of his engagement, he had experienced his first manic episode and was hospitalized when his behavior became erratic. The manic depression had been successfully managed with lithium, but the preexisting social anxiety became acute. In most social situations, or in anticipation of social situations, Bob would become so anxious that he would literally be drenched in sweat. His shame and fear of becoming anxious resulted in his avoiding contacts with many colleagues, which severely hampered his ability to complete assignments. His resulting anxiety over his low productivity or over a forced meeting led to bouts of insomnia. The lack of sleep, in turn, frequently brought on a migraine headache that prevented him from going to work. Bob's frequent absences from work exacerbated his general state of anxiety about his job performance and his fear of losing his job. Except for a brief involvement in a therapy group following his hospitalization, Bob had not received treatment for either the manic-depressive illness or the anxiety disorders.

In the initial session, in addition to helping Bob get a clearer picture of the circular, reinforcing nature of his symptoms and behavior, which in itself brought him a measure of relief and hope, the occupational social worker carefully explored his fears and anxieties about being involved in a therapeutic relationship with a female worker because Bob had avoided all relationships with women since his fiancée broke off their engagement; he was acutely anxious when meeting new people and in the presence of women. The techniques of progressive relaxation, deep breathing, and cognitive restructuring were also introduced and practiced in the session to provide some immediate reduction of Bob's debilitating anxiety states.

The agreed-on initial goals were to reduce Bob's anxiety at bedtime and to develop strategies for managing his social anxiety at work. Because Bob had gained some relief from his insomnia and could immediately see the benefit of the deep breathing exercises and cognitive restructuring techniques in managing social contacts at work, he was motivated to continue the work of identifying dysfunctional thoughts and the automatic "self-statements" that exacerbated his anxiety and the process of decentering (moving from an egocentric perspective to more realistic perceptions of himself, others, and the world). For example, when asked to rate the experience of becoming anxious and sweating in a social situation on a scale of 1 to 10, Bob initially rated it "above a 10." As he learned to shift his focus from himself to the other person, while not exaggerating the other person's negative reaction to his anxiety, his rating of this experience eventually dropped to 3.

When Bob was able to meet with his supervisors on schedule and to attend some social activities and become friends with a female colleague, the focus of treatment shifted to developing problem-solving skills and to working through his feelings of loss and anger and his misconceptions about his chronic mental illness. Thus, when it became evident that his productivity problems at work were also due to a supervisor's management style, not just to Bob's anxiety and excessive absences, Bob learned to generate solutions, anticipate obstacles, and choose the solution that was most likely to alter the difficult work situation. After eight sessions, Bob agreed to join a psychoeducational group for people with anxiety disorders, which he had been unable to consider at the beginning of treatment. Two sessions were devoted to helping him prepare for the highly anxiety-provoking prospect of sharing his feelings with others. Bob quickly became a valued member of the group because of his mastery of relaxation techniques and his willingness to discuss his symptoms and their precipitants. This group experience helped him to develop a more realistic perspective on his symptoms, which he had assumed were unique to him, and increased his developing positive self-regard.

Bob completed the four sessions of the group and was seen for one individual follow-up session two months after his termination with the group. His insomnia and headaches had diminished to the point that he anticipated being able to take a vacation for the first time. He was also able to continue on the reduced dosage of medications that had been previously worked out with his physician during his individual sessions. Social situations continued to precipitate anxiety states, but Bob thought that he now had the ability to prevent these states from escalating out of control. He continued to use a problem-solving approach at work instead of his previous method of coping with job difficulties through avoidance, and this approach also reduced his nighttime anxiety states.

Planned Short-term Practice Models

Most brief treatment models take a pragmatically eclectic or integrated approach to treatment interventions, using cognitive, behavioral, family systems, and psychodynamic techniques to facilitate the resolution of problems (Parad & Parad, 1990). The task-centered approach, for example, which is the most widely used planned, short-term, solution-focused social work practice model, does not stipulate what the specific intervention should be, although it makes liberal use of cognitive–behavioral techniques to facilitate the collaborative effort toward completing tasks (Kanter, 1983; Reid, 1987). The task-centered model is a planned intervention of eight to 12 sessions over a period of three to four months during which one or two target problems are selected as the foci that are maintained throughout. To resolve problems, the worker uses certain intervention strategies: preparation for anticipated obstacles; implementation strategies, such as rehearsal, anticipatory guidance, and guided practice (homework assignments); and follow-up through the review of tasks and the analysis of feelings, distorted perceptions, or dysfunctional communication and behavioral patterns that are creating obstacles to change (Hepworth & Larsen, 1990; Reid, 1987).

The task-centered, planned, short-term approach has been adapted for work with families and groups. It is used to help families and members of a group with such interpersonal problems as deficient conflict- and problem-solving skills, negative styles of influence, distorted or unrealistic expectations of others, dysfunctional interaction patterns and alignments, and the inability to meet the need for affection and attachment (Hepworth & Larsen, 1990; Reid, 1987). Problems are redefined in interactional terms, and tasks are assigned that address the specific interactional problems. For example, tasks are assigned to strengthen the marital dyad and child–peer relationships when a dysfunctional parent–child alignment exists. This solution-focused treatment approach is also well suited to "crisis group counseling" for survivors of a trauma because it offers group members the opportunity to share their experiences while learning ways to process and integrate the traumatic experience. As incidents of violence and accidents increase in the workplace, the group modality may be the most efficient and effective way to prevent maladaptive stress reactions in groups of people who are exposed to the same stressors (Hillenberg & Wolf, 1988; Parad, 1988).

Other cognitive, behavioral, and cognitive–behavioral techniques are useful for counseling individuals, families, and groups in the workplace. For example, cognitive restructuring is "particularly relevant for problems associated with low self-esteem; distorted perceptions in interpersonal relationships; unrealistic expectations of self, others, and life in general; irrational fears, anxiety, and depression" (Hepworth & Larsen, 1990, p. 21). Cognitive restructuring involves assisting clients to be aware of their dysfunctional thoughts and the impact of these thoughts on their feelings and behavior and then helping them to develop more realistic, functional cognitive sets. Reframing, a family therapy technique that is a form of cognitive restructuring, is useful in helping clients and their families to see their situation in a different way, which can help move them out of impasses and ready them to change their behavior and interactions (Webb, 1990).

Cognitive therapy techniques are frequently combined with such behavioral techniques as assertiveness training, relaxation training, or behavioral rehearsal for a more rapid improvement in targeted problems. Recently, the subjective and objective techniques have been combined in intervention strategies, such as stress-inoculation training and self-instruction training (Fischer, 1986). These cognitive–behavioral techniques are effective in managing anger and reducing anxiety and stress.

In stress inoculation, for example, the client gradually gains mastery over impulsive behavior by learning about the individual physical, emotional, and cognitive responses to stresses, that is, learning to recognize self-statements, perceptions, and interpretations that influence his or her physiological and emotional responses to stressful situations. The client then learns to use more constructive cognitive sets; to recognize situations that arouse tension and anger; and to respond more constructively to arousal situations, such as the use of relaxation techniques, and then practices the new cognitive–affective–behavioral tasks before applying them to real-life situations, such as coping with an abrasive colleague or supervisor (Hepworth & Larsen, 1990).

Other planned short-term treatment models, for example, I-D-E (Budman & Gurman, 1988) and Eclectic Time-Limited Therapy (Fuhriman, Paul, & Burlingame, 1986), have a stronger psychodynamic influence and are most useful with characterological, life-transition, or developmental issues, especially unresolved losses. The foci in these models are usually developed from core conflicts that are themes that have a strong affective meaning and behavioral response for the client. The mechanisms for change in these treatment models include identifying conflicting or ambivalent feelings, providing an opportunity for their expression, and increasing the client's understanding and awareness of how these core conflicts negatively affect various areas of functioning, particularly interpersonal functioning.

These mechanisms of change are combined with specific tasks that are designed to enhance coping strategies. Thus, with an issue of unresolved loss, the social worker helps the client to identify the troubling event and to assess its meaning and impact; normalizes for the client his or her responses to the event; encourages the process of grieving, including the expression of feelings about the loss; engages members of the client's interpersonal system, if possible, to aid in this grieving process; and helps the client to accept the loss and the altered state of well-being through the assignment of specific tasks, for example, visiting the grave site or viewing photographs of the deceased (Budman & Gurman, 1988; Golan, 1981).

Crisis Intervention

Crisis intervention is a special form of time-limited work that differs from brief counseling mainly in the magnitude of the stressor event, the severity of the client's reaction to the stressor, and the intensity of the social worker's response to the client's distress. A crisis is a biopsychosocial phenomenon in which the client is faced with a stressor that he or she experiences as overwhelming and for which the client's usual coping strategies are not sufficient. The result is a state of disequilibrium, characterized by objective and subjective states of distress. The objective manifestations, such as the inability to concentrate, diminished performance, irritability, and increased conflict with co-workers, frequently lead to a worker being referred to the occupational social worker by concerned supervisors or co-workers. In a crisis, the worker is often self-referred because of the level of subjective distress. Clients in crisis frequently report feeling anxious, bewildered, confused, immobilized, helpless, hopeless, panicked, and unable to sleep or eat (Lukton, 1982).

The client's level of distress requires that the social worker respond as rapidly as possible, particularly if the client is at risk of harming himself or herself or someone else. To understand why this client has not been able to cope with this event or to resolve the problem, the social worker must make a quick assessment of the nature of the precipitating event, the meaning or perception of the event to the client and client system, and the resources or strengths of the individual within his or her total environment (Aguilera, 1990; Sussal & Ojakian, 1988). The worker then must work quickly to prevent a long-term maladaptive response to the stressor event, to return the individual to his or her previous level of coping, and perhaps to help him or her develop better coping responses to future stresses. In the initial sessions, the social worker is active and supportive, bringing cognitive clarity and understanding to a confused or disorganized client, while normalizing the stress response and offering hope and encouragement and the opportunity to ventilate painful feelings (Hillenberg & Wolf, 1988; Tabachnick, 1990).

The resolution of the crisis generally requires that the individual accomplish two sets of tasks—the instrumental–behavioral and the expressive–personal. In the personal tasks, the individual must cognitively and affectively process the changed sets of assumptions about himself or herself and his or her relationships and view of the world and future. For example, the client in crisis will have to work through painful feelings of loss, diminished self-esteem, and diminished sense of competence to define a new state of well-being, whether the precipitating event is the loss of a valued relationship or the loss of a job. At the same time, the client will often have to adjust to changes in the environment, in role, or in status or learn new problem-solving skills (Golan, 1981).

On the basis of the assessment, the social worker helps the client to identify the tasks that need to be accomplished and provides the information, guidance, and support necessary for the client to master the tasks. Again, he or she needs to be flexible in the length and frequency of sessions, the selection of who will be seen, and the choice of intervention techniques. Thus, if the client's family members are also responding maladaptively to the crisis because of preexisting dysfunctional communication patterns, negative styles of influence, or the inability to recognize and tolerate feelings, it may be necessary to work with the family on tasks related to these problem areas (Parad & Parad, 1990).

Clients in crisis are generally seen more intensively at the beginning of the contact, often several times per week, and then there is a tapering off as the crisis state diminishes. At the beginning of each session, the client's current psychological status and progress in achieving the tasks are reviewed, and at the end of the session, it is helpful to summarize the major issues worked on to help the client stay focused on the salient issues and to give him or her an immediate sense of accomplishment. The rehearsal of new behaviors, anticipatory guidance of responses to stresses, and the assignment of homework tasks are useful intervention techniques with the demoralized, disorganized client in crisis. Planned follow-up calls or visits after termination are often made to monitor the client's postcrisis adjustment (Parad & Parad, 1990).

Single-Session Therapy

For clients with circumscribed problems, good prior functioning, or a preference for limited contact, it is possible to do effective work in a single session if a systematic intervention is followed. Also, many of the theoretical and technical principles of single-session work can be adapted to the assessment–referral model. If these principles are followed, it is likely that there will be a higher rate of successful referrals or that more clients will gain relief or begin to resolve a problem, even though they are being seen only for assessment and referral.

Many of the principles of time-limited work previously discussed are necessary for single-session work: rapid assessment, early identification of a focus, setting minimal yet pivotal goals and tasks, building on a client's strengths, fostering the client's readiness to change through reframing problems in terms that indicate the direction of the change needed, maintaining a high level of activity, and empowering clients by mobilizing their capacity to manage their lives (Bloom, 1981; Talmon, 1990). In this approach, the counselor again must quickly establish a positive working relationship with the client; be directive but highly sensitive to the client's unexpressed needs and concerns; and be comfortable with the role of facilitator of the process of change, rather than the architect of change. Planned follow-up contact is also an intervention strategy in single-session work. The following case illustrates the process of working within a single-session framework.

Mrs. Jones was referred by the administrator of the city school–crossing guards. For the past three months, Mrs. Jones had become increasingly agitated and suspicious, demanding that the administrator intervene with what Mrs. Jones perceived to be harassment by her immediate supervisor. She claimed that ever since a child had been struck by a car after she had left her post at the appointed time, her supervisor had blamed her for the accident and now was constantly checking up on her when she was on duty. Her supervisor denied the allegation. The administrator suggested that Mrs. Jones go for an evaluation to determine whether it would be advisable for her to take some time off from work to reduce her level of distress.

Mrs. Jones, who is 57, married, and the mother of five grown children, presented as anxious, confused, and concerned about her current emotional state. She reported that she was having increasing difficulty concentrating, sleeping, and eating. She was constantly preoccupied with what she felt was her supervisor's unfair accusation about her being at fault for the child's injury and with his unwarranted surveillance of her. The assessment indicated that Mrs. Jones had functioned well before this event. She was an esteemed member of her community, someone everyone in the neighborhood turned to for advice and help and had, until the accident, been active in her church and in a number of community organizations. This was the first time she had ever encountered any negative feedback either on the job or in her family or community relationships.

Given her previous high level of functioning and her immediate response to clarification and cognitive restructuring, a contract for one session (and a follow-up session) was set. The focus of the session was on Mrs. Jones's dependence on positive feedback from everyone to feel positive about herself. She and the social worker reviewed her past accomplishments and her current strengths and looked at her tendency toward selective abstraction (focusing on the one negative evaluation and ignoring all her previous accomplishments). They examined the impact of her magnification of the supervisor's negative evaluation on her mood and ability to function. Mrs. Jones could see that she might not be able to influence the supervisor's opinion, but that she could control how she felt by not obsessing about it. She was encouraged to return to her church and community activities and to use the support of her family when she found herself preoccupied with the supervisor's opinion of her. At the end of the two-hour session, Mrs. Jones reported that she felt greatly relieved that she was not going crazy and felt as if an immense burden had been lifted from her. She wanted to return to work and she gave the social worker permission to contact the administrator, who was informed that Mrs. Jones could and should return to work.

The following week, Mrs. Jones called to report that she was sleeping and eating well, had returned to her usual activities, and was again enjoying being a crossing guard. At the one-month follow-up visit, Mrs. Jones had a bright affect, was no longer agitated, reported that she continued to feel better and was no longer concerned with the supervisor and recognized that he may only have blamed her *initially*, but once the facts were reviewed, had no longer considered her at fault.

Conclusion

Employer and union programs offering counseling in the workplace present good opportunities for early intervention with and the rapid reconstitution of workers who are experiencing emotional and behavioral difficulties. By working in a planned, structured, problem-focused manner, the occupational social worker can quickly reduce the client's level of distress, increase his or her ability to cope with the current stress and future stresses, and enhance his or her social functioning. Such structured, time-limited interventions have been found to be as efficient as long-term or open-ended treatment for problems in living, as well as cost efficient (Orlinsky & Howard, 1986; Reid & Hanrahan, 1982; Reid & Shyne, 1969). However, their effectiveness is contingent on the occupational social worker's understanding and acceptance of the theoretical tenets and mastery of the technical skills of short-term therapy.

As the principles and techniques of brief treatment are better articulated, more clearly differentiated from open-ended practice techniques, and more grounded in empirical research, the social work profession may move closer to resolving one dilemma. Is it better to offer high-quality service to fewer clients or to offer less intense services to a greater number of clients, or is it possible that with advances in knowledge and refinements in techniques, fewer sessions will not have to mean lesser quality?

The metamodel presented here can serve as an introduction to the theoretical and technical principles of time-limited work. The next level of mastery for the occupational social worker is to become skilled in specific techniques from a broad range of practice models to be able to devise flexible, multimodal intervention plans. The challenge for the future for occupational social workers will be to be able to apply this eclectic approach in a systematic fashion. The greater precision in the matching of clients' problems and characteristics to specific techniques and modalities of intervention will lead to increased effectiveness of treatment and improved cost effectiveness. However, this systematizing of intervention strategies must continue to be grounded in the particular interests and needs of the worker and the workplace.

References

Aguilera, D. C. (1990). *Crisis intervention: Theory and methodology*. St. Louis: C. V. Mosby.

Bloom, B. L. (1981). Focused single-session therapy: Initial development and evaluation. In S. H. Budman (Ed.), *Forms of brief therapy* (pp. 167–216). New York: Guilford Press.

Budman, S. H., & Gurman, A. S. (1988). *Theory and practice of brief therapy*. New York: Guilford Press.

Compton, B. R., & Galaway, B. (1989). *Social work processes*. Belmont, CA: Wadsworth.

De Shazer, S., Berg, I. K., Lipchik, E., Nunnally, E., Molnar, A., Gingerich, W., & Weiner-Davis, M. (1986). Brief therapy: Focused solution development. *Family Process, 25*, 207–222.

Fischer, J. (1986). Eclectic casework. In J. C. Norcross (Ed.), *Handbook of eclectic psychotherapy* (pp. 302–352). New York: Brunner/Mazel.

Fleisher, D., & Kaplan, B. H. (1988). Employee assistance/counseling typologies. In G. M. Gould and M. L. Smith (Eds.), *Social work in the workplace* (pp. 31–44). New York: Springer.

Fortune, A. (1985). Planning, duration, and termination of treatment. *Social Service Review, 59,* 647–661.

Fuhriman, A., Paul, S. C., & Burlingame, G. M. (1986). Eclectic time-limited therapy. In J. C. Norcross (Ed.), *Handbook of eclectic psychotherapy* (pp. 226–258). New York: Brunner/Mazel.

Germain, C., & Gitterman, A. (1980). *The life model of social work practice.* New York: Columbia University Press.

Golan, N. (1981). Building competence in transitional and crisis situations. In A. N. Maluccio (Ed.), *Promoting competence in clients: A new/old approach to social work practice* (pp. 74–102). New York: Free Press.

Gold, N. (1990). Motivation: The critical but unexplored component of social work practice. *Social Work, 35,* 49–56.

Grinnell, R. M., Kyte, N. S., & Bostwick, G. J. (1981). Environmental modification. In A. N. Maluccio (Ed.), *Promoting competence in clients: A new/old approach to social work practice* (pp. 152–183). New York: Free Press.

Hartman, A. (1978). Diagrammatic assessment of family relationships. *Social Casework, 59,* 465–476.

Hepworth, D., & Larsen, J. (1990). *Direct social work practice: Theory and skills.* Belmont, CA: Wadsworth.

Hillenberg, J. B., & Wolf, K. L. (1988). Psychological impact of traumatic events: Implications for employee assistance intervention. *Employee Assistance Quarterly, 4*(2), 1–11.

Hudson, W. W. (1982). *The Clinical Measurement Package: A field manual.* Homewood, IL: Dorsey Press.

Kanter, J. (1983). Reevaluation of task-centered social work practice. *Clinical Social Work Journal, 11,* 228–243.

Lukton, R. (1982). Myths and realities of crisis intervention. *Social Casework, 63,* 276–285.

Mann, J. (1981). The core of time-limited psychotherapy: Time and the central issue. In S. Budman (Ed.), *Forms of brief therapy* (pp. 25–44). New York: Guilford Press.

Moore-Kirkland, J. (1981). Mobilizing motivation: From theory to practice. In A. N. Maluccio (Ed.), *Promoting competence in clients: A new/old approach to social work practice.* New York: Free Press.

Orlinsky, D. E., & Howard, K. I. (1986). Process and outcome in psychotherapy. In S. L. Garfield & A. E. Bergin (Eds.), *Handbook of psychotherapy and behavior change* (3rd ed., pp. 311–381). New York: John Wiley & Sons.

Parad, H. (1988). Time-limited crisis therapy in the workplace: An eclectic perspective. In G. Gould and M. Smith (Eds.), *Social work in the workplace* (pp. 63–74). New York: Springer.

Parad, H., & Parad, L. (Eds.). (1990). *Crisis intervention: Book 2*. Milwaukee: Family Service America.

Reid, W. J. (1987). Task-centered approach. In A. Minahan (Ed.-in-Chief), *Encyclopedia of social work* (Vol. 2, pp. 757–765). Washington, DC: National Association of Social Workers.

Reid, W. J., & Hanrahan, P. (1982). Recent evaluations of social work: Grounds for optimism. *Social Work, 27*, 328–340.

Reid, W. J., & Shyne, A. (1969). *Brief and extended casework*. New York: Columbia University Press.

Rooney, R. (1988). Socialization strategies for involuntary clients. *Social Casework, 69*, 131–140.

Rosen, A., Proctor, E. K., & Livne, S. (1985). Planning and direct practice. *Social Service Review, 59*, 161–177.

Rutter, M. (1986). Meyerian psychobiology, personality development, and the role of life experiences. *American Journal of Psychiatry, 143*, 1077–1087.

Singh, R. N. (1982). Brief interviews: Approaches, techniques, and effectiveness. *Social Casework, 63*, 599–606.

Strupp, H., & Binder, J. L. (1984). *Psychotherapy in a new key: A guide to time-limited dynamic psychotherapy*. New York: Basic Books.

Sue, S., & Zane, N. (1987). The role of culture and cultural techniques in psychotherapy: A critique and reformulation. *American Psychologist, 42*, 37–45.

Sussal, C. M., & Ojakian, E. (1988). Crisis intervention in the workplace. *Employee Assistance Quarterly, 4*(1), 71–85.

Tabachnick, N. (1990). Crisis and adult development: A psychoanalytic perspective. In H. Parad & L. Parad (Eds.), *Crisis intervention: Book 2* (pp. 193–208). Milwaukee: Family Service America.

Talmon, M. (1990). *Single session therapy*. San Francisco: Jossey-Bass.

Tolson, E. R. (1988). *The metamodel and clinical social work*. New York: Columbia University Press.

Vigilante, F. W., & Mailick, M. D. (1988). Needs-resource evaluation in the assessment process. *Social Work, 33*, 101–104.

Webb, W. (1990). Cognitive behavior therapy: Application for employee assistance counselors. *Employee Assistance Quarterly, 5*(3), 55–65.

Weick, A., Rapp, C., Sullivan, W. P., & Kisthardt, W. (1989). A strengths perspective for social work practice. *Social Work, 34*, 350–354.

Yamatani, H. (1988). Client assessment in an industrial setting: A cross-sectional method. *Social Work, 33*, 34–37.

CHAPTER 12

Serving the Substance Abuser in the Workplace

Meredith Hanson

> The last thing to go for an alcoholic is work. The family, your health, everything can go, but work remains. When work goes, you hit rock bottom. Rock bottom.
>
> —Jason Robards
> *The Courage to Change*

Alcoholism and other forms of substance abuse are major social and public health problems in the United States. It is estimated that 5 percent to 10 percent of the U.S. adult population will suffer from alcoholism at some point in their lives (for example, Schuckit, 1989). The lifetime prevalence of other types of drug abuse–dependence has been found to be as high as 5.9 percent (Helzer & Przybeck, 1988). In addition, the lives of thousands of individuals who do not misuse alcohol or other drugs are disrupted by their association with substance abusers.

The most recent epidemiological data reveal that since 1985 there has been a downward trend in the use of alcohol and other drugs by the general population (National Institute on Alcohol Abuse and Alcoholism [NIAAA], 1989, 1990; National Institute on Drug Abuse [NIDA], 1991). Yet, many experts believe that "the level of drug use in the United States is higher than that in any other industrial nation. More than one half of American youth try an illicit drug before they finish high school. An estimated 14.5 million Americans used a drug illicitly in the month prior to being surveyed in the 1988 National Household Survey on Drug Abuse" (Adams, Blanken, Ferguson, & Kopstein, 1989, p. 1). Furthermore, some evidence suggests that despite the overall downward trend in substance use, there may be an increase in multiple substance-related problems in the nation (see, for example, Hasin, Grant, Harford, Hilton, & Endicott, 1990).

Some research (such as Kandel, 1980) has suggested that unemployed persons have the highest rates of substance use, whereas other reports (including Nelson, 1981; Potter & Orfali, 1990) have found that the substance use patterns of employed and unemployed individuals are comparable. All agree, however, that the majority of abusers of alcohol and other drugs are in the work force. From 5 percent to 10 percent of all workers who are employed full time are heavy consumers of alcohol (Kopstein & Gfroerer, 1991). An estimated 10.1 million American workers use *illicit* substances (Scanlon, 1991), and reports sponsored by the federal government have stated that "as many as 20 percent of all American workers [have used] illegal drugs *on the job* [italics added]" (*National Drug Control Strategy*, 1989, p. 56) and that 5 percent of the work force is addicted (Backer, 1987).

The seriousness with which business executives and employers view substance use by members of the work force is underscored by the findings of a 1987 poll by *Fortune* magazine, in which substance abuse was identified as the second-most-pressing problem faced by business and industry; only the federal deficit was viewed with more concern (Sprinzen, 1988, cited in O'Hara & Backer, 1989). Productivity losses that are due to substance abuse cost American business around $100 billion per year (Walsh & Gust, 1986). Substance users are more likely than are other employees to be involved in accidents and fatalities in the workplace (Aumann & Murray, 1986; Baker, Samkoff, Russel, & Van Buren, 1982; Podolsky & Richards, 1985). They experience greater job turnover (Kandel & Yamaguchi, 1987) and have higher rates of absenteeism (Cannella, 1987; Trice & Roman, 1978). Major safety and security risks result from the sale of illegal drugs at the work site (Castro & DeQuine, cited in DiNitto, 1988; Hode, 1990; Marrone, 1988).

With executive order 12564, issued September 1986, former President Ronald Reagan set forth standards and procedures that required the federal government—the country's largest employer—to establish a drug-free federal workplace (NIDA, 1989). The Drug Free Workplace Act of 1988 extended this policy to all federal contractors and grantees receiving payments of $25,000 or more by compelling them to take specific actions to ensure that their work sites were drug free. With the implementation of the National Drug Control Strategy in 1989, *all* private workplaces were encouraged to develop similar policies and procedures (*National Drug Control Strategy*, 1989). The double message contained in these mandates and regulations is that the use of illegal substances must not be tolerated in work organizations, but that assistance should be offered to any employee who has a problem with alcohol or other substances. The presence of official directives such as these gives sanction to social work intervention with substance abusers in the workplace. These directives reinforce the need to protect the rights of all members of work organizations—employees, managers, and union members—when developing initiatives to promote and create substance-free working environments (Akabas & Hanson, 1989).

From the epidemiological evidence and the responses of business leaders, the government, and unions, it is apparent that substance abuse presents major problems for work organizations. Although it is unclear how and to what extent working conditions actually contribute to substance abuse, the economic and human costs of substance abuse are indisputable (Gust & Walsh, 1989; Plant, 1979; Trice & Roman, 1978; Whitehead & Simpkins, 1983). A significant number of American workers abuse substances or are affected by substance abuse–related difficulties that extend into the workplace. Governmental regulations and standards encourage and, in some cases, require employers to establish substance-free working environments. Thus, knowledge and skills that are relevant for practice with substance abusers are essential for social workers who are employed in work organizations (Akabas & Kurzman, 1982).

History of Responses to Substance Abuse in the Workplace

U.S. employers recognized the adverse effects of substance abuse on their employees' work performance as far back as the early 1800s, when owners of small businesses and farmers expressed their distress about their workers' excessive drinking; such concerns were among the driving forces in the emergence of the American temperance movement (Metzger, 1988). In the late 19th century, U.S. capitalists became troubled about the disorderly actions of men whose excessive drinking upset the operations of their factories. In response, they hired welfare secretaries (the first occupational social workers) to socialize new immigrant workers and to create a "new, improved, loyal" work force who would be content and have little desire to unionize (Googins & Godfrey, 1985; Popple, 1981; Straussner, 1990). Among the services offered to workers were educational programs, medical care, and "wholesome" recreational activities to replace alcohol consumption. The official organs of companies, such as Sears and Roebuck, inveighed against drinking and urged workers to substitute the virtues of diligence and thrift for the evils of drink (Emanet & Jeuck, 1950; Googins & Godfrey, 1985). Other companies, like the Ford Motor Company, hired investigators who probed workers' alcohol consumption during their off-hours (Brandes, 1976).

In the 1940s, occupational alcoholism programs (OAPs) were developed in large business firms to respond to the alcohol-related problems of workers.

These programs were staffed primarily by recovering alcoholics who were affiliated with Alcoholics Anonymous (AA). They trained supervisors to recognize the signs and symptoms of alcoholism manifested by their supervisees (for example, a flushed complexion, tremors, bloodshot eyes, unexplained mood swings, absenteeism, and declining work performance), to document their observations, and to confront their supervisees constructively about their deteriorating conditions (Trice & Schonbruun, 1981; Trice & Sonnenstuhl, 1985). It was assumed that poor work performance was an early sign of alcohol-related problems. By pairing confrontation about declining work performance with the offer of assistance, the OAPs believed that workers could be motivated to accept help for drinking-related problems. According to Roman (1981, p. 247), the essence of this type of constructive confrontation was "crisis precipitation, believed to be necessary to counteract the effects of alcohol dependency by increasing the costs associated with drinking."

As OAPs developed, it was recognized that supervisors were poor diagnosticians and that their authority did not encompass their supervisees' substance use except as it affected the quality of the supervisees' work. Consequently, supervisors were instructed to focus on work performance, to document their observations, to provide time limits for improved performance, and to suggest professional assistance for employees whose substance use affected their functioning on the job. According to Scanlon (1991), the change in focus to work performance was important because it permitted the earlier identification of troubled workers, frequently before they started to drink or use drugs on the job. The threat of job loss remained a major force to precipitate crisis and to mobilize workers to take responsibility for their substance use (Roman, 1981; Trice & Roman, 1978). The objective of the confrontation was to convince workers to accept referrals for assistance, not to diagnose or treat the substance abuse.

Currently, employee assistance programs (EAPs) and union-based member assistance programs (MAPs) are the predominant means used to respond to substance abuse in the workplace. In the early 1970s, the development of EAPs was spurred by the establishment of NIAAA, which created an occupational programs branch to promote the creation of work-based assistance programs (Seymour & Smith, 1990).

According to Roman (1981), NIAAA's program recommendations represented both a continuity and a discontinuity with past intervention efforts in the workplace. Continuity was reflected in the institute's assertions that (1) supervisors' attention to deteriorating work performance was the best means for identifying troubled employees and (2) supervisors' confrontation of employees about poor work performance was critical to mobilize employees to take responsibility for their addictions and to seek help. Discontinuity was evident in the institute's efforts to broaden the concept of the program to encompass "behavioral–medical" problems other than alcoholism. Thus, although they evolved from OAPs, most EAPs and MAPs are multiple-issue programs that assist troubled employees who are experiencing a range of difficulties besides substance abuse.

According to McClellan and Miller (1988), as the organization of the workplace, the nature of social controls on employees, and the roles of supervisors have changed, corresponding changes have occurred in EAPs. As a result of the changes in EAPs, the needs of work organizations and employees are met in new ways. Today, employees are likely to seek assistance without being confronted by their supervisors and to request aid for problems other than substance abuse (Bayer & Barkin, 1990). Consequently, workers who are reluctant to admit to or deny the existence of substance abuse problems may be identified earlier and assisted when they seek help for other difficulties that may be the consequences of substance abuse. Furthermore, with the shift in focus, employees' substance abuse is more likely to be viewed within the context of the workers' total lives, making referral, assessment, and assistance more relevant to their concerns.

Aiding Substance Abusers in the Workplace

Social workers who are employed in work organizations must be skilled and knowledgeable about substance abuse. Their primary functions include the early identification, assessment, mobilization, and referral of substance-abusing employees, as well as the reintegration of treated substance abusers into the workplace. To carry out their roles, occupational social workers must maintain a dual focus on both the individual worker and the organizational–environmental context; they must be adept at micro- and macro-level intervention.

Conceptual Framework

The substance abuse field is characterized by numerous divergent explanations of substance abuse (Hanson, 1991). Although the disease model of addictions prevails among professionals, other models that stress social, cultural, and or psychological forces have strong support. Each model highlights important factors that contribute to the development of substance abuse; each is limited to the extent that it oversimplifies addictive behavior. Taken together, the models underscore the fact that substance abuse is a biopsychosocial syndrome in which multiple factors from the person–environment context interact sequentially and simultaneously not only to predispose some persons to substance abuse, but to influence the emergence and progression of the condition (Galizio & Maisto, 1985; Kissin & Hanson,

1982; Wallace, 1989). Within this framework, substance abuse is conceptualized as a transactional phenomenon that emerges when vulnerable individuals (such as genetically predisposed persons) encounter situations that precipitate substance use (for example, situations characterized by pressures and opportunities to use alcohol and other drugs).

Under certain conditions (for example, to relieve stress or feelings of powerlessness), substance use may be functional for workers (Corneil, 1987; Shain, 1979). In other circumstances, it may be encouraged and normalized by the work environment (Fine, Akabas, & Bellinger, 1982). To be effective, occupational social workers must adopt conceptual frameworks that draw their attention to individuals' total life contexts and that permit them to understand substance abuse as a function of the dynamic tensions existing in those contexts (Hanson, 1991).

According to Corneil (1987, p. 34), a disease-based individual model of substance abuse "forms the basis for the classic EAP activities of documentation, coercion, referral and treatment of the individual. There are few if any activities related to changing the work organization or its social structures." A biopsychosocial perspective, in contrast, is sufficiently broad to include the organizational and environmental factors that may contribute to substance abuse in the workplace. It does not minimize the disease aspects of substance abuse, but it facilitates occupational social workers' thinking about the person–environment context and empowers them to intervene with both workers and work organizations.

Early Identification and Intervention

A major reason for the success of workplace intervention is that substance-abusing employees are identified early, often before they become debilitated by the chronic effects of substance abuse and lose the support of the work organization (Nathan, 1984). Because many substance abusers do not acknowledge that they have substance use problems, case finding is critical.

Occupational social workers can facilitate the early identification of substance abusers in several ways:

1. Through training, they can prepare supervisors and other key personnel to recognize troubled employees, systematically document observations of poor performance, approach the employees constructively around their work performance, and encourage them to seek assistance. They also can counter any tendency by members of the work organization to respond judgmentally to substance abuse or to collude with substance abusers and hence enable them to continue their substance abuse.

2. By contributing to the development of policy, occupational social workers can ensure that work organizations respond humanely to substance abusers (Akabas & Hanson, 1989). If employees believe that they are valued by their companies and that they will be supported in their recovery, they may be more apt to seek assistance when they realize that they have substance use–related difficulties.

3. Through educational campaigns and health-promotion initiatives, occupational social workers can increase the entire work organization's awareness of the signs, symptoms, and consequences of substance abuse. Employees who respond to educational campaigns may recognize their substance-abuse patterns and voluntarily seek assistance. Effective organization-level initiatives such as these will combat institutional and individual barriers that impede the recognition of substance abuse by employees and allow and encourage it to continue (Googins, 1984; Johnson Institute, 1990).

4. By routinely incorporating questions about substance use in all their screening interviews, occupational social workers can identify the substance abuse problems of employees who seek help with other concerns. By remaining alert to the signs and symptoms of substance use, by being sensitive to the meanings of substance use and the risks for abuse among different cultural groups, and by intervening positively when they observe their clients' problems with substance use, occupational social workers can help their clients openly examine their substance use and determine whether they should obtain further help.

Outreach and case-finding efforts are particularly important for identifying women substance abusers and facilitating their entry to treatment. Women encounter stigma and other institutional barriers (such as inappropriate treatment arrangements, the lack of social and emotional support, and poor child care facilities) that discourage them from seeking and receiving assistance (Beckman, 1984; Gutierrez, 1990; Vannicelli, 1984a). In addition, because of the lack of systematic research on interventions with women, myths arise that women have poorer prognoses and are "more difficult" clients than are men. In contrast to the prevailing myths, the available evidence suggests that once women enter treatment, the outcomes of their treatment are comparable to, if not better than, those of men (Vannicelli, 1984b). Findings such as these highlight the need for occupational social workers to be sensitive to the attitudes and obstacles that women face in the workplace. If they can respond to women's needs and remove the barriers women encounter, their women clients are likely to respond more favorably to efforts to assist them.

Mobilization

Employees seek help under a variety of circumstances. Some recognize that they have a substance abuse problem and voluntarily request assistance. Others seek help for other concerns and may be unaware of their substance-related difficulties. Still others are in jeopardy of losing their jobs and are required to seek assistance. Thus, when they engage clients, occupational social workers must attempt to understand their clients' perceptions of their needs, as well as their motivations and readiness to address their substance use. The first task of intervention is not to "treat" clients, but to facilitate their decision to engage in a partnership with the occupational social worker to deal with their concerns.

When employees meet with EAP professionals for the first time, they may be in various stages of change (Prochaska, DiClemente, & Norcross, 1992). They may not recognize that they have a substance use problem; they may be "contemplating" the existence of a problem; they may be convinced that they have a problem, but are unsure about whether to do anything about it; or they may be certain that a problem exists and are seeking assistance to resolve it. Intervention strategies must vary according to the clients' stages of change. For example, immediate referral to a drug detoxification facility or to a self-help group may be an appropriate intervention for employees who recognize that they have a substance abuse problem and are ready to take action to eliminate it. The same strategy will fail, however, with employees who do not believe that they have substance-related difficulties.

According to Miller (1983, 1989), several interview strategies are useful to mobilize individuals to address their substance use. First, through reflective, empathic listening, occupational social workers can encourage clients to explore their thoughts, feelings, and conflicts about their substance use. Second, with awareness-building techniques (for example, using the clients' statements that may suggest a difficulty with substance use, presenting them with objective data to support the presence of such a problem, and eliciting self-motivational statements), occupational social workers can increase the clients' dissonance, which will motivate the clients to change. Third, by supporting clients' self-esteem and reinforcing their sense of self-efficacy (for instance, by actively involving them in the interview process, by communicating acceptance and respect, and by avoiding labels), occupational social workers can direct the clients' dissonance toward abstinence. Fourth, by helping clients to develop a range of alternative responses to their situations, occupational social workers can encourage clients to remain active partners in the therapeutic process and to take responsibility for their recovery.

To mobilize clients to seek assistance for substance abuse, occupational social workers must link substance use with the clients' presenting concerns (such as the possibility of losing their jobs or financial distress). In addition, they must highlight the potential adverse consequences of continued substance use and the failure to seek assistance (King, 1986). Finally, they should not attack defense mechanisms, such as denial, early in the process, but should work around these mechanisms in their efforts to clarify the clients' substance use patterns and to encourage them to seek additional assistance (Gallant, 1987; Miller, 1983). Aggressive "third-degree" tactics rarely encourage individuals to be candid about their substance use.

Referral

Once employees have accepted the need for substance abuse treatment, occupational social workers should refer them to the appropriate level of care. A diversified service delivery system exists in most communities to meet the needs of substance abusers (Hanson, 1991). Although they are not part of the formal service delivery system, *self-help groups*, including AA, Al Anon, and Narcotics Anonymous, have reached the greatest number of substance abusers. *Drug and alcohol detoxification units* are available to help drug-dependent clients withdraw from addictive substances without developing the drugs' particular withdrawal syndromes. *Inpatient rehabilitation and residential treatment facilities* exist for persons who do not require drug detoxification, but who need brief periods of care in protected environments. *Therapeutic communities and halfway houses* offer care for persons who are more enmeshed in addictive life-styles and who require extensive and intensive social therapy. *Outpatient clinics* provide aftercare services to clients who are able to remain abstinent in the community, but require ongoing support to maintain sobriety.

Not all treatment facilities are equally effective for all substance abusers. Therefore, referrals must be based on differential assessments and service plans that are congruent with the needs of individual clients (Marlatt, 1988; Moos, Finney, & Cronkite, 1990). Occupational social workers must be familiar with the range of options for assistance that exist in their communities. They also must maintain links with the various treatment facilities to ensure that their clients receive the aid that they require and to facilitate the planning and delivery of treatment.

Reintegration into the Workplace

The reintegration of clients into the workplace is essential to support their recovery. Organizational factors, such as drinking cultures, occupational stresses, and supervisory biases, may precipitate relapse. In addition, many supervisors and co-workers do not recognize the seriousness of substance abuse or the fact that recovery continues when employees return to work. Therefore, it is important that, if the client's permission can be obtained, social workers attempt to prepare organizational members for the return of recovering employees. Meetings with managers, supervisors, and union representatives can alert them to the particular problems that recovering employees encounter and can enlist their support. The creation of support groups for recovering substance abusers can provide additional assistance.

Work-reentry contracts (Morse, 1988) and back-to-work conferences (Singer, 1986) are useful tools to help recovering individuals structure their return to work. In such contracts and conferences, the responsibilities of the employees, the occupational social workers, and other key organizational members can be delineated; contingency plans can be established; follow-up procedures can be specified; and options for additional assistance can be clarified. Because all relevant parties are involved in the contracts and meet face to face in the conferences, confusion is minimized and reintegration into the workplace is supported (Schram, 1991).

During these conferences, occupational social workers must encourage all parties to discuss their concerns about the employees' past work performance and conditions on the job that may prove to be problems for workers returning after a period of absence. For example, the employees' anxiety about their ability to maintain their previous workload immediately on their return to work can be addressed, ways to handle co-workers' questions about the employees' absence can be planned, and temporary adjustments in work assignments can be considered.

In these meetings, explicit agreements should be negotiated between the workers, supervisors, and other participants. Supervisors should agree to notify the employees and perhaps the social worker and union representatives immediately if they observe difficulties in the employees' work performance; employees should agree to inform the supervisors, occupational social workers, and or union representatives if they feel undue stress on their jobs; and social workers should agree to meet with the employees to help them resolve the difficulties they encounter.

The intent of these meetings and negotiations is to keep lines of communication open and to clarify the rights and responsibilities of all parties. When they are successfully implemented, the participants report that the process of reintegrating the employees into the workplace is enhanced (Schram, 1991).

Confidentiality

Ensuring privacy and confidentiality is fundamental to the helping process and is a way that occupational social workers communicate respect for clients. Assurances of confidentiality are especially important at the work site and with substance abusers, who not only may experience feelings of shame and stigma associated with substance abuse, but may face difficulties that may jeopardize their employment. Without guarantees that privacy will be respected and ensured, it is unreasonable to expect clients to be candid about their substance abuse and the problems it poses for them.

Model plans for establishing substance abuse programs in the workplace contain detailed instructions for the maintenance of confidentiality in record keeping and in contacts with clients (see, for example, NIDA, 1989). In addition, the federal government has established regulations that prohibit the unauthorized disclosure (disclosure that the client has not authorized) of records or other materials that provide information on the substance abuse of any client in a federally assisted substance abuse program. Although exceptions can be made in cases of criminal activity on the program's premises and initial reports of suspected child abuse, the federal regulations generally apply "whether or not the person seeking information already has the information, has other means of obtaining it, enjoys official status, has obtained a subpoena or warrant, or is authorized by state law" (Confidentiality of Alcohol and Drug Abuse Patient Records, 42 CFR Part 2, Secs. 2.13 (b); 2.20, cited in Legal Action Center, 1988).

Because of the legal sanctions that require strict confidentiality when assisting substance abusers, it is imperative that social workers familiarize themselves with the various laws that apply. Because of the nature of the problems that substance-abusing employees encounter, it is crucial that social workers initiate discussions regarding confidentiality and privacy in the beginning phase of their work with clients.

Assisting Significant Others
Substance abuse by employees profoundly affects the lives of family members and other persons with whom the employees come in contact. In addition, many employees who do not abuse alcohol or other drugs are associates of substance abusers. Often, in their attempts to adjust to the presence of substance abuse or to help the substance abuser, associates actually create situations that enable or encourage the continued misuse of substances. For example, supervisors may excuse occasional lapses in performance related to some employees' substance use by citing the "domestic problems" these employees are experiencing. They may explain away substance use as the employees' "personal business." Employed spouses may tolerate continued substance abuse and avoid confronting their substance-abusing mates because they feel sorry for them. In short, they do the wrong thing for the right reasons. Rather than helping substance abusers face the

destructive reality of their addictions, such responses are conspiratorial in that they enable the addictive cycle to continue.

Occupational social workers can assist persons whose lives are disrupted by another's substance abuse in a number of ways. First, they must educate them about the destructive effects of substance abuse for both substance abusers and their associates. Second, they can help family members and significant others to understand the specific ways in which they may be enabling the person's continued substance abuse. Once family members and associates become aware of the systemic nature of substance abuse and how they are entrapped in the addictive cycle, they can become meaningful partners in the intervention process. They can be helped to take steps that extract them from their codependent patterns and encourage the substance abusers to take responsibility for their addiction and seek assistance.

Several useful guides are available for intervention with family members and associates of substance abusers (see, for example, Gallant, 1987; Johnson, 1986; Picard, 1989). In general, they suggest the following:

1. The significant others must be helped to strengthen their own self-esteem and coping responses and to disengage from the substance abuser and develop their own strengths.

2. The transactions between the significant others and the substance abusers must be addressed. Maladaptive communication patterns must be neutralized and "disenabled," and skills in problem solving, conflict resolution, and other types of communication must be developed.

3. Through the use of planned confrontations of the substance abusers by the significant others and by changing systemic patterns that support continued substance abuse, substance abusers can be induced to seek assistance and to eliminate their substance use (Thomas & Yoshioka, 1989).

Drug Testing

Concern about the impact of illegal drugs such as marijuana and cocaine on work organizations has led some employers to adopt drug-testing procedures to identify users of illicit drugs. Drug-testing programs are not widespread, yet. Most exist in large companies with 1,000 or more employees, and most are aimed at job applicants rather than at employees (U.S. Bureau of Labor Statistics, 1989). However, as employers attempt to comply with legislation, such as the Drug Free Workplace Act of 1988, and to respond to other pressures to create drug-free work environments, the number of such programs will increase.

The presence of drug-testing programs creates major dilemmas for helping professionals (Hanson, 1993). Although the number of drug-testing programs has increased, serious questions have been raised about the efficacy of preemployment drug screening for predicting applicants' work performance (Zwerling, Ryan, & Orav, 1990). Also, arguments have been made that most drug-testing programs may violate employees' rights (Baumrin, 1990). To aid occupational social workers who are employed by work-site assistance programs, the National Association of Social Workers issued drug-testing guidelines (Danto, Chenoweth, Foster, Livingston, & Straussner, 1989).

Although they usually are not directly involved with the administration and interpretation of drug tests, occupational social workers must be familiar with them, so they can understand their value and their limitations. To be effective, drug testing must not be used punitively or in isolation from other employee services. Most experts assert that it must be part of a comprehensive program that is designed to address substance abuse problems and that the results of tests without other corroborating information have little value (de Bernardo, 1988; Hawks & Chiang, 1986). Therefore, occupational social workers must advocate on behalf of employees so that test results are used as clinical tools to increase employees' awareness of their substance use; to mobilize them to seek assistance; and to monitor their recovery, rather than to separate them from the workplace. In short, they must endeavor to balance deterrent interventions with preventive and rehabilitative initiatives.

Case Illustration

The following case example illustrates the process of identifying, mobilizing, and assisting employees whose substance use is affecting their work performance. It demonstrates that social workers must maintain a dual focus on employees and work organizations and highlights useful practice strategies.

James Rose was a 34-year-old single white man, who worked for 10 years as a dietary aide in the kitchen of a large metropolitan hospital. He lived with his elderly mother in a small apartment in a working-class section of the city. He was referred to the EAP by his supervisor following a formal counseling session in which he was confronted about his poor work performance. As was documented in the supervisor's report, Mr. Rose had missed over 10 days of work because of "illness" in the past three months (he never supplied medical verification of an illness), he was late for work frequently, he did not follow assigned work instructions, and he was observed with alcohol on his breath and acting intoxicated (slurred speech and an unsteady gait) on at least three occasions (he was sent home from work each time).

The supervisor noted that unless Mr. Rose's attendance and work performance improved in the next three months, she would institute formal disciplinary action. She also recommended that the EAP explore with him any personal problems that might be affecting his work performance.

When he introduced himself to Mr. Rose, the occupational social worker informed Mr. Rose about his role as social worker in the EAP. He stated that he was an employee of the hospital, just like Mr. Rose, and that part of his function was to address any problems or issues that were interfering with Mr. Rose's job performance. He also informed Mr. Rose that by law social workers are required to keep information they obtain confidential and that he would release no information about their meetings without Mr. Rose's permission.

Mr. Rose was angry about the circumstances surrounding his meeting with the social worker. He insisted that he had "no problem other than that woman [his supervisor] who is always on my back." He also stated that he did not want any union involvement because "I can handle this myself."

It was clear to the social worker that Mr. Rose was in the "precontemplation" stage of change (Prochaska et al., 1992); that is, he did not accept that he had a substance abuse–related difficulty. Instead of challenging Mr. Rose directly (Gallant, 1987), the social worker asked him to clarify what he meant when he said that the supervisor was "always on his back." When Mr. Rose offered no specifics, the social worker attempted to introduce reality information from the workplace by suggesting that they explore the supervisor's list of Mr. Rose's problems in performing his job.

Following Miller's (1983) motivational interviewing strategies, the social worker elicited Mr. Rose's reactions to each citation by the supervisor. No attempt was made to pass judgment on the supervisor's comments. Instead, the social worker made comments like the following: "On March 1 your supervisor reported that she sent you home because you were staggering in the kitchen and you had alcohol on your breath. Tell me more about what happened." As he reviewed the list, Mr. Rose acknowledged that each incident had occurred, but that none was "that serious." The social worker proceeded to explore with Mr. Rose what his options were. He asked, "What do you think might happen if you do nothing and go back to work?" Mr. Rose acknowledged that he might lose his job and that he did not want that to happen. Once he admitted that losing his job would be "serious," he agreed to work with the social worker to "avoid losing my job." By helping Mr. Rose to think through the logical consequences of his actions, the social worker was able to elicit self-motivational statements (Miller, 1983). By actively involving Mr. Rose in the decision-making process, the social worker reinforced Mr. Rose's sense of self-efficacy and self-esteem. He also helped to empower Mr. Rose to take the necessary steps to address his substance use difficulties.

The social worker conducted a substance-use history as part of his assessment interview. The history revealed that Mr. Rose began drinking alcoholic beverages at age 11. For the past five years, he drank daily (primarily beer and rum) with his co-workers and other friends. He could not recall the last time he went for more than a day without drinking. He said that sometimes he felt "edgy" when he did not drink and that he felt "more normal (you know, more like myself)" when he drank. He admitted to no other substance use, except for experimentation with marijuana when he was a teenager ("I stopped it; it made me paranoid"). His father died of cirrhosis of the liver 10 years before, but he was aware of no other family member who experienced a substance abuse problem. Mr. Rose had no experience with alcoholism treatment; he had never attended AA.

The social worker presented the results of the assessment interview to Mr. Rose. Together, they reviewed the "evidence," including Mr. Rose's own statements that he drank on a daily basis and that he was in jeopardy of losing his job. When he was asked for his interpretation, Mr. Rose responded that he had better do something and "do it now." The social worker agreed with him and suggested that he might want to make an appointment with an alcoholism treatment facility "to get a more thorough evaluation." Mr. Rose agreed reluctantly, and an appointment was made for the following day.

When Mr. Rose appeared at the treatment facility, it was determined that he should be admitted to the hospital for alcohol detoxification and short-term inpatient alcoholism rehabilitation. With Mr. Rose's permission, the social worker contacted Mr. Rose's supervisor, the department head, and the shop steward. In the course of their discussions, it was observed that several of the dietary workers had been referred for substance abuse treatment and that many drank during their lunch breaks. Because it was apparent that organizational-level intervention was needed, preliminary plans were developed to conduct supervisory training sessions and to hold some departmentwide classes on substance abuse education that all employees would be given release time to attend.

Before Mr. Rose returned to work following his hospitalization, a back-to-work conference was arranged and a work reentry contract was developed (Morse, 1988; Singer, 1986). As part of the contract, Mr. Rose agreed to attend an outpatient alcoholism clinic, as well as regular AA meetings. The social worker agreed to meet with him once a week for six months to respond to any work-related issues that might arise. A meeting was set up between Mr. Rose, his supervisor, his shop steward, and the social worker to review the working conditions and to help Mr. Rose improve his job performance. The supervisor agreed to adjust Mr. Rose's lunch break to permit him to attend an AA group that met three times a week at the hospital; she also agreed to inform Mr. Rose immediately if she observed any deterioration in his work performance.

During the six-month monitoring period, Mr. Rose's work performance remained satisfactory and he remained alcohol free. A one-year follow-up revealed that Mr. Rose had a brief relapse, following the death of his mother. However, he reestablished sobriety, remained active in AA, and experienced no new difficulties at work.

This case example illustrates the process of aiding substance abusers in the workplace. A dual focus was maintained on the client's transactions within his environmental context. The occupational social worker used the client's poor job performance as reality information to mobilize him to seek assistance for a substance abuse problem. Specific data about the client's work performance, as well as his own statements, were used to increase his awareness and to encourage him to obtain additional help. When the client acknowledged that his substance use was a problem, the occupational social worker helped him explore his options. Once the client entered the treatment facility, linkages were maintained, and efforts were made to intervene in the work organization to prepare it for the client's return. A work-reentry contract was used to help the client become reintegrated into the workplace. By working with the employee and members of the work organization, the occupational social worker was able to design and implement a successful assistance plan.

Conclusion

Substance abuse poses major problems for work organizations. Regardless of the associations between occupational characteristics and substance abuse, it is clear that many American workers have substance use problems and that their difficulties adversely affect their work performance. To intervene effectively with substance abusers in the workplace, occupational social workers must maintain a dual focus on individuals and organizations. Such a perspective ensures that they understand the biopsychosocial nature of substance abuse, that they accurately assess the transactional dynamics that contribute to the development and maintenance of substance abuse, and that they develop meaningful initiatives to eliminate substance abuse patterns and support substance-free work organizations.

References

Adams, E. H., Blanken, A. J., Ferguson, L. D., & Kopstein, A. (1989). *Overview of selected drug trends*. Rockville, MD: National Institute on Drug Abuse.

Akabas, S. H., & Hanson, M. (1989). Organizational implications of drug abuse programming: Making the organization work for you. In National Institute on Drug Abuse, *Drug abuse curriculum for employee assistance program professionals* (DHHS Publication No. ADM 89-1587). Rockville, MD: National Institute on Drug Abuse.

Akabas, S. H., & Kurzman, P. A. (1982). The industrial social welfare specialist: What's so special? In S. H. Akabas & P. A. Kurzman (Eds.), *Work, workers, and work organizations* (pp. 197–235). Englewood Cliffs, NJ: Prentice Hall.

Aumann, G., & Murray, T. H. (1986, October). Striking a moral balance in worksite screening. *Business and Health*, pp. 10–12.

Backer, T. E. (1987). *Strategic planning for workplace drug abuse programs*. Rockville, MD: National Institute on Drug Abuse.

Baker, S. P., Samkoff, J. S., Russel, S. F., & Van Buren, C. B. (1982). Fatal occupational injuries. *Journal of the American Medical Association, 64*, 692–697.

Baumrin, B. H. (1990). To test or not to test? Social welfare versus worker freedom. *Journal of Psychoactive Drugs, 22*, 485–487.

Bayer, G. A., & Barkin, A. C. (1990). Employee assistance program utilization: Comparison of referral sources and problems. *Employee Assistance Quarterly, 5*(4), 63–70.

Beckman, L. J. (1984). Analysis of the suitability of treatment resources for women. *Substance and Alcohol Actions/Misuse, 5*, 21–27.

Brandes, S. D. (1976). *American welfare capitalism, 1880–1940*. Chicago: University of Chicago Press.

Cannella, J. M. (1987). Drug abuse in the workplace: An industry's point of view. *Clinical Chemistry, 33*, 61B–65B.

Corneil, D. W. (1987). Alcohol in employment settings: The results of the WHO/ILO international review. *Employee Assistance Quarterly, 3*(2), 5–48.

Danto, E., Chenoweth, R., Foster, B., Livingston, S. T., & Straussner, S. L. A. (1989, February). *Drug-testing in the workplace: Guidelines for the profession*. New York: National Association of Social Workers, New York City Chapter, Task Force on Drug-Testing in the Workplace.

de Bernardo, M. A. (1988). *Drug abuse in the workplace: An employer's guide for prevention* (2nd ed.). Washington, DC: U.S. Chamber of Commerce.

DiNitto, D. M. (1988). Drunk, drugged, and on the job. In G. M. Gould & M. L. Smith (Eds.), *Social work in the workplace: Practice and principles* (pp. 75–95). New York: Springer.

Emanet, B., & Jeuck, J. (1950). *Catalogues and counters: A history of Sears Roebuck and Co.* Chicago: University of Chicago Press.

Fine, M., Akabas, S. H., & Bellinger, S. (1982). Cultures of drinking: A workplace perspective. *Social Work, 27*, 436–440.

Galizio, M., & Maisto, S. A. (1985). Toward a biopsychosocial theory of substance abuse. In M. Galizio, & S. A. Maisto (Eds.), *Determinants of substance abuse: Biological, psychological, and environmental factors* (pp. 425–429). New York: Plenum.

Gallant, D. M. (1987). *Alcoholism: A guide to diagnosis, intervention, and treatment.* New York: W. W. Norton.

Googins, B. (1984). Avoidance of the alcoholic client. *Social Work, 29,* 161–166.

Googins, B., & Godfrey, J. (1985). The evolution of occupational social work. *Social Work, 30,* 396–402.

Gust, S. W., & Walsh, J. M. (Eds.). (1989). *Drugs in the workplace: Research and evaluation data* (NIDA Research Monograph 91). Rockville, MD: National Institute on Drug Abuse.

Gutierrez, L. M. (1990). Working with women of color: An empowerment perspective. *Social Work, 35,* 149–153.

Hanson, M. (1991). Alcoholism and other drug addictions. In A. Gitterman (Ed.), *Handbook of social work practice with vulnerable populations* (pp. 65–100). New York: Columbia University Press.

Hanson, M. (1993, May). *Overview and perspectives on drug and alcohol testing in the workplace.* Paper presented at the International Tripartite Experts Meeting on Drug and Alcohol Testing in the Workplace, Oslo (Honefoss), Norway.

Hasin, D., Grant, B., Harford, T., Hilton, M., & Endicott, J. (1990). Multiple alcohol-related problems in the United States: On the rise? *Journal of Studies on Alcohol, 51,* 485–493.

Hawks, R. L., & Chiang, C. N. (Eds.). (1986). *Urine testing for drugs of abuse* (NIDA Research Monograph 73). Rockville, MD: National Institute on Drug Abuse.

Helzer, J. E., & Przybeck, T. R. (1988). The co-occurrence of alcoholism with other psychiatric disorders in the general population and its impact on treatment. *Journal of Studies on Alcohol, 49,* 219–224.

Hode, N. L. (1990). Drugs in the workplace: New York State is meeting the challenge. *Employee Benefits Journal, 15*(1), 21–25, 32.

Johnson, V. E. (1986). *Intervention.* Minneapolis: Johnson Institute.

Johnson Institute. (1990). *Enabling in the workplace.* Minneapolis: Author.

Kandel, D. B. (1980). Drug and drinking behavior among youth. *Annual Review of Sociology, 6,* 235–285.

Kandel, D. B., & Yamaguchi, K. (1987). Job mobility and drug use: An event history analysis. *American Journal of Sociology, 92,* 836–878.

King, B. L. (1986). Decision making in the intervention process. *Alcoholism Treatment Quarterly, 3*(3), 5–22.

Kissin, B., & Hanson, M. (1982). The bio-psycho-social perspective in alcoholism. In J. Solomon (Ed.), *Alcoholism and clinical psychiatry* (pp. 1–19). New York: Plenum.

Kopstein, A., & Gfroerer, J. (1991). Drug use patterns and demographics of employed drug users: Data from the 1988 national household survey of drug abuse. In S. W. Gust, J. M. Walsh, L. B. Thomas, & D. J. Crouch (Eds.), *Drugs in the workplace: Research and evaluation data, volume 2* (pp. 11–24). Rockville, MD: National Institute on Drug Abuse.

Legal Action Center. (1988). *Confidentiality: A guide to the new federal regulations.* New York: Author.

Marlatt, G. A. (1988). Matching clients to treatment: Treatment models and stages of change. In D. M. Donovan & G. A. Marlatt (Eds.), *Assessment of addictive behaviors* (pp. 474–483). New York: Guilford Press.

Marrone, M. (1988). Drugs in the workplace: No quick fix. *Security, 25*(9), 62–64.

McClellan, K., & Miller, R. E. (1988). EAPs in transition: Purpose and scope of services. *Employee Assistance Quarterly, 3*(3–4), 25–42.

Metzger, L. (1988). *From denial to recovery.* San Francisco: Jossey-Bass.

Miller, W. R. (1983). Motivational interviewing with problem drinkers. *Behavioural Psychotherapy, 11*, 147–172.

Miller, W. R. (1989). Increasing motivation for change. In R. K. Hester & W. R. Miller (Eds.), *Handbook of alcoholism treatment approaches* (pp. 67–80). New York: Pergamon Press.

Moos, R. H., Finney, J. W., & Cronkite, R. C. (1990). *Alcoholism treatment: Context, process, and outcome.* New York: Oxford University Press.

Morse, G. A. (1988). Work reentry contracting. *Professional Counselor, 3*(2), 47–48.

Nathan, P. E. (1984). Alcoholism prevention in the workplace: Three examples. In P. M. Miller, & T. D. Nirenberg (Eds.), *Prevention of alcohol abuse* (pp. 387–405). New York: Plenum.

National drug control strategy. (1989). Washington, DC: U.S. Government Printing Office.

National Institute on Alcohol Abuse and Alcoholism. (1989). *Apparent per capita alcohol consumption: National, state and regional trends, 1977–1987* (Surveillance Report No. 13). Rockville, MD: Author.

National Institute on Alcohol Abuse and Alcoholism. (1990). *Alcohol and health: Seventh special report to the U.S. Congress from the Secretary of Health and Human Services.* Rockville, MD: Author.

National Institute on Drug Abuse. (1989). *Model plan for a comprehensive drug-free workplace program.* Rockville, MD: Author.

National Institute on Drug Abuse. (1991). *National household survey on drug abuse: Main findings, 1990.* Rockville, MD: Author.

Nelson, J. E. (1981). Drug abusers on the job. *Occupational Medicine, 23*, 403–408.

O'Hara, K., & Backer, T. E. (1989). Index of survey research studies on workplace drug abuse and EAPs. *Employee Assistance Quarterly, 4*(3), 79–100.

Picard, F. L. (1989). *Family intervention: Ending the cycle of addiction and co-dependency.* Hillsboro, OR: Beyond Words Publishing.

Plant, M. A. (1979). *Drinking careers.* London: Tavistock.

Podolsky, D. M., & Richards, D. (1985). Investigating the role of substance abuse in occupational injuries. *Alcohol Health and Research World, 9*(4), 42–45.

Popple, P. R. (1981). Social work practice in business and industry, 1875–1930. *Social Service Review, 55*, 257–269.

Potter, B. A., & Orfali, J. S. (1990). *Drug testing at work: A guide for employers and employees.* Berkeley, CA: Ronin.

Prochaska, J. O., DiClemente, C. C., & Norcross, J. C. (1992). In search of how people change. *American Psychologist, 47,* 1102–1114.

Roman, P. M. (1981). From employee alcoholism to employee assistance: Deemphasis on prevention and alcohol problems in work-based programs. *Journal of Studies on Alcohol, 42,* 244–272.

Scanlon, W. F. (1991). *Alcoholism and drug abuse in the workplace* (2nd ed.). New York: Praeger.

Schram, D. (1991). Making supervisor referrals work. *EAP Digest, 11*(2), 29, 56–58.

Schuckit, M. A. (1989). *Drug and alcohol abuse: A clinical guide to diagnosis and treatment* (3rd ed.). New York: Plenum.

Seymour, R. B., & Smith, D. E. (1990). Identifying and responding to drug abuse in the workplace. *Journal of Psychoactive Drugs, 22,* 383–405.

Shain, M. (1979). *Occupational programming: The state of the art as seen through the literature reviews and current studies.* Toronto: ARF Books.

Singer, G. (1986). Return to work conference eases the way. *EAP Digest, 6*(3), 45.

Straussner, S. L. A. (1990). Occupational social work today: An overview. In S. L. A. Straussner (Ed.), *Occupational social work today* (pp. 1–17). New York: Haworth Press.

Thomas, E. J., & Yoshioka, M. R. (1989). Spouse interventive confrontations in unilateral family therapy for alcohol abuse. *Social Casework, 70,* 340–347.

Trice, H. M., & Roman, P. M. (1978). *Spirits and demons at work: Alcohol and other drugs on the job* (2nd ed.). Ithaca: New York School of Industrial and Labor Relations, Cornell University.

Trice, H. M., & Schonbruun, M. (1981). A history of job-based alcoholism programs, 1900–1955. *Journal of Drug Issues, 11,* 171–198.

Trice, H. M., & Sonnenstuhl, W. J. (1985). Constructive confrontation and counseling. *EAP Digest, 5*(3), 31–36.

U.S. Bureau of Labor Statistics. (1989). *Survey of employer anti-drug programs* (Report 760). Washington, DC: U.S. Department of Labor.

Vannicelli, M. (1984a). Barriers to treatment of alcoholic women. *Substance and Alcohol Actions/Misuse, 5,* 29–37.

Vannicelli, M. (1984b). Treatment outcomes of alcoholic women: The state of the art in relation to sex bias and expectancy effects. In S. C. Wilsnack & L. J. Beckman (Eds.), *Alcohol problems in women* (pp. 369–412). New York: Guilford Press.

Wallace, J. (1989). A biopsychosocial model of alcoholism. *Social Casework, 70,* 325–332.

Walsh, J. M., & Gust, S. W. (1986). *Consensus summary: Interdisciplinary approaches to the problem of drug abuse in the workplace.* Rockville, MD: National Institute on Drug Abuse.

Whitehead, P. C., & Simpkins, J. (1983). Occupational factors in alcoholism. In
    B. Kissin & H. Begleiter (Eds.), *The biology of alcoholism: Vol 6. The pathogen-
    esis of alcoholism; psychosocial factors* (pp. 405–453). New York: Plenum.

Zwerling, C., Ryan, J., & Orav, E. J. (1990). The efficacy of preemployment drug
    screening for marijuana and cocaine in predicting employment outcome.
    Journal of the American Medical Association, 264, 2639–2643.

CHAPTER 13

Managing Disability in the Workplace

A ROLE FOR SOCIAL WORKERS

Sheila H. Akabas and Lauren B. Gates

A former cancer patient reminisced with a social worker:
"I really died twice—once when I got the diagnosis and the
second time when my boss heard about it and fired me."
—Quoted in Frances Feldman
Work and Cancer Health History:
A Study of Blue-Collar Workers

"Americans with disabilities are the largest, poorest, least employed, and least educated minority in America" (West, 1991, p. xi). Depending on the definition of disability, they have been estimated to number from 37 million (with functional limitations) to 120 million (with impairments) (National Institute on Disability and Rehabilitation Research, 1993; West, 1991). They are also a diverse minority. They include both men and women; all ages, from newborns to the aged; all ethnic groups; immigrants and Native Americans; and employed executives and welfare recipients as well as numerous other groups. Although social workers have given attention to some, such as those who suffer from mental illness or are substance abusers, it is surprising that they have not focused on serving the needs of all people with disabilities, given the magnitude and diversity of the population.

This same inattention typifies occupational social work's response to disability in the workplace. In general, social service providers and EAP personnel have not considered the problems of physical disability to be a priority (Akabas & Krauskopf, 1989). Traditionally, those with disabilities were placed on some income maintenance scheme (Social Security disability insurance, workers' compensation, or short- or long-term disability benefits) and were left to solve other problems accompanying their disabilities on their own or with assistance from agencies outside the workplace. Recently, the disabilities of the work force have been of greater interest to employers because of pressures to contain costs, humanitarian concerns, the potential to influence the productivity of the work force, and the imperatives of the Americans with Disabilities Act of 1990.

Some employers have begun to assist their employees who become disabled, but their efforts have had limited success because they tend to be unsystematic, uncoordinated, or lack the professional expertise needed to deal with the issues that workers with disabilities and the systems that employ them are likely to experience. The current understanding of the issue of disability in the workplace suggests that social workers, through their historic and traditional practice of case management (Leukefeld, 1990), have the ideal model for helping deal with it. Furthermore, through participation in employee assistance programs (EAPs) or their union counterparts, member assistance programs (MAPs), social workers, more than any other personnel in the world of work, are ideally located to help with the problems of disability and the need of the workplace to accommodate employees with disabilities. The appropriate clients for their attention are both individual employees and the work organization. An expanded role for social workers in managing disability in the workplace can both provide a vehicle for containing health care and disability costs incurred by employers and enhance the well-being of workers.

This chapter presents the rationale for such a direction, reviews research findings, and describes the components of a disability-management initiative and the specific activities in which social workers can engage to support the needs of workers with disabilities and their workplaces. Much of the support for these recommendations is derived from applied research and demonstration programs carried out by the Center for Social Policy and Practice in the Workplace of the Columbia University School of Social Work, in alliance with practitioners in many and varied field sites. These efforts have been funded, in part, by the National Institute of Disability and Rehabilitation Research of the U.S. Department of Education.

Rationale

The relationship of the world of work to the issue of disability is extensive and systemic. Not only do persons with disabilities seek employment daily, but the occurrence of disability is an everyday event in the workplace. In 1987, more than 6 million cases of reportable occupational injuries and illness were recorded by the U.S. Department of Labor, and these cases caused more than 50 million lost days of work (McCurdy, Schenker, & Samuels, 1991). In addition, the workplace is faced with the worsening of disability among those who are already disabled or an increase in their functional problems because of changes in technology or job assignments. Likewise, disability among family members is responsible for untold days of lost time among the employed work force. Research suggests that when a child with a disability is born to previously employed parents, one parent is likely to drop out of the labor force (Krauskopf & Akabas, 1988). Working women, when faced with the needs of their fragile, disabled parents, are likely to terminate their work roles about 50 percent of the time (Brody, n.d.).

The high cost of disability in the workplace may be seen in the many days of lost time resulting from these complex causal patterns, as well as in the loss of productivity related to dysfunctional performance. The constantly escalating expenses involved in health care are another disability-related cost. The long-term human cost in the loss of both purpose and income when workers with disabilities are not maintained at or returned to work can barely be estimated. Employers and trade unions recognize the importance of developing aggressive strategies to manage these costs. Prevention that reduces the occurrence of disability and programs that promote the maintenance at or early return to work of employees who experience disability are two preferred solutions to this problem. Child care and elder care services are responsive to the question of support for disabled dependent relatives. Managed health care is yet another modality for attacking the cost involved in disability.

Additional concerns involve the humanitarian imperatives that accompany disability. Those with a disability are the "worthy poor." There is a societal expectation that they will receive care, and employers and trade unions cannot ignore them with impunity. When a disability arises "out of and in the course of employment," workers' compensation laws in each state prescribe the medical care, income maintenance, and lump-sum compensation that employees with disabilities will receive.

The employer has a major responsibility for the remediation or support of employees who are injured or made ill by work. This expectation resembles the one faced by industries that pollute the environment, which are expected to restore the environment and to prevent further damage to it. By the same reasoning, one would expect employing organizations to provide maximum physical and mental restoration and reemployment to those who become disabled in the course of an industrial accident or as a result of a work-connected illness.

Equally important is the concern over the waste of human resources when persons with disabilities are employed at less than their full capacity. Human resources are expected to become more scarce as we approach the year 2000. Thus, minimizing waste has become an economic as well as a moral imperative (Johnston, 1987).

However, the passage of the Americans with Disabilities Act (ADA) in 1990 has moved this issue to the forefront. The act assures civil rights to Americans with disabilities in much the same manner that Title VII of the Civil Rights Act of 1964 did so for women and minorities. Employment provisions of ADA make it a matter of national policy to ensure that all Americans, regardless of their disability, can participate in the mainstream of life, *including the world of work*. ADA mandates that persons with disabilities be hired, maintained in their jobs, or returned to work. By training, skill, knowledge, competence, and "turf," the occupational social worker is the obvious professional to participate in the achievement of these outcomes.

Disability

Disability is an amorphic concept, usually defined in the eyes of the beholder. Disability-rights advocates often claim that disability is a social construct, "a product of the interaction between the individual and the environment" (Hahn, 1984, p. 10). Support for this concept comes from social scientists, for instance, a historian's view that disability "represents a social judgment and, in some cases, a personal choice" (Berkowitz, 1987, p. 3). The ever-practical economists provide another description, namely, that disability is "the loss of the ability to perform socially accepted or prescribed tasks and roles due to a medically definable condition" (Berkowitz & Hill, 1986, p. 4).

Perhaps the most relevant definition for purposes of this chapter is the one set forth in ADA, which characterizes disability as

- A physical or mental impairment that substantially limits one or more of the major life activities of such individuals;
- A record of such an impairment; or
- Being regarded as having such an impairment ("Regulations," 1992, p. 396).

The act excludes *present* (but not past) substance abusers. An employee or job applicant is protected under the act if he or she is "otherwise qualified" and can, "with reasonable accommodation," perform the "essential functions" of the job.

Although many adults with ADA-defined disabilities are in the workplace, the majority are unemployed. A 1986 Harris poll (Harris, 1986) found that two-thirds of all persons ages 16 to 65 with a disability were unemployed and that two-thirds of them would prefer to work, despite the many financial disincentives in doing so. With the mandate of ADA, these persons are likely to apply for jobs, and those who are already employed can be expected to become more vocal in their demands to remain in the workplace and to be accommodated when and however it is necessary. The challenge and opportunity these persons present to occupational social workers is limited only by the professional imagination.

Research Findings

Employment for persons with disabilities has been the subject of research for several decades. Studies have found that, when appropriately placed, such persons are as productive as their nondisabled peers and their work is well regarded by their supervisors (E. I. Du Pont, 1990; Weiner, Akabas, & Sommer, 1973). The job maintenance of those who are employed results in significant cost savings (Hill & Gipson, 1990). Accommodations that are needed to achieve these results are usually without cost or require a modest investment; for example, a 1982 study (Collignon, 1986) found that 51 percent of all reported accommodations are no-cost items and that an additional 30 percent cost less than $500.

In 1987, the Center for Social Policy and Practice in the Workplace, funded in part by the National Institute of Disability and Rehabilitation Research, conducted a national survey of 1,000 EAPs and MAPs (Akabas & Krauskopf, 1989). The purpose of the survey was to determine the role that EAPs–MAPs play, and may potentially play, in how employing organizations manage employees who become disabled. The research team expected that EAPs might play a significant role in the management of disability in the workplace because persons with new or worsening physical or mental disabilities often need help managing work roles and, therefore, would be logical candidates for the attention of EAPs. Furthermore, because the literature suggests that the continued employment of this population requires case management (Schwartz, Watson, Galvin, & Lipoff, 1989), the staffing patterns (the majority of the staffs are social workers) and practice model (typically information, referral, and monitoring) of EAPs implied that they could perform the case management function in disability management efforts.

The findings disproved the hypothesis. Instead, most EAPs were found to be firmly rooted in, and to largely restrict themselves to, handling mental illness and substance abuse problems. However, although the duration of the EAPs ranged from six months to 27 years, the mean duration was only 7 years—just long enough to establish a firm place for an EAP, but not enough time to expand its role. The likelihood that an EAP was involved in disability management (43 percent of respondents made such a claim) not only increased with its age, but such involvement significantly increased the likelihood of interest in greater involvement. All the respondents reported that an average of 5 percent of their clients presented with problems of physical disability. Even those EAPs that were not focused on physical disability served some who would benefit from disability management.

The study team concluded that although EAPs were poised to extend their activities to disability management, they generally have not aggressively offered disability management strategies. However, the survey did identify the many components of disability management that EAPs already have that they could use to move into this arena:

- Counseling professionals are on staff in most units.
- Most units report to human resources or medical departments, which traditionally monitor disability.
- Most units are well integrated in the total organization. That is, they collaborate with other important actors that would be needed in a disability management effort.
- Most units have ties with significant medical resources in the community.
- EAPs are ongoing structures that are regarded as referral sources for workers with problems.
- The kinds of services EAPs offer are relevant to persons with physical disabilities.
- Workers with disabilities can be expected to seek the assistance of EAPs because EAPs have a reputation for maintaining confidentiality.

Other research done at the Center for Social Policy and Practice in the Workplace and reported elsewhere (Akabas, Gates, & Galvin, 1992) found that early identification and intervention can limit the long-term negative impact of a disability. A workplace that conveys an attitude of caring and provides transitional employment and accommodated work opportunities is likely to achieve a higher rate of maintaining employees with disabilities in or returning them to their jobs and to contain the escalating costs of medical care and benefit payments as a result. The center's studies have shown that those who return to work on the date set by their physicians cost an average of $2,717 (Akabas & Gates, 1991), compared to $2,051 for those who return earlier than expected. On the other hand, for those who return after the expected date or whose physicians never set a return date (a frequent situation), these average costs increase significantly to $3,805 and $4,902, respectively.

A key to optimizing the return date in Akabas and Gates's study of 258 newly disabled unionized workers in a variety of industries in six locations across the United States was an initial interview that identified the workers' presenting needs in relation to jobs, medical care, and family and financial problems and then attempted to remediate those gaps that interfered with the workers' retention of their jobs. It would be difficult to describe a task more appropriate to the case management function of a social worker in an EAP–MAP or in a community facility or agency that provides contractual services to employees with disabilities.

Disability Management

Disability management is an initiative that marshals all systems in an organization to be responsive to the issue of disability within the setting. According to Akabas et al. (1992), the components of a disability management program include the following:

- conducting a needs assessment
- appointing a coordinating committee
- developing policies and procedures
- designating a case manager
- establishing mechanisms for early case finding
- providing transitional and accommodated employment options
- offering training to those with new, program-related responsibilities
- setting up a data collection and evaluation method
- preventing disability.

Many of these roles can be carried out by social workers who have some connections with the world of work. Other social workers can be partners in efforts that involve other workplace actors.

As with the development of any program, the first step is to identify the situation and define the problem to which the effort is designed to respond. One of the reasons that disability management has received scant attention is that information on disability is either not systematically recorded or is dispersed so widely within most work organizations that no one pays much attention to it. Organizing support for an effort requires someone to make the issue visible by gathering appropriate information in a *needs assessment*. Who are the workers with disabilities in the organization? With what frequency does disability occur? How is it dealt with now, and with what outcomes? What costs are involved? Does the organization's handling of disability meet legal requirements? Is it equal to the best practice of comparable organizations? Who are the key actors in the setting in relation to the issue?

Answers to these questions can help establish the context for an initiative, identify who should be invited to participate, and provide baseline data against which future activity can be measured. At this point, the social worker will have to decide whether to be the leader or remain behind the scenes, encouraging the effort and doing the vital but less visible work (Akabas & Hanson, 1989; Brager & Holloway, 1978; Resnick & Patti, 1980). In either case, a *coordinating committee* to establish policies, implement the program, and serve as the guardian of the effort is needed. It should include all those with key roles, whether in favor of a disability management initiative or opposed, so the support is readily available and opponents are co-opted—available to be influenced, rather than to engage in hidden activities to undermine the effort.

A *policy must be established and procedures developed* for implementing the program. The policy must fit with existing policies at the workplace—recruitment, affirmative action, benefits—as well as provisions in the collective bargaining contract. In keeping with the regulations of ADA, a policy that encourages the continuing and accommodated employment of workers with disabilities is advisable. When employees are represented by a union, the participation of the union is essential. In some organized settings, it is the union that administers the benefit program through the collectively bargained health and welfare trust fund. Social workers within these union settings are in an ideal position to provide leadership to a disability management program.

Procedures must establish the roles of the various parties. Who will identify the candidates for the program? What are the responsibilities of the supervisor? How much work must an individual be able to do to be eligible to return to work? For example, should someone with cancer who needs two days off a month for chemotherapy be returned to work? How about someone with multiple sclerosis or AIDS who fatigues easily and can work only five hours a day during an exacerbation of his or her condition? Should someone with a back injury return to work only when fully functional or be provided with light work immediately? If the latter, what kind of work should be available? These are examples of the kind of questions that policy and program planners must answer. They will differ for each setting, depending on the type of work, the characteristics of the labor force, other policies at the setting, and the availability of community resources and services at the workplace, as well as many other features.

Once these issues are settled, *mechanisms for early case finding* must be identified at the site. The EAP itself can become a vital resource for case finding and can act as the case manager in a service delivery scheme. Workers with physical problems can be encouraged to refer themselves to the unit, and supervisors can be trained to refer employees who are experiencing difficulties that derive from physical sources, as well as from substance abuse and mental illness. Notification of the availability of help and an invitation to make use of it can accompany a check for disability payments or the first workers' compensation benefit.

The *case management process* starts with a thorough assessment of the individual and identification of the services that must be organized to make maintenance at or return to work likely. The EAP must make a distinction between early return to work and the optimum timing of a return. Returning too early can precipitate a recurrence of the symptomatology that caused the lost time in the first place. For example, someone who has had a coronary bypass will almost certainly be able to return to work. The date of that return would be different for a clerical worker and a truck driver, and there is an optimum time for each when work will foster further recovery. Research has substantiated that those who return after coronary problems improve more and have a longer life expectancy than do those with the same symptomatology who remain unemployed (Debusk, Dennis, & Sidney, 1988).

Nonetheless, the right of individuals to self-determination in relation to employment following the onset of a disability is basic to social work ethics. Timing can be affected by the emotional response to the onset of disability, which varies with the individual. Few presenting problems require a more sensitive evaluation. Individuals who are experiencing a disability undergo the gamut of emotions: fear about the course of the disability, concerns about self-worth, worry about family and finances, interest in maintaining a work role, concern about rejection, and so on. The accommodations needed to preserve the productivity of particular individuals are also highly variable, requiring a reconciliation between the nature of the disability and the nature of the work. Flexibility about the length of the workday, the means used to accomplish the work, and the physical accommodations available (such as ramps and technology to compensate for hearing or visual impairments) will influence the timing of the return.

The availability of transitional jobs that are reserved for those who are recovering from disabilities and the extent of accommodated work arrangements constitute *employment options* that influence the disability management initiative. The ability of the case manager to negotiate these arrangements, often with assistance from the supervisor and the affirmative action officer or benefits manager, is an important determinant of the employment outcome of the individual who is experiencing the onset or worsening of a disability.

It is clear from the foregoing that different persons in the work setting have to assume new tasks or roles to implement a disability management program. *Training* is an important component of the development of any program that awards new responsibilities, and disability management is no exception. Those in a position to do early case identification need training in how to do so. Those who must provide work accommodations need training in that arena. Those who serve on the coordinating committee need training in handling the policy and procedural issues that arise. Everyone involved needs training in the gathering and analysis of data. Here, too, the social workers' abilities to identify the content of and develop and implement training are valuable to the achievement of the initiative.

From the time of the initial needs assessment, information and its evaluation serve a vital role in the development of a disability management program. *Systems of data collection and analysis* need to be built in, so the activity can be monitored and feedback can be obtained for improving the program. Moreover, if the disability is a result of activity in the workplace, an analysis of the data can identify opportunities for *prevention*. Over the long run, the preservation of the disability management program, like most work-situated social service endeavors, will depend on the ability to document its effectiveness. Both human and cost-benefit analyses are warranted. A program that helps individuals to remain in the labor force deserves its own reward. But when that effort can document the cost-saving nature of its outcomes, an effect that many disability management initiatives have achieved, it becomes an economic as well as a moral imperative.

Services to Individuals with Disabilities

The reader would do well to contemplate the experience that accompanies the onset of a disability. At one moment an individual is an active member of the work force, earning a livelihood. Then, within an instant, or slowly, but progressively, the person's ability to maintain a work role is thrown into question. Several income maintenance systems come into play at such a time. If the employee has had an accident in the workplace, workers' compensation benefits may be forthcoming. If the cause is not work related, but the individual lives in one of the states in which a statewide disability program is in effect (California, New Jersey, New York, Rhode Island, or Wisconsin) or works for one of the countless companies or is a member of a union that provides disability payments as part of its benefits package, some short- and perhaps long-term income coverage will be available.

The individual will face the realization that his or her job is at risk, an extremely threatening reality for anyone, but even more so if the individual has dependents. Often, the result of this scenario is the desire to protect the disability-benefit payment, rather than to return to work because of the underlying fear that he or she will not be able to perform the usual activities of the job. Hester and Decelles (1985) found that of the almost 600,000 workers annually who leave their jobs for at least five months because of a disability, less than half ever return to work.

This scenario can be altered by a disability management program that includes sensitive responsiveness to the individual. An initiative can alleviate the fear and depression that may accompany the inability to work and carry the message that the workplace is responsive to individuals and would welcome their return to work. Intervention can also deal with the attending physician, who may be overly cautious about recommending that the person return to work because of the physician's ignorance of the tasks of the person's job (or the accommodations possible) or a mistaken belief that the employee is served better by drawing benefits than by working.

These same issues confront a worker who is experiencing limitations, but has not yet left employment. Such a person may present at a community facility for treatment or go to an EAP for advice. The social worker in either location should initiate disability management planning. Research indicates that the earlier the intervention–rehabilitation–accommodation process begins, the greater its chance for success. It is easier to maintain a person at a specific job than to introduce him or her to another position; it is easier to maintain a worker's connection with the workplace through the employer of record than to obtain his or her reemployment with a new employer.

Unions are particularly valuable advocates of the needs of workers who are facing disability. They are an important ally in gaining the trust of a worker with a disability—trust that is so essential to the effectiveness of disability management. Akabas (1986, p. 34) summarized the reasons for unions' interests:

- How the needs of workers with disabilities are to be handled is covered in many collective bargaining agreements.

- Rehabilitation and job maintenance are a matter of right in labor's traditional concern for individual welfare.

- Protecting and promoting the employment rights of any one group strengthens the rights of all.

- The onset of disability can cause problems at the worksite that can be mitigated by active disability management strategies.

- Job maintenance is a means of helping long-term union members, thereby increasing loyalty and protecting an employer's experienced work force.

- All workers are subject to becoming disabled, so all will feel more secure if newly disabled workers are protected.

- Union involvement in return-to-work initiatives can eliminate the misconception that unions protect workers at the expense of employers.

An intake interview is the essential first step in formulating a plan of intervention. It must be carried out while reassuring the individual that participation will not jeopardize his or her benefits and that information will remain confidential unless the person gives explicit permission to share the information as part of the intervention. Remembering that the individual probably is unaccustomed to asking for help and may have difficulty doing so (Landy, 1960) will help establish the appropriate context. Interviews can take place over the phone or in person when it is feasible to bring the employee in for the interview. The interviewer should identify any problems in the areas of the job, health care, family relationships, and financial considerations that affect the employee's return to work. (A software package, available from the Center for Social Policy and Practice in the Workplace, Columbia University, called INSTASCAN, provides a framework for carrying out the interview and automatically identifies first-stage intervention strategies.)

A great many strategies for removing these potential barriers to reemployment must be devised. They may include counseling on personal and family issues, helping with financial management and obtaining assistance from outside resources, negotiating light-duty or flextime employment or the transfer to another job, and training the employee to carry out specific discussions with the physician on the timing and circumstances appropriate for his or her return to work. A few examples will help clarify the possibilities.

Disability can interfere with an employee's ability to perform the tasks of the job, follow various aspects of the routine, or manage the physical environment and interpersonal relationships of the job (Akabas et al., 1992). Job-related interventions usually involve some type of temporary or permanent accommodation to alleviate these problems. The social worker can convene a team that includes the individual worker with the disability; the supervisor; representatives of relevant departments, such as the equal employment opportunity, medical, and benefits departments; and the union, if the employee is a member. Serving as chair, catalyst, negotiator, or advocate, the social worker can help establish a plan that will allow the worker to return to work.

The plan may involve reduced hours of work per day to avoid rush-hour traffic or to allow time off to pursue required medical care. It may also involve a temporary or permanent reassignment. The ADA regulations require "reasonable accommodation" for an "otherwise qualified" individual with a disability. An individual who has already occupied a particular job is, prima facie, qualified. Often workers are too fearful or embarrassed, however, to share, without encouragement, their knowledge of how they could be accommodated to do their jobs.

The occupational social worker can help information flow more freely and can interpret and negotiate around it in the interest of the worker and the employer. Within the framework of ADA, reasonable accommodation may include the removal from the job (and its reassignment) that portion of the function that the disability makes difficult, for example, telephone answering for a stock clerk who becomes hearing impaired, provided that telephone work is not an "essential function" of the job (usually defined as more than 10 percent of the requirements of the task).

The case management function of the social worker extends to other arenas as well. Workers follow medical advice in their return-to-work behavior. Akabas and Gates (1991) found that 90 percent of employees return to work at the time their physicians recommend, even though physicians rarely have any clear notion of the nature of a patient's work and the accommodations that are possible. The social worker, with the employee's informed consent, may discuss the functional requirements for the performance of the job with the physician. Better yet, the social worker may help the employee capture sufficient time and attention from the physician to discuss it directly. Learning to communicate effectively with a treating physician can be a coping skill of lifelong value.

Financial and family issues may arise at the time of a disability. Mortgage payments continue and car loans must be repaid, regardless of the employees' reduced income. The occupational social worker may provide budget counseling; help negotiate an extended loan-repayment schedule; or explore, with the individual, the income maintenance options available. When concerns about health and changes in familial roles accompany the onset of the disability, referrals to mental health services may be indicated. The practitioner requires extensive assessment skills and a network of contacts with community resources to succeed in the case management function.

Of course, these case management skills are not unique to social workers in the world of work. Professionals in community agencies can use them to help clients who, following the onset or worsening of a disability, find the workplace unresponsive to their needs. Gaining an understanding of the problem, through the client's eyes, is the first step in the advocacy process that a community-based social worker can undertake (Akabas, 1990; McGowan, 1987).

ADA gives the social worker a strong base for negotiating with the workplace to meet the employee–client's needs. For example, a social worker at a hospital oncology service or from Cancer Care may help develop a plan for an employee–client's release from work for chemotherapy. A professional from the Arthritis Foundation may help a client–employee whose work is customarily done while standing to negotiate a physical accommodation that would provide a high stool.

Numerous other workplace responses will occur to the reader. The point here is that one does not have to be in the workplace to help a worker make the employer more responsive to his or her needs and situation. What is necessary is permission from the employee, an understanding of the presenting problem, clarity of the sanction for advocacy (the provisions of ADA), and a willingness to reach out to the unfamiliar territory of the world of work. Thereafter, the steps in advocacy involve identifying the goal and the probable resistance to it; designing a strategy that will surmount that resistance; enlisting the key actors in the workplace and the necessary resources; and finally, implementing the strategy and monitoring it, over time, to ensure its outcome. Through these steps, social workers can help reintegrate workers who are experiencing the onset of a disability to the workplace.

Social Work Skills and Knowledge

Logan's (1988, p. 111) observation regarding services to deaf people— "Attending to problems and needs generated by the handicapping condition of deafness is not something on which the social work profession has much of a track record"—is probably applicable to social work practice in relation to all physical disabilities. Although social workers pride themselves on using biopsychosocial assessment as the basis for direct practice, little attention is directed to the biological context—the physical condition of clients. Involvement in disability management elevates the importance of biological knowledge. Understanding the impact of a rotor-cuff injury of the shoulder or of repetitive-motion tasks on carpal tunnel syndrome, for example, becomes more than a matter of curiosity. Knowing the course of multiple sclerosis or the usual schedule of recuperation from bypass surgery constitutes essential data for carrying out a significant aspect of disability management.

Disability management presents the occupational social worker with an opportunity to serve individual employees and to influence policy decisions at the same time. The bevy of knowledge and skills required to assume such roles, however, require some redirection from other customary activities of EAP personnel. "Although the diagnosis of a chronic condition or impairment may be a medical task, the outcome—disabling or not—is shaped by individual attitudes, personal values, and social circumstances" (Mudrick,

1991, p. 495). The occupational social worker who would seek to influence the employment outcome of persons with disabilities must be able to adopt a systems approach to practice. This approach requires the professional to move easily among the skills of assessment, referral, counseling, mediation, interdisciplinary collaboration, and advocacy. Administrative responsibilities may include the ability to alert the employing organization and the individual with a disability to the effects of legislation and its accompanying regulations. To assume a leadership position in disability management at the workplace, the social worker will also need the technical capacity to develop computer systems and interpret the data forthcoming from those systems.

Disability management is frequently a new initiative in a workplace, which usually means that new expectations are added to the roles of many persons within the organization. By attending to the training needs of these numerous individuals, the social worker can make an important contribution to support the implementation of the initiative and to ensure that it receives ongoing attention. The capacity to offer that assistance can significantly expand his or her influence in the organization.

As the population ages, the incidence of disability among employed persons will increase. As ADA and other legislative actions open employment to people with disabilities, its prevalence in the workplace will expand. EAP practitioners are strategically placed to contribute to the effective integration of people with disabilities into the world of work. Assuming a responsible role in managing disability in the workplace is compatible with the values of social work and the knowledge and skill bases of the profession. The outcome of such activities will enhance the well-being of individuals, the productivity and profitability of the American workplace, and the contribution of the social work profession to the world of work. It is rare for a profession to be offered such a win-win opportunity.

References

Akabas, S. (1986). Disability management: A longstanding trade union mission with some new initiatives. *Journal of Applied Rehabilitation Counseling, 17*(3), 33–37.

Akabas, S. (1990). Reconciling the demands of work with the needs of families. *Families in Society, 71,* 366–371.

Akabas, S., & Gates, L. (1991). *Disability management: Labor initiatives in early intervention, final report.* New York: Center for Social Policy and Practice in the Workplace, Columbia University School of Social Work.

Akabas, S., Gates, L., & Galvin, D. (1992). *Disability management: A complete system for reducing costs, increasing productivity, meeting employee needs and ensuring legal compliance.* New York: AMACOM.

Akabas, S., & Hanson, M. (1989). Organizational implications of drug abuse programming: Making the organization work for you. In *Drug abuse curriculum for employee assistance professionals* (pp. III-1–III-57). Rockville, MD: National Institute on Drug Abuse.

Akabas, S., & Krauskopf, M. (1989). *Managing disability costs at the worksite: The role of employee assistance programs in disability management.* New York: Center for Social Policy and Practice in the Workplace, Columbia University.

Berkowitz, E. D. (1987). *Disabled policy: America's programs for the handicapped.* Cambridge, England: Cambridge University Press.

Berkowitz, M., & Hill, M. A. (Eds.). (1986). *Disability and the labor market.* Ithaca, NY: ILR Press.

Brager, G., & Holloway, S. (1978). *Changing human service organizations: Politics and practice.* New York: Free Press.

Brody, E. M. (n.d.). *Women-in-the-middle: The mental health effects of parent care.* Bethesda, MD: National Institute of Mental Health, Office of the Associate Director for Special Populations.

Collignon, F. (1986). The role of reasonable accommodation in employing disabled persons in private industry. In M. Berkowitz & M. A. Hill (Eds.), *Disability and the labor market* (pp. 196–241). Ithaca, NY: ILR Press.

Debusk, R., Dennis, C., & Sidney, S. (1988). New inroads in return to work. *Business and Health, 6*(7), 32–35.

E. I. Du Pont de Nemours & Co. (1990). *Equal to the task.* Wilmington, DE: Author.

Hahn, H. (1984). *The issue of equality: European perceptions of employment for disabled persons.* New York: World Rehabilitation Fund.

Harris, L. (1986). *The ICD survey of disabled Americans: Bringing disabled Americans into the mainstream.* New York: Louis Harris & Associates.

Hester, E., & Decelles, P. (1985). *The worker who becomes disabled: A handbook of incidence and outcomes.* Topeka, KS: Menninger Foundation.

Hill, S., & Gipson, K. (1990). How Weyerhaeuser improved its workers' compensation program. *Business and Health, 8*(5), 38–44.

Johnston, W. B. (1987). *Workforce 2000: Work and workers for the twenty-first century.* Indianapolis, IN: Hudson Institute.

Krauskopf, M., & Akabas, S. (1988). Children with disabilities: A family/workplace partnership in problem resolution. *Social Work Papers, 21,* 28–35.

Landy, D. (1960). Problems of the person seeking help in our culture. *Social welfare forum, 1960* (pp. 127–145). New York: Columbia University Press.

Leukefeld, C. G. (1990). Case management: A social work tradition. *Health and Social Work, 15,* 175–179.

Logan, S. (1988). Social services for deaf and hearing impaired clients: A review of the literature. *Health and Social Work, 13,* 106–113.

McCurdy, S. A., Schenker, M. B., & Samuels, S. J. (1991). Reporting of occupational injury and illness in the semiconductor manufacturing industry. *American Journal of Public Health, 81*(1), 85–89.

McGowan, B. (1987). Advocacy. In A. Minahan (Ed.-in-Chief), *Encyclopedia of social work* (18th ed., Vol. 2, pp. 89–95). Silver Spring, MD: National Association of Social Workers.

Mudrick, N. A. (1991). An underdeveloped role for occupational social work: Facilitating the employment of people with disabilities. *Social Work, 36,* 490–495.

National Institute on Disability and Rehabilitation Research. (1993). *Rehab brief: Disability statistics* (Vol. 14). Washington, DC: U.S. Department of Education.

Regulations to implement the equal employment provisions of the Americans with Disabilities Act of 1990: Definitions (rev.). (1992, July 1). *Federal Register, 56*(144), Section 1630.2.

Resnick, H., & Patti, R. (Eds.). (1980). *Change from within: Humanizing social welfare organizations.* Philadelphia: Temple University Press.

Schwartz, G., Watson, S., Galvin, D., & Lipoff, E. (1989). *The disability management sourcebook.* Washington, DC: The Washington Business Group on Health.

Weiner, H. J., Akabas, S. H., & Sommer, J. J. (1973). *Mental health care in the world of work.* New York: Association Press.

West, J. (Ed.). (1991). *The Americans with Disabilities Act.* New York: The Millbank Fund.

CHAPTER 14

The Older Worker and Service Delivery at the Workplace

Cynthia Stuen and Barbara Drahus Worden

I don't know what this thing is: retire. I think to live is to work.

—Kirk Douglas
The Ragman's Son: An Autobiography

The American work force is aging. By the year 2000, 49 percent of the work force will be ages 35 to 54, a startling 14 percent increase over the 35 percent it was in 1988. The aging work force reflects the general trend toward an aging population in the United States. The current 33 million Americans age 65 and over constitute nearly 13 percent of the general population, in contrast to 4 percent of the population in 1900 (Soldo & Agree, 1988).

Two factors that have been attributed to the "graying" of the population have significance for the workplace. First, because of their increased life expectancy primarily because of medical advances, older adults may have to continue working to supplement their incomes during their prolonged period of retirement or may choose to continue to work beyond age 65, at least part-time, if they feel healthy enough to do so. Furthermore, with the elimination of the mandatory retirement age and the gradual increase in the qualifying age for full retirement benefits under Social Security, older workers will have greater incentives to continue working. Second, with the declining birthrate will come a decline in both the number of young adults

---

The authors gratefully acknowedge the research assistance of Martha Stokes, MS.

joining the labor force and the ratio of workers to retirees at a time when there are concerns about the increased cost of Social Security. These factors will make older adults a more attractive labor pool from which to recruit, retain, or retool.

According to a major national survey by Louis Harris and Associates (undated), more than 1.9 million unemployed older Americans ages 50 to 64 are ready and able to go back to work. This figure is almost three times the official U.S. Bureau of Labor Statistics estimate of 630,000 and represents about 24 percent of those not currently working (McNaught, Barth, & Henderson, 1991). Although there has been an overall trend toward early retirement, part-time work has increased among older adults age 65 and over. From 1960 to 1986, the proportion of older men working part-time rose from 43 to 61 percent and that of older women, from 30 to 48 percent.

An important symbiotic trend is evolving whereby older workers who are willing and able to work or need to do so are being seen as a solution to the projected labor shortages in many industries and occupations, the increased costs of labor, and the diminished levels of skills of an increasingly undereducated work force. Recognition of the life-transition issues that are prevalent among older adults is important for providing successful occupational social work interventions to maximize the resources of older workers. These issues may range from preretirement planning, which includes concerns about the meaning of work, adequate income, and health status, to caregiving for dependent older relatives. This chapter reviews the laws, entitlements, and legal issues that affect older workers; addresses the needs of special populations of older workers who are at risk of unemployment; reviews the literature on attitudes of and job productivity among older workers; identifies new roles and resources for older workers; and discusses the implications of the gerontological occupational social work field for practice and research.

Laws, Entitlements, and Legal Issues

The definition of "older workers" varies, from workers who have reached retirement age to a group of middle-aged workers who have difficulty keeping or finding jobs because of their age. Various laws and entitlements define older workers differently, and each has policy implications for the utilization and retention of older workers in the labor force.

The Social Security Act of 1935 provided public recognition of the need for income in old age. A floor of income protection for retired workers was the original intent of this legislation, which was modeled on German and English social policies (eligibility was expanded to survivors and dependents in 1939 and to workers with disabilities in 1956). Otto Von Bismarck, chancellor of Germany in the late 1800s, is credited with the introduction of a separate legal status for the elderly into western social policy. In 1889, Germany adopted the Old Age and Survivors Pension Act for financial support of its older citizens, starting at age 65—an arbitrary age, selected by Bismarck, who was 74 at the time.

According to Wilbur Cohen (cited in Cain, 1976, p. 181), age 65 was selected as the age of eligibility for Social Security benefits without much debate:

> The simple fact is that at no time in 1934 did the staff or members of the Committee on Economic Security deem feasible any other age than 65 as the eligible age for receipt of old age insurance benefits. There is, therefore, very little material available to analyze the economic, social, gerontological or other reasons for the selection of this particular age or of any proposals for voluntary retirement or of any flexible retirement program in relation to the disability of an individual.

Social Security benefits at reduced levels are available to workers who retire as early as age 62, and full benefits are available at age 65. The 1983 amendments to the Social Security Act mandated that the age of eligibility for full retirement benefits will be gradually raised from 65 to 67 (age 66 for those born between 1943 and 1960 and age 67 for those born after 1960). These changes were made because of the concern by some that Social Security benefits should be cut and the retirement age increased so that older workers will remain in the labor force and hence contribute to the nation's production of goods and services in response to the burgeoning federal deficit. At the same time, public and private employers have been offering retirement-incentive programs to encourage employees' early retirement, and their accelerated efforts in this regard have contributed, at least in part, to the long-run trend toward early retirement (Moon & Hushbeck, 1989; Mutschler, 1986). There is, however, some evidence that the trend toward early retirement may be diminishing as older workers are coming to be seen as a valuable, alternative supply of labor for current or anticipated shortages.

The Employee Retirement Income Security Act (ERISA) of 1974 and its amendments protect the private pensions of workers by requiring all pension plans to give their participants the right to accrued benefits at a designated age, regardless of whether the pensioners are still employed at that time. This legislation will have even more significance for future cohorts of workers because fewer than 30 percent of older adults now receive income from private pensions (Rix, 1990).

Under the provisions of the Age Discrimination in Employment Act (ADEA), an older worker is someone age 40 and over. ADEA was enacted in 1967 to promote the employment of older persons on the basis of their ability, rather than their age; it prohibits age-related discrimination in compensation for and the terms, conditions, and privileges of employment. The 1978 amendments to the act extended the minimum permissible mandatory retirement age to 70 and abolished mandatory retirement for most federal employees. Proponents of extending the retirement age beyond age 65 argued successfully that the increasing life spans and better health among older people, coupled with demographic projections of potential labor shortages because of the trends toward early retirement and a lower birthrate, logically led to the extension of the age of retirement. Business leaders and college administrators voiced opposition to this plan. Among their unsuccessful arguments was the belief that the age limit of 65 was a fair and equitable policy that allowed older workers to retire with dignity and did not clog promotion ladders or reduce opportunities for women, minorities, and younger employees. Since January 1987, older persons, with few exceptions, have been legally entitled to remain at work for as long as they wish, assuming that their performance is adequate (Rix, 1990).

Age discrimination did not disappear with the passage of ADEA, however. Some of the reasons cited in the literature from the employer's perspective are the prevailing stereotypical attitudes that older workers are recalcitrant, untrainable, and unreliable; the continuation of early retirement incentive programs and of the preference for younger workers when jobs become available; and the weak administration and enforcement procedures of the act (Wineman, 1990).

From the employee's perspective, early retirement (withdrawal from the labor force before age 65) has become the norm for men, reflecting improvements in employees' retirement resources (Social Security, pensions, and accumulated wealth) and, in some cases, health problems. Some retirements, however, are not strictly voluntary, but are a response to the actual or probable loss of jobs. Workers may prefer another choice, such as phased retirement, part-time employment, or opportunities for second careers.

The Job Training Partnership Act (JTPA) of 1982 is the largest government-sponsored job training program. Although it is primarily a program for youths, older workers have been served under JTPA's Title II-A block grant to the states and through a 3 percent set-aside specifically targeted to persons age 55 and over. The goal of JTPA is to afford job training to economically disadvantaged individuals and others who face severe barriers to employment. However, the restrictive income criterion for JTPA has meant that a large number of middle-aged and older workers who could benefit from the updating of their skills are not qualified.

Age 55 and over also designates an older worker in Title V of the Senior Community Service Employment Program (SCSEP), established under the

Older Americans Act of 1965. SCSEP authorizes part-time community service employment to disadvantaged older workers with incomes no higher than 125 percent of the poverty level. Its objectives are to provide training to older people, serve as a source of current income, and place older people in public and nonprofit community service organizations. SCSEP participants are largely female (70 percent), minority (37 percent), poorly educated (50 percent have less than a high school education), and over age 65 (more than 50 percent) (Rix, 1990).

As Coberly (1991) pointed out, both the Older Americans Act and the ADEA were passed in the 1960s, when retirement was perceived as involuntary, resulting from mandatory employment practices, poor health, or age discrimination. Careful study of decisions to retire in the 1980s suggests that the majority of older workers retired because it was advantageous to do so. Economic impact studies of retirement have shown that older workers were penalized by both private pension plans and the Social Security system if they worked beyond normal and often early retirement ages (Quinn, Burkhauser, & Myers, 1990).

From the employer's perspective, health insurance costs and the role of Medicare are important considerations in hiring or retaining older workers. For example, with the passage of the Tax Equity and Fiscal Responsibility Act of 1982, older workers receive, in effect, no Medicare benefits until their employee health insurance benefits are exhausted. This act creates an economic disincentive for employers to hire or retain older workers (Root & Zarrugh, 1987). Hence, changes in laws, regulations, and entitlements can have a profound impact on how mutually beneficial it is for employers and older workers to work together or sever their ties.

Special Populations: Women and Minorities

Although the overall participation of older men in the labor force has decreased since the turn of the century, that of women ages 45 to 64 has increased, but the rates of both women and men in the post-65 age group have declined (see Table 1). The effect of these trends is that the labor force of older workers is increasingly female. The percentage of midlife and older women who are seeking jobs is increasing, as is that of women who choose to remain in their jobs even when they are able to retire (National Council on Aging, 1986). Contributing to this growth are increased life expectancy; changing values toward women's roles; the increased opportunity for advanced educational opportunities for women; and the post–World War II baby boomers, who are turning 40 and thus swelling the ranks of older workers, including a growing number of women.

Table 1
Labor Force Participation Rates of Men and Women Aged 45–64 and
65 and Over, Selected Years, Actual 1900–1989 and Projected 2000
(in percentages)

	MEN				WOMEN			
YEAR	45–64	45–54	55–64	65 AND OVER	45–64	45–54	55–64	65 AND OVER
1900	90.3	—	—	63.1	13.6	—	—	8.3
1920	90.7	—	—	55.6	16.5	—	—	7.3
1930	91.0	—	—	54.0	18.0	—	—	7.3
1940	89.4	—	—	42.2	20.0	—	—	6.0
1944	93.5	—	—	50.9	31.2	—	—	9.6
1950	91.9	95.8	86.9	45.8	33.1	38.0	27.0	9.5
1960	91.9	95.7	86.8	33.1	44.3	49.8	37.2	10.8
1970	89.3	94.3	83.0	26.8	49.3	54.4	43.0	9.7
1980	82.0	91.2	72.1	19.0	50.7	59.9	41.3	8.1
1989	80.2	91.1	67.2	16.6	58.5	70.5	45.0	8.4
2000	81.8	90.5	68.1	14.7	65.5	76.5	49.0	7.6

NOTE: Figures for 1900–1940 are from decennial censuses; figures for 1944–1989 are from current population surveys.

SOURCES: Fullerton, (1989), U.S. Bureau of the Census (1965), and U.S. Department of Labor (1985, 1990).

The double jeopardy of age and gender presents special barriers for women in the workplace. Not only are ageism and sexism still present in the workplace, but "research on job searching among older adults shows that age discrimination affects women at an earlier age than men" (Rothstein, 1988, p. 179). How can it be that the vast majority of women in today's work force are clustered in the lower-paying jobs when discrimination based on age and gender is illegal? Some 60 percent of all female workers are in retail sales, administrative support, and services—jobs at the lower end of pay scales (Herz, 1988).

Continuity in the labor force is another area in which women workers differ from their male counterparts. Women continue to assume the primary responsibilities for the care of their homes and children, and the caregiving role often requires them to move in and out of the labor force. Even when their children are launched, middle-aged daughters and daughters-in-law then must often care for their older relatives. This phenomenon of caring for both the younger and older generations has caused middle-aged women to be called the "sandwich" generation (Brody, 1981). It directly affects women's Social Security and pension benefits; in fact, private pension plans still do not cover half the women in the work force (Rix, 1990). Hence, many women find it necessary to continue to work because they need to supplement their smaller pensions and social security payments, compared to those of men.

Occupational social workers should recognize that older women who are in the labor force today experienced a different workplace in their early and middle years and have seen many changes. For example, during the Great Depression, many states proposed legislation to ban married women from employment (Shaw, 1985). The women of the baby-boom cohort, in contrast, have been exposed to the women's rights movement and have had more educational and job opportunities and therefore come to the workplace with different expectations.

Displaced homemakers—women whose principal job has been home-making and who have lost their main source of income through divorce, separation, widowhood, or the disability or long-term unemployment of their husbands—are a growing pool of older workers. Uhlenberg and Myers (1981) estimated that in the future, as many as half the people age 65 and over will have been divorced. Furthermore, the number of divorced people who will not remarry will also increase (Hess & Waring, 1983). The economic implications of divorce or the other factors just mentioned often necessitate that these women work. A national network has emerged to represent the estimated 11 million women (6 million over age 65) who have lost the support of their husbands and need employment (Miller, 1989). The Displaced Homemakers Network, with approximately 1,000 local chapters, recognizes that, because of their age and the lack of work experience and skills, displaced homemakers face multiple barriers to entering or reentering the labor force.

People of color face circumstances that are similar to those faced by older female workers. Unemployment is a greater problem for middle-aged and older black men than it is for white men, and the same holds true for black women. Male workers of color often are clustered at the low end of the pay scale, have not had the educational opportunities afforded their white male counterparts, and have been victims of discrimination in the workplace. Women of color who want to work face even more barriers—the triple jeopardies of ageism, sexism, and racism.

Working out of economic necessity is a more prevalent issue for people of color. The poverty rates of women and older people of color are much higher than those of white men. In contrast to the poverty rate of 12.4 percent for all older adults, the poverty rates of black and Hispanic elderly people are 31 percent and 22.5 percent, respectively (U.S. Senate, 1987–88). A survey of black persons age 60 and over and their labor force interests revealed that 25.5 percent of the 165 people who were surveyed preferred to work (Crawley, 1992). Among this group who wanted to work, more than one-third viewed finances as their greatest concern, but financial incentives were not the only reason they were working; 43 percent worked for personal satisfaction or the sense of accomplishment they felt.

Refugees are a population that is sometimes overlooked. The rates of placement of older refugees into the labor force were significantly lower than were those for younger refugees by the New York State Department of Social Services (Bloom & Kurzman, 1986, 1987). The reasons cited for these lower rates were that older refugees are less acculturated; many are further isolated when they assume the role of caretakers in their extended families; and they often experience depression, loneliness, and isolation. An Older Refugee Employment Assistance Program provides valuable strategies for occupational social workers to incorporate when serving a population of older refugee workers.

Attitudes, Aptitude, and Training

Attitudes about older workers vary. Although many employers espouse the virtues of older workers, some of their practices are still biased against older workers; they make neither jobs nor opportunities for retooling and or advancement available to them. The American Association of Retired Persons (AARP, 1988, 1989) conducted two major public opinion polls to examine the attitudes and practices of businesses toward older workers. The findings of these polls must be considered in the context of the following economic, demographic, and social forces: (1) cost cutting and technology as top priorities; (2) the rising costs of health care; (3) the restructuring of the labor force, with growth in the low-wage service sector; (4) the view that the 50-plus age group is an attractive consumer segment (but not an employee pool), and (5) the fact that employers are not attuned to employees' needs and to older people who want to work part-time.

The AARP polls yielded a number of interesting findings. First, positive attitudes toward older workers were high in both the 1988 and 1989 polls, and there was an increased appreciation for the "work ethic" that is charac-teristic of older workers, who are dependable, reliable, and punctual. However, some age discrimination was still reported. Second, despite these positive attitudes, the issue of whether older workers can adapt to new technology and concerns about the costs of their health benefits appears to impede the full utilization of older workers in American businesses. Third, companies have had little or no progress in implementing programs to use older workers more fully. Fourth, the largest companies (1,000 or more employees) continue to display the least positive attitudes toward older workers. Human resources decision makers in the largest companies give older workers less credit for their work ethic, are more critical of their ability to adapt to technology and other areas, and are keenly aware of the costs of health insurance, all of which are reflected in the companies' policies on providing incentives for early retirement.

Last, older workers view themselves as having superior work habits and a greater commitment to work than management recognizes. They also believe that they are seen as expensive, in terms of both salaries and benefits. They regard themselves as an untapped resource and are frustrated about the lack of opportunity to maximize their contribution (AARP, 1989).

Issues of productivity have long been associated with decisions to hire or retain older workers. The findings of studies on the relationship between workers' age and productivity have varied, but none of the studies has shown any clear evidence of higher or lower productivity associated with any age group (U.S. Senate, 1984). Variations in productivity *within* age groups are more common than among them.

Concerns about job-related injuries are related to productivity. A comparison of older and younger workers revealed that, although older workers sustain fewer on-the-job injuries than do younger workers, the severity of their injuries tends to be greater, and although absences for job-related injuries tend to be longer, avoidable work absences decrease with age. Furthermore, job-turnover rates are lower and job stability after training is greater among older workers (Davies & Sparrow, 1985).

Some employers have taken a shortsighted view, not wanting to spend money on retraining older workers, perhaps because of ageist views that stereotype older adults as being less able to acquire new skills. Although the length of time it takes to learn some new tasks and to acquire some new skills may be a little longer for older than for younger workers, older workers can and do learn (Hartley, Hartley, & Johnson, 1984; Poon, 1987; Sterns & Doverspike, 1988). Knowles (1988) pointed out that the costs of retraining existing older workers should include recognition of the costly and risky replacement expenses, which involve recruiting, relocating, and training new workers. Root and Zarrugh (1987) noted that older workers may be excluded from training opportunities because it is assumed that the investment will have a shorter payback period than for younger workers. But higher turnover rates and the short half-life of many new technologies suggest that the exclusion of older workers generally is based on age stereotyping rather than on a cost-benefit rationale.

A study released by the Commonwealth Fund (1991) provided the first detailed economic evidence that older workers can be trained in new technologies, are flexible about work assignments and schedules, have lower rates of turnover and absenteeism, and are often better salespeople than are their younger colleagues. The following is one case from that study:

Days Inns of America began hiring older workers (individuals age 50 and over) as reservations agents in 1986 due to difficulty recruiting younger workers and their nearly 100 percent turnover. The company's nationwide reservations system, divided in two locations, is a sophisticated 24 hour a day telecommunications operation handling 23,500 calls a day. The research analyzed one center and compared the costs and benefits of hiring older versus younger workers. It found:

- Older workers can be trained to operate sophisticated computer software in the same time as younger workers: 2 weeks.
- Older workers stay on the job much longer than younger workers, an average of 3 years compared to 1 year. This results in average training and recruiting costs per hire of $618 for older workers, compared to $1,742 for younger workers.
- Older workers are better sales people than younger workers. They generate additional revenue by booking more reservations than younger workers, although they take longer to handle each call to the reservation center.
- Older workers participate in all three shifts. (Commonwealth Fund, 1991, p. 3)

Other companies have been leaders in training older workers: The Travelers companies train returning retirees in keyboard skills and office technology, AT&T trains for its emerging technologies in the communications field, and Control Data Corporation encourages workers ages 30 to 55 to consider new opportunities for employment within the company. The National Caucus and Center on Black Aged sponsors a 26-week training course to prepare older workers to become housing managers (Rix, 1990).

Educational institutions have also provided leadership in and conducted research on the retraining and retooling of older workers. Some colleges and universities have developed specialized courses for older adults to utilize their retired faculty in community service projects, for pay or on a volunteer basis. For example, Seniors Teaching Seniors was created at Columbia University to train older adults to become effective communicators of their skills and expertise to strengthen the existing network of senior center programs (Stuen, Kaye, & Monk, 1983). The Retired Faculty Linkage project, another Columbia University initiative, grew out of a survey that found that 60 percent of the retired faculty remained in the university environs and were interested in being involved in consulting, advising, and lecturing at community organizations (Stuen & Kaye, 1984). Emeriti institutes, lifelong learning centers, college after 60, and reduced or free tuition for older adults all provide opportunities for older adults to retool or renew, using the resources of academic institutions.

New Roles and Costs

Given the emerging economic and business trends, the next decade must be a time of reconciling ageist assumptions and demographic imperatives with the need of the workplace to create viable solutions that benefit both employers and older workers. Choices for older workers, such as job sharing, part-time work, flextime schedules, flexplaces (alternative work sites), phased retirement options, and job redesign, which also may benefit younger workers, are slowly becoming available.

An examination of the database of the National Older Worker Information System (NOWIS) (which documents private-sector initiatives) shows that hiring programs for older workers are primarily for part-time clerical and service positions. Hiring for full-time work is limited and has little applicability for blue-collar or nonclerical, white-collar workers who were displaced before retirement.

The costs of compensating older workers are a concern of management (U.S. Senate, 1984). Older workers are often the most senior (and hence are at higher salary levels), so it is always tempting to consider replacing them with lower-paid younger workers. Caution must be exercised with this strategy, however, for it may be more costly to hire, relocate, and train a new person than to retrain or retool an older worker.

The expense of health benefits is another concern of management because the costs of health benefits for older workers are higher than for younger workers. Although the collective conscience of employers may be lagging in the ability to separate fact from fiction about older workers, Root and Zarrugh (1987) pointed out that some employee-benefit regulations may lower the costs of employing older workers. For example, ADEA permits the exclusion from a pension plan of a newly hired worker who is within five years of the normal retirement age of 60 or older. Also, employers can cease adding pension income for workers once the workers reach the normal retirement age. Provisions under ADEA also allow employers to provide less in the way of benefits to older workers as long as what they pay for those benefits is the same for younger and older workers.

Resources for Older Workers and Volunteers

A number of national and regional initiatives address issues that are related to the employment of older workers and retirees and the use of volunteers. A brief highlight of some of them will give the occupational social worker an idea of the available resources to pursue. This listing reflects the diversity of older workers, which includes individuals who are making midlife career changes, workers who are contemplating retirement, retirees who are returning to the work force full- or part-time, displaced workers who have been wrenched from their accustomed employment, and persons who have had little or no work experience outside the home.

- Ability Based on Long Experience (Operation ABLE) is an umbrella organization of services that helps persons over age 50 find employment. It originated in Chicago, and there are similar organizations in many other cities.

- Prime Time Productivity, a program of the National Council on Aging, offers program development and training services to help businesses mold a work force for America 2000 and publishes a newsletter, *The Aging Workforce*.

- AARP established the Worker Equity Department to promote job opportunities for older workers and to assess the impact of an aging work force on society. It publishes many print and video resources, including a newsletter, *Working Age*.

- Promoting Older Women's Employment Rights is a coalition of women's rights organizations and organizations of older people that promotes the rights of midlife and older women in all areas of employment and training.

- The National Clearinghouse on State and Local Older Worker Programs, operated by the National State Units on Aging, provides technical assistance to professionals in programs for older workers with job development, recruitment, training, and retention.

- NOWIS is a computerized database that provides information about corporate employment practices and programs for older workers.

- Forty Plus is a career-center program for executives and professionals aged 40 and over. Its office staff provide support services to members while they look for work and teach them job-search skills.

- ACTION, the federal government's domestic volunteer agency, has a number of programs for volunteers, some with paid stipends for older adults. These programs include the Retired Senior Volunteer Service, which provides opportunities for volunteers in the community; the Senior Companion Program for low-income older adults, to help other adults remain independent in the community; the Foster Grandparent Program, offering older adults a chance to provide companionship to children; and Volunteers in Service to America, whose participants help to alleviate poverty.

- The Service Corps of Retired Executives provides American businesspeople, particularly in small businesses, with counseling and training from retired executives, who share their expertise.

- Labor unions, such as the Amalgamated Clothing and Textile Workers Union; the American Federation of State, County, and Municipal Employees; the International Brotherhood of Teamsters; and the United Auto Workers, provide leadership in protecting the jobs of older workers and advocating work alternatives to accommodate older workers' needs. These unions also offer professional occupational social work services to current workers and to retirees. Many have started support groups to address the caregiving demands of older workers, to provide access to community aging networks and to help retirees to continue to be involved in union activities.

Gerontological Occupational Social Work

Older adults are part of the world of work today and reflect a growing representation of minority groups, women, and persons with disabling conditions. As Kurzman and Akabas (1981, p. 53) pointed out, "the world of work is a functional community that provides easy access to a large population in its natural life space and offers an opportunity to develop a universal service delivery system unencumbered by eligibility and categorical requirements." The occupational social worker can be a facilitator and enabler for older workers through a variety of interventions, including individual and group service modalities. In addition, his or her general knowledge of the employing organization or union can clarify and stimulate work options that may expand and lengthen the older worker's productive years on the job. Therefore, although the occupational social worker needs to see the employing organization as a target for change, the workplace remains an important vehicle for service delivery (Crawley, 1987).

While working with policy issues that affect the older worker and providing direct services, the occupational social worker must simultaneously assess and intervene on several levels to do the following:

1. evaluate the individual employee's motivation and capacity to fulfill the role of worker, as well as the personal meaning of work to that individual

2. ensure that the organization's formal personnel policies do not promote age stereotyping

3. influence the informal attitudes that are perpetuated by personnel employees, trainers, and managers in the recruitment, hiring, training, and retention of older workers

4. if unionized, advance the union's mandate to negotiate for and serve the needs of its older and retired members.

Unions see older workers and retirees as a valued constituency because of their long-standing philosophy of "social unionism." This philosophy reinforces the belief system among older members that the union is a way of life, rather than merely an economic system (Wineman, 1990). This mutual identification ensures a loyal and steady dues-paying population and promotes strong ties to the union, while setting an example for younger union members. Many older and retired union members see these benefits as their right, an entitlement earned through long years of active membership. They can accept services more readily because they feel they belong and generally do not see themselves as "charity cases" (Habib & Gutwell, 1985).

Some direct services provided to this population are concrete: transportation and home-care arrangements, information on and services for elder care, housing and legal advocacy, assistance in applying for entitlements, and escort services. When union members retire, outreach programs that focus on decreasing their social isolation and easing the disengagement process are often successful (Habib & Gutwell, 1985; Wineman, 1990).

The occupational social worker also must assess the organization's commitment to retain and, if necessary, retrain, the older worker. Too often, career development and training opportunities are established solely for young workers, and older workers are overlooked. Second-career positions, as well as part-time and flextime options for the older employee who is willing and able to continue in the work force, can add valuable skills and organizational memory that the organization may need to manage technological change. Organizational strategies that promote early retirement have been successful, but in some cases encourage older workers to leave the work force before they are ready and to face a retirement transition for which they are unprepared (Rosen & Jerdee, 1985). In turn, the employer is robbed of stable and skilled employees and may face a shortage of replacement workers.

The diversity of the older adult population is apparent when one realizes that old age spans nearly 40 years and everyone does not age uniformly. Chronological age is not always a good indicator of overall health or functional status. However, chronic conditions, such as arthritis, hypertensive disease, heart disease, and hearing and visual impairments increase sharply with age. Although the majority of older workers do not report disabling conditions that interfere with their work, as age increases so do the rates of disability. Workers ages 65 to 69 are three times as likely as are workers ages 45 to 54 and six times as likely as are those ages 35 to 44 to report severe functional limitations (Berkowitz, 1988). These limitations include impairments in seeing, hearing, speaking, lifting or carrying, walking, using stairs, and getting around both outside and inside, all of which can obviously affect work performance. However, Berkowitz also noted that although health and functioning may not improve with age, older people gain knowledge and wisdom that perhaps offset some of the age-related changes, such as reduced speed or reaction time.

The graying of America affects the workplace in a dimension other than the employment of older workers. As the population ages, younger workers will be increasingly faced with concerns about caring for their older, often fragile, family members. Elder care is predicted to be the most needed benefit in the 1990s and offers a challenge to occupational social workers in their provision of direct services and their knowledge of community caregiving resources (Winfield, 1988, p. 237; see also Chapter 9). Many employers turn to their EAPs for assistance with elder care (Wagner, 1989). The social work role can vary from education, in which the worker coordinates information and referral services, to in-depth, individualized case assessment, counseling, and management for employees, regardless of their age, who are responsible for caring for older adults. Other services offered by occupational social workers may include transportation, home care, housing and legal advocacy, entitlement counseling, and escort services.

Another issue for occupational social workers is related to anticipated life transitions, particularly retirement. An understanding of normative family relationships and aging processes can guide social workers to anticipate the types of services that older workers will need to remain productive on their jobs and eventually to make a healthy transition to retirement. In addressing the family issues of older workers, social workers can offer seminars that cover health-management issues, changes in family relationships, the effects of the aging process on health and well-being, and caregiving support. These are all salient topics for older workers that touch on specific life- and family-stage transitions (Feit & Tate, 1986).

Because the transition to a nonwork status may be stressful for some older workers, it is important to offer preretirement planning programs in the workplace, preferably early enough in the careers of workers that they have time to plan. Assessing the adequacy of a worker's projected retirement income is an important early endeavor and one that needs to be done with awareness of legislation, particularly regarding pension coverage, as was highlighted in the section on legislation. Preretirement programs vary in their duration and content and the times when they are offered, but common topics include financial planning, life-style considerations, interpersonal relationships, role changes, living arrangements, and health education. Monk (1990) identified three major tasks for social workers who do preretirement counseling. *Developmental tasks* involve selling the idea of preretirement preparation and ensuring ongoing offerings. *Educational tasks* entail helping the retiree adjust to retirement by providing useful information and links to community resources. *Therapeutic assistance* is offered to retirees who may have a negative experience and or an unrealistic expectation with regard to retirement that may require counseling.

Postretirement programs, more frequently found in union settings, may be as formal as a retiree service department or as informal as bringing retirees together six months after retirement to explore how the transition has gone; to offer additional assistance, if needed; or to promote social activities and bonding. Other work organizations have retiree clubs, through which they maintain a tie with retirees, and provide opportunities for retirees to volunteer in workplace or community service activities.

The meaning of work, identity with a work role, and adjustment to retirement in the context of a worker's role in his or her family network, community, and the society at large are intricately related. As this country's work force ages, occupational social workers can continue to be at the forefront in responding to the needs of the diverse population of older workers in the workplace.

Implications for Research and Practice

Research on social theories of aging has proliferated in the past three decades. Many traditional theories, such as disengagement, activity, exchange, and subculture, have been attacked as inadequate for explaining and predicting the behavior of older persons. The major criticism has been that these theories focus on individual difficulties in adjusting to old age and do not seek to understand the aging experience (Passuth & Bengston, 1988).

Ryder (1965) and Schaie (1965) recognized the importance of looking at older adults in terms of specific age-period cohorts. Much of what is known about the retirement process is derived from their studies of men who were born in the first 20 years of this century. The data collected on this specific cohort, however, *cannot* form the basis of a theory of retirement because it offers little variation (Campbell & O'Rand, 1988). The gerontological social worker recognizes that no single theory can explain all social phenomena, but as research endeavors continue, a greater awareness of the individual, cultural, and contextual factors—which include historical, political, and economic features—must guide theory building about aging. Social work researchers have much to contribute to this process and should be encouraged to conduct research on the employment of older adults.

Although planning for late life includes some predictable and probable occurrences, Safford (1988) pointed out that it is not possible to project illness, disability, or social or financial losses. What is inevitable, she noted, is change itself and that planning for change is an important component for preparing for late life. Enabling older workers to plan for changes, some inevitable and predictable, some not, is a challenge for occupational social workers who are preparing to meet the needs of an aging work force in the next decade. In addition to providing services, occupational social workers must participate in needs-assessment and data-collection efforts to document the needs of older workers in the workplace: those who are preparing for retirement; retirees; those who want to reenter the labor market; and those who want alternatives to employment, such as volunteer opportunities.

A significant human resources issue is an employee's entitlement to existing benefits, pension plans, or other forms of deferred payments. Occupational social workers can be involved in this issue on several levels. On the individual level, they can encourage all older workers to be aware of their entitlements and existing plans and to determine if these plans are adequate for future needs. On an organizational level, they should ensure that all new employees receive material on benefits, compensation, and health insurance plans so that careful planning can begin early.

Through direct service experience with older workers, occupational social workers can identify policy-level issues that are of concern to policymakers, employers, and unions. Advocacy for legislative and policy changes that do not deter older workers from participating in the labor force, while being cognizant of the needs of employers, is an important arena in which the occupational social worker should engage.

To bring about organizational change, social workers must establish strong links to and among departments. They can be involved in (1) the evaluation of benefit packages to assess the impact on coverage for older workers and their families, (2) the examination of personnel policies to ensure the inclusion of age-neutral standards, (3) the implementation of programs that address the psychosocial and retirement needs of older workers, and (4) the continued review of current legislation that affects the rights of older workers.

The goal should be a mutually beneficial environment for the older worker and the employer in light of increasing numbers of and longevity among older adults and the workplace's need for trained, dependable, and flexible workers. Furthermore, awareness that many of the innovations in work that are applicable to older workers may also be beneficial to younger workers may create a more sensitive and productive workplace milieu across the life span.

References

American Association of Retired Persons. (1988). Aging work force. *Working Age, 4,* 4.

American Association of Retired Persons. (1989). *Business and older workers: Current perceptions and new directions for the 1990s.* Washington, DC: Author.

Berkowitz, M. (1988). Functioning ability and job performance as workers age. In M. E. Borus, H. S. Parnes, S. H. Sandell, & B. Seidman (Eds.), *The older worker*. Madison, WI: Industrial Relations Research Association.

Bloom, J. E., & Kurzman, P. A. (1986, October). *Evaluation report of the networking vocational services for older refugees project*. Albany, NY: Welfare Research.

Bloom, J. E., & Kurzman, P. A. (1987, February). *Networking vocational services for older refugees project: Evaluation report for the extension period, September 1– November 30, 1986*. Albany, NY: Welfare Research.

Brody, E. M. (1981). Women in the middle and family help to older people. *The Gerontologist, 21*, 471–480.

Cain, L. D. (1976). The growing importance of legal age in determining the status of the elderly. In R. T. Atchley & M. M. Seltzer (Eds.), *The sociology of age* (pp. 180–191). Belmont, CA: Wadsworth.

Campbell, R. T., & O'Rand, A. M. (1988). Settings and sequences: The heuristics of aging research. In J. E. Birren & V. L. Bengston (Eds.), *Emergent theories of aging* (pp. 58–79). New York: Springer.

Coberly, S. (1991). Older workers and the Older Americans Act. *Generations, 15*, 27–30.

Commonwealth Fund. (1991). *Americans over 55 at work program: Three case studies*. New York: Commonwealth Fund.

Crawley, B. (1987). Social work roles in employment and training programs for older workers. *Social Work Papers, 20*(1).

Crawley, B. (1992). The transformation of the American labor force: Elder African-Americans and occupational social work. *Social Work, 37*, 41–46.

Davies, D. R., & Sparrow, P. R. (1985). Age and work behavior. In N. Charness (Ed.), *Aging and human performance* (pp. 3–23). Chichester, England: John Wiley & Sons.

Feit, M. D., & Tate, N. P. (1986). Health and mental health issues in preretirement programs. *Employee Assistance Quarterly, 1*(3), 49–56.

Fullerton, H. V., Jr. (1989). New labor force projections, spanning 1988 to 2000. *Monthly Labor Review, 112*, 3–12.

Habib, M., & Gutwell, S. (1985). The union setting: Working with retirees. *Journal of Gerontological Social Work, 8*, 247–255.

Hartley, A. A., Hartley, J. T., & Johnson, S. A. (1984). The older adult as computer user. In P. K. Robinson, J. E. Livingston, & J. E. Birren (Eds.), *Aging and technological advances* (pp. 51–71). New York: Plenum.

Herz, D. (1988). Employment characteristics of older women, 1987. *Monthly Labor Review, 111*, 3–12.

Hess, B., & Waring, J. (1983). Family relationships of older women: A women's issue. In E. Markson (Ed.), *Older women* (pp. 227–251). Lexington, MA: Lexington Books.

Knowles, D. E. (1988). Auditing the company for age discrimination. In H. Axel (Ed.), *Employing older Americans: Opportunities and constraints* (pp. 28–29). New York: The Conference Board.

Kurzman, P. A., & Akabas, S. H. (1981). Industrial social work as an arena for practice. *Social Work, 26,* 52–60.

Louis Harris and Associates. (undated). *Older Americans: Ready and able to work.* New York: Author.

McNaught, W., Barth, M. C., & Henderson, P. H. (1991). The human resource potential of Americans over 50. *Human Resource Management, 28,* 455–473.

Miller, J. (1989). Displaced homemakers in the employment and training system. In S. L. Harlan & R. J. Steinberg (Eds.), *Job training for women: The promise and limits of public policies* (pp. 18–26). Philadelphia: Temple University Press.

Monk, A. (1990). Pre-retirement planning programs. In A. Monk (Ed.), *Handbook of gerontological services* (2nd ed., pp. 400–419). New York: Columbia University Press.

Moon, M., & Hushbeck, J. (1989). Options for extending work life. *Generations, 2,* 27–30.

Mutschler, P. H. (1986). How golden a handshake? Reactions to early retirement incentive plans. *Compensation and Benefits Management, 4,* 277–283.

National Council on Aging. (1986). Diverse programs nationwide lead to beneficial exchange. *Perspectives on Aging,* 10–13.

Passuth, P. M., & Bengston, V. L. (1988). Sociological theories of aging: Current perspectives and future directions. In J. E. Birren & V. L. Bengston (Eds.), *Emergent theories of aging* (pp. 333–355). New York: Springer.

Poon, L. N. (1987). Learning. In G. Maddox (Ed.), *Encyclopedia of aging* (pp. 18–26). New York: Springer.

Quinn, J. F., Burkhauser, R. U., & Myers, D. C. (1990). *Passing the torch: The influence of economic incentives on work and retirement.* Kalamazoo, MI: W. E. Upjohn Institute for Retirement Research.

Rix, S. E. (1990). *Older workers.* Santa Barbara, CA: ABC-CLIO.

Root, L. S., & Zarrugh, L. H. (1987). Private-sector employment practices for older workers. In S. H. Sandell (Ed.), *The problem isn't age: Work and older Americans* (pp. 177–191). New York: Praeger.

Rosen, B., & Jerdee, T. H. (1985). *Older employees: New roles for valued resources.* Homewood, IL: Dow Jones-Irwin.

Rothstein, F. (Ed.). (1988). *Commitment to an aging workforce: Strategies and models for helping older workers achieve full potential.* Washington, DC: National Council on Aging.

Ryder, N. B. (1965). The cohort as a concept in the study of social change. *American Sociological Review, 30,* 843–861.

Safford, F. (1988). Value of gerontology for occupational social work. *Social Work, 33,* 42–45.

Schaie, K. W. (1965). A general model for the study of developmental problems. *Psychological Bulletin, 64,* 92–107.

Shaw, L. B. (1985). *Older women at work.* Washington, DC: Women's Research and Education Institute.

Soldo, B. J., & Agree, E. M. (1988, September). America's elderly [Entire issue]. *Population Bulletin, 43.*

Sterns, H. L., & Doverspike, D. (1988). Training and developing the older worker: Implications for human resource management. In H. Dennis (Ed.), *Fourteen steps in managing an older workforce* (pp. 97–110). Lexington, MA: Lexington Books.

Stuen, C., & Kaye, L. W. (1984). Creating educational alliances between retired academics, community agencies and elderly neighborhood residents. *Community Services Catalyst, 14,* 21–24.

Stuen, C., Kaye, L. W., & Monk, A. (1983). A demonstration program for training senior teachers. *Lifelong learning: An omnibus of practice and research,* 7, 15–27.

Uhlenberg, P., & Myers, M. (1981). Divorce and the elderly. *The Gerontologist,* 21, 276–282.

U.S. Bureau of the Census. (1965). *The statistical history of the United States from colonial times to the present.* Stamford, CT: Fairfield.

U.S. Department of Labor, Bureau of Labor Statistics. (1985). *Handbook of labor statistics.* Washington, DC: U.S. Government Printing Office.

U.S. Department of Labor, Bureau of Labor Statistics. (1990). *Employment and earnings.* Washington, DC: U.S. Government Printing Office.

U.S. Senate. (1984). *The costs of employing older workers: An information paper.* Washington, DC: U.S. Government Printing Office.

U.S. Senate, Special Committee on Aging, in conjunction with the American Association of Retired Persons, the Federal Council on Aging, and the U.S. Administration on Aging. (1987–88). *Aging America: Trends and projections.* Washington, DC: U.S. Department of Health & Human Services.

Wagner, D. (1989). *Employees and eldercare: Designing effective responses for the workplace.* Bridgeport, CT: Center for the Study of Aging, University of Bridgeport.

Wineman, J. (1990). Services to older and retired workers. In A. Monk (Ed.), *Handbook of gerontological services* (2nd ed., pp. 377–399). New York: Columbia University Press.

Winfield, F. E. (Ed.). (1988). *The work and family sourcebook.* New York: Panel.

CHAPTER 15

Military Social Work as Occupational Practice

Jesse J. Harris

I don't like work . . . no man does—but I like what is *in*
the work—the chance to find yourself, your own reality.
—Joseph Conrad
Heart of Darkness

The military is an industry, employing workers called "soldiers" (the term
used here to refer to all uniformed members of the armed forces). The men
and women who wear the uniform of the U.S. armed forces perform many
jobs that require a wide range of skills. Among them are administrators,
cooks, physicians, maintenance personnel, pilots, tank drivers, infantrymen,
secretaries, scientists, logisticians, submariners, teachers, and engineers. All
the military specialties require a higher degree of skill and knowledge than
they did a generation ago.

The U.S. Department of Defense (DOD) is one of the largest employers
in the U.S. government. In recent years, during periods of peace, DOD has
carried more than 2 million armed forces personnel on its payroll: 750,193
in the army, 581,903 in the navy, 195,903 in the marines, and 543,091 in the
air force. During periods of mobilization, DOD adds reserve and National
Guard units to its active force *(Defense Almanac,* 1990).

Kurzman and Akabas (1981) defined occupational social work broadly
enough to make the case that the military is an appropriate setting for
occupational social work. Just as social workers who choose a traditional
industrial setting for their practice must reorient their thinking in light of the
non–human services nature of the host setting, so must those who choose to

practice in a military setting. The dilemmas and issues that confront social workers as they attempt to work with managers, union representatives, and workers are similar in many ways to the issues confronting military social workers, who must intervene with the command (managers) and the troops (workers).

There is a need for social workers to work in this government-sponsored occupational setting, and it is appropriate for them to do so. However, social workers who choose to work in this environment, either as uniformed personnel or as civilians, must understand and be sensitive to its unique culture, which has a set of values and traditions that set it apart from the larger society (Kurzman, 1983; Masi, 1982; Ortiz & Bassoff, 1987; Smith, 1985). Balgopal's (1989, p. 437) caution that social workers need to be aware of their institutions' expectations is appropriate advice for anyone who works in a military setting:

> Industry has a special stake in employee performance; it will, understandably, seek clinical expertise that visibly contributes to this goal and question that which does not. Under such scrutiny, social workers should not enter occupational settings without developing a heightened attention to the environmental perspective.

The majority of social workers in the military are civilians. Through the years, the numbers have fluctuated, depending on the personnel policies in effect at any given time. Except in combat zones, civilian and uniformed social workers work together and under similar conditions. Therefore, in this chapter, the term *social worker* is used for both, and distinctions between the two are made only when necessary.

Background

The Military System

The military is a hierarchical system composed of officers, noncommissioned officers, and enlisted personnel. It has a definite rank structure that is essential background information for everyone who interacts in that system. Only chaplains and attorneys enjoy privileged communication in the armed services; social workers do not, and the commander may request feedback from social workers concerning a soldier's fitness for duty. Thus, issues of confidentiality can be a problem in some cases. The fact that it is not unusual for soldiers to be *ordered* to go to a mental health clinic raises the issue of involuntary treatment.

This occupation has a unique mission. All members of the armed forces take an oath to "protect and defend the Constitution of the United States against all enemies foreign and domestic" (United States Code 16, sec. 118, 1949). This oath places each participant under obligations that are unique and that may be ideologically problematic for some social workers. Those who are antimilitary would do themselves and their clients a disservice to practice in a military environment. On the other hand, social workers must be cautious of stereotypes. The clients are, after all, the youngsters next door who joined the service.

Ever since the introduction of the all-volunteer army, the military has had to compete with the civilian market for skilled and qualified men and women. Its ability to attract and retain these individuals has varied over the past decades and has depended, in part, on its popularity and the economy. Keeping pace with civilian wage scales has presented the military and Congress with a challenge. On the other hand, the benefits provided have helped to attract and retain a substantial number of young men and women in the active and reserve forces. These benefits include allowances for subsistence and housing, the GI bill, and an attractive retirement at a young age. In addition, there are commissary and post or base exchange privileges and medical benefits for both the soldiers and their families that continue after retirement. Titmuss (1968, p. 192) referred to such benefits as "occupational welfare," the submerged part of the "iceberg phenomena of social welfare"; similarly, these military benefits are the result of the soldier's status, achievement, and record.

The Stress of the Military

Soldiers must train for war. Occupational specialty notwithstanding, soldiers train and operate in a variety of terrains and climatic conditions. In addition to the potential of enduring physical hardships, they and their families must be prepared to endure separations because soldiers are on duty 24 hours a day. Although family members generally accept this fact, the uncertainty of duty hours adds to the stress they experience.

Members of the armed forces represent a microcosm of America. The vast majority of military personnel and their families are able to adjust to the military life-style and find it rewarding, but some do not. The stress on military personnel and their families has been the subject of considerable research (see, for example, Bowen & Orthner, 1989; Jensen, Lewis, & Xenakis, 1986; Martin & Ickovics, 1987; Orthner & Pittman, 1986; Segal, 1986; Westbrook, 1980).

Like all managers, DOD managers are concerned with helping their personnel cope with a wide range of problems, including substance abuse, absenteeism (AWOL), and illness associated with stress, that could interfere with productivity. Although the terms *employee assistance program* (EAP) and *occupational social work* are not used in the military, as a semi-self-contained occupational society, the military needs human resources experts to staff its workplace programs that are equivalent to an EAP.

The soldiers have their personal, social, and family needs as workers met, in part, by fellow soldiers (workers) who are retained by their employer to meet the human service needs of the individuals and the human service agenda of the employing organization. These personnel are social work officers (with MSWs) in medical units and civilian social workers who are employed by or on contract to the DOD. They may work as part of a team with psychiatrists, psychologists, nurses, physicians, and other helping professionals.

Social Work in the Military: A Brief History

This country has a proud history of supporting its military personnel. McNelis (1987) noted that the commitment to support soldiers and the beginnings of social services in the military can be traced to the Civil War, when volunteers visited hospitalized Union soldiers. This same commitment was clearly documented during World War I, when social work services were provided by the Red Cross. The Red Cross continued to staff military hospitals with social workers until the end of World War II (Masi, 1982).

Several significant events validated the importance of social work and elevated its standing in the military. Following the onset of World War II, the civilian social work community established liaisons with military psychiatrists to determine the most effective use of professional social workers who were entering the army. This effort resulted in the establishment of the army's first Mental Hygiene Consultative Service, which was staffed by social workers in enlisted status at Fort Monmouth, New Jersey, in October 1942. Thus, psychiatric social work was recognized by the army as a legitimate occupation that was relevant to the military mission (Ross, 1946). By the end of World War II, 711 social workers had served in enlisted status. In June 1945, the military social work program was incorporated into the army's Surgeon General's Office. In 1946, the first social worker was commissioned as an army officer, and uniformed social work officers began to staff military hospitals.

In 1947 the air force became a separate service, and in 1952 instituted its social work program. The air force currently has a program that is comparable in size to the army's.

The navy had no social workers in uniform until 1980. Before then, the program was staffed by Red Cross and civilian social workers. Its current program, although small in relation to those of the other services, is dynamic and provides services similar to those of the army and the air force. In addition, the navy is responsible for social work policy for the marines and their families.

During the 1960s and 1970s, army social workers attempted to broaden the scope of their practice from its psychiatric–medical base. They were instrumental in establishing nonmedical occupational social work services— Army Community Service (ACS); race relations, organizational effectiveness, correctional rehabilitation, and drug and alcohol prevention programs; and child advocacy. "This social action swing reflected the social work values in the civilian community and the educational thrust of the schools of social work" (Hamlin, Timberlake, Jentsch, & Van Vranken, 1982, p. 3).

Following the Vietnam War, the army experienced significant cutbacks in personnel, among them social workers in nonmedical settings. However, the need for the community aspect of social work remained, and many of these slots were subsequently filled by civilian social workers who were hired by the military, but not as sources of medical personnel. By the beginning of the 1980s, army social work officers were predominately back in the medical field (Hamlin et al., 1982).

Role of the Military Social Worker

Wherever soldiers serve, social work support is not far behind. Military social workers are assigned to health care settings, including hospitals; mental health clinics; substance abuse programs; correctional settings, such as military prisons and stockades; and family support centers. Senior social workers are assigned to high-level administrative and staff positions in the Pentagon and major command headquarters, where they are responsible for formulating and implementing policies and programs. Social workers are also on the faculties of military schools and are engaged in research. In short, civilian and uniformed social workers are assigned to various units worldwide in support of soldiers and their families.

Family Programs

A comprehensive family focus characterizes military social work practice. The worker and family receive sponsored medical care; a housing allowance; cost-of-living allowances; and dental, drug, and optical services. There are also family-centered programs and services. This family focus is expanding because the military, which had been perceived as a single man's service, suddenly found that its demographics had changed.

The deployment of units to the Dominican Republic and to Vietnam resulted in a massive call-up of personnel into the military services. The army, which had the largest number of personnel (and thus the largest number of family members) recognized the potential value of having centers where people could go for information and direct services. Thus, in 1965, under the auspices of the army adjutant general, ACS was established. Shortly thereafter, a network of 162 centers was established throughout the army. As the experience and value of the ACS centers became clear, other services began to examine their need for a similar structure. Thus, the Civilian Health and Medical Program of the Uniformed Services (CHAMPUS) was created in 1966 in response to the increase in personnel and need for coverage.

In 1973, the army changed to an all-volunteer force—a change that would soon alter the demography of the services forever. One of the major changes was the increase in young married families. For example, the army had 67,000 married soldiers in 1940 and 500,000 married soldiers with 1.7 million family members in 1965. As of 1989, the army had over 1.2 family members, not including the reserve components; the navy 720,399 family members; the marines 211,890; and the air force 836,059. Thus, in addition to its uniformed personnel, the DOD has 2,770,606 family members to serve, including "dual-career families," in which both the husbands and wives are in military service (*Defense Almanac*, 1990, p. 25).

The increase in families has major implications for policymakers. Research indicates that the key to retaining high-quality personnel in the services is to provide an acceptable quality of life for their families (Baker, 1985; Faris, 1984; Hosek, Antel, & Peterson, 1989; Leider, 1978). If the family is dissatisfied, the chances of retaining the service person are greatly diminished (Pittman & Orthner, 1986).

In the early 1980s, the services held major conferences to identify and address problems that family members face, and family members participated in these conferences. The army leadership responded by acknowledging the importance of the families in the mission of total readiness and by instituting plans to improve the quality of family life. The chief of staff for the army declared "that there is a partnership between the military and the family" (Chief of Staff, 1983, p. 8).

Out of an air force conference came the beginnings of the Air Force Family Support Centers. The air force is unique in that the majority of its combat personnel are officers who are more likely to be older and to be married than are enlisted personnel. Unlike the Army Family Support Centers, the Air Force Family Support Centers are not involved in counseling services; their mission is family and community education, and their primary tasks are managing volunteer resources and providing relocation and transition assistance and support to spouses.

By late 1990, all branches of the armed forces had such centers. There were 166 Army Community Services Centers, 75 Navy Family Support Centers,

104 Air Force Family Support Centers, and 18 Marine Corps Family Support Centers ("Family Centers," 1990).

In further recognition of the importance of families to the uniformed services, DOD combined two of its major departments, the Military Family Resource Center and the Office of Family Policy, to establish the Office of Family Policy and Support. This office has responsibility for family advocacy for the military, as well as oversight for child care, adoption, family support centers, employment of spouses, relocation, information and referral, and child custody for all the uniformed services. Some of the leading programs of the family support centers that social workers staff are these:

Information, referral, and follow-up. This program provides commanders, service members, and families with information on military and civilian community resources. The social worker and other personnel participate in long-range community planning by identifying duplications and gaps in the service delivery system (*Army Community Service Program*, 1986).

Relocation assistance. This program provides information, guidance, and assistance to support soldiers and their families when they are required to relocate from one military community to another. Those involved in relocation assistance may also be called on to help with the unique problems that occur when an entire unit deploys with its families (*Army Community Service Program*, 1986).

Exceptional Family Member Program (EFMP). The Education for All Handicapped Children Act of 1975 (P.L. 94-142) requires that all handicapped children receive free appropriate public education, including special education and certain related services. The EFMP, working in concert with other military and civilian agencies, provides comprehensive educational, community support, and personnel-type services for families with special needs. It considers the special education and medical needs of the exceptional family member during the assignment process and assigns military members to areas where these special needs can be accommodated (*Exceptional Family Member Program*, 1986).

The air force instituted the Children Have a Potential (CHAP) program as early as 1961. The purpose of CHAP is to provide assistance to families whose children are physically, mentally, or emotionally disabled.

The Family Advocacy Program. The objectives of the Family Advocacy Program are to encourage the reporting of all instances of violence and abuse—child and spouse abuse; child sexual abuse; child neglect; and institutional abuse, such as may occur in day care centers—to ensure the prompt investigation of all cases of abuse, to protect victims of abuse, and to treat all family members who are affected by or involved in abuse, so they can be restored to a healthy state. The family support centers are responsible for prevention; community education; liaison with community and military services and support services, such as temporary shelter; and short-term crisis intervention. Treatment is the responsibility of the installation hospital (*Army Family Advocacy Program*, 1987).

Foster care. Temporary foster care is provided to children when parents are unable to maintain a home for them. This care is provided under local, state, or host-nation agreements, if available. In many cases, temporary foster care is provided by other military families on the military installation (*Army Community Service Program*, 1986).

Consumer affairs and financial assistance. The inexperience and youth of many of the soldiers and their spouses have resulted in the need to teach them basic financial skills, such as budgeting. In addition, some family support centers provide financial assistance, including debt liquidation, and specific information on local products and services that are available at the installation and in the surrounding communities (*Army Community Service Program*, 1986).

Employment of family members. The nomadic life-style of military families often militates against career planning for spouses. The Family Member Employment Program consists of employment education, volunteer resources, training workshops, private sector job banks, individual job-search assistance, and counseling to identify skills (*Army Community Service Program*, 1986).

Many of the programs that are provided by family support centers are the direct result of the U.S. Army's White Paper (Chief of Staff, 1983) and the changing climate in the nation with respect to women's rights, the emphasis on families, and the realization that the soldiers will not perform well if their families are dissatisfied with the quality of their lives.

Social Work in Health and Mental Health Care Settings

Medical and dental services are seen as a right for every uniformed member of the armed forces. However, the administration and structure of social work services in hospitals differ by service. For example, in the army and navy, social work is a separate and independent service. The roles of social workers in army hospitals mirror those of social workers in civilian settings: discharge planning, family advocacy, and community assessment. Other services have placed a greater emphasis on inpatient and outpatient mental health services. For example, social workers in air force hospitals have traditionally supported the departments of psychiatry.

Substance abuse programs started with the need to respond to the growing substance abuse problem in this country during the Vietnam War era as a result of the counterculture. In 1970, Congress passed the Comprehensive Alcohol

Abuse and Alcoholism Prevention, Treatment, and Rehabilitation Act (P.L. 91-616 and 92-129), mandating that the armed forces identify, treat, and rehabilitate drug- and alcohol-dependent soldiers. Each branch of service admitted to the Senate that its substance abuse problem was of epidemic proportions (Cangianelli, 1990). Social workers are involved in alcohol and drug programs as part of an interdisciplinary team and work in outpatient and residential settings. On some installations, substance abuse programs are also available to civilian employees (Rozan, 1983).

Social Work in Research

Social workers have a rich history of contributing to the knowledge base of the military services on such issues as family well-being, the performance and satisfaction of soldiers, child welfare, and the profession of social work in military settings. Many of the studies have been the result of doctoral dissertations by military social workers, and others have come from social workers who were assigned to units that specialize in research. Many have contributed to the civilian literature (Hamlin et al., 1982; Harris & Segal, 1985; Martin & Ickovics, 1987; McNelis, 1987; Rothberg, Harris, Jellen, & Pickle, 1985).

Social Work in Health Promotion

All members of the military are expected to maintain a state of good physical fitness, partly because of the nature of their mission and partly because they may be deployed to regions in which debilitating diseases may be prevalent (Rothberg et al., 1985). Therefore, periodic physical examinations are required. Most of the services require a test to determine one's fitness for duty in terms of meeting standards of weight, physical strength, and endurance. Some services require that personnel be released from active duty if they are unable to meet these standards.

When the civilian job sector began to emphasize physical fitness, the military services reexamined the status of their members' health and found that their soldiers were not as "fit" as they should be. As a result, DOD issued *Directive 1010.10* in 1986 that established a health promotion policy whose purpose was to increase military readiness by improving and maintaining the quality of life of its personnel ("Health Promotion," 1986). The policy included smoking prevention and cessation, physical fitness, nutrition, stress management, alcohol and drug abuse prevention, and early identification of hypertension.

This policy resulted in the creation of a fitness program throughout the DOD. A major part of the program was remedial fitness for soldiers whose physical fitness was below standard. Some of these remedial fitness programs enlist the use of social workers.

Family Support Groups

A relatively new concept in the uniformed services is that of family support groups, which are vehicles for the exchange of information, support, and comfort during times of crises and are similar to self-help or mutual-aid groups. The concept of the family support group received its greatest boost when troops were sent to the Sinai Desert for peacekeeping duty; such groups were also found to be effective during the Grenada operation. There is growing research interest in military family support groups (Military Family Resource Center, 1987; 1990).

During the Persian Gulf War, families reported that their ability to cope with the stress of deployment would be improved if they could get timely and accurate information on the soldiers' status and mission by being involved in an active family support group and having access to family support centers. They reported that they were experiencing stress from concern for the welfare of the soldiers, uncertainty about how long the deployment would last, the lack of consistent contact with the soldiers, financial changes caused by the deployment, role overload, negative rumors, and concern for how the deployment was affecting their children ("Army studies," 1991; "ARPERCEN Supports Desert Storm," 1991; "Community Support for Desert Storm," 1991; "Family Support for Desert Shield," 1990). The soldiers reported that they felt better knowing that their families were involved in support groups.

Support groups are governed and operated by family members and sanctioned and supported by the installation commander. Social workers and chaplains are in demand as consultants.

Military Social Work and National Emergencies

Military social workers, like their counterparts in civilian uniformed settings, such as fire and police departments, have a responsibility for trauma counseling and crisis debriefing. The knowledge and skill to help individuals and families with loss, relocation, family separation, and the experience of constant physical danger are imbedded in their social work expertise (Brunstein & Kilpatrick, 1988; Cornell, 1991; Engel, 1991; Wagner, 1983). The ultimate role of the social worker in the DOD establishment, of course, is to provide for the needs of the soldiers and their families when the nation is involved in armed conflict or other emergencies. DOD social workers have met that challenge. For example, they provided assistance to families and staff after peacekeeping forces of the 101st Airborne Division were killed in a tragic plane crash in Newfoundland, crisis intervention at the Rhiemstein Air Show after flaming debris from a plane crash engulfed spectators, and the needed interventions for military members and their families after the raid on Libya (personal communication with Colonel J. Cox, U.S. Air Force, August 1991). When the navy ship U.S. *Stark* was accidentally fired upon, a social worker was a member of a team that landed on its deck while the ship was still burning (personal communication with Colonel Gregory Myer, February 1990).

Military Social Work in the Combat Arena

Many social workers served with the troops in Vietnam; with the multinational peacekeeping forces in the Sinai Peninsula (Harris & Segal 1985; Segal, Harris, Rothberg, & Marlow, 1984); in Grenada and Panama; and, most recently, in the Persian Gulf. They were involved in a variety of supportive roles, working with mental health teams that included psychiatrists, psychologists, and enlisted personnel who were trained in mental health techniques. Together, the team members provided a consultation program that included assessment, prevention, and command management of psychiatric casualties. They served as clinical social workers in direct support of combat units, as medical social workers in hospital settings, and as counselors in substance abuse treatment centers. During the Vietnam War an army social worker was given one of this nation's highest awards for bravery, the Silver Star.

Social workers provided group and individual therapy to personnel who returned with unresolved issues around their battlefield experiences. Along with other members of the health team, they briefed commanders on the symptoms of posttraumatic stress disorder (Engel, 1991).

Conclusion

The future of the human services in the military ultimately depends on the decisions of the U.S. Congress and the economic and political forces that drive its decisions. Social workers have served soldiers and their families during periods of peace and war. But, it cannot be denied that the primary mission of the military is to fight and defend. Although it is an unpleasant thought, the structure and function of the military of the future will be dictated by projected battlefield scenarios. Technological advances have changed the nature of warfare. As this "industry" "re-tools," its employees must understand its impact on them and their families. The armed forces of the future will move with lightning speed and with a destructive force that may result in a higher rate of medical and psychiatric casualties than in past conflicts.

The helping skills needed will require social workers to operate in or close to the zone of battle as team members with other than the traditional mental health disciplines. Furthermore, social workers will have to be sensitive to the impact of the rapid deployment of forces on young soldiers and their families. Support groups will continue to be significant to families whose soldiers may be deployed into battle with fewer than 24 hours' notice.

The lessons of the Persian Gulf War have yet to be fully digested. Unlike other conflicts, Operation Desert Storm raised issues related to families that the military and the nation had not been exposed to previously. For example, it is now clear that greater attention must to be given to the family issues of reserve and National Guard units when these soldiers are called to active duty, not the least of which is the financial loss experienced by some families. It is also clear that as the number of dual-career families increases and as mothers as well as fathers are called to arms, military social workers may need to work more closely with civilian social service agencies to ensure the well-being of the children who are left behind. As a result of 24-hour media coverage during Operation Desert Storm, the public became acutely aware of the horror of war. Social workers in the future may find it necessary to provide at least consultation to civilian-sector support groups.

The changing nature of world diplomacy will require that social workers be skilled in areas that may be unfamiliar to them. For example, in recent years, military social workers have served as members of crises response teams that accompanied many of the U.S. citizens held hostage by terrorists from their release points to safe territory. The release of hostages from Iran and Lebanon; the hijacking of TWA 847 in Athens, Greece; and the hijacking of the Italian cruise liner *Achille Lauro* are but a few examples.

It is clear that the emphasis on families, family advocacy, and family services will continue and that social workers will play a major role in program planning and intervention. It is also clear that there will be a need for social workers with a cross-cultural orientation. The changing demography in American society is reflected in the military. One can anticipate an increase in women, single parents, minorities, and immigrants. The military family structure will reflect the family in the civilian sector. Consequently, the social fabric of the military community may be significantly different.

Social work in military hospitals is becoming more like that in the civilian sector. The ability to work with young families who are affected by the illness of their members will continue to be a challenge. But social workers must also appreciate the impact of illness or death on a soldier's unit. Command consultation may be desirable. The military will continue to seek social workers with expertise in substance abuse.

The military has been and will continue to be one of the leading users of computers and computer applications. Social workers on most posts and in most hospitals will be expected to be computer literate and to learn sophisticated information management methods and adopt new computer technologies.

In recent years the military has become more "civilianized." There has been an increase in the number of civilian social workers at the MSW level as well. There is no reason to believe that this trend will change. The military has increasingly sought outside expertise as new and increasingly complex issues arise and when the available personnel are insufficient to meet growing needs. EAPs have and will continue to contract with the military services.

The military is a microcosm of the larger society, and it has been found that the productivity of soldiers increases if they are given the right mix of reinforcements and motivation. The government has, through a mixture of monetary incentives and fringe benefits, attempted to attract and retain the best personnel. But it has also recognized that there are many intangibles involved in maintaining a well-motivated and highly productive military force. The ultimate occupational hazard for those in uniform is to become casualties of war. Nothing will destroy the morale of soldiers faster than the lack of confidence that they or their families will be cared for should the unforeseen occur.

Military social workers will continue to be expected to serve as consultants on a number of human service and human relations issues. Consequently, it is expected that those who have skills in policymaking and planning will be needed by the DOD. Social workers must have the expertise to move into policymaking positions to examine the future implications for military family life. Indeed, for the occupational social worker in military service, the program development and policy perspective may become all the more central, as civilian, contract, and self-help groups take ever-increasing responsibility for direct services.

References

Army Community Service Program (AR 608-1). (1986, March). Washington, DC: U.S. Department of the Army.

Army Family Advocacy Program (AR 608-18). (1987, September). Washington, DC: U.S. Department of the Army.

Army studies Desert Storm families. (1991). *Army Families, 10*(1), 1–2.

ARPERCEN supports Desert Storm. (1991). *Army Echoes, 35*(1), 4.

Baker, H. B. (1985). Antecareer crises: Military recruiting and the youthful job applicant. *Armed Forces and Society, 11,* 565–580.

Balgopal, P. R. (1989). Occupational social work: An expanded clinical perspective. *Social Work, 34,* 437–442.

Bowen, G. R., & Orthner, D. K. (1989). *The organization family: Work and family linkages in the U.S. military.* New York: Praeger.

Brunstein, S., & Kilpatrick, M. A. (1988). Counseling survivors of workplace accidents. In G. M. Gould & M. L. Smith (Eds.), *Social work in the workplace* (pp. 96–108). New York: Springer.

Cangianelli, L. A. (1990, March). The navy drug and alcohol abuse program. *EAPA Exchange,* pp. 14–17.

Chief of Staff, U.S. Army. (1983). *White paper 1983, the army family* (Miscellaneous Publication 4-3). Washington, DC: U.S. Government Printing Office.

Community support for Desert Storm. (1991). *Army Echoes, 35*(1), 5.

Cornell, W. (1991). Fire department trauma. *Employee Assistance, 3*(10), 28–33.

Defense Almanac. (1990, November–December), pp. 24–25.

Engel, F. (1991). Post-traumatic stress disorder. *Employee Assistance, 3*(10), 34–37.

Exceptional Family Member Program (AR 600-75). (1986, March). Washington, DC: U.S. Department of the Army.

Family centers. (1990, December). *Military Family,* p. 13.

Family support for Desert Shield remains high priority (1990, December). *Military Family,* p. 1.

Faris J. (1984). Economic and non-economic factors of personnel recruitment and retention in the AVF. *Armed Forces and Society, 10,* 252–253.

Hamlin, E. R. II, Timberlake, E. M., Jentsch, D. P., & Van Vranken, E. W. (1982). *U.S. Army social work in the 1980s.* Washington, DC: U.S. Government Printing Office.

Harris, J., & Segal D. (1985). Observations from the Sinai: The boredom factor. *Armed Forces and Society, 11,* 235–248.

Health promotion. (1986, March 11). *Department of Defense directive 1010.10.* Washington, DC: U.S. Department of Defense.

Hosek, J., Antel, J., & Peterson, C. (1989). Who stays, who leaves? Attrition among first-term enlistees. *Armed Forces and Society, 15,* 389–409.

Jensen, P. S., Lewis, R., & Xenakis, S. (1986). The military family review. *Journal of the American Academy of Child Psychiatry, 25,* 225–234.

Kurzman, P. A. (1983). Ethical issues in industrial social work practice. *Social Casework, 64,* 105–111.

Kurzman, P. A., & Akabas, S. H. (1981). Industrial social work as an arena for practice. *Social Work, 26,* 52–60.

Leider L. (1978). Muddling through won't do. In J. B. Keely (Ed.), *The all volunteer force and American society* (pp. 183–204). Charlottesville: University of Virginia Press.

Martin, J. A., & Ickovics, J. R. (1987). The effects of stress on the psychological well-being of army wives: Initial findings from a longitudinal study. *Journal of Human Stress, 13,* 108–115.

Masi, D. A. (1982). *Human services in industry.* Baltimore, MD: Sheppard Pratt.

McNelis, P. (1987). Military social work. In A. Minahan (Ed.-in-Chief), *Encyclopedia of social work,* 18th ed. (Vol. 2, pp. 154–161). Silver Spring, MD: National Association of Social Workers.

Military Family Resource Center. (1987). *Bibliography resource: Support groups.* Arlington, VA: Author.

Military Family Resource Center. (1990). Support groups or agencies? In *Bibliography: Military research and literature.* Arlington, VA: Author.

Orthner, D. K., & Pittman, J. (1986). Family contributions to work commitment. *Journal of Marriage and the Family, 48,* 573–581.

Ortiz, E. T., & Bassoff, B. Z. (1987). Military EAPs: Family service roles for social workers. *Employee Assistance Quarterly, 2*(3), 55–67.

Pittman, J. F., & Orthner, D. (1986). Predictors of spousal support for the work commitments of husbands. *Journal of Marriage and the Family, 50,* 335–348.

Ross, E. (1946). *Psychiatric social work* (Technical Bulletin No. 154). Washington, DC: U.S. Department of the Army.

Rothberg, J. M., Harris, J., Jellen, L., & Pickle, R. (1985). Illness and health of the U.S. battalion in the Sinai MFO deployment. *Armed Forces and Society, 11,* 413–425.

Rozan, J. (1983, January–February). Disposition of repeaters in the army alcohol and drug abuse prevention program. *EAP Digest,* pp. 18–22.

Segal, D., Harris, J., Rothberg, J., & Marlow, D. (1984). Paratroopers as peacekeepers. *Armed Forces and Society, 10,* 487–506.

Segal, M. W. (1986). Enlisted family life in the U.S. Army: A portrait of a community. In *Life in the Rank and File* (pp. 184–211). Washington, DC: Pergamon-Brassey's International Defense Publishers.

Smith, M. L. (1985). Social work in the military: An occupational social work perspective. In *Social work papers* (Vol. 19, pp. 46–55). Los Angeles: University of Southern California Press.

Titmuss, R. M. (1968). *Commitment to welfare.* New York: Pantheon.

United States Code, 16, sec. 188, 1949.

Wagner, M. (1983). Trauma counselling and law enforcement. In R. J. Thomlison (Ed.), *Perspectives on industrial social work practice* (pp. 133–139). Ottawa: Family Service Canada.

Westbrook, S. D. (1980). Sociopolitical alienation and military efficiency. *Armed Forces and Society, 7,* 170–189.

PART 4

MANAGEMENT AND POLICY INITIATIVES

Introduction to Part 4

In this final part of the volume, it seems almost superfluous to argue that the way work is managed has a formative impact on the way people live and that the policy of the workplace has a formative impact on the way people deal with social problems in this society. What is surprising, and therefore makes the chapters in this part vital, is the magnitude of that impact. Parenthetically, these chapters seek to alert social workers to the importance of playing a more active role in the workplace's management and policy initiatives.

There is convincing evidence of the importance of public services to the well-being of society. No one could survive without schools, hospitals, welfare departments, dependent care services, and the like. Women are the predominant workers in those arenas, particularly at the lower levels. As observers noted recently, they are held in these positions by the phenomenon of the "sticky floor," that is, low-level essential jobs that no one else wants to do but that no society can manage without, the caring jobs that are seen as "women's work" and offer no career ladder. In their struggle to earn more and to have more promotional opportunities, a few women have moved beyond the boundaries of the glass walls of occupational segregation. In Chapter 16, Barbara Levy Simon and Sheila H. Akabas focus on women who hold high-risk public service jobs in work arenas that have long been dominated by men—the armed services, police, fire, and corrections work. Here there are no sticky floors that limit the opportunity and pay of the workers. Instead, women encounter traditions and co-workers who would bar the way were it not for the pressure of affirmative action legislation and the potential shortage of workers.

But though admission has begun, the token newcomers in these positions are severely tried, according to the authors. These women are under constant scrutiny that *compounds* the stress of high-risk work or predictable public interest in those whose pay derives from public taxation. Leaving behind support networks of women colleagues, these workers experience isolation, trivialization, scapegoating, and constant tests of competence that make satisfactory performance harder to achieve than the already-difficult situation faced by their male co-workers. The authors understand that the need is not only to serve the women but to change the work environment. They recommend a full array of interventions for social work attention, starting with an aggressive campaign to enlist more women in the services. They conclude that changes in the management of these workplaces and in social policy will be necessary if women are to take their place in a gender-integrated public sector that heretofore has been men's exclusive domain. Without such help, women will always be circumscribed by the sticky floor and glass walls of their present occupational isolation.

Chapter 17, by Lee Schore and Jerry Atkin, provides convincing evidence that the world of work is fraught with stress that requires attention from professional social workers. These authors make a case for the need to reframe the problem and reshape the workplace to overcome the internalized damage that that stress is doing to workers. These authors suggest a new partnership between social workers and unions, claiming the contribution of trade unions to the empowerment of workers and of the ameliorative power of delivering individual and group services to alleviate stress through that source. Believing that the way work is organized has negative consequences for health, they promote a model that combines clinical and organizing skills. The steps of the model include reinforcing dignity and respect, validating experience and feeling, normalizing people's experience, exposing the causes of stress, attacking social myths, using the new information gained to reframe the problem, and then helping people develop individual and collective strategies to solve problems and overcome obstacles.

Schore and Atkin review the former strategies against stress—relaxation, modification of nutrition and exercise patterns, and information about stress—and conclude that these interventions attack symptoms only. Working collaboratively and organizing social support, they conclude, deals with the source of the stress rather than its symptoms. Their model incorporates the union. They believe that "unions are an appropriate place to develop these programs because it is their role to protect their members and to maintain health and safety standards." Effective services must be work- and worker centered and based on a treatment strategy that "validates workers' culture and experience . . . [to] empower workers to assert themselves to gain greater control over their working conditions [to] reduce both stress and self-blame." They report on the successful application of their model in individual and group situations.

A reading of Chapter 18, by Lawrence S. Root, helps explain why workers accept stressful work circumstances and why women are willing to enter the dangerous world of high-risk jobs, where they are seen only as tokens. Those jobs at least avoid the unemployment and underemployment, if not turbulent and unsatisfying employment, that are too often the lot of today's workers. Root expresses concern for the great changes in the workplace: decreasing manufacturing jobs; more layoffs and plant closings; the increased supply of low-paid service jobs, part-time jobs, and contingent employment; and the growing need for education to qualify for any new job. Nonetheless, he acknowledges that the workplace is the source in this society, not only of employment, but of protection for well-being because it is the origin of most benefits, in addition to wages. He traces the long history of social work's involvement in employment issues, dating to the pioneering work of the 19th century with immigrant and low-wage workers. He concludes that as long as the rhetoric of national politics employs market mechanisms, professionals who are concerned with a social welfare agenda must be involved with policy and practice in the world of work.

Root makes suggestions for such involvement at all levels. For reaching out to the individual, he directs our attention to job-search assistance, training, and educational counseling. For help with more thematic issues, such as the balance between family and work, he recommends an alliance with representatives of personnel, to turn social workers' "sensing" of the problem into remedial policy. Finally, as a true policy advocate, he points out the importance of social work's involvement in community economic development policy in order to have a lasting impact on the causes of the problem of underemployment and unemployment. In short, he makes clear that a societywide perspective and the development of effective coalitions are necessary for social work in the modern era.

The question of whether and how services are provided by employers, particularly the owners of small businesses, is explored by Kurt Spitzer and Alison Favorini in Chapter 19. This chapter reports on an analysis of existing EAP services, reviews research findings on the efficacy of different models in meeting needs in the workplace, and discusses the authors' research on external providers in Michigan. Findings from all sources are interesting but inconclusive. The basic theme that emerges from the chapter is "it depends." The advantages of the internal model of EAPs are greater for large settings than for smaller ones; the gains through the external provision of EAP services occur most extensively when the product is custom tailored to the idiosyncratic nature of the setting.

The authors consider the implications of their findings and conclude that EAPs are likely to continue to expand because they represent the mutuality of interests among many parties—the employer, chambers of commerce, and external providers of services. They are a socially valuable and acceptable tool for reducing poor performance and absenteeism, for meeting drug-free workplace regulations, and for containing costs—the main goals of employers.

Projecting into the future, Spitzer and Favorini note a dramatically changing workplace and believe that an "occupational service center" is the next evolutionary step. Such a center would offer a comprehensive program in almost a cradle-to-grave involvement in the lives of workers, from child care to postretirement resources and from diversity and sensitivity training to the promotion of health. Their model suggests that social workers will have a significant role in helping employers deal with the social and personal problems of the work force of the next century.

The final chapter, Chapter 20, by David Bargal, examines how likely it is that occupational social workers will have such a role in the United States by building a predictive model for their influence based on a comparative analysis of the role of occupational social workers in the Netherlands, Germany, Israel, and Australia. The author cites three important dimensions in determining the extent and influence of social work in the workplace—the societal–workplace characteristics, the professional and academic character of occupational social work, and its workplace repertoire and domain.

Bargal finds that in each of the countries under consideration, some component is lacking to ensure real power and growth for occupational social work. Among the countries he studied, he is more optimistic about the outcome in the Netherlands and Israel than in Germany and Australia, largely because the social climate is most conducive in those two countries. The positive factors he identifies in the Netherlands and Israel as helping to establish occupational social work, particularly its advocacy and policy aspects, are that trade unions have an important degree of power and the country is committed to a welfare state. Given this analysis, he is not sanguine about possibilities in the United States. The significant changes that are occurring in American economic life, however, leave Bargal somewhat hopeful that occupational social work will be able to seize the moment as it were, to overcome the drag of a "highly competitive economic market and weak unions." However, to do so he believes will require improved professional training, a more scholarly professional culture, and greater integration with management and labor. This challenging note, which reinforces the need for influence in managing workplaces and social policy, seems a fitting end to the contributions to this volume.

CHAPTER 16

Women Workers in High-Risk Public Service

TOKENS UNDER STRESS

Barbara Levy Simon and Sheila H. Akabas

> The true history of a nation can never be known unless
> we know about the work lives of the laboring popula-
> tion. . . . the quality of the lives of these working men
> and women are the primary measure of the success of a
> democratic society.
> —Eli Ginzberg and Hyman Berman
> *The American Worker in the 20th Century*

Myriad writers, social reformers, and scientists have explored and recorded the terrible toll that hazardous jobs take on women workers. Following the tradition of earlier pioneers like Alice Hamilton, Upton Sinclair, and George Orwell, contemporary researchers have conducted systematic studies of the traumata encountered in high-risk workplaces (Cooper & Payne, 1980; Hartsough & Myers, 1985; Karasek, Theorell, Schwartz, Peiper, & Michael, 1982; Quick, Bhagat, Dalton, & Quick, 1987; Shostak, 1980). A variety of stressors have been examined, among them, work load, the pace of work, the routinization of work, the degree of an individual worker's control over the work process, environmental hazards of the workplace, and rotating shifts (House, 1981; Lawson, 1987; Quick et al., 1987).

Within this promising arena of studies of occupational stress, many questions remain unanswered, indeed, still unasked, concerning the experience and the consequences of working in one particularly dangerous trade—public service that is charged with protecting the physical welfare of the public. Police officers, soldiers and sailors, prison guards, and firefighters are employed to confront and eliminate threats to the public welfare. High risks accompany their daily responsibilities, and it is not surprising that high levels of stress and traumatic stress reactions do so, as well (Lawson, 1987; Peterson, 1982; Van Maanen, 1975; Yoder, Adams, & Prince, 1983). In their recent work with police officers and firefighters, the authors have observed directly the obvious physical and emotional costs to workers of facing catastrophe on a daily basis—costs that are extreme and pervasive enough to merit much more detailed empirical analysis in the future and to require the institutionalization of preventive interventions, such as the debriefing sessions held for police officers in the Chicago Police Department who encounter violence or death on the job (Wagner, 1982).

Yet, even more inchoate than the current state of understanding of the occupational stress experienced by public servants in high-risk occupations is the limited knowledge base on women who work in these four branches of dangerous public services. Relative newcomers to these occupations, women have served as fully integrated participants in regular police forces, fire departments, prison guard units, and military divisions for fewer than 20 years in the United States. Given the 200-year history of these public services in the United States, women's integrated participation has been brief and recent in the extreme.

Correspondingly, research concerning the work experience and occupational stress of female prison guards, police officers, firefighters, and soldiers and sailors is still rudimentary and sketchy, despite a few excellent pioneer publications (Feinman, 1985; Horne, 1980; Morris, 1987; Pollock, 1986; Zimmer, 1986). Still at the exploratory stage, scholarship about token women in high-risk public services necessarily relies primarily on anecdotal evidence and case studies, for want of other data. Newspapers and magazines have therefore become invaluable contemporary texts about the occupational stressors on token women and their male colleagues. In formulating the speculations that follow, the authors have called on journalistic anecdotes, material from case studies, autobiographical accounts, their own observations as consultants with hazardous public services, and the nascent scholarly literature on stress and reactions to stress among token women in blue-collar trades and among token minorities. In addition, studies of stress among nurses have proved directly pertinent to this investigation because many nurses, like women in high-risk public services, work with death, burns, and severe injuries on rotating shifts in hierarchical and male-dominated workplaces while juggling the primary responsibilities for households, children, and often elderly parents (Akabas, 1988; Smith, Colligan, Frockt, & Tasto, 1979).

This chapter is part of a beginning phase of what the authors trust shall become a long and rich tradition of naturalistic and experimental inquiry into the consequences for women and minorities of integrating and working in dangerous public services. Only with such an understanding of consequences can leaders of public services identify and mitigate salient stressors.

Stressors Affecting All Public Servants

Public Service as a Stressor

For all men and women who work in public services responsible for public safety, several occupational stressors are predictable. Accountable to all citizens, taxpayers, and elected officials, public servants are subject to constant scrutiny by the media and designated authorities. They also endure the ongoing threat of budgetary reductions and consequent understaffing. In election years or at other opportune times, public services are likely scapegoats for financial shortfalls, municipal mishaps, or unforeseen catastrophes.

It is not surprising that high-risk public services turn against each other in the light and heat of public inspection, community blame, and fiscal cutbacks. Police chiefs denigrate fire departments; the army belittles the navy. Fire chiefs and navy admirals take the same internecine tack. Stress, in sum, arises from multiple sources—the public; the media; the legislative, executive, and judicial branches of government; and other rival public services.

Dangerous Work as a Stressor

High-risk work carries with it a host of predictable stressors for all its employees. Three basic kinds of stress-producing pressures, according to Hartsough and Myers (1985), accompany dangerous public service: "event" stressors, occupational stressors, and organizational stressors. Event stressors include (1) the personal losses and injuries that occur in hazardous physical work; (2) the traumatic stimuli of horrible acts, sights, smells, and sounds that a worker may frequently find in disasters, fires, scenes of crime, war, and prisons; and (3) the inevitable failures and errors that take place when workers try to reduce violence and destruction in chaotic or disastrous circumstances. For example, rescue workers who search over a series of days and nights for a lost child, only to find him or her dead from exposure to the elements, undergo not only the horror of discovering a dead innocent, but the extreme disappointment that attends occupational failure to which life and death are linked. Self-doubt and self-blame surface at these times for even the most seasoned public servants (Hartsough & Myers, 1985). Such event stressors are traumata that, according to Janoff-Bulman (1985), can shatter fundamental unexamined assumptions about oneself and the world that most people rely on as everyday articles of faith. One's belief in her or his personal invulnerability, self-worth, and the comprehensibility of the universe may be severely threatened by the death of a co-worker, an injury, a costly miscalculation on the job, or the inability to contain mayhem (Hartsough & Myers, 1985; Janoff-Bulman, 1985).

Compounding this damage to soldiers and sailors, prison guards, police officers, and firefighters are chronic occupational stressors that are associated with particular catastrophes. The disruption of routines of sleep and eating that crisis calls and shift work regularly impose on these workers foster sleep deprivation, inadequate nutrition, digestive problems, mood disorders, and relational conflicts (Akabas, 1988; Akabas & Pirie, 1989; Smith et al., 1979). Workers in high-risk trades also endure particularly intense time pressures on the job because deaths and significant injuries can result from tiny delays in their performance or from moments of indecision. Work loads also constitute an occupational hazard for employees in high-risk public services. In the line work of the military, prisons, and police and fire departments, employees face two sorts of stressors related to work load—they are either overworked or underworked most of the time, with little ability to control the volume or pace of the demands made on them. Crises, whether violence, crime, fires, or chemical spills, often overwork public servants past the point of exhaustion. Such periods of overwork are then followed by concentrated and indeterminate stretches of inaction and boredom, with little for workers to do but wait for the next alarm, as in the case of emergency medical service workers. Both crises and inactivity appear to tax the mind and body immeasurably (Hartsough & Myers, 1985).

Coercive Organizations as Stressors

In addition, organizational stressors influence the welfare of police officers, prison guards, soldiers and sailors, and firefighters daily. All four of these public services are conducted in military or paramilitary organizations that are, in Etzioni's (1961) words, "coercive organizations" that have formal chains of command, impose strict penalties for errors or deviations from established procedures, and discourage questions or suggestions from line workers. As the "job strain model" of Karasek et al. (1982) indicates, this combination of a high demand for productivity and low control over the nature of one's work in contexts that require much activity and initiative is the precise formula for creating the highest possible levels of stress among workers. Such organizations call on the stick much more than the carrot in maintaining order and excellence in their ranks and, consequently, rely on fear of superiors as a regular source of motivation in the workplace.

In high-risk trades organized in military or paramilitary fashion, the fear of danger, as well as the fear of organizational punishment, fuels a solidarity among frontline personnel that is indispensable to the teamwork and bravery required in such jobs (Gouldner, 1954). Although the fear of punishment and death on the job fosters obedience, unity, and courage, fear as daily fare also erodes workers' physiological, emotional, and cognitive well-being (Hartsough & Myers, 1985; Haynes, LaCroix, & Lippin, 1987). Women, whose exclusion from organized athletics and military service has, until recently, left them much less experienced than their male peers in working in coercive formal organizations, are especially vulnerable to the initial shock of coming under paramilitary or military rule (Peterson, 1982).

Stressors Affecting Token Women in High-Risk Public Services

Token Status as a Stressor

Occupational segregation by gender, pervasive in the U.S. labor market, continues to confine most working women to fewer than 30 of 400 occupational categories (Blau & Ferber, 1987). Token status is a major source of stress for women minorities in any "skewed" work force, one that consists of a majority group of at least 85 percent of the job occupants and a minority group of 15 percent or less of the job category (Kanter, 1977a). No occupations have been more effective than high-risk public services in excluding and discouraging women from joining. The representation of women among firefighters, police officers, prison guards, and combat forces remains disproportionately small, despite a geometric progression of increases since the early 1970s. In 1991, only 1.4 percent of the firefighters and 10.3 percent of the police officers and detectives were women (U.S. Bureau of the Census, 1992, p. 394). In December 1987, 10.5 percent of U.S. military officers and 10.2 percent of the military enlisted personnel were women (U.S. Department of Defense, 1988, p. 30). Women made up only 17.8 percent of all correctional officers in prisons and jails in 1983, including those who staffed women's institutions (U.S. Bureau of Labor Statistics, 1985, p. 51).

The work and bearing of token women in any male-dominated trade are far more visible than are those of their male colleagues, subjecting female participants to discrepant amounts of scrutiny. The newer the token is to a work context, the greater her visibility (Alexander & Thoits, 1985). Such visibility creates a variety of performance pressures for token women. The actions of each woman at work become public demonstrations and tests of competence by which all women in the chosen trade are judged. Thus, the woman quickly becomes a symbol of womanhood's strengths and limitations, rather than just another individual who is trying to learn and perform a job. This involuntary and constant burden of proving all women's worth is a stressor that induces the woman to act with greater caution on the job than she might otherwise adopt (Schollaert, 1988). Because the woman's mistakes receive heightened attention that puts the reputation of women workers as a group at risk, the woman is reluctant to learn through the trial-and-error experimentation that characterizes most apprentices' approach to on-the-job training (O'Farrell, 1982). Indeed, token workers with whom the authors work have reported few opportunities for informal learning on the job, the sine qua non of on-the-job training, because few majority-group veterans are willing to act as informal mentors to them in the glare of the spotlight that relentlessly and inevitably focuses on the token women.

Token women appear to respond to their unusual visibility with either a strategy of underachievement that is intended to avoid trouble and limelight or a strategy of overachievement, with the attendant physical and mental costs that excessive chronic effort and self-conscious performance entail. Studies of the disproportionate rates of mental illness and of institutionalization among ethnic minorities who live as tokens in their neighborhoods are suggestive of the damage wrought by excessive visibility and resultant circumspection.

In addition to experiencing unusual visibility at work, tokens encounter the proclivity of majority group members to heighten the boundary between majority and minority groups in the workplace. This "polarization," in the words of Kanter (1977b), takes the form of majority members' perceptual exaggeration of the differences between the behavior of the majority group and that of the minority group and minimization of the intragroup differences among majority members and among tokens. Male members who constitute the overwhelming majority of an occupation like soldiering, for example, tend to view men's job performance as monolithically competent while finding women's performance uniformly substandard.

This boundary-heightening process inspires members of the majority group to identify the salience and homogeneity of the informal majority culture of the workplace through rituals, pranks, vocabulary, and jokes that underscore the solidarity among majority members and the unacceptability of tokens (Morse & Furst, 1982). Through shunning behavior, harassment, assault, sabotage, and the creation of a climate of sexual harassment, majority members keep tokens out of the informal networks in which indispensable training, bonding, and the collective release of occupational tension and stress occur (Long & Porter, 1984; O'Farrell, 1982; O'Farrell & Harlan,

1982; Schollaert, 1988; Yoder, 1985). Should scapegoating provoke an observable response from a token—anger, retaliation, tears, silent withdrawal, psychosomatic symptoms, absenteeism, or a request for a transfer or leave of absence—the scapegoaters, incited by the success of their campaign, increase their hostility in the hopes of forcing the token's resignation and of gaining the protection that the reputation of being a unit to which it is unwise to assign a minority member or a woman provides.

In one common version of harassment, explicitly sexual pictures were displayed on the walls of firehouses and pornographic movies were shown in fire stations during tours of duty in Los Angeles. Women firefighters protested that such materials fueled contempt for female firefighters and encouraged sexual harassers in the workplace. The president of the Los Angeles Fire Commission agreed and banned all sexually explicit materials, gestures, and behaviors (Kendall, 1988). Even more destructive than specific sexual insinuations, suggestions, or overtures is a climate of sexual harassment—sustained by off-color jokes, stories, gossip, gestures, insinuations, noises, films, and pictures—that inevitably trivializes token women workers and puts each of them through an ordeal of debasement that is prolonged and isolating. Unlike traditional forms of hazing for all new members of a club or workplace that bind cohorts of newcomers and that serve as shared experiential bridges with earlier generations of people who have weathered the same tests and humiliations, sexual harassment is directed only at the few who are female and thereby underscores the irreversible differences between male veterans and female rookies (Van Maanen, 1975). Such a process can only be exclusionary in nature, intention, and effect.

Tokens are also subject to stereotyping processes in the workplace. Calling on preconceived role definitions borrowed from patriarchal family life, majority-group members expect women tokens to play out limited and caricatured occupational roles that replicate one or more of four prevailing stereotypes of women—that of mother, seductress, mascot, or Amazon (Gutek & Morasch, 1982; Kanter, 1977a; Laws, 1975). Tokens respond to these forms of role entrapment with a continuum of behaviors, including outright rejection of stereotyped expectations, time-consuming and exhausting efforts to disprove stereotypic misconceptions, resigned enactment of assigned roles, psychological internalization of designated roles, or feigned submission and frivolity with inward rebellion (Kanter, 1977a; O'Farrell, 1982). Each of these paths proves psychologically costly to the token woman worker and results in a diminished sense of self-worth, which, in turn, reduces her capacity to perform (Yoder, 1985).

The recency of token women's entrance into high-risk public service jobs poses distinct disadvantages. The less seniority one has, the less desirable are one's work shifts, assignments, locations, and vacation options. Ill-fitting equipment and clothing designed for male bodies slow down token women's performance and add to the danger of already dangerous work (Morse & Furst, 1982). Inadequate bathroom and shower facilities in previously all-male work domains make basic personal hygiene a difficult and contentious matter. The shortage of female role models and mentors on police and firefighting forces, military units, and prison guard staffs exacerbates token women's pain, which emanates from isolation, self-doubt, and harassment and reduces their faith that hard work will result in successful careers for them in public service, a belief that expectancy theorists argue is necessary for sustained achievement (O'Farrell, 1982; Schollaert, 1988; Van Maanen, 1975; Yoder, Adams, Grove, & Priest, 1985).

Anticipatory socialization, the preparatory learning that occurs in one's family, neighborhood, school, athletic team, or peer network teaches broad societal expectations and specific behavioral guidelines for performing a job (Van Maanen, 1976). The recency of women's entry into high-risk public services puts women at a disadvantage by making it unlikely that they will have personally known women who have performed the jobs they are about to enter and making anticipatory socialization improbable and "reality shock" likely during the first months on their jobs (Hughes, 1958; Van Maanen, 1976). The absence of informed anticipation before entry into public service leaves women "rookies" unusually vulnerable to disappointment when their expectations about the work and work context are discrepant with everyday realities. The recent entrance of a small number of women to high-risk public services also leaves many of them without the support and responsiveness of unions because male domination characterizes these unions' leadership and rank and file as thoroughly as it does the work sites (O'Farrell, 1982).

African American, Hispanic, and Asian American women who work in high-risk public services confront all the stressors that token white women face, as well as others that surround members of racial minorities in the workplace. "Double" tokens must endure two clusters of stereotypes: extreme isolation on the job and the pressures of performing as the symbolic representatives of two denigrated groups. To compound the difficulties of token minority women, their "healthy cultural suspiciousness and adaptive response to the experience of racism" (Parson, 1985, p. 322) is often understood by white co-workers and supervisors to be unprovoked hostility, paranoia, or a refusal to become part of the team. Unlike Irish American women in fire departments and police forces, who understand intuitively the subcultural conventions of the many Irish American men represented in these public services and whose humor and mannerisms are recognizable to the men, women of African American, Hispanic, and Asian backgrounds are thoroughly unfamiliar to the male majorities. In the words of one black woman firefighter with whom the authors worked, "White women have only to prove that they are as tough as men; black women have first of all to prove that they are human beings."

Family–Work Conflicts as Stressors

Women who take jobs in high-risk, male-dominated public services increase dramatically their chances of experiencing conflicts between the demands of the workplace and those of their families and of losing some of the social supports that they have previously relied on as "stress buffers" (House, 1981). The exigencies of shift work disrupt women's and men's participation in extended family groups, recreational and cultural activities, clubs, church and volunteer activities, sports, and even friendships. For a woman who has primary parental responsibility for young children while working rotating shifts, logistical difficulties and conflicting demands for her time and attention are everyday stressors. If she is the sole parent through divorce, separation, widowhood, or design, the pressures and counterpressures become especially extreme. It is probable that she will find neither time nor opportunity for any activity but work and parenting. If she also has caregiving responsibilities for an elderly parent, stress levels can result in mental and physical exhaustion and illness (Brody, 1985; Simon, 1986).

Indeed, evidence is mounting of the increase in "Superwomen" illnesses— stress-induced conditions of married and single mothers who bear much responsibility on the job and at home with little authority or control in either domain. Rates of cardiovascular morbidity, cancer, miscarriages, and mental depression are disproportionately high among married working mothers in white, blue-collar households, in which gender roles remain most sharply differentiated and, consequently, in which family responsibilities are least shared by husbands (Haynes & Feinleib, 1984; Haynes et al., 1987; Verbrugge, 1983). Working mothers of preschoolers appear to be particularly stressed and especially vulnerable to stress-related illness (Sales & Frieze, 1984).

It is clear from the authors' discussions with women police officers and firefighters that some husbands disapprove of their wives' entry into dangerous or traditionally male work. The loss of a husband's or boyfriend's approval of one's work and the threat of the loss of his cooperation in managing the balance between work and family roles quickly become acute sources of distress (Barnett, Beiner, & Baruch, 1987; Rosen, 1987). In couples in which both members are employed in the same high-risk public service, dual harassment is reported. The husband is taunted for "allowing" his wife to violate traditional gender and marital roles, and the wife is harassed for intruding on male terrain.

Women's entry into jobs in male-dominated work domains also requires that they leave behind support networks of women colleagues in their former work settings. Women who are accustomed to working in sex-segregated jobs, the vast majority of women working in the United States, report that the absence or scarcity of other women in their new jobs is one of the most painful parts of their occupational transition (Kessler-Harris, 1982; O'Farrell, 1982; O'Farrell & Harlan, 1982).

Differential Physical Readiness as a Stressor

Traditional gender-role socialization has ensured that most women public servants who enter high-risk occupations prove significantly less fit for the physically punishing dimensions of their jobs than do their male counter-parts. Most female rookies on police, fire, and military forces arrive with demonstrably less physical strength and confidence in their physical capacities than do entering men, many of whom were athletes throughout their youth and have predicated their sense of manhood, in part, on physical risk taking and demonstrations of strength since early childhood.

Compounding this differential readiness of men and women who are new to public service is the physiological fact that once they are on the force, women have a more difficult time than do men building and maintaining upper body strength. The male musculature, denser and longer than that of females, is more easily kept strong through systematic exercise. Women, of course, can build and sustain excellent levels of physical strength, but must work harder than men at the same exercises to do so (Clarke, 1986; Heyward, Johannes-Ellis, & Romer, 1986; Misner, Plowman, & Boileau, 1987).

At the same time, token status makes working out on the job more difficult for women than for men. Exercise rooms at the work site are a traditional male preserve, from which many women public servants are warned or kept off by overt and covert tactics. Thus, the workers with the greatest need to lift weights and exercise on the job are those with the least opportunity to do so.

Stress Reactions of Token Women Workers

There are available no systematic epidemiological studies that quantify the proportion of women soldiers, prison guards, police officers, and firefighters who remain healthy and emotionally unaffected by the multiple stressors they necessarily encounter as female tokens in dangerous work. Clearly, some token women workers adapt to these occupations and conditions in a resilient and relaxed way. Others have noted the onset of physical symptoms, emotional difficulties, or behavioral problems after they entered high-risk public services (Morse & Furst, 1982; O'Farrell, 1982; Schollaert, 1988; Vitters & Kinzer, 1977; Yoder, 1985).

Women in high-risk public services have reported a long list of physical stress reactions to their token status and dangerous work, including disrupted menstrual cycles, nausea, exhaustion, eye and skin infections, rashes, migraines, ulcers, colitis, muscle spasms, backaches, blackouts, allergies, hypertension, hyperventilation, and chronic diarrhea. Emotional reactions documented among token women workers are equally various. Women have reported indications of situational or chronic depression and rage states whose symptoms include weeping spells; the inability to get out of bed, make minor decisions, or concentrate; withdrawal from favorite friends and family members; apathy; a prolonged feeling of emotional numbness; unprecedented mood swings; and obsessive thought patterns (Morse & Furst, 1982; Yoder, 1985). For example, one woman firefighter spoke of her repetitive fantasies of being "pushed into a fire."

Behavioral problems also are found among token women workers in high-risk public services. After entering such jobs, some women noted marked weight gain or loss, anorexia, bulimia, drug abuse, alcoholism, sexual difficulties, sleeping disorders, and frequent arguments with intimates (Morse & Furst, 1982; O'Farrell & Harlan, 1982; Yoder, 1985). Another common behavioral response is to quit the job. Attrition rates of women in high-risk public services are high. For example, 35.1 percent of the female midshipmen at Annapolis between 1980 and 1987 left before graduation, compared with 22.9 percent of the men (Schollaert, 1988), and 50 percent of the women cadets at West Point in the class of 1980 quit, compared with 40 percent of the men (Yoder et al., 1983).

Major Stressors: "Stressful Life Events" or "Daily Hassles"?

Investigators of traumatic and posttraumatic stress reactions have tended to fall into one of two theoretical camps—those who have restricted their definition of significant stressors to "life events" that are life threatening and catastrophic and those who include in their category of significant stressors both catastrophic life events and less dramatic difficulties, such as the erosion over time of support networks and the accrued daily aggravations internalized on a hostile work crew (Miller, 1988). The former group of theoreticians designates as major stressors only events that are sufficiently potent unto themselves to cause physical or emotional illness in previously well people. The latter group also includes processes that trigger the formation or advance the development of illness in people who are predisposed to dysfunction by prolonged exposure to environmental, familial, or occupational difficulties.

It is obvious that the catalog of stressors that the authors have compiled that affect token women workers in high-risk public services includes a combination of catastrophic and accrued daily pressures. At the same time that they may risk separation or divorce, injury, sabotage, and death on the job by entering high-risk, traditionally male domains, these token women workers also undergo shifts in their support networks, sleep patterns, and the balance of their work and family responsibilities. Both catastrophe and accumulated strain, in short, figure as traumatic factors in their lives.

Recommended Interventions in the Workplace

Despite the weight and intensity of interests and influences that perpetuate tokenism and its ills, the incentives for remediation are compelling. A work environment that is replete with pent-up hostility is costly to all participants and expensive to the public that funds it. Hence, in addition to the moral and legal arguments that support equity, decency, and protection from harm and for public pace setting in developing an integrated labor force, there are imperatives of cost saving and increased productivity. By the simple laws of supply and demand, recruiting from a larger pool will provide either a choice of equally qualified applicants for less pay or a choice of superior applicants for the same pay. The marginal productivity of each newly hired person is thereby increased. In addition, because the cumulative tension of a hostile work environment compromises the health of all participants, a better-integrated work force should result in reduced medical care costs for all.

Therefore, the litany of contributing causes invokes an equally varied roster of short- and long-term responses to the needs of the parties. Overall, a strategy for ameliorating the stress experienced by token women in high-risk jobs combines primary and secondary prevention that is targeted at individual, organizational, and community perceptions and behavior. Some of the components of such a plan are detailed in the next section. Such a strategy is in the interest of public policy, community welfare, productive efficiency, and the well-being of all employees in the work setting.

Primary Prevention Initiatives

The linchpin of any effort to resolve the problem of the stress of token women in high-risk public services is to end their token status; this can occur only when a steady stream of women apply and qualify for these jobs. In the short run, the investment of resources with which to carry out an aggressive, focused, and community-based recruitment campaign may be helpful if it is followed by organizationally and community-sponsored training programs that hone the skills that interested women would need to pass the preentry written and physical examinations. The effectiveness of such efforts, unfortunately, has been limited.

Therefore, the achievement of a large pool of successful female candidates awaits a broad-gauged *community* drive that would engage the public in a redefinition of these jobs so that young women would be socialized to think of such occupations as appropriate career goals and the rest of society's members would affirm that definition. Included in such a campaign would be the use of public relations tools, from television spots by persons whom young people respect for their achievements to bold programs of encouragement in black churches, from comic books depicting female heroines in these jobs to children's books carrying out the same message. Mass advertising and outreach teams can visit schools and other community facilities to augment more targeted initiatives. The proliferation of women's sports programs and competitions and the encouragement of women to enter scientific fields of inquiry are important related initiatives that merit the support of those who seek the gender integration of work forces. Coalitions among groups that are working for the advancement of women in sports, science, and public service are advisable.

Forceful articulation and support from the highest level of *governmental leadership*, although politically hazardous because of the expected initial resistance from the community and employing organizations, is a vital ingredient to the success of this strategy. Furthermore, such leadership must be mirrored by the equal commitment of political leaders and their managerial representatives and union counterparts at each lower governmental level. By speech and action, visible public figures can model this public redefinition and thereby help alter the pool of persons who apply for these positions. Moreover, primary prevention on a community basis can be promoted by affirmative action legislation and concomitant regulations to support proactive enforcement and the recruitment and appointment of women to public service high-risk jobs.

Within specific *employing organizations*, the management's allocation of resources and application of sanctions determine the climate in the workplace. Management can promote prevention by auditing its own house—examining attitudinal and structural patterns that affect the working conditions and pay of all, with special attention to the design of jobs and the delegation of tasks to teams of workers so they do not have a negative impact on the opportunities of any particular group in the work force. Attention paid to the systems of performance appraisal and of promotions and other rewards, to ensure that they reflect the value that management places on a discrimination-free workplace, will stimulate a climate that enhances the growth and development of all members of the organization. Conversely, punishment for violators should leave no doubt about the seriousness of organizational enforcement.

Strengthening the "host"—in this case the individual entrant into the work organization—is another primary prevention strategy. Preentry education in general problem-solving skills and coping behavior, together with role rehearsal that realistically anticipates what to expect on the job, can help women handle the work environment effectively (Long & Porter, 1984).

Secondary Prevention

Short of achieving significant gender integration, there are a multitude of strategies that, by intercepting conditions before they worsen, can reduce the stress now experienced by token women. At the community level, the ready availability of services, such as day care and elder care, that lighten the conflicts between the demands of work and family can help women reserve sufficient energy to cope with the difficulties of tokenism in the workplace.

Within the employing organization itself, education for members of both token and majority groups is a promising road on which to reduce the stress experienced by all participants. Training for majority-group men—peers, supervisors, and union representatives—that is organizationally sponsored should help them understand the range of formal and informal prejudicial attitudes and discriminatory behaviors; the experience of being a token in a workplace; the necessary components to create a supportive work climate; and their own responsibilities in preventing, identifying, and resolving situations involving harassment. Obviously any new entrants to the organization, male or female, require exposure to the policy of preventing and eradicating discrimination. Special assistance should be provided to supervisors who are given the responsibility of supervising a work force of both men and women for the first time. Mentoring by colleagues who have already gained facility with such a charge has proved extremely helpful. Performance appraisals that include formal criteria for evaluating demonstrable levels of competence in cooperating with and managing diverse groups of workers offer structural support for managerial intent, provided that these appraisals are backed by a system of rewards and penalties that are closely linked to performance ratings.

Experience suggests that discrimination and harassment are ongoing problems that are not easily checked through a single application of any particular intervention. Above all, organizations need to develop a continuous awareness of the possible problems that may develop and the commitment and capacity to respond when problems become manifest. Furthermore, token women, like all workers, find that being able to do their jobs well gives them the strength to face the difficulties represented by their status as tokens. Their receipt of information and training in skills that enhance their on-the-job performance not only increases their own sense of well-being, but may help lay to rest one precipitant of harassment—lingering doubts about whether women can do these jobs.

In many settings, employee assistance programs (EAPs) with the so-called broad-brush ability to deal with the mental health needs of an organization's labor force have been designated to monitor sexual harassment, to provide supportive counseling to individuals, and to offer consultation and mediation to groups in crisis situations. Because of their multiple functions and wide-ranging interactions, members of EAP staffs often gain a keen sense of their organization's structure and dynamics. Consequently, they may be able to intercept any worsening of a situation by serving as liaisons to officers of departments of human resource management, training, and benefits and other key actors who are concerned with the changing needs of token women (L. Miller, 1981). In high-risk public service settings, EAP staff should be prepared to act as advocates for these women.

For individual women, two sources—EAPs and self-help groups—are particularly valuable secondary prevention activities. Individual counseling from EAPs, especially when modeled as a trauma-debriefing experience that utilizes a systems approach to helping an individual understand the intersections and conflicts among personal, familial, organizational, and community forces, can assist the token woman in a variety of ways. Counseling can help her to develop productive behaviors of self-care, physical fitness, adequate rest, and good nutrition, as well as to reconstruct her perceptions of the work environment and reestablish her sense of competence (Akabas, Grube, & Krauskopf, 1989; Brunstein & Kilpatrick, 1988). Mutual aid groups of peers can also mitigate the physical and emotional damage of tokenism. Such groups assist women to understand their situation, receive and give help, confirm members' sense of rights and obligations vis-à-vis employers and unions, promote the learning of new coping and problem-solving skills, and identify useful resources. Women military personnel, firefighters, police officers, and prison guards have underscored the salience of such groups in their efforts to reduce their own sense of isolation and marginality on the job (Feinman, 1985; Martin, 1980; Morris, 1987; Pollock, 1986; Schollaert, 1988; Yoder, 1985; Zimmer, 1986).

Five years ago, the U.S. Department of Labor (1988, p. 1) reported that "much has been written about the progress women have made in entering many professional occupations such as engineering, medicine and law.

However, similar progress has not been made in the skilled trades and other manual occupations. Women continue to be dramatically underrepresented." This challenge still faces those who employ women in high-risk public service occupations. Federal, state, county, and municipal employers in the United States have broken important ground on many social issues of equity and safety in the workplace. Occupational integration of women and men provides yet another opportunity, and, indeed, an imperative, for public leadership. In a work force that is rapidly changing and that will include a majority of women by the year 2005, a much larger proportion of women will be needed just to fill the available jobs (Johnston, 1987). To go beyond the mere filling of vacancies—to reduce the costly waste of tokenism and replace it with the achievement of building a productive, efficient, and cost-effective work force in high-risk public service jobs—gender integration becomes a mandate.

References

Akabas, S. H. (1988). Women, work and mental health: Room for improvement. *Journal of Primary Prevention, 9*(1–2), 130–140.

Akabas, S. H., Grube, B., & Krauskopf, M. (1989). Sexual harassment. *Employee Assistance, 2*(1), 8–15.

Akabas, S. H., & Pirie, V. (1989). *Impact of shift work on employee well-being: A manual for discussion leaders.* New York: Center for Social Policy and Practice in the Workplace, Columbia University School of Social Work.

Alexander, V. D., & Thoits, P. A. (1985). Token achievement: An examination of proportional representation and performance outcomes. *Social Forces, 64,* 332–340.

Barnett, R. C., Beiner, L., & Baruch, G. K. (Eds.). (1987). *Gender and stress.* New York: Free Press.

Blau, F. D., & Ferber, M. A. (1987). Occupations and earnings of women workers. In K. S. Koziara, M. H. Moskow, & L. D. Tanner (Eds.), *Working women: Past, present, future* (pp. 37–68). Washington, DC: Industrial Relations Research Association.

Brody, E. M. (1985). Parent care as a normative family stress. *The Gerontologist, 25,* 19–29.

Brunstein, S., & Kilpatrick, M. A. (1988). Counseling survivors of workplace accidents and disasters. In G. M. Gould & M. L. Smith (Eds.), *Social work in the workplace* (pp. 96–108). New York: Springer.

Clarke, D. H. (1986). Sex differences in strength and fatigability. *Research Quarterly for Exercise and Sport, 57,* 144–149.

Cooper, C. L., & Payne, R. (Eds.). (1980). *Current concerns on occupational stress.* New York: John Wiley & Sons.

Etzioni, A. (1961). *A comparative analysis of complex organizations.* New York: Free Press.

Feinman, C. (1985). *Women in the criminal justice system* (2nd ed.). New York: Praeger.

Gouldner, A. (1954). *Patterns of industrial bureaucracy.* New York: Free Press.

Gutek, B. A., & Morasch, B. (1982). Sex-ratios, sex-role spillover, and sexual harassment of women at work. *Journal of Social Issues, 38*(4), 55–74.

Hartsough, D. M., & Myers, D. G. (1985). *Disaster work and mental health.* Washington, DC: U.S. Government Printing Office.

Haynes, S. G., & Feinleib, M. (1984). Clerical work and coronary heart disease in women: Prospective findings from the Framingham study. In B. G. F. Cohen (Ed.), *Human aspects of office automation* (pp. 239–255). Amsterdam: Elsevier Science Publishers.

Haynes, S. G., LaCroix, A. Z., & Lippin, T. (1987). The effect of high job demands and low control on the health of employed women. In J. C. Quick, R. S. Bhagat, J. E., Dalton, & J. D. Quick (Eds.), *Work stress: Health care systems in the workplace* (pp. 93–110). New York: Praeger.

Heyward, V. H., Johannes-Ellis, S. M., & Romer, J. F. (1986). Gender differences in strength. *Research Quarterly for Exercise and Sport, 57,* 154–159.

Horne, P. (1980). *Women in law enforcement.* Springfield, IL: Charles C Thomas.

House, J. S. (1981). *Work stress and social support.* Reading, MA: Addison-Wesley.

Hughes, E. C. (1958). *Men and their work.* Glencoe, IL: Free Press.

Janoff-Bulman, R. (1985). The aftermath of victimization: Rebuilding shattered assumptions. In C. R. Figley (Ed.), *Trauma and its wake: The study and treatment of post-traumatic stress disorder* (pp. 15–35). New York: Brunner/ Mazel.

Johnston, W. B. (1987). *Workforce 2000: Work and workers for the 21st century.* Indianapolis, IN: Hudson Institute.

Kanter, R. M. (1977a). Some effects of proportions on group life: Skewed sex ratios and responses to token women. *American Journal of Sociology, 82,* 964–990.

Kanter, R. M. (1977b). *Women and men of the corporation.* New York: Basic Books.

Karasek, R., Theorell, T., Schwartz, J. E., Peiper, C., & Michael, J. E. (1982). *Job characteristics of occupations in relation to the prevalence of myocardial infarction in the U.S. Health Examination Survey.* Unpublished manuscript.

Kendall, J. (1988, January 8). Ban on explicit sex material in L.A. firehouses sought. *The Los Angeles Times,* p. II-4.

Kessler-Harris, A. (1982). *Out to work: A history of wage-earning women in the United States.* New York: Oxford University Press.

Laws, J. L. (1975). The psychology of tokenism: An analysis. *Sex Roles, 1*(1), 51–67.

Lawson, B. Z. (1987). Work-related post-traumatic stress reactions: The hidden dimension. *National Health Line, 12,* 250–261.

Long, J., & Porter, K. L. (1984). Multiple roles of midlife women: A case for new directions in theory, research, and policy. In G. Baruch & J. Brooks-Gunn (Eds.), *Women in midlife* (pp. 109–159). New York: Plenum Press.

Martin, S. E. (1980). *Breaking and entering: Policewomen on patrol.* Berkeley: University of California Press.

Miller, L. (1981). Giving a helping hand with personal problems. *Advanced Management Journal, 46*(2), 49–55.

Miller, T. W. (1988). Advances in understanding the impact of stressful life events on health. *Hospital and Community Psychiatry, 39,* 615–622.

Misner, J. E., Plowman, S. A., & Boileau, R. A. (1987). Performance differences between males and females on simulated firefighting tasks. *Journal of Occupational Medicine, 29,* 801–805.

Morris, A. (1987). *Women, crime and criminal justice.* Cambridge, MA: Basil Blackwell.

Morse, D. R., & Furst, M. L. (1982). *Women under stress.* New York: Van Nostrand Reinhold.

O'Farrell, B. (1982). Women and non-traditional blue collar jobs in the 1980s: An overview. In P. A. Wallace (Ed.), *Women in the workplace* (pp. 135–164). Boston: Auburn House.

O'Farrell, B., & Harlan, S. L. (1982). Craftworkers and clerks: The effect of male co-worker hostility on women's satisfaction with non-traditional jobs. *Social Problems, 29,* 252–265.

Parson, E. R. (1985). Ethnicity and traumatic stress: The intersecting point in psychotherapy. In C. R. Figley (Ed.), *Trauma and its wake* (pp. 314–337). New York: Brunner/Mazel.

Peterson, C. B. (1982). Doing time with the boys. In B. R. Price & N. J. Sokoloff (Eds.), *The criminal justice system and women* (pp. 437–462). New York: Clark Boardman.

Pollock, J. M. (1986). *Sex and supervision: Guarding male and female inmates.* Westport, CT: Greenwood Press.

Quick, J. C., Bhagat, R. S., Dalton, J. E., & Quick, J. D. (Eds.). (1987). *Work stress: Health care systems in the workplace.* New York: Praeger.

Rosen, E. I. (1987). *Bitter choices: Blue-collar women in and out of work.* Chicago: University of Chicago Press.

Sales, E., & Frieze, I. H. (1984). Women and work: Implications for mental health. In L. Walker (Ed.), *Women and mental health policy* (pp. 229–246). Beverly Hills, CA: Sage Publications.

Schollaert, S. (1988, August). Nobody asked me either, but . . . *Proceedings* (U.S. Naval Academy), p. 94.

Shostak, A. B. (1980). *Blue-collar stress.* Reading, MA: Addison-Wesley.

Simon, B. L. (1986). Never-married women as caregivers: Some costs and benefits. *Affilia, Journal of Women and Social Work, 1*(3), 29–42.

Smith, M., Colligan, M., Frockt, J., & Tasto, D. (1979). Occupational injury rates among nurses as a function of shift schedule. *Journal of Safety Research, 11,* 181–187.

U.S. Bureau of the Census. (1992). *Statistical abstract of the United States: 1992* (112th ed.). Washington, DC: U.S. Government Printing Office.

U.S. Bureau of Labor Statistics. (1985). *Handbook of labor statistics* (Bulletin 2217). Washington, DC: U.S. Government Printing Office.

U.S. Department of Defense. (1988, September–October). *Defense 88 almanac.* Washington, DC: U.S. Government Printing Office.

U.S. Department of Labor. (1988). *Employment of women in nontraditional jobs, 1983–1988* (Bureau of Labor Statistics, Report No. 756). Washington, DC: U.S. Government Printing Office.

Van Maanen, J. (1975). Police socialization: A longitudinal examination of job attitudes in an urban police department. *Administrative Science Quarterly, 20,* 207–228.

Van Maanen, J. (1976). Breaking in: Socialization to work. In R. Dubin (Ed.), *Handbook of work, organization, and society* (pp. 67–130). Chicago: Rand McNally.

Verbrugge, L. M. (1983). Multiple roles and physical health of women and men. *Journal of Health and Social Behavior, 24,* 16–29.

Vitters, A. G., & Kinzer, N. S. (1977). *Report of the admission of women to the U.S. Military Academy (Project Athena).* Unpublished manuscript, U.S. Military Academy, West Point, NY.

Wagner, M. (1982). Counseling police officers. *Practice Digest, 5*(2), 30–31.

Yoder, J. D. (1985). An academic woman as a token: A case study. *Journal of Social Issues, 41*(4), 61–72.

Yoder, J. D., Adams, J., Grove, S., & Priest, R. F. (1985). To teach is to learn: Overcoming tokenism with mentors. *Psychology of Women Quarterly, 9*(1), 119–131.

Yoder, J. D., Adams, J., & Prince, H. T. (1983). The price of a token. *Journal of Political and Military Sociology, 11,* 325–337.

Zimmer, L. E. (1986). *Women guarding men.* Chicago: University of Chicago Press.

CHAPTER 17

Stress in the Workplace

A RESPONSE FROM UNION MEMBER ASSISTANCE PROGRAMS

Lee Schore and Jerry Atkin

> Without work, all life goes rotten. When work is
> meaningless, life withers and dies.
>
> —Albert Camus
> *The Stranger*

Social work has a long history of providing services to working people in workplaces and in union halls as advocates, organizers, and clinicians (Reynolds, 1934/1982). Over time the nature of work has significantly changed, and these changes require new approaches to serving working people. The current restructuring of the economy from manufacturing to service and information industries, coupled with the increasing use of new technology, has transformed the workplace and the skills required. One of the by-products of these changes has been a greater awareness of the effects of working conditions on individual workers, their families, and their communities. These changes place new demands on workers and present new challenges to social work to respond to the human consequences of these changes.

Work stress has become a key issue because of its impact on the physical and psychological well-being of workers and on productivity. Research on job stress, which originally focused on exposure to chemicals and other physical stressors, has been broadened over the past 20 years to include the contribution of psychosocial stressors and social conditions in the workplace to physical and psychological disease (Tesh, 1988). Psychosocial stressors are those aspects of the organization of work and work environments that are neither physical nor biochemical, but have a direct impact on the health and well-being of workers. They include conflict with supervisors or co-workers, the lack of control over the work process, the underutilization of skills, shift work and overtime, divisions at the workplace (racism, sexism, classism, homophobia, and ageism), the lack of advancement opportunities, job insecurity, and the impact of work on family life.

From a public health perspective, work and working conditions are viewed as an arena of crucial human activity that broadly influences the psychological health and well-being of individuals, families, and communities (U.S. Public Health Service, 1991). The causes of stress in the workplace are now understood to exist within the total system of the workplace and to have an impact that reaches beyond the workplace to affect family and community systems (Akabas, 1990).

This approach, which looks at work and work stress holistically as it is rooted in the totality of people's lives, reflects a clear social work perspective. The social work profession historically has emphasized the complex social transactions between individuals and their environment with the goal of improving the quality of people's lives and their ability to function effectively and to act decisively. This way of looking at social interactions is an ideal, practical, and analytic tool for addressing the emerging issues of work and workplace stress that this society confronts. By combining clinical insights, social analysis, and organizing skills, social workers can make an invaluable contribution by providing effective treatment for the problems that workers face and by using this perspective to heighten social awareness of the role of work in determining the quality of life for individuals, families, and communities (Perlman, 1982). Long-range goals of social work practice in this area should include education and advocacy directed toward shaping corporate and public policy to transform work and workplaces into healthy, productive, and satisfying extensions of social life.

The Impact of Workplace Stress

A survey conducted by the Northwestern National Life Insurance Company (Dewey, 1991) indicated that 70 percent of the workers surveyed said that job stress caused frequent health problems and made them less productive; one-third said they expected to burn out on the job in the near future, and a similar percentage had thought seriously about quitting their jobs during the past year because of job stress. The proportion of workers who reported that their jobs were highly stressful (46 percent) doubled between 1985 and 1992. The survey also noted that the lack of personal control on the job was the single largest cause of burnout. In a survey conducted by the National Career Development Association (1990), 48 percent of the workers surveyed said that job stress had a significant impact on their lives, both on and off the job. Twenty-five percent reported that it affected their off-the-job relationships, and 36 percent (42 percent of those with children) frequently experienced conflict between work and family life.

Grippa and Durbin (1986) reported that compensation claims for job-related stress disabilities tripled between 1980 and 1986, and Minter (1991) quoted insurance industry sources as saying that "gradual mental stress" accounts for 11 percent of all workers' compensation claims. As a further indication of the seriousness of this job-stress epidemic, Freudenheim (1987) estimated that the cost of job stress to U.S. businesses may run as high as $150 billion per year.

To deal with the effects of such stress on workers and productivity, a variety of services have been implemented, primarily by business and insurance companies, but the development of these services has been uneven and narrow. A survey by the U.S. Public Health Service (1991) found that only 26.6 percent of the work sites that were surveyed provided stress services and that these services mainly included the provision of information, special places to relax, and stress-reduction classes; only 10 percent of the work sites provided stress counseling.

This chapter discusses (1) the evolution of the concept of workplace stress, with an emphasis on current research on psychosocial stressors; (2) approaches to stress management in the workplace; (3) a model for chronic work-stress interventions; (4) a union-based membership assistance program (MAP) that deals with issues of workplace stress; and (5) an in-depth case study of the impact of work stress on an individual and his family. The MAP presented here goes beyond traditional stress services to offer individual and group counseling as part of a larger constellation of support services that are provided by social workers with both clinical and organizing skills. The services are based on a model that validates the workers' culture and experience and uses information and social support to develop treatment strategies. The underlying goal is to overcome the internalized effects of stress and to enable workers to assert some control over the sources of the stress by using their individual and collective strength to bring about change in the workplace.

Changing Concept of Occupational Stress

The basis of the original studies of occupational stress was the pioneering work of Selye (1936/1976) who proposed the first comprehensive medical model, the generalized stress syndrome, to describe the effect of stress on the human body. Selye's work established that stressors in the environment have a direct impact on both physiological and psychological functioning. Early work in the field of occupational stress focused on biochemical stressors related to the exposure to toxic materials in the work environment. In the past 25 years, the focus has shifted to psychosocial stressors that reflect the organization of work.

McGrath (1970) and Frankenhaeuser and Gardell (1976) conducted the first studies of psychosocial stressors in relation to work overload and work underload, and House (1981) examined social support as an intervention to mediate the effects of stress. Karasek (1979, 1989), working in both Sweden and the United States, began to investigate the relationship between job-decision latitude (workers' ability to control the way in which work tasks are performed), the level of physical and psychological demands, and stress symptoms. Wallin and Wright's (1986) research correlated dull and repetitive work with low motivation, low self-esteem, and apathy.

Karasek and Theorell (1990) pointed out that the stressful way in which work is organized has negative consequences not only for the health of workers, but for productivity. They suggested that attention to psychosocial stress and the organization of work might influence low productivity, the decline in the quality of goods, the impersonality of services, and the emphasis on short-term profits at the expense of ingenuity and the long-term utility of products.

Karasek and Theorell (1990) amply documented that jobs with high demand and low job-decision latitude are the most stressful. Measures as widely disparate as the rate of symptoms of heart disease among workers (Karasek, 1989) and workers' level of citizenship activity in the community (Karasek & Theorell, 1990) are affected by how psychologically demanding jobs are and how much control workers have over how their work is accomplished. Increasing the level of decision latitude reduces stress, promotes health and greater participation in family and social life, and has as its logical outcome the involvement of workers in redesigning the work process and, ultimately, the workplace.

Closely linked to decision latitude is the issue of the use of skills. Research (Karasek & Theorell, 1990; Kasl, 1989) has demonstrated that whereas the underutilization of skills increases levels of stress, opportunities to use skills and to develop new ones reduce stress and increase productivity and workers' self-concept. Jobs that provide these opportunities are generally those in which workers have decision latitude and control over the work process. These findings are consistent with those of Lerner (1985), who found that programs that empower workers to assert themselves to gain greater control over their working conditions reduce both stress and self-blame.

Stress Management in the Workplace

The economic cost of stress has been the primary motivation for employers and insurance companies to initiate stress-management programs. The goal of most of these programs is to help workers adjust to the effects of stress and to take action to reduce the symptoms of stress. This approach views occupational stress as an individual problem and implies that the inability to handle stress is the fault of the worker.

Karasek and Theorell (1990) observed that, although there has been general agreement that stress is the result of something in the environment that affects individuals, traditional responses primarily help individuals to manage the level of stress caused by the environment. These programs assume that people can use a series of techniques (relaxation exercises, attitudinal shifts, biofeedback, and time management) to enable them to cope with environmental stress. Until recently, the impact of the redesign of jobs on stress in the workplace received little attention.

In 1987, a National Institute of Occupational Safety and Health (NIOSH) publication (Murphy & Schoenborn, 1987) concluded that traditional stress-management approaches are severely limited because no effort is made to remove or reduce the sources of stress at work. By targeting workers, these approaches blame the victims and place the responsibility for dealing with stress on the individual. The NIOSH publication suggested that a more appropriate application of stress management would be as a complement to the redesign of jobs or organizational change. Such interventions include workers' participation in the planning and production process, the adjustment of workloads and work roles, and greater training and advancement opportunities. All these recommendations focus on workers having more control and acting more directly to shape working conditions.

Some stress programs in the labor movement have attempted to address the concerns raised by NIOSH. They incorporate some of the same techniques (information, relaxation exercises, and modification of nutrition and exercise patterns), but also make it clear that this approach only relieves the symptoms of stress and is not a solution to the problem. The roles of the social workers in these programs are to provide direct services and to act as enablers who support workers in taking the more active role implicit in NIOSH's recommendations.

Starting from the premise that stress is real, not an attitude or a personal "problem," and that the sources of stress are in the work environment, these programs help people bring about changes in stressful conditions and situations at work. Some strategies are based on what an individual can do alone, though the emphasis is always on working collaboratively with others to accomplish the desired change. Because apathy and feelings of powerlessness are two common reactions to stress (Lerner, 1985), working with others on the resolution of the problem is, in itself, an important way to reduce stress.

The Role of Social Support

Although work was probably more physically oppressive and, therefore, more stressful in the past, the effects were buffered by social support in the workplace, the family, and the community. Today, workers are more vulnerable to the effects of stress because they are often cut off from these natural support systems and because many jobs have been "deskilled" and routinized (Braverman, 1974). Therefore, a critical task of social workers who provide stress services is to activate and re-create social support structures, both on and off the job.

Social support is generally defined as the experience of belonging to groups of people who understand, support, and value you. Sources of social support can be found in the workplace, the union, the family, or in religious or other community groups. Social support in the workplace has been shown to be an important buffer between stressors and physical or emotional illness (Karasek, Triantis, & Chaudhry, 1982; LaRocco, House, & French, 1980). Karasek and Theorell (1990) cited evidence from the U.S. Department of Labor's *Quality of Employment Surveys* (1972, 1977) that found that the incidence of depression among the workers who were surveyed rose from 12 percent in workplaces with high levels of social support to 26.8 percent in workplaces with low levels of such support.

Johnson (1989), working with Swedish researchers, explored the effect of social relations and social support in the workplace on stress and health. He found that social support has a positive effect on health by (1) meeting the basic human need for companionship and group affiliation, (2) serving as a resource to moderate the impact of job demands, (3) promoting active or passive patterns of behavior and hence influencing adult socialization, and (4) providing a collective coping system that protects groups of workers against structural demands and pressures.

Thus, control over the work process and social support in the work setting are two major psychosocial resources that can modify the potentially stressful demands and pressures of the modern workplace (Johnson, 1989; Marmott & Theorell, 1988).

The Role of Social Work

Union programs may approach stress in a comprehensive way that includes (1) education about stress; (2) the relief of symptoms of stress in individuals; (3) the development of social support structures as a basis for mediating the effects of stress; and (4) the mobilization of workers, using the resources and protection of the union, to bring about changes that address the root causes of stress in the workplace. Social work practice that incorporates clinical insights into the nature of psychosocial stressors and an understanding of organizing and organizations is the perfect combination of skills to develop worker-centered, responsive services in unions.

A Model for Dealing with Chronic Stress in the Workplace

The model presented in this chapter was developed to deal with workers who suffer from chronic workplace stress. Rosch and Pelletier (1987) pointed out that, although there are many short-term stress-wellness programs for ancillary stress-related problems, such as substance abuse, overeating, and marital difficulties, few programs are designed to treat workers who are suffering from prolonged and aggravated occupational stress. By the time a condition has moved into the crisis phase, a worker is being treated for the symptoms (for example, high blood pressure, ulcers, and chronic low back pain), but the source is not addressed directly. The effects of chronic stress sometimes are also masked because they are cumulative and may lead to a sequence of events that obscure the roots of the problem, so that the client is treated as a "troubled worker."

Unions are an appropriate place to develop these programs because it is their role to protect their members and to maintain health and safety standards. One of the difficulties that workers face in changing the stressful conditions of their workplaces is that these conditions produce reactions (anger, fatigue, apathy, and low self-esteem) that make it much more difficult to act to change them. Therefore, it is necessary for social workers to provide both needed treatment and the support that will make it possible for people to act on their own behalf.

The social work model for providing the services and interventions described in this chapter is derived from work done at the Institute for Labor and Mental Health and the Center for Working Life (CWL), a community-based nonprofit organization in Oakland, California, between 1980 and 1990. The model is based on the premise that effective services must be work- and worker-centered, that is, they must be based on an understanding of the culture of work and workers, and this understanding must be used as the cornerstone of both mental health and organizing interventions (Schore 1987, 1990).

Basic Steps of the Model

The basic steps of the model involve (1) reinforcing dignity and respect; (2) validating experiences and feelings; (3) normalizing people's experiences; (4) discovering the causes of stress; (5) exposing social myths; (6) using the information gained to reframe the problem; and (7) helping people to develop strategies, individually and collectively, to solve problems and to overcome obstacles.

Reinforcing dignity and respect. The first step involves the nonjudgmental acceptance of people and the problems they face in a way that recognizes and reaffirms their dignity and pride as workers. This dignity and respect is often denied in daily interactions within the workplace and is a major source of perceptions of powerlessness, self-blame, and low self-esteem.

Validating experiences and feelings. Rather than ask people to deny or ignore their experiences and feelings, this model recognizes the need to validate them. If people feel angry and frustrated, it is necessary to address their experiences and their feelings about them. Otherwise, the feelings become an internalized obstacle to taking action.

Normalizing and destigmatizing experience. Often people think they are the only ones who are experiencing difficulty and that there is something "wrong" with them. Acknowledging that others have had the same experiences and feelings is an important step in breaking down the isolation that intensifies the effects of stress and self-blame. Removing the stigma of personal failure is a major step in reducing stress.

Discovering the causes of stress. After showing that the reactions to stress that people experience are normal, not the result of personal shortcomings, this model provides information about the causes and consequences of stress with an emphasis on the impact of psychosocial stressors that originate in the organization of work and the workplace.

Exposing social myths. The next step involves exposing social myths that reinforce the idea that stress in the workplace is an individual problem and personal failure. Examining myths of meritocracy and the social myths that reinforce competitive individualism, racism, sexism, and classism moves problems away from the purely personal and locates them in a larger social context in which they can be dealt with actively.

Reframing problems. After the social worker validates workers' experiences and feelings, destigmatizes the experience of seeking help, and shows the common root of problems in a larger social context, workers can move past the emotional barriers to reframe their problems. They can analyze both the symptoms and the causes of workplace stress in a new context.

Developing action strategies. The ultimate goal is to help people, individually and collectively, gain the information, support, and skills necessary to initiate concrete plans to respond to workplace stress and its effects on them, both on and off the job.

The aim of this model is to democratize the delivery of services. When possible, meetings take place in supportive union-identified environments, no compulsion is involved, and people are not required to identify themselves as weak or needy to be served. In most service delivery and therapeutic settings, there is a separation and imbalance of power between the professional staff and the person receiving services. This model attempts to create a more democratic pattern that reflects the mutuality of the interactions. Clinical interventions take place within this framework.

Member Assistance Programs

MAPs, the union-based equivalent of employee assistance programs (EAPs), provide a wide range of counseling and support services, including (1) information and educational services; (2) workshops and seminars on stress, drug and alcohol abuse, and single parenthood or other family issues; (3) ongoing stress-reduction groups; (4) individual, couple, and family counseling; and (5) mediation in the workplace. Whereas EAPs treat the symptoms of stress and usually approach stress as an individual problem, MAPs deal not only with the needs of the individual, but with the environmental causes of stress. This latter perspective views the removal of a source of stress as superior to dealing with the symptoms created by it (Matteson & Ivancevich, 1987). The attempt to link individual concerns with collective concerns through the union distinguishes the approach of the MAP from that of the traditional EAP.

MAPs use a social work approach that combines counseling with advocacy and organizing. They can also be a vehicle for developing programs that go beyond the individual "troubled worker" to address the issues of the "troubled workplace" (Kurzman & Akabas, 1981; Rothman, 1982). Combining MAPs with social work provides a vehicle to deal with the health and welfare of the work force and the effects of work roles and work organizations on individuals and their families (Briar, 1988).

Because the union is a worker-identified organization that protects workers' rights and is a source of collective strength and social support, the effectiveness of MAPs is enhanced. Basing stress and mental health services in the union also creates a greater sense of trust around issues of confidentiality. People who may not feel free to discuss work situations in a management-based EAP may feel freer to do so in a MAP. The union also provides a base for initiating concrete action.

The SEIU 790 MAP

The Service Employees International Union (SEIU) Local 790 MAP in Oakland, California, uses the services of CWL, which works closely with the staff of the union to offer multilevel support services, including (1) individual and family counseling; (2) ongoing stress groups; (3) consultation and training with union staff and officers; (4) seminars and workshops on workplace stress for the membership; and (5) the development of new union services, such as workplace literacy programs and support groups for women who are experiencing sexual harassment, members who are HIV-positive, single parents, caretakers of elderly parents, and preretirees.

Members become aware of the services through articles in the union newspaper and from other members, shop stewards and union staff, and contact with CWL staff at the workshops and seminars conducted at different work sites. The premise on which the program is based is that the union understands that working conditions are stressful and difficult and that it is part of the union's responsibility to maintain workers' health and safety. Thus, the MAP is designed not for "workers with problems," but as a basic union benefit available to all members because all members are affected by the stressful conditions of their jobs.

Access to MAP services removes one of the perceived obstacles that often prevents people from using EAPs—the fear that management will learn that they are receiving services and use this knowledge against them. Hence, members who have a choice of using either the company EAP or the union MAP often choose the MAP. Other factors that make services accessible and effective include (1) the destigmatization of the use of MAP services, (2) the focus on a work- and worker-centered approach, (3) the availability of services throughout the day and during evening and weekend hours, (4) the guarantee of confidentiality at the work site because management is not involved in the delivery of services, and (5) the identification of the services with the union that negotiates for their collective interests.

Identifying workplace stress as a union issue that affects all members and providing information and services to help people deal with it causes the services to be linked with and integrated into the union's structure. The case example that follows is typical of the interrelationship between MAP services and the role of the union.

Impact of Work Issues: A Case Study

The effects of workplace stress often show up in problems at home and are identified as "marital problems." Once the problem has been identified in this way, "troubled workers" are seen as bringing their problems from home to the workplace, where they interfere with the workers' job performance. The symptom may get treated, but the problem does not go away. This was the case for M, a middle-aged man who works in the print shop of a public agency.

When M sought out the MAP, he had been experiencing family problems for over a year. His wife had been ill and hospitalized several times with a job-related back injury. M was supportive of and sympathetic to his wife's condition and had taken on most of the household chores. Nevertheless, there was a great deal of tension in the home. Sometimes M was impatient and erratically angry, whereas at other times he was withdrawn and depressed. His relationships with his wife and daughters had deteriorated and become unbearable.

Simultaneously M's job had changed. During a restructuring of the agency, a young, inexperienced woman was brought in to supervise the unit that M had been running for over 10 years, causing his job to be "deskilled" to that of a machine operator. M fought with the new supervisor daily, felt undermined on the job, and was on the verge of quitting. At his wife's urging, he had sought help from the agency's EAP. After three sessions, his marital situation was identified as the source of his problem, and he was referred to the psychological services of his health maintenance organization (HMO) for family counseling. When he tried to talk about the impact of the new situation at work, he was told that his anger toward his female supervisor was really an expression of anger toward women, specifically his wife, as well as his mother and sister. M and his wife remained in counseling at the HMO, and the tension at home temporarily subsided, although M continued to be depressed.

Reframing the Problem

During this time, M attended a workshop on stress on the job sponsored by the union. This workshop looked specifically at the workplace as a source of stress and identified anger resulting from self-blame as one of the primary sources of workplace stress. During a small-group session in the workshop, workers were asked to talk about what drove them "crazy" in their workplaces. Listening to other workers describe feelings similar to his had a profound effect on M. He later said, "It was like a heavy cloak that had been draped on my shoulders slipped off and I could stand up straight again, and when I did, I realized how much I hurt from being stooped over so long."

As a result, M decided to seek assistance from the MAP, even though he described himself as "shrink shy" after his experience with the EAP. In the first session, he was asked to describe what was happening at work. He told of having been apprenticed to his former supervisor, who taught him everything about running the print shop and then retired, leaving M in charge of the shop, which he had run efficiently for the past 10 years. As a result of changes in upper-management personnel, M was suddenly placed under the direction of a new supervisor, who had been an executive administrative assistant and had no experience in printing or supervision. Rather than letting M set the priorities for his work, she would tell him what had to be done and in what order. Often that order required changing colors on a print machine several times a day, instead of ordering jobs that use the same color to run in sequence. The result—extra work and slowed production—was then blamed on M's not cooperating with the supervisor.

The counselor's first response was to validate M's feelings by stating the obvious: "You must be pretty angry getting jerked around like that every day." M's response was to begin to weep. He said to the counselor, "You mean I'm not crazy?" The counselor's response was to accept the validity of the feelings expressed about the work situation without "psychologizing" it. The source of the problem as M presented it was not that M had marital problems or that the supervisor was female, but that the supervisor was acting arbitrarily and taking away the control that was necessary for M to do his job efficiently and in a satisfying manner.

The initial intervention consisted of providing a safe place where M could vent much of the frustration he felt on the job, have his feelings validated and normalized, and gain some understanding of the sources of the powerlessness he was experiencing. A later session, held with M's wife, helped her understand why the situation at work was having such an impact on M and why he simply could not forget about it when he came home. At that time, M's wife, a nurse, was on a disability leave from her job because of her back problem. Her job had also been stressful, and she was in the process of seeking compensation for her injury. Her case had been held up in legal procedures because the hospital administrators were contending that her injury was the result of lifting a patient improperly. When she was able to relate to M as a "worker," who was going through a similar experience of being "blamed" for events beyond his control, she became a more active ally in his struggle.

Getting Social Support and Taking Action

The effect of this support enabled M to talk with his union shop steward and to file a grievance on some of the work issues in the print shop. At a union meeting, he initiated a discussion of stress, described his own experience, and suggested that others who were having similar experiences get together with him to find support and begin to plan to change the working conditions that were affecting them. The response to his presentation became the basis for a 12-week stress group that was designed and facilitated jointly by M and the CWL staff. A format of weekly topics, with material assigned to prepare for the discussions, focused on how issues were reflected in each person's work life. The topics included the physiology of stress, the psychology of stress, the organization of work, divisions in the workplace, and work and family life. The group produced a series of recommendations that the union took to the bargaining table, and some of the recommendations resulted in significant changes in the workplace.

Mental Health Outcomes

M's depression lifted as he focused directly on the cause of his anger and responsive action. The key to M's improvement was overcoming the self-blame that left him feeling that he was the source of the problem, that there was something wrong with him. This feeling unfortunately had been reinforced by the EAP, his supervisor, the HMO psychologist, and his family. Until M was able to get support for the real anger he was experiencing daily at work and to find a way to begin to change that situation, he was unable to separate his powerlessness and anger about his work situation from the powerlessness he experienced in not being able to help his wife in her workers' compensation case. This sense of powerlessness had immobilized him and left him emotionally crippled.

The impact of the work situation on M was rooted in the lack of control he was experiencing on the job and the resultant loss of esteem, identity, and pride. M had gone from a highly respected and skilled worker, who enjoyed his work, to an "incompetent worker with a bad attitude," who hated going to work but felt trapped in this hopeless situation because of his wife's illness. His anger had been displaced onto himself, and he was left feeling incapable of taking control of a situation that he perceived as being "out of control." He eventually won his grievance at work and had some of his responsibilities on the job reinstated. He also received a lot of recognition for helping other workers understand their own workplace stress and its effect on them and on their families. Building on his rediscovered sense of competence and power, he also succeeded in finding a new lawyer for his wife's case, which was settled favorably.

M continued to see a MAP counselor from time to time during the 18-month process just described to receive encouragement and support and to solve new problems. As a result of the trust he developed in the counselor and his increased emotional strength, he was able to begin to look beyond his anger from the workplace and deal with some of the underlying unresolved conflicts in his life that had been triggered by the working conditions and had contributed to the intense pain he had experienced.

This case illustrates a treatment modality that used an understanding of the worker in the environment as the basis for interventions. These interventions included involving the family, building social support, and helping the worker identify and act on the source of the problems he and his family were facing. The function of the social worker changed many times in the course of this case, but it included the role of educator, trainer, cofacilitator, counselor, mediator, advocate, problem solver, and therapist. The union, as the provider of the service and as a source of the actual power to bring about changes in the conditions that were the source of the problem, played an important role.

This case is presented in detail because there are many "Ms" in workplaces, people whose home life is profoundly affected by their daily experience at work and its impact on their self-esteem (Rubin, 1976). Understanding the impact of work on their lives is a critical element in providing appropriate and effective services.

Workplace Stress and Beyond

Using a comprehensive perspective on the interaction of social and psychological factors, social workers need to be involved in developing and delivering accessible, effective individual and group stress services that protect workers from the effects of stress and that remove the causes of stress in the workplace. At both the practice and policy levels, the alliance of labor and social work is an important partnership for the development of creative and innovative models of practice. These models incorporate the traditional spirit of social work and the historical role of unions in protecting the rights of workers. This partnership represents an important resource in the effort to develop public and corporate policies that will redefine the nature of the workplace and the relationship among work, family, and society.

References

Akabas, S. H. (1990). Reconciling the needs of work with the needs of families. *Families in Society: The Journal of Contemporary Human Services, 71*, 366–371.

Braverman, H. (1974). *Labor and monopoly capital*. New York: Monthly Review Press.

Briar, K. H. (1988). *Social work and the unemployed*. Silver Spring, MD: National Association of Social Workers.

Dewey, B. (1991, May 8). Stressed workers are ready to quit. *Oakland Tribune*.

Frankenhaeuser, M., & Gardell, B. (1976). Underload and overload in working life: Outline of a multi-disciplinary work. *Journal of Human Stress, 2*, 34–46.

Freudenheim, M. (1987, May 26). Business and health, *New York Times*.

Grippa, A. J., & Durbin, D. (1986). Worker compensation occupational disease claims. *National Council Compensation Insurance Digest, 1*(2), 15–23.

House, H. S. (1981). *Work stress and social support*. Reading, MA: Addison-Wesley.

Johnson, J. V. (1989). Collective control: Strategies for survival in the workplace. *International Journal of Health Services, 19*, 469–480.

Karasek, R. A. (1979). Job decision latitude, job demands and mental strain: Implications for job redesign. *Administrative Science Quarterly, 24,* 285–307.

Karasek, R. A. (1989). Control in the workplace and its health-related aspects. In S. L. Sauter, J. J. Hurrell, & C. C. Cooper (Eds.), *Job control and worker health* (pp. 129–159). London: John Wiley & Sons.

Karasek, R. A., & Theorell, T. (1990). *Healthy work: Stress, productivity, and the reconstruction of working life.* New York: Basic Books.

Karasek, R. A., Triantis, K., & Chaudhry, S. (1982). Co-worker and supervisor support as moderators of associations between task characteristics and mental strain. *Journal of Occupational Behavior, 3,* 147–160.

Kasl, S. V. (1989). An epidemiological perspective on the role of control in health. In S. L. Sauter, J. J. Hurrell, & C. C. Cooper (Eds.), *Job control and worker health* (pp. 161–181). London: John Wiley & Sons.

Kurzman, P. A., & Akabas, S. H. (1981). Industrial social work as an arena for practice. *Social Work, 26,* 52–60.

LaRocco, J., House, J., & French, J. (1980). Social support, occupational stress and health. *Journal of Health and Social Behavior, 21,* 202–218.

Lerner, M. (1985). *Occupational stress groups and the psychodynamics of work.* Oakland, CA: Institute for Labor and Mental Health.

Marmott, M. G., & Theorell, T. (1988). Social class and cardiovascular disease: The contributions of work. *International Journal of Health Services, 18,* 659–674.

Matteson, M. T., & Ivancevich, J. M. (1987). *Controlling work stress: Effective human resource and management strategies.* San Francisco: Jossey-Bass.

McGrath, J. E. (1970). A conceptual formulation for research of stress. In J. McGrath (Ed.), *Social and psychological factors in stress.* New York: Holt, Rinehart & Winston.

Minter, S. G. (1991). Relieving workplace stress. *Occupational Hazards, 53*(4), 38–42.

Murphy, L. R., & Schoenborn, T. F. (Eds.). (1987). *Stress management in work settings.* Cincinnati, OH: National Institute of Occupational Safety and Health.

National Career Development Association. (1990). *A national survey of working America.* Washington, DC: Author.

Perlman, H. H. (1982). The client as worker: A look at an overlooked role. In S. H. Akabas & P. A. Kurzman (Eds.), *Work, workers, and work organizations* (pp. 90–116). Englewood Cliffs, NJ: Prentice Hall.

Reynolds, B. C. (1982). *Between client and community: A study in responsibility in social case work.* Silver Spring, MD: National Association of Social Workers. (Original work published 1934)

Rosch, P., & Pelletier, K. (1987). Designing workplace stress management programs. In L. R. Murphy & T. F. Schoenborn (Eds.), *Stress management in work settings* (pp. 69–91). Cincinnati, OH: National Institute of Occupational Safety and Health.

Rothman, J. (1982). Taking account of the workplace in community organization practice. In S. H. Akabas & P. A. Kurzman (Eds.), *Work, workers, and work organizations*. (pp. 176–196). Englewood Cliffs, NJ: Prentice Hall.

Rubin, L. B. (1976). *Worlds of pain: Life in the working-class family*. New York: Basic Books.

Schore, L. (1987). The mental health effects of work: An issue for social work education. *Catalyst, 21*, 43–52.

Schore, L. (1990). Issues of work, workers and therapy. In T. Kupers (Ed.), *Using psychodynamic principles in public mental health: New directions in mental health services* (pp. 93–101). San Francisco: Jossey-Bass.

Selye, H. (1976). *The stress of life*. New York: McGraw-Hill. (Original work published 1936)

Tesh, S. N. (1988). Air traffic control and stress. In S. N. Tesh, *Hidden arguments* (pp. 105–130). New Brunswick, NJ: Rutgers University Press.

U.S. Department of Labor. (1972). *Quality of Employment Survey*. Ann Arbor: University of Michigan Survey Research Center.

U.S. Department of Labor. (1977). *Quality of Employment Survey*. Ann Arbor: University of Michigan Survey Research Center.

U.S. Public Health Service, Office of Disease Prevention and Health Promotion. (1991). *The role of the workplace in mental health: Prevention report*. Washington, DC: Author.

Wallin, L., & Wright, I. (1986). Psychosocial aspects of the work environment: A group approach. *Journal of Occupational Medicine, 28*, 384–393.

CHAPTER 18

Unemployment and Underemployment

A POLICY AND PROGRAM–DEVELOPMENT PERSPECTIVE

Lawrence S. Root

> A man willing to work, and unable to find work, is
> perhaps the saddest sight that fortune's inequality
> exhibits under the sun.
>
> —Thomas Carlyle
> *Chartism*

Mist blurs the outlines of the sprawling factory complex on the edge of Saginaw, Michigan. It is dawn, but the plant has not slept. Three shifts keep operations going throughout the night. Thousands of workers will pass through the gates today, to make gears, pumps, and axles in the multiple plants that make up this sprawling production facility.

These workers are "aristocrats" of the blue-collar work force. They work hard, in demanding jobs, but their wages and benefits are the envy of other industrial workers. Collective bargaining has created a miniature social welfare system for them, with a variety of services, such as employee assistance, legal insurance, child care, and educational counseling (Root, 1982).

On the other side of town, there is another story. Where other workers once poured steel, the furnaces are banked and cooled. Automation, foreign competition, and the movement of production to more modern facilities have closed plants for workers who once thought they were settled for life in their jobs. These workers face job searches, retraining, and relocation. Some will land on their feet, with new jobs that rival their former positions. For others, their future will be in low-paying service jobs, in part-time positions, as involuntary "early retirees," or as the long-term unemployed.

These two contrasting realities in Saginaw suggest a contemporary agenda for occupational social work—an agenda with roots in historical social work roles, but one that demands adjustments to new realities. On the one hand, there is the developed industrial social welfare system, in which the employment relationship is the vehicle for the provision of social welfare services. Even in this favored setting, pressures of shift work and the competing responsibilities of job and family create a need for occupational social work. These programs are explored in other chapters in this book. This chapter addresses the challenges presented by a turbulent employment environment in which job loss, low-wage–low-benefit employment, and ongoing job insecurity create demands for different interventions. Unlike previous downturns, layoffs have increasingly become a reality for white-collar as well as blue-collar workers. Corporate downsizing is reaching further into the ranks of the white-collar work force (see, for example, Stern, 1992).

This chapter begins with a discussion of employment issues and current labor market changes that affect the well-being of workers and their families. It then considers social work interventions in terms of three targets: individuals, employers–unions, and communities. Finally, it looks at barriers to the creation of services to address these employment-related problems and the prospects for expanding such initiatives.

Social Work, Employment, and Unemployment

Responses to the problems of employment and unemployment have been an important part of the history of modern social work. The settlement house movement was one precedent for employment-related social work. Pioneering social workers in East London, on New York's Lower East Side, and on the South Side of Chicago constantly confronted the problems of low-wage and unstable employment (Davis, 1967). Immigrants, including new arrivals from rural America, faced a variety of social and economic demands, often without the supports of their families and communities. Settlement house workers sought to humanize the environment of the emerging industrial structure, to soften the hard edges of urban capitalism. To do so, they provided a range of interventions, from English-language classes and day care to local economic development to advocacy of standards for occupational health and safety. Some of the most enduring contributions of Jane Addams, the nation's most visible settlement worker, were in the areas of workers' health and safety (reducing the risks of phosphorous poisoning in the making of matches, for example) and the regulation of child labor (Addams, 1910/1990).

Settlement house activism in the United States arose in response to social needs in a rapidly changing environment. Immigration and industrialization were changing the face of urban America. Between 1880 and 1920, the population of the United States doubled, with an average of a half million new immigrants arriving every year. During that time, the proportion of the population who were living in cities went from 28 percent to 51 percent (U.S. Bureau of the Census, 1975).

In retrospect, the magnitude and impact of these changes stand out in bold relief. Contemporary changes in the economic and employment environment are more difficult to discern. New technologies and the internationalization of economic life may prove to have as profound effects on employment and social welfare. These changes have important implications for the structure and operation of the labor market. Domestic producers are finding that they must compete with foreign production sites, where hourly labor costs are a fraction of those in the United States. Jobs are being lost not only to overseas competitors, but to U.S. companies who move their operations abroad to find a less costly production environment.

The U.S. system of employee benefits is also causing turbulence in the job market. Health insurance and pension costs are influencing employers to avoid these expenses through the increased use of contractual and part-time workers. In this way, employment is being stripped of important elements and families are losing basic protection against the loss of income and the cost of medical care. These changes in economic patterns are transforming employment relationships and creating the need for new approaches to occupational social work.

Employment and Social Welfare: A Changing Reality

Social work has a fundamental interest in and commitment to income-support programs, but *employment* is the primary source of income for individuals and families. Public assistance programs may blunt the worst effects of poverty, but they operate "at the margin." Even in the most advanced social welfare systems, such programs only ameliorate the problems of poverty; they do not greatly affect the overall distribution of income. Access to employment opportunities remains the cornerstone of individual economic security; poverty and inequality of income are primarily a function of the labor market.

When one considers the impact of economic changes on social welfare, two related areas of change stand out: changes in family composition and changes in employment opportunities. Although these two areas are related, they can be considered separately to understand their implications for occupational social work.

Two trends in family composition are particularly important for understanding the relationship between social welfare and employment: the increase in single-parent families and the growing difficulty of making ends meet on a single income. In 1970, 87.1 percent of the families with children under age 18 had two parents in their households. By 1991, that figure had dropped to 71.1 percent (U.S. Bureau of the Census, 1992). This increase in single-parent households has come at a time when it is often necessary to have two full-time workers in a family to rise out of poverty. Almost 14 percent of the families with only one full-time worker have household incomes that are less than half the median household income (a measure of relative poverty). Among African American families, 28.1 percent of single-earner households live in relative poverty.

The incidence of poverty has not been static. In recent years, the distribution of income has become more polarized. For families with children under age 18, 29.1 percent now have household incomes that are less than half the median income in the country, compared to 21.2 percent in the mid-1960s. If one considers only those families that are *not* headed by a married couple, 63.0 percent have incomes that are less than half the median income. This measure of relative poverty is much larger for African Americans and Hispanic single-parent families—80.3 percent and 79.4 percent, respectively (U.S. Bureau of the Census, 1991).

The demographics of families suggest a double-edged problem. First, there are more single-parent families. Second, it has become more difficult to rise out of poverty on a single income.

These trends in poverty are related to changes in job opportunities. The principal manifestation of these problems is unemployment, which presents a range of threats to the individual and his or her family. In addition to the loss of income and benefits, the inability to find a job undercuts one's concept of self-worth and identity. This combination of economic and psychological pressures increases the impact of job loss.

Unemployment has long been recognized as a key stressor, having a negative impact on physical and mental health. A review of the literature identified 250 publications dealing with these social costs of economic changes (Gordus & McAlinden, 1984)—ranging from quantitative studies that examine correlations between mental health indicators and the economy (see, for example, Brenner, 1973) to case studies of the impact of layoffs on individuals (see, for example, Beckett, 1988; Buss & Redburn, 1983).

Official statistics suggest that about 6.5 million Americans were unemployed in 1989, representing about 6.8 percent of the civilian labor force (U.S. Bureau of Labor Statistics, 1992). If one looks at groups within the population, one sees a much higher official unemployment rate for minorities and for young people. For example, the official unemployment rate for African American male teenagers was over 40 percent.

The phenomenon of unemployment is usually categorized in terms of its cause. In practice, the lines between these different types of unemployment may blur. But thinking in terms of the causes of unemployment is the key to evaluating possible interventions.

Individual job seekers often spend time conducting a job search. This type of unemployment is referred to as *frictional unemployment*. It is usually thought to be short-term, and assistance with the job search is the principal intervention to address this type of unemployment.

Seasonal unemployment refers to unemployment resulting from jobs that are active only during certain seasons of the year. For example, jobs that are dependent on the weather or tourism tend to have long periods of idleness in the off-season. Diversifying the economic base in an area or retraining workers for new positions are interventions associated with seasonal unemployment.

During periods of economic downturn, employers often suspend hiring and may lay workers off. Unemployment arising from these changes in the business cycle is termed *cyclical unemployment*. The assumption is that the jobs that are lost will return when the economy "heats up" again. Interventions include macroeconomic policies to stimulate an economic recovery and to provide income support in the meantime.

Unemployment that arises from the fact that the jobs that exist do not match the skills of those seeking employment is referred to as *structural unemployment*. In such cases, training–retraining interventions are typical.

Some analysts believe that the U.S. economy is experiencing a long-term failure to generate sufficient jobs. This assessment suggests a fifth category: *chronic unemployment*, or "growth-gap unemployment" (Sherraden, 1985). The creation of jobs, including public service employment, is one response to such unemployment.

As was mentioned earlier, the negative effects of unemployment on physical and mental health have been well documented. The sense of self-blame and powerlessness is well known to all who have worked with individuals who are unemployed (Briar, 1988; Maurer, 1979). Large-scale layoffs or plant closings add to the dilemmas facing the unemployed. First, they disrupt long-term employment relationships, forcing individuals into a job search after many years of secure employment. These individuals have the added problem of having to look for jobs at a time when there is increased competition for jobs by other workers.

Some of the effects of layoffs can be seen in the increase in prime-age adults (ages 25–44) who have been unemployed for a long time. Statistics from the United States and from Western Europe show increases in the proportion of the long-term unemployed who are in this age group. For example, in 1979, prime-age adults were 35.9 percent of the long-term unemployed in the United States, 23.7 percent in the United Kingdom, and 23.8 percent in West Germany. In 1986, the percentages rose to 51.9 percent in the United States, 42.6 percent in the United Kingdom, and 42.9 percent in West Germany) (Organization for Economic Cooperation and Development [OECD], 1988). Although changes in the population associated with the baby-boom generation may account for some of this increase, the growth in the percentage of prime-age adults who are among the long-term unemployed is striking, especially when one considers that "discouraged workers" (individuals who have given up looking for jobs) are not counted as unemployed.

Whereas unemployment may be the single most critical problem facing workers, other changes taking place in the employment relationship are influencing the need for occupational social work, including those described below.

Fewer Manufacturing Jobs

The loss of manufacturing jobs has been described as a process of "deindustrialization" in the United States, although the extent of industrial erosion is a matter of debate (Bluestone & Harrison, 1982; Staudohar & Brown, 1987). The proportion of the nonagricultural work force in manufacturing (both durable and nondurable products) decreased from 31 percent in 1960 to 17 percent by 1990 (U.S. Office of the President, 1992, Table B-41). In practical terms, this decrease has meant a loss of jobs that traditionally were relatively high-paying but that did not require a college education. The reduction in the number of such positions has effectively eliminated a rung in the ladder that took previous generations out of poverty.

Increases in Service-Sector Jobs

In the past 20 years, employment in the service sector has increased from one-quarter to one-third of the work force. This change presents a mixed picture. Although there are high-wage–high-benefit service jobs, these positions require a college or graduate education. A far larger number of the service-sector jobs have been created at the lower end of the employment scale. Those jobs, with less stringent educational requirements, offer lower pay and fewer employee benefits than did the manufacturing jobs that these workers might have held in a previous generation. It is estimated that the earnings of over 5 million workers are at or below the minimum wage. Service employees are much more likely to be at this level (Haugen & Mellor, 1990).

Increased Importance of Education

There is a growing differential between the wages of college graduates and those with less education. This differential appears to reflect stagnant wage levels for those without a college education, rather than a sharp increase in wages for the college-educated.

Technological change has itself worked to squeeze low-skill workers out of higher-paying jobs. The day-to-day technologies of production in manu-facturing demand more highly educated workers than was previously the case. Many manufacturing jobs that formerly did not require more than the most basic educational skills have been replaced by jobs that require the ability to read manuals, follow detailed written procedures, and interpret graphic output (*America's Choice*, 1990).

The pace of change in the workplace has also become an important factor in planning for human resources. Employers need a work force that is capable of adapting rapidly to new technologies. Workers who lose their jobs in this changing environment may find that they do not have the requisite skills to move into new positions.

Layoffs and Plant Closings

In addition to the effects on individuals just discussed, large-scale layoffs have broader effects. The loss of a local plant decreases the fiscal base of a region—both tax revenues and contributions to voluntary agencies—at the same time that demands for social welfare services are increasing.

A side effect of the increase in layoffs and plant closings is a correspond-ing increase in job insecurity even among those who are not directly involved. Long-term workers who thought that they would work at a company until they retired may now think that their plans for the future are in jeopardy. This fear can increase tensions both on the job and at home.

Increases in Part-time and Contingent Employment

Part-time employment is attractive to companies that are facing large benefit costs for their full-time workers. In addition, using part-timers increases flexibility in the management of human resources. Similar advantages have made "contingent workers" (that is, workers who are employed on contract or through a third party) an appealing option for employers. So-called employee-leasing firms grew from under 200 in the mid-1980s to over 1,000 in 1992, employing a million people. The rapid increase in the number of leasing companies has been accompanied by increased problems of person-nel administration (for example, see Meier, 1992).

From the perspective of the employee, part-time and contingent employ-ment can be a problem (Levitan & Conway, 1992). Part-timers tend to receive lower pay and have less job security than do full-timers. Even more important, however, is the lack of employee benefits in most part-time positions. Without health insurance and pension plans, part-time positions leave employees and their families vulnerable to the loss of income and high health care costs. Although some workers prefer to work part-time, half the increase in part-time employment from 1969 to 1979 and *all* the increase since then has reflected the dearth of full-time work ("involuntary part-time employment") (Tilly, 1991).

These changes in the environment suggest needed directions for occupational social work. With this context in mind, the author now turns to considerations of different approaches to intervention.

Interventions in a Changing Occupational Environment

Occupational social work interventions can be understood in terms of targets and links among those targets. Interventions can be targeted to the individual (and his or her family), the workplace (the employer and union), and the community. The links among these three also provide a means for understanding interventions. To explore this idea, the author first discusses the targeting of programs and then looks at the links established among them.

Targeting the Individual

Programs targeted to individuals address both employment options and support for individuals (and their families) who are experiencing unemployment and other problems. As was mentioned in the discussion of unemployment, the appropriate intervention depends on the origins of the employment problem. *Job-search assistance*, for example, is a primary programmatic response to frictional unemployment. Employers may take the initiative in such assistance through the use of *outplacement* programs that tend to use freestanding companies that work with employees to find alternative employment.

Many programs combine logistic or instrumental assistance with a focus on *empowerment* and *encouragement* of the individual. These programs encourage individuals to build on their strengths, often strengths of which they were not consciously aware. Peer-group interventions are particularly important in this regard. *Job clubs* are an example of an approach in which groups of job-seekers meet regularly, sharing emotional support as well as practical assistance (such as information about job-search experiences, tips, prospects, help in writing résumés, and access to telephones for job inquiries). Research suggests that such programs can be effective (and cost-effective) in helping individuals find employment (Bloom, 1990).

If unemployment is thought to arise from a mismatch between the skills of job seekers and the needs of employers ("structural unemployment"), interventions like education and training are appropriate. The increased importance of education in employment places a greater premium on programs that encourage individuals to finish high school. These programs are a form of primary prevention, seeking to encourage adequate educational preparation before young people enter the labor force. They include direct efforts for high-risk youths, such as early interventions based on school performance, and programs that decrease the need to drop out (including programs to discourage unwanted teenage pregnancies).

Training programs, for those who have already left school, have long been a response to unemployment. The Manpower Development and Training Act (1962), the Vocational Education Act (1963), and the Economic Opportunity Act (1964) all created federally based training programs to address skill building and employability. Residential programs, such as the Job Corps, built on models developed during the Great Depression and sought to improve the skills of poor youths through intensive, broad-based training. Ten years later, these training efforts were consolidated under the "block-grant" strategy in the Comprehensive Employment and Training Act (CETA) (1973). CETA also included a provision for public employment programs that rapidly became a major expenditure and source of employment in urban America. CETA was eventually replaced in the 1980s with the Job Training Partnership Act (1982), which further decentralized training efforts and eliminated public employment and income support for those being trained.

Some analysts, such as Bovard (1989), have suggested that the federal training efforts over the past 25 years have had no major successes. Retraining programs for displaced workers have received mixed reviews from researchers. For example, some greater successes are reported when the training is specifically geared to the local labor market, rather than being targeted more generally (see, for example, Leigh, 1990). The outcomes of other approaches varied with the target group. The National Supported Work Demonstration, for example, focused on the trainees' readiness for jobs and increasing responsibility. This project had some success increasing the employment of women who had been long-term AFDC recipients, but it had no success with other groups, such as unemployed youths or former drug users (see Manpower Demonstration Research Corporation, 1980).

Job development is another intervention that is relevant to occupational social work. It can be done on a one-to-one level (developing jobs for specific individuals) or more generally targeted toward the expansion of job opportunities in an area. In the former case, it involves the marketing of an individual, essentially providing a potential employer with the reasons for giving that person a chance to prove his or her ability to contribute. General job development, discussed later, is more closely associated with targeting the community.

Many occupational social work interventions attempt to improve the functioning of individuals and their families. The loss of a job creates intense tensions for workers and their families. Social workers generally play important roles—as advocates, counselors, sources of information, and consultants—in helping to maintain equilibrium during this period of stress, providing support as well as help with the practical problems associated with the loss of a job (Briar, 1988; Foster & Schore, 1990; Straussner, 1990).

Targeting the Employer and the Union

Making changes in the employment setting is another target for occupational social work. Services, such as EAPs, are typically targeted to individuals and families, but a social worker in the workplace can be a change agent, stimulating consideration of changes in personnel policies that may preserve jobs and or help employees who are in jeopardy to maintain their work roles. For example, occupational social workers can play a role in developing flextime programs for those who are balancing work and family commitments. Benefit policies also provide a venue for the application of social work principles (see, for example, Balgopal & Pirzynski, 1990) and in dealing with human resources policies related to minorities, women, the disabled, and other vulnerable groups in the work force (see Crawley, 1992; Gettman & Pena, 1986; Poverny & Finch, 1988).

Occupational social workers traditionally have not been involved in personnel planning decisions, but they can help employers review the differential effects of downsizing and consider alternative criteria for those decisions. The concern with maintaining a stable and loyal work force may open up new roles (U.S. Department of Labor, 1992). For example, interest in family–work connections can be seen in the emerging role of the *work–family manager*. Although these positions are still new and not widespread, they provide a model that reflects an organizational role for occupational social work. Practitioners provide individual services; however, they report that their most important roles are in the areas of organizational policy and organizational change (Johnson & Rose, 1992).

Increasing the skills and flexibility of current workers is a major prevention initiative to avoid future unemployment. Employers' and unions' initiatives have expanded *training opportunities* in many settings. Although training for specific job-related skills has traditionally been the focus of workplace training, more extensive and varied educational opportunities have become increasingly common as well. For example, collective bargaining in the auto industry has expanded tuition benefits to courses that are not directly related to the demands of the workplace. Although these more general educational programs may improve workers' job performance (for example, help workers develop skills that make them more intellectually active and receptive to new technologies), they are a new form of employee benefit that goes beyond training for jobs.

This new direction in workplace educational opportunities has taken a step further with the introduction of *on-site educational counseling* for auto workers. For example, the University of Michigan School of Social Work is working with the United Auto Workers (UAW) and with General Motors (GM) and Ford to develop a broad-based educational counseling program. Working in partnership with the joint union–management team and the local plants, these educational counseling programs offer a new model for providing decentralized social services based in the workplace. Full-time professional counselors who are employed by the School of Social Work assist UAW members at GM and Ford facilities to define their educational goals and to implement plans for reaching those goals.

These educational counselors generally have backgrounds in education or social work, and all have experience working with nontraditional learners. Workers may be engaging in "second-chance" educational programs, remediating earlier educational deficits (Levitan & Shapiro, 1987), or they may simply be following their interests, using the educational benefits to enhance the quality of their lives. The types of educational goals range from improving basic reading and mathematics skills, to completing high school, to obtaining college and graduate degrees. Employees may be motivated by vocational interests (such as planning for part-time positions after they retire or a concern about expanding options in case of a layoff) or by personal interests. The positive impact of these educational experiences can be an important motivator for other family members; for example, one employee wanted to get his college degree as an example to his children, to encourage their own educational ambitions.

Targeting the Community

Social work interventions can address programs on the community level, including voluntary-sector programs, and policies that govern employment-related activities. The occupational social worker in such situations could be involved in the design and delivery of services, as well as in advocating for community involvement in addressing employment problems.

A number of social welfare policies have a direct impact on employment and the consequences of unemployment. As an advocate, the occupational social worker can seek to change policies, such as *disability benefits* that do not take age into account and *public assistance* that discourages work efforts that have an adverse effect on those who experience employment problems.

In addition to such broad policy changes, there are also community-based initiatives. Many programs targeted to individuals also require program development and advocacy targeted to local communities. *Job creation*, politically unpopular in the United States, continues to be a temporary policy response in Europe (OECD, 1988). Future initiatives could include job-creation schemes tied to the goals of developing human resources (for instance, enhancing people's readiness to take jobs and combined employment-training programs).

Some local communities are developing *legislation on plant closings.* Cross-national models exist for the regulation of large-scale layoffs and plant closings, but there is still resistance to similar public policies in the United States (Root, 1987). Although there is strong support for "free-market" solutions, community initiatives can provide a check on private economic decision making, which has a profound localized impact on communities (Portz, 1990; Schlack, 1991). Requiring advance notification of intended plant closings, for example, appears to be a significant factor in improving employment opportunities for the workers who are affected (Nord & Ting, 1991).

Community development is a critical aspect of creating job opportunities, especially when local industries are experiencing economic distress. Approaches can be direct (for example, providing seed money for the development of new industries) or indirect (for instance, providing tax incentives to attract business). Such local community development efforts have the negative impact of creating competition between localities in pursuit of new businesses. This competition may not have any real positive effects on employment. Rather, it may reduce local revenues while simply reshuffling unemployment among geographic areas.

Community development, however, can be more creative than simply giving tax breaks to new businesses. Communities can devise local economic development plans that enhance the levels of skills of the local work force and provide noncash assistance to prospective businesses that are seeking new locations for expansion. Businesses can assume a partnership role with their communities in attracting prospective new employers (Carroll, 1987). The quality of life in an area, including a well-developed social service structure, may be another important factor in attracting new economic investment.

An Agenda for Occupational Social Work

This chapter began by reviewing changes in the workplace and their impact on the social welfare of individuals and families and then discussed the targeting of interventions. These points are highlighted in Table 1. The interventions suggest a variety of roles for the occupational social worker: counselor, advocate, program developer, human resource manager, and community planner. But to think realistically about an agenda, one must consider the support for developing such interventions.

Social work, as a field, is characterized by a separation between the direct beneficiaries of programs and payment for the services rendered. Programs for the poor and the disenfranchised are seldom paid for directly by the

Table 1
Changes in the Workplace and Social Work Interventions

CHANGE IN THE WORKPLACE	IMPLICATIONS	INTERVENTIONS
Unemployment	Loss of income and benefits Loss of sense of confidence and identity Family tension-friction	Unemployment benefits, supplemental employment benefits, severance pay Job-search services Job clubs–peer support Relocation services Support services for individuals and their families (including support for dependent-care responsibilities) Coordination with local social service agencies
Decrease in manu-facturing jobs	Lower wages and benefits Impact on community if other jobs are not available locally	Advocacy for public programs Community development and economic stimulation
Increase in service-sector jobs	Increased gap between "good" jobs and "bad" jobs Increased low-pay–low-benefit jobs	Increase in the minimum wage Efforts to improve the quality of jobs—unionization
Increased importance of education	Greater difficulty for those with less education to get jobs with good wages and benefits	Improved educational opportunities Efforts to encourage "at-risk" students to stay in school or otherwise gain needed skills Upgrading the skills of current workers
Layoffs and plant closings	Loss of jobs by long-term workers Loss of the local tax base Loss of opportunities for new job entrants	Advocacy for alternatives to reductions in the work force Advance notification for individual planning

(continued)

Table 1
Continued

CHANGE IN THE WORKPLACE	IMPLICATIONS	INTERVENTIONS
Layoffs and plant closings (*continued*)	Tension in the workplace and in family life Low morale on the job	Community development for economic opportunities Revenue sharing for relieving local tax losses Retirement–preretirement planning EAPs Alternative career planning Educational opportunities Outplacement programs
Part-time and contingent employment	Low wages No benefits or shallow benefits Marginal attachment to the labor force	Advocacy for higher wages and benefits Prorated benefits Reorganized–new public benefit programs

individuals who are served. When payments *are* made, they represent only a small proportion of the overall cost of providing the services. An agenda for occupational social work must be developed in light of the ability and willingness of employers and communities to support interventions and would include a consideration of the links among individuals, employers–unions, and public policy.

The links among the targets of interventions and some examples of them are displayed in Figure 1. Communities that are affected by decreased job opportunities can develop a variety of programs to help individuals and their families. Employers and unions also can take an active role in assisting their members or employees who are threatened with the loss of jobs. The extent to which they all do so depends both on resources and expectations. These two factors are not independent. The availability of resources for social welfare depends on the priorities placed on such activities. And priorities are a function of societal expectations for employers and for community services.

The adoption of new human resource programs, such as educational counseling, reflects changing standards of what constitutes an enlightened personnel policy. Although cost-benefit analyses are a factor, the diffusion of innovations is as much a result of changing standards of what constitute appropriate and

Figure 1
Occupational Social Work Targets and Paths

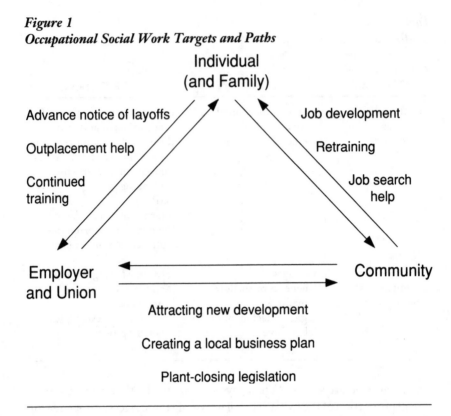

competitive practices by employers. Public policies reflect (and, in turn, influence) changing expectations for business and for government.

Several barriers hinder the movement toward a comprehensive agenda for occupational social work. First, there is the prevalent orientation in the United States toward laissez-faire governmental policies, particularly with regard to the regulation of private-sector businesses. The rhetoric of national politics continues to emphasize market mechanisms, minimizing the role of public policy in ensuring basic social welfare. This view of a limited governmental role is reinforced by a parallel distrust of the *ability* of government to effect positive changes.

A second barrier is economic stagnation. Without a growing economy, resources for new initiatives must be drawn from competing areas. In such a situation, it is more difficult to identify and mobilize resources for innovation.

A third barrier is the perception of social work, both within and outside the profession. Social workers have been involved in a wide range of social welfare activities, but the public impression (and the impression of employers and unions) continues to pigeonhole social workers as providers of either relief services to the destitute or psychological counseling to troubled individuals and families. The application of social work practice to workplace issues has not been a major focus of the profession until recently.

These barriers to the expansion of an occupational social work agenda suggest an additional agenda item for occupational social work: building effective coalitions that can work for enhanced social welfare services. The expansion of meaningful social work programs, both in the workplace and in the community, depends on the fostering of societywide perspectives to support the development of programs. Garnering this support is the first order of business for the entire profession and a necessary step in integrating occupational issues into the social welfare enterprise.

References

Addams, J. (1990). *Twenty years at Hull House*. Urbana: University of Illinois Press. (Original work published 1910)

America's choice: High wages or low skills. (1990). Rochester, NY: National Center on Education and the Economy.

Balgopal, P. R., & Pirzynski, J. E. (1990). An analysis of preretirement plans: Challenges for occupational social work. *Employee Assistance Quarterly, 5*(3), 13–31.

Beckett, J. O. (1988). Plant closings: How older workers are affected. *Social Work, 33*, 29–33.

Bloom, H. S. (1990). *Back to work: Testing reemployment services for displaced workers*. Kalamazoo, MI: W. E. Upjohn Institute for Employment Research.

Bluestone, B., & Harrison, B. (1982). *The deindustrialization of America*. New York: Basic Books.

Bovard, J. (1989). The failure of federal job-training. *Society, 26*(4), 57–84.

Brenner, M. H. (1973). *Mental illness and the economy*. Cambridge, MA: Harvard University Press.

Briar, K. H. (1988). *Social work and the unemployed*. Silver Spring, MD: National Association of Social Workers.

Buss, T. F., & Redburn, F. S. (1983). *Mass unemployment: Plant closings and community mental health*. Beverly Hills, CA: Sage Publications.

Carroll, A. B. (1987). Management's social responsibilities. In P. D. Staudohar & H. E. Brown (Eds.), *Deindustrialization and plant closure* (pp. 167–181). Lexington, MA: Lexington Books.

Crawley, B. (1992). The transformation of the American labor force: Elder African Americans and occupational social work. *Social Work, 37*, 41–46.

Davis, A. F. (1967). *Spearheads for reform*. New York: Oxford University Press.

Foster, B., & Schore, L. (1990). Job loss and the occupational social worker. In S. L. A. Straussner (Ed.), *Occupational social work today* (pp. 77–97). New York: Haworth Press.

Gettman, D., & Pena, D. G. (1986). Women, mental health and the workplace in a transnational setting. *Social Work, 31*, 5–11.

Googins, B. K., & Burden, D. (1987). Vulnerability of working parents: Balancing work and home roles. *Social Work, 32*, 295–300.

Gordus, J. P., & McAlinden, S. P. (1984). *Economic change, physical illness, mental illness, and social deviance.* (Hearings before the Joint Economic Committee, U.S. Congress). Washington, DC: U.S. Government Printing Office.

Haugen, S. E., & Mellor, E. F. (1990). Estimating the number of minimum wage workers. *Monthly Labor Review, 113*(1), 70–74.

Johnson, A. A., & Rose, K. L. (1992). *The emerging role of the work-family manager* (Report No. 987). New York: The Conference Board.

Leigh, D. E. (1990). *Does training work for displaced workers?* Kalamazoo, MI: W. E. Upjohn Institute for Employment Research.

Levitan, S. A., & Conway, E. A. (1992). Part-timers living on half rations. In B. D. Warme, K. L. P. Lundy, & L. A. Lundy (Eds.), *Working part-time: Risks and opportunities* (pp. 45–60). New York: Praeger.

Levitan, S. A., & Shapiro, I. (1987). *Working but poor.* Baltimore, MD: Johns Hopkins Press.

Manpower Demonstration Research Corporation. (1980). *Summary and findings of the National Supported Work Demonstration.* Cambridge, MA: Balinger.

Maurer, H. (1979). *Not working: An oral history of the unemployed.* New York: Holt, Rinehart & Winston.

Meier, B. (1992, March 20). Some "worker leasing" programs defraud insurers and employers. *New York Times*, p. 1.

Nord, S., & Ting, Y. (1991). The impact of advance notice of plant closings on earnings and the probability of unemployment. *Industrial and Labor Relations Review, 44*, 681–691.

Organization for Economic Cooperation and Development. (1988). *Measures to assist the long-term unemployed: Recent experience in some OECD countries.* Paris: Author.

Portz, J. (1990). *The politics of plant closings.* Lawrence: University of Kansas Press.

Poverny, L. M., & Finch, W. A., Jr. (1988). Integrating work-related issues on gay and lesbian employees into occupational social work practice. *Employee Assistance Quarterly, 4*(2), 15–29.

Root, L. S. (1982). *Fringe benefits: Social insurance in the steel industry.* Beverly Hills, CA: Sage Publications.

Root, L. S. (1987). Britain's redundancy payments for displaced workers. *Monthly Labor Review, 110*(6), 18–23.

Schlack, R. F. (1991). Plant closings: A community's bill of rights. *Journal of Economic Literature, 25*, 511–518.

Sherraden, M. W. (1985). Chronic unemployment: A social work perspective. *Social Work, 30,* 403–408.

Staudohar, P. D., & Brown, H. E. (Eds.). (1987). *Deindustrialization and plant closure.* Lexington, MA: Lexington Books.

Stern, G. (1992, August 24). After the fall: White-collar workers face tougher time after their layoffs. *Wall Street Journal,* p. A1.

Straussner, S. L. A. (Ed.). (1990). *Occupational social work today.* New York: Haworth Press.

Tilly, C. (1991). Reasons for continuing growth of part-time employment. *Monthly Labor Review, 114*(3), 10–18.

U.S. Bureau of the Census. (1975). *Historical statistics of the United States.* Washington, DC: U.S. Government Printing Office.

U.S. Bureau of the Census. (1991). *Trends in relative income: 1964 to 1989, Current Population Reports* (Series P-60, No. 177). Washington, DC: U.S. Government Printing Office.

U.S. Bureau of the Census. (1992). *Household and family characteristics, current population reports* (Series P-20, No. 458). Washington, DC: U.S. Government Printing Office.

U.S. Bureau of Labor Statistics. (1992). *Employment and earnings* (whole issue), *39*(11).

U.S. Department of Labor, Bureau of Labor-Management Relations and Cooperative Programs. (1992). *Work and family provisions in major collective bargaining agreements* (BLMR 144). Washington, DC: Author.

U.S. Office of the President. (1992). *Economic report of the president.* Washington, DC: U.S. Government Printing Office.

CHAPTER **19**

The Emergence of External
Employee Assistance Programs

Kurt Spitzer and Alison Favorini

> In America, as in most modern societies, work is the
> most widely accepted indicator of social usefulness and
> thus the best indicator of individual respect and identity
> . . . which are universal human needs.
> —Herbert Gans
> *More Equality*

The past few years have produced a significant growth in the number of employee assistance programs (EAPs). In 1973, the National Institute on Alcohol Abuse and Alcoholism (NIAAA, 1981) estimated that there were 500 programs in the country; by 1981, the Washington Business Group on Health placed the number at over 5,000 (Klarreich, DiGiuseppe, & DiMattia, 1987). By 1988, the number of programs was conservatively estimated to be 15,000 to 20,000 nationwide (Morrall, 1988). Increasingly, employers are becoming aware of the benefits of a healthier and more productive work force and are discovering the potential of EAPs to help contain rising health care costs. The societal mandate for a drug-free workplace has been another strong reason for the increase in EAPs.

Rather than develop EAPs themselves, most businesses contract for external employee assistance services offered by a wide variety of EAP providers, such as independent firms that specialize in providing such

The authors gratefully acknowledge the contribution of their student, Mary Kraft, in searching the literature for appropriate articles and studies and Sylvia Nykanen and Delores Robinson for word-processing assistance.

services, hospitals and health care organizations, chemical dependence treatment programs, and community mental health or family service centers (Blair, 1987). Most employers find the external EAP approach preferable to administering internal programs, including hiring and supervising EAP staff and dealing with potential liability issues. Some external EAP providers have been in business since the early 1970s, but most of the programs have been instituted in the past few years. Although these programs are beginning to have a significant influence on today's workplace, the literature on them is sparse. This chapter presents the findings of the authors' survey of the practices and trends among external EAP programs in Michigan in 1990, along with a report of the need for employee assistance services by workers in small manufacturing companies in a Detroit area community, based on a needs-assessment survey conducted in 1989. Because of the dearth of information on EAPs for small businesses, these findings should be of value in understanding issues involved in providing external EAPs to small manufacturing companies.

The chapter begins with a discussion of some of the pros and cons of external versus internal programs and trends in the delivery of services by external EAPs, including a brief summary of the limited body of empirical literature. It then presents the findings of a survey of external EAPs in Michigan and the preliminary findings of a survey of small businesses, along with the implications for practice, and describes a comprehensive needs assessment instrument for tailoring external EAPs to the needs of the changing work force. Finally, it discusses the implications of emerging trends in the EAP field for occupational social work.

Advantages and Disadvantages of External Models

A number of writers have identified the advantages and disadvantages of external and internal models in relation to the range of services provided, tailoring services to employees' needs, confidentiality, effecting organizational change, implementing programs and integrating them into the workplace, and cost considerations. As Googins and Godfrey (1987, p. 121) pointed out:

> Whereas the indigenous program may rely on one or two individuals, the contracted program can provide a greater array of skills and treatment resources. Consequently, the services of the larger treatment staff can be channeled to meet the particular needs of the troubled employee or even organization needs. . . . [Similarly] the contracted design allows the smaller company to take advantage of an array of services without having to pay for full-time [in-house] staff.

According to Blair (1987), the issue of confidentiality for users of in-house programs is frequently a source of great concern. The awareness that staff members of an internal EAP work directly for the same employing organization indeed may become an impediment to some employees' use of the program, although there is little evidence of violations of confidentiality in internal programs.

Conversely, Blair stated that for some employees, internal EAPs may instill greater confidence in the program, because "the EAP person is here and understands the kinds of problems we have" (Blair, 1987, p. 13). The internal EAP offers greater accessibility, and its location at the work site enhances its staff's knowledge of the company and makes the program more visible to employees (Hofmann, 1988). These advantages may allow the internal EAP to function as an agent of organizational change and may increase referrals to it (Googins, 1989). Some external EAPs have recognized the importance of this dynamic and have tried to incorporate these aspects into the design of their programs. For example, external EAPs that serve hourly and salaried employees in separate programs at a major automotive company have set up on-site offices in the plants or union halls and have employed EAP counselors with personal experience in the industry. This practice has enabled them to integrate their programs into the workplace and force strong linkages with workers, supervisory staff, and department heads. Googins (1989, p. 25) observed that "without a regular and planned-for presence and interaction of the EAP at the worksite, there is a counseling service, but not an EAP." Although some external EAP providers have been creative in establishing their presence in the work site, this is not usually a strength of external models when compared to internal programs (Hofmann, 1988).

In addition to greater perceived confidentiality, a number of other advantages of external EAPs have been identified in the literature. For example, some authorities contend that external EAPs are less costly (Duvall, 1986; Hofmann, 1988), offer a better risk-management strategy by minimizing the client company's liability (Straussner, 1988a), provide better supervision to their counselors, and are less likely to place the EAP counselor in conflict-of-interest situations (Hofmann, 1988; Leeman, 1974). Some companies are replacing internal EAPs with external ones to cut costs, often as part of an overall cost-containment or downsizing process or when their internal EAP coordinators retire or otherwise leave the companies (Koca, 1986; "What Services?" 1989). As the result of extensive experience working with a wide array of organizations, seasoned external providers are more likely to implement programs rapidly because of their solid knowledge of the essential components and policies of EAPs and their ability to mobilize staff.

A significant development in the workplace has been the increased emphasis in promoting healthy life-styles for employees through such avenues as stress management, fitness, health-risk appraisal, and follow-up. The "megabrush" approach of Erfurt, Foote, and Heirich (1990) integrates these preventive services with more traditional EAP case-finding and counseling techniques. In most cases, the external EAP is in a better position than is the internal EAP to provide a broad range of comprehensive services, such as 24-hour emergency coverage; wellness programs; consultation on regulations for a drug-free workplace; resources for dependent care; and, increasingly, managed mental health care.

Large external EAP providers are in an excellent position to offer services to companies with a geographically dispersed work force, especially if they are national firms. Consequently, there has been a growth in the number of national and multistate providers and a trend toward the merger or acquisition of providers. This trend has been accelerated by the entry of large managed behavioral health care companies into the EAP market, a development that raises many questions about whether the welfare of employees will remain the primary focus of EAPs.

In addition, the demand for a wider array of services to a geographically dispersed work force, combined with the recognition that internal and external EAPs each have particular advantages, has given rise to blended models in which internal programs contract for many services, large external providers contract with local service providers for postassessment counseling and treatment, and external providers establish on-site outreach and counseling. The field is in a state of flux, which has resulted in the "unbundling" of services and "wrap-around" arrangements (both of which involve subcontracting for selected services) and "introduction services" (which offer one or two services to introduce a company and its employees to EAP services)—all in an effort to tailor programs to the needs of an employer while remaining competitive in this evolving and challenging market (see Bernstein, 1989). To gain access to desired services but maintain control over their quality, selection of providers, and administration, the Fort Worth Division of General Dynamics retained an internal EAP coordinator who oversees the central diagnostic and referral and other services provided by the company's external provider (Anderson, 1989). In contrast, ARCO established its EAP in 1973, when there were no national providers, and thus its internal program contracts individually with service providers in each of its locations (Durkin, 1990); this EAP also has been involved in structuring managed mental health care for the company. Thus, creative EAP professionals have combined the strengths of both models—internal and external—when desirable.

Concurrent with these developments, prospective providers of EAP services and companies that are interested in contracting for EAP services now have access to a number of guidelines for planning a program, choosing a provider, and developing a contract (see Chiabotta, 1985; "Getting Down to Brass Tacks," 1989; Hellan & Campbell, 1981; Keohane & Newman, 1984; Koca, 1986; Leeman, 1974; Offield, 1988).

Review of Empirical Research on External EAPs

Research comparing external and internal programs has been limited, but whatever exists has been useful in identifying and documenting the differences and comparative advantages and disadvantages of the two models. Straussner (1988a, 1988b), in a study conducted in 1983–84, compared 15 internal and eight external management-sponsored programs in the New York City metropolitan area (45 percent of the management-sponsored, private-sector EAPs in the area)—a purposive sample stratified by size of company, type of industry, and program auspices (internal versus external). She reported that the mean cost per employee was significantly higher in contracted programs than in internal EAPs ($25.60 per employee per year versus $7.40) and that in-house programs were more flexible in adapting services to the needs of their organizations. On the other hand, contractual EAPs reported more frequently to management and implemented programs more rapidly because they had larger, more experienced staffs that could focus simultaneously on planning and developing programs and on assessment and counseling. External programs also reported fewer problems with confidentiality than did internal EAPs.

Also, according to Straussner (1988a, 1988b), in-house programs were viewed more favorably by unions, had greater familiarity with the work environment, and thus were in a better position to advocate for employees. However, 50 percent of the external programs offered easily accessible on-site locations and were more likely to provide 24-hour hotline and emergency services. An average of 5.7 percent of the eligible employees used contracted EAPs in a 12-month period, compared to 3.8 percent of the employees in the in-house programs. Consistent with other studies, 75 percent of the clients in contracted programs were self-referred compared to 44 percent in internal programs, and the internal programs served more alcoholics, whereas the contracted programs saw more clients for mental health and legal difficulties. The external programs also provided more professional expertise, greater availability to family members, and more referral options and reported greater utilization by higher-level workers. Conversely, internal programs were used more by minorities and lower-level employees, whereas external programs tended to be underutilized by minority-group workers.

Although firms with internal and external EAPs were comparable in size and the types of industries they served, the generalizability of Straussner's results may be limited by the size of the companies that were studied (the median was over 10,000 employees), the inclusion of only employers in the New York City metropolitan area, and the selection of only management-sponsored, private-sector programs. Furthermore, unions were more involved in planning the internal programs; none of the external programs reported involving unions either in program planning or in training sessions. Thus, the external programs in Straussner's study may not be typical of currently operating external EAPs. Also, the findings on the relative costs of external and internal EAPs must be interpreted with caution because some of the in-house programs did not include overhead in their cost estimates and because the relative costs of internal and external EAPs may have changed in the past 10 years.

In 1988, the Bureau of Labor Statistics conducted a two-stage survey of a nationwide, stratified, random sample of 7,502 U.S. businesses to determine the prevalence of EAPs and drug testing (U.S. Department of Labor, 1989). The survey found that of the EAPs established in 6.5 percent of these businesses, 55.5 percent were contractual and 44.5 percent were in-house. The prevalence of EAPs was strongly associated with organizational size: Less than 10 percent of the firms with under 50 employees reported having EAPs, whereas about three-quarters of those with 1,000 or more employees had instituted EAPs. Only the largest firms (5,000 or more employees) were more likely to have *internal* programs than external programs. As Blum and Roman (1987, p. 95) observed: "Where it was once believed that the adoption of external programs would be limited to small organizations, this has changed dramatically. Today, organizations that employ more than 1,000 workers commonly have external EAP contracts, and numerous large multi-location companies provide nationwide EAP services through external contracts." It is interesting to note that external EAPs were especially prevalent in manufacturing (72.5 percent), whereas service industries reported relatively high rates of internal programs (52 percent). When the respondents were queried about whether their EAPs provided hotlines, drug awareness programs, family services, counseling, referral, and follow-up, small establishments (except those with under 10 employees) were almost as likely as were large firms to provide these services. These results are probably not due to a response bias because the response rate was high (above 85 percent) owing to the assertive follow-up of nonrespondents.

Sudduth (1984) examined employees' duration of employment, the prevalence of chemical dependence in the caseloads, and the source of referrals in six EAPs that were classified as internal (one firm, 433 cases), external with a local vendor (three firms, 459 cases), or external with a distant vendor (two firms, 205 cases). (The geographic location and types of industries were not specified in the report, but the length of the EAPs' operation was given and internal EAPs were not appreciably older.) Because information on the size and nature of the companies' work forces was not provided, it is difficult to interpret the results of the study or to draw conclusions with confidence. However, one finding that was pronounced and consistent with other research was the significantly higher level of supervisory referrals and lower self-referrals to the internal EAPs, compared to the five firms with external EAPs.

When a large utility company with a four-year-old internal EAP added an external program as well in 1985, Harlow (1987) studied the transition process to see whether the two EAPs served different populations of clients (most previous research had found that internal EAPs had higher proportions of substance abuse and job-jeopardy referrals than did external EAPs). Drawing random samples of clients using the internal EAP before and after the external EAP was introduced, Harlow compared these populations of clients with each other and the employees served by the two programs during the first year of the external EAP's operation.

Although the 1984 and 1985 caseloads of the *internal* EAP did not differ significantly on most demographic and job characteristics or presenting problems, the 1985 caseload of the *external* EAP included significantly more marital and family problems (59 percent versus 23 percent in the internal program in 1985) and significantly fewer substance abuse referrals (11.6 percent versus 31 percent in the internal program). The internal EAP program had three times as many referrals from supervisors as did the external EAP, whereas self-referred individuals gravitated to the external EAP. Harlow concluded that the internal program may have become identified with job-jeopardy and chemical dependence referrals and that the employees and their families may have thought that they would be afforded greater confidentiality if they used the external program. Older, higher-status, and white-collar staff tended to prefer the external EAP, whereas younger, blue-collar, and minority employees were more often found in the internal EAP's caseload. Apparently management preferred the internal EAP for supervisors' referrals, and employees and their families, especially white-collar workers, favored the external program. These results confirm the EAP-utilization patterns found in other studies. Harlow suggested that external EAPs may need to provide postreferral feedback to supervisors to inspire confidence in their programs.

In a much larger study conducted in six states in 1985, Blum and Roman (1987) gathered on-site data in 480 private-sector firms with at least 500 employees and EAPs. One-third of these EAPs were external, and they tended to be found in somewhat smaller companies. Employees with alcohol problems made up 37 percent of the caseloads of the internal EAPs, on average, compared to 24 percent of the caseloads of external EAPs. The internal EAP cases were more often supervisor referred (48 percent versus 39 percent self-referrals), whereas external EAPs more often saw self-referred clients (51 percent versus 37 percent supervisor referred). The report did not indicate how informal referrals by supervisors were classified. Internal EAPs reported somewhat better program outcomes for clients with alcohol problems: 68 percent of these clients were performing adequately on the job within 12 months, compared to 60 percent of the clients in external EAPs. The authors do not state whether the sample of businesses was random and whether the internal and external EAPs differed according to the types of firms or utilization rates (the percentage of the firms' employees using the EAPs). In discussing the advantages of internal and external EAPs, Blum and Roman noted that it is impossible to generalize about the relative costs of the two models because the comparison is dependent on the context.

In another, more recent study (Schneider & Colan, 1990), 94 EAPs were chosen from five states in a multistage probability sampling process that was designed to represent the five major regions of the nation. The authors reported preliminary results comparing the 39 internal and 34 external EAPs (21 programs involving features of both models were not included). The host firms of the internal and external EAPs were of comparable size; no information was given concerning whether the internal and external EAPs differed on types of industries, management versus union sponsorship, or public-private–sector status. The external EAPs were significantly newer, served more suburban employees, had trained supervisors more often in the past year (97 percent versus 77 percent of internal EAPs), and had higher utilization rates than did the internal EAPs (5.7 percent versus 4.0 percent, p = .08). As in earlier studies (Blum & Roman, 1987; Straussner, 1988a, 1988b; Sudduth, 1984), the rates of referral by supervisors were higher for internal (29 percent) than for external EAPs (19 percent), but when the informal referrals by supervisors were omitted, the rates were the same in the two models. Comparable rates of chemically dependent employees (35 percent) were seen in both types of programs, in contrast to earlier research that found more such referrals in internal programs. Furthermore, compared to external programs, administrators of internal EAPs more often reported that the lack of time or staff resources prevented them from doing more supervisor training. This finding is consistent with Straussner's (1988a) observation that members of internal staffs may be under more stress, partly because they perform more roles and partly because the size of staffs has not kept pace with the growth of caseloads.

In summary, empirical studies comparing internal and external EAPs suggest the following conclusions:

1. External EAPs are now more prevalent than are internal programs (U.S. Department of Labor, 1989).

2. Internal EAPs tend to be older and serve more clients who are in jeopardy of losing their jobs, are chemically dependent, and are blue-collar workers, whereas external EAPs tend to be newer and attract more clients with mental health and family problems, self-referrals, and white-collar workers.

3. External EAPs are perceived to be more confidential and tend to have higher utilization rates than do internal EAPs (cf. Schneider & Colan, 1990; Straussner, 1988a, 1988b), but internal EAPs appear to attract more referrals from supervisors. It may be that the greater visibility of internal programs and the presence of internal EAP coordinators on site are more successful in overcoming the reluctance of supervisors to refer employees.

4. Therefore, external EAP providers need to, and apparently do (cf. Schneider & Colan, 1990), conduct more supervisor training, probably in an effort to inspire supervisors' confidence in the programs and in the value of making referrals.

5. Data on the relative costs of internal versus external EAPs are mixed and not necessarily consistent with the conventional wisdom that internal EAPs are costlier.

These findings, of course, must be viewed in the larger context of increasing competition among providers; the demand for containing the costs of benefits; the requirements for a drug-free workplace; employees' desire for more services; and the consequent increase in external EAP providers, especially large regional and national employee assistance organizations that are capable of responding to these forces.

Survey of External EAP Providers

Although most of the research has focused on comparisons of external and internal EAPs in relation to issues of confidentiality, accessibility, comparative costs, and scope of services provided, little is known about the characteristics of external EAP providers in relation to the composition of their staffs, the specific services they provide, their fee structures, and number and types of client organizations they serve. Because of the sparseness of empirical research on providers of external EAPs in these areas, the authors conducted a survey of a representative group of these providers to obtain a more accurate profile of these organizations and their services. The sampling unit in this study was the provider, not the client company.

Method

In July 1990, the Michigan Office of Substance Abuse Services, in cooperation with the Michigan chapter of the Employee Assistance Professionals Association (EAPA) and of the Employee Assistance Society of North America (EASNA), published a directory of internal and external EAPs in Michigan. Because the directory identified whether programs were internal or external, the authors were able to define a sampling frame including all 79 external EAPs that were listed. They then designed a survey to poll these organizations concerning several major areas of interest: auspices of the external EAP; type of clientele served; credentials of the provider staff; types of services provided; the basis for fees; attitudes of prospective clients toward EAPs; marketing techniques utilized; and perceptions of trends in the employee assistance field, particularly in relation to small businesses. The survey was six pages long and was estimated to take 10 to 15 minutes to complete.

In October 1990, the survey was sent to the specified contact person in each of 79 external EAPs identified in the directory, with a cover letter explaining the purpose of the survey, encouraging the respondent's cooperation, and assuring that the organization's identity and individual responses would be kept confidential. Three weeks after the first copies of the survey were mailed, second copies were sent, reminding the contact persons to complete and mail them if they had not already done so. This two-wave strategy yielded a return of 50 surveys, for a response rate of 63 percent. The respondents were assured confidentiality by not putting their organizations' names on the questionnaires. With few exceptions, the responses to individual profiles were complete and appeared to be answered accurately. The respondents were representative of the geographic distribution of external EAPs in Michigan, except for a slight overrepresentation of EAPs from the northern part of the state.

Results

Nature and staff of responding organizations
One-third of the organizations identified themselves as exclusively EAP providers, either single-site (20.4 percent) or regional–national (12.2 percent) providers. The majority of respondents (53 percent) stated that their EAP component was part of a larger organization providing chemical dependence (22.4 percent), mental health (12.2 percent), or family services

(10.2 percent) or was part of a hospital or other medical facility (8.2 percent). Seven respondents (14.3 percent) indicated other auspices, typically a private consulting firm or human resource development organization. More than half the respondents (56 percent) had begun providing external EAP services within the past five years (1985 or later), although 22 percent had initiated external services before 1980.

The organizations varied considerably in the composition and size of their staffs. The average size of their staffs, including support staffs, was 6.9 full-time equivalent members (range: .3–44) (two agencies that had clearly included the entire agency staff [not just the EAP staff] were eliminated from these statistics). Nearly half the organizations (47 percent) had three or fewer staff members, one-quarter reported four to nine, and 28 percent had 10 or more. These totals included clinical, managerial, and support staff. A typical (median) staff configuration included 2.5 clinical staff, no nonclinical managers, and one support staff person.

More than three-quarters of the providers had at least one MSW on staff, and half reported having one or more psychologists. The great majority of professional staff in these organizations had college degrees (91 percent), 58 percent of whom had MSWs. Nearly three-quarters of the professional staffs (72 percent) had other credentials or certification, such as ACSW (34 percent), CEAP (14 percent), CSW (34 percent), CAC (9 percent), or a board-certified social work diplomate (4 percent) (because of a typographical error on the questionnaire, in which CAC was spelled CCAC, the number of CACs may have been underreported). About half (48 percent) of the providers used only credentialed staff, and more than three-quarters (78 percent) reported that at least half their staffs had one or more of the foregoing five credentials or certifications. Therefore, in most cases the organizations appeared to be staffed with appropriately trained and credentialed clinical staffs, consistent with the standards of professional associations, such as EASNA (1990).

Types of organizations served

There was considerable diversity in the number and type of client organizations served. One question asked how many contracts and less formal provider arrangements the external EAP had in 1980, 1985, and 1990. The tremendous growth in EAPs was evident in the answers to this question. In 1980, these external EAPs served a total of 223 client organizations; in 1985, they served 625; and in 1990, they served 2,173—a nearly tenfold increase from a decade earlier. These totals exclude three consortia serving about 7,000 small businesses in the state. The number of formal contracts grew at a faster rate than did the less formal referral arrangements: The proportion of firms served under contract was 47 percent in 1980, 71 percent in 1985, and 84 percent in 1990. The average number of contracts held increased from 11.7 in 1980 to 24.1 in 1985 to 36.8 in 1990. In 1990 the total number of organizations served per provider ranged from one to 800, even when consortia were counted as one client. However, it is important to note that the *median* number of firms served was just *six*, even in 1990. Therefore, the mean for the large clientele for 1990 (44.3 firms) is accounted for primarily by the rapid growth of a few large firms.

The nature of organizations served by these external EAPs varied, but manufacturers were the most prevalent (see Table 1). These figures suggest that most providers served several types of organizations. Another dimension of client firms, and one of special interest here, is the *size* of the organizations served (see Table 2). The most prevalent size of the client companies was 100 to 249 employees; more than one-quarter of all the client companies fell in this range. Excluding two consortia serving thousands of very small firms, one-third of the client companies had fewer than 100 employees (two providers serving very large consortia of extremely small firms did not include these companies when answering the question on size of firms). Although more than one-quarter of the providers served firms of under 100 workers, only 14 percent reported serving small-business *consortia*, which suggests that this type of service may be less common than serving

---

Table 1
Types of Client Firms Served by External EAPs (N = 50)

SECTOR	PERCENTAGE OF EAP PROVIDERS SERVING THIS SECTOR
Manufacturing	84
Government	54
Educational–school systems	48
Other service industries[a]	48
Hospital–medical organizations	46
Transportation–utilities	46
Finance, insurance, real estate	40
Social service organizations	38
Communications	36
Retail, wholesale, trade	30
Mining, construction	22

[a]This sector includes personal services, entertainment, repairs, legal, and business services, among others.

Table 2
Sizes of Firms Served by External EAP Providers

SIZE OF CLIENT FIRM	PERCENTAGE OF ALL FIRMS SERVED	PERCENTAGE OF PROVIDERS SERVING THIS SIZE FIRM
1–9 employees	3.5	27
10–49 employees	12.4	49
50–99 employees	18.2	67
100–249 employees	28.6	69
250–499 employees	18.1	64
500–999 employees	8.9	40
1,000–4,999 employees	7.4	51
5,000 or more employees	2.9	24

small businesses individually. The seven providers serving consortia served a total of 10 consortia averaging over 600 members apiece (this average excludes one consortium with 3,000 law firms of the state bar association). One-third of the consortia were sponsored by the Chamber of Commerce, and half were sponsored by trade or professional associations. Larger EAP providers (with at least 10 staff members) were three times as likely to have consortia among their clientele than were smaller ones.

Because the major market of expansion for EAPs is with small businesses, the respondents were asked to identify services that are particularly needed for businesses with under 50 employees. It was somewhat surprising that only 20 percent of the responses involved needs specific to small businesses (such as offering consortia, low-cost services, fee-for-service arrangements). The majority of responses to this question involved the needs of *any* business contracting for EAP services, such as supervisory training, education and prevention, and assessment and referral. Therefore, most respondents did not consider the needs of small businesses to be especially unique. On the basis of the authors' survey of small businesses in one community in Michigan (reported later), this perception may not be accurate.

Services provided
About two-thirds of the providers (65 percent) did at least some EAP business on a capitation basis (charging per company employee, regardless of the number actually using the service), and a similar proportion (67 percent) did at least some business on the basis of the actual services that were utilized. On average, 48 percent of the business was done on a capitation basis, 42 percent on a service-utilization basis, and 10 percent on some other

basis (for example, a flat fee *not* based on the number of employees). About one-fifth (19 percent) of the providers reported offering a standard package of services to all clients, but most (81 percent) reported tailoring services to their customers' specifications.

The average number of services offered by providers was 13.4, indicating a broad range of available services. Fifteen of the services were reportedly provided by at least half the responding organizations. The services that were offered most often were supervisory training (94 percent), chemical dependence services (88 percent), short-term counseling (four sessions or fewer, 82 percent), crisis intervention (80 percent), mental health services (78 percent), family or marital counseling (74 percent), and stress-management workshops (74 percent). The proportion of firms giving short-term counseling was much higher than in a 1986 survey of EAP professionals, which included both internal and external programs (82 percent versus 58 percent; McClellan & Miller, 1988). Only 22 percent of the respondents reported offering drug-testing services, which is consistent with the prevalent view that EAPs should not enter that arena. Reflecting the current trends toward cost containment and healthy life-styles, managed care was offered by 42 percent of the EAP providers and wellness services were offered by 52 percent. Eight organizations mentioned offering other services that were not listed on the questionnaire, including information on and assistance in establishing a drug-free workplace (mentioned by two) and information on dependent care (mentioned by one). It is noteworthy that only 18 percent of the respondents provided reports on *cost savings* to management, perhaps because of their lack of access to cost data for the companies. Evidence from other sources suggests that employers also do not track EAP cost savings as assiduously as one would expect.

Some of the respondents (13 percent) provided no ongoing counseling to employees, doing only assessment and referral. Among those offering counseling, the average number of sessions provided, including assessment, was 4.1 (range: 1–20) and the average maximum offered was 6.5 sessions, with 23 percent of the EAPs reporting no cap on the number of sessions provided. Nearly half (47 percent) of the organizations reported that they will offer more than eight counseling sessions, if needed.

In summary, the range of services offered by these external EAPs was extensive and is probably more comprehensive than noted here because not all possible services were listed on the questionnaire.

Promotion of EAP services
A significant majority of respondents thought it was easier to promote EAP services—both contractual services (83 percent) and services on a referral

basis (84 percent)—in 1990 than it was in 1980, or whenever they began to operate. Organizations also were asked to indicate the three most important reasons that companies decide to establish EAPs and comparable reasons for *not* establishing such programs. Among the reasons for establishing EAPs, the most-often mentioned were (1) to reduce absenteeism, accidents, and poor job performance (68 percent); (2) regulations for establishing a drug-work workplace (62 percent); and (3) anticipated cost savings (52 percent). These goals are similar to those identified by McClellan and Miller (1988) in a survey of both internal and external EAPs. The perception that cost savings are a major motivation for employers contrasts with the finding that only one in five EAPs reported on such savings. Other reasons given for the establishment of EAPs were the publicity regarding drugs in the workplace (38 percent), to reduce the time that supervisors spend on troubled employees (28 percent), the desire for a healthier work force (26 percent), and the concern for the welfare of employees (14 percent). The reasons that were considered most salient in decisions *not* to establish EAPs included (1) "don't perceive a need for service" (92 percent), (2) the lack of information about the benefits of EAPs (68 percent), and (3) concerns about costs (52 percent). All three of these reasons suggest a general lack of information about the payoffs of EAPs among companies without these services.

These external providers were asked to identify the two main reasons they believe companies prefer external to internal services, when they do. The most prominent reason was the perception of greater confidentiality (mentioned by 75 percent), followed by the decreased need to maintain in-house EAP expertise (55 percent), the perception that external EAPs are less costly (39 percent), and access to a broader range of services (29 percent).

Trends in the delivery of EAP services
The respondents were asked to identify trends in services requested by businesses. Among nine possible choices, three were most often mentioned: (1) assistance in establishing a drug-free workplace (81 percent), (2) the greater emphasis on cost containment (64 percent), and (3) more requests for EAP-provided managed care (57 percent). Other possible service choices included case management, prevention and wellness, a broader range of services, more flexibility in service packages, and drug testing. The respondents were also asked to rank the top three trends they perceived in the field. The three trends that received the highest average ranks were cost containment (1.6), requests for case management services (1.7, mentioned by 49 percent), and managed care services (1.9). It is noteworthy that only 23 percent mentioned "more requests for drug testing" and that that service had the lowest average rank (2.4). These three trends highlight the need for knowledge and expertise in managed care and other cost-containment

methods, case management, and regulations on establishing a drug-free workplace among those who market external EAP services (cf. McClellan & Miller, 1988).

Selected results, by the size of EAP organizations
Beyond this descriptive analysis, the authors examined how size of the EAP provider affects other factors. For this purpose, they divided the EAP organizations into three categories according to size: small (3 or fewer staff members), medium (4 to 9 staff members), and large (10 or more staff members). The large EAP organizations had been providing external services significantly longer than had the others (since 1979, on average, compared to 1985 for small firms; ANOVA, $p < .0005$). They also did a significantly greater share of business on a capitation basis (91 percent versus 29 percent for small- and 51 percent for medium-sized organizations), offered significantly more services (15.7 on average versus 11.7 in small EAPs; $p < .02$). It is interesting to note that the small EAP providers tended to offer fewer consulting sessions and to have a lower maximum, although these differences were not significant. Larger firms were significantly more likely to be freestanding EAP providers and not part of another organization (46.2 percent of large versus 28.6 percent of small providers). As was noted earlier, larger EAPs were three to four times as likely as were small or medium-sized EAPs to serve small-business consortia. On the one hand, large providers were in a better position to provide coverage over a greater geographic area. On the other hand, the authors thought that larger companies would be less interested in doing the tailoring that might be needed to serve small businesses; however, this did not appear to be an impediment to providing such services.

Summary of Findings
The results of the survey revealed that external EAPs grew significantly from 1980 to 1990 and suggested that these organizations were serving a variety of client organizations, were providing a broad range of services, and generally were staffed with appropriately credentialed providers.

With regard to external services for small businesses, the survey found the following:

- One-third of the client firms of providers had fewer than 100 employees. Small businesses were therefore underrepresented compared to their numbers among all businesses. It is evident that serving small businesses is a potential area of growth for external EAPs.

- Most of the needs of the small businesses identified by the respondents were similar to those identified in the literature for employers of any size. It is likely that the respondents' perception of the similarities of the needs of small and large businesses is not entirely accurate. Although it was not specifically included in the questionnaire, one or two providers mentioned that small companies had asked for help in designing or modifying benefits packages, which may be another special need of small businesses that do not have this internal human resources expertise.

• Services to small-business consortia were more likely to be provided by the larger external EAP providers.

Reaching Out to Small Businesses

Although the number of companies that used EAPs increased markedly from 1980 to 1990, employees of small companies continue to be a large underserved population. An estimated 5 percent of companies with fewer than 100 employees and only 38 percent of companies with 100 to 1,000 employees offered EAP services as of 1988 (Vinton & Brennan, 1988). And in the authors' survey, one-third of the client firms of EAP providers in Michigan were small businesses of under 100 employees.

It goes without saying that workers in small and medium-sized companies that make up 99 percent of the nation's employers (Freudenheim, 1989) and almost half the nation's employees are certainly not exempt from the human and personal problems of workers in larger companies. This fact was clearly borne out in the authors' survey of small manufacturing companies in an industrial community in the Detroit area that they conducted with support from the Chamber of Commerce. The survey sought to determine the nature of personal and workplace problems experienced by the workers in these companies and the feasibility of developing an EAP for this business community.

The survey team interviewed the owners or executive officers of 68 companies at their work sites that were selected from a membership list supplied by the Chamber of Commerce. They found that 60 percent of the companies had fewer than 25 workers and were family-operated businesses. Most of the companies had a mix of skilled workers, such as tool and die makers, and transient unskilled laborers. Many of these workers had extensive individual and family difficulties, as well as alcoholism problems, for which they were probably not seeking or receiving any assistance from the public or private social service sector. If they could go to an accessible and cost-free EAP, they would be more likely to link with an appropriate service program as a result of a self-referral or supervisor's referral to the EAP.

Interviews with company officials sought their impressions of the problems of workers that had the greatest impact on productivity and on workers' well-being. The respondents were presented with the Problem-Severity Index, which lists 12 commonly encountered problems in the workplace, and were asked to rank them according to the severity of the impact on their workplace. They identified tardiness, low productivity, preoccupation with family problems, and absenteeism, in that order, as the most serious problems, followed by poor-quality workmanship and alcoholic behavior.

The research team also asked how these problems were being handled and discovered that there were basically two approaches in most of the companies. Unskilled workers with problems that affected productivity usually were quickly dismissed and replaced with new workers. Skilled workers; workers who were part of the family operating the business; and long-term, valued employees often were retained even when the problems continued or got worse. Because the effects of an impaired worker are often more devastating to overall production in a small company than in a large company, the continuation of such a situation can have major economic consequences. In one instance, an employee whose drinking severely affected his work performance was retained for 15 years in a family business that had all the characteristics of a codependent family system, with enabling behavior, including many well-intentioned but ineffective discussions with him by supervisors in the hopes of controlling his dysfunctional behavior.

The authors believe that outreach to small businesses can best be accomplished through contact with trade associations, especially chambers of commerce. Increasingly, these associations have served as catalysts as they have become aware of the opportunities for cost savings through the development of employee assistance services for their members. Recognizing that EAP services are as strong or as weak as the availability of community treatment resources to which EAPs can refer workers, chambers of commerce and trade associations are often instrumental in putting together EAP and health insurance packages that include provisions for inpatient and outpatient mental health and chemical dependence treatment for their constituent companies.

In essence, interests and needs of employers, trade associations, and external EAPs are coming together, and for external EAPs, this mutuality of needs and interests means extended opportunities for delivering services. However, these needs or the ways in which they can be addressed are not always evident to chambers of commerce or business organizations. Therefore, external EAPs have developed active marketing strategies and have played a major role in developing programs to reach out to and educate the business community. Although it can be argued that such strategies are largely in the EAP purveyors' economic interests, their outreach benefits many employees, including workers who are employed by small businesses.

Recently, the scope of EAP services has been extended to include wellness and health-promotion programs for both small-business consortia and for individual firms. The states of Michigan and New York, for example, have provided incentives in the form of small grants for employers to provide such programs, and companies have often combined these programs with traditional EAP counseling for employees with early- or late-stage mental health or substance abuse problems. The emerging EAP packages are thus providing employee assistance services at the primary, as well as the secondary and tertiary levels of prevention.

For the EAP services for small companies to be utilized, EAPs need to develop individualized approaches to address the needs, realities, and culture of each workplace, which are usually different from those of larger businesses. These differences need to be reflected in the EAPs' outreach efforts as well. In the authors' contacts with owners of small businesses, they learned quickly that their approach needed to be informal and personalized, and EAPs have told the authors that the responsiveness of small businesses to marketing outreach is usually more related to the interpersonal approach of the EAP representatives than to more objective presentations of cost-benefit data.

Describing the program of Lincoln EAP in Nebraska, 46 percent of whose contracts are with small companies of up to 100 employees, Vinton and Brennan (1988) identified fundamental differences in the ways that EAP firms need to relate to small businesses compared with larger companies. With regard to the culture of the workplace, small businesses are frequently family operated and employees and employers have close ties to the community, including local political leaders. Unlike the corporate culture, there are frequently no written statements regarding employees' conduct or personnel policies. Job responsibilities are not formally defined, and workers often carry several job assignments. Often there is no human resources staff, so EAPs need to provide a broader array of services. When marketing services, the EAP representative often can go straight to the top, and the decision to implement an EAP is usually not a long drawn-out process, as it often is in a large corporation.

Vinton and Brennan's description of small business culture and ways of working with small companies is congruent with the findings and experiences in the authors' survey of small businesses even though the companies were primarily in the manufacturing sector and Vinton and Brennan studied a mix of service and industrial organizations. Therefore, Vinton and Brennan's observations seem to be indicative of small-business culture in general and should be useful for EAPs that are reaching out to this sector of the business community.

Emergence of Occupational Service Centers

In the future, occupational social workers can expect to be called on to provide consultation regarding companies' needs for employee assistance and wellness services and to offer guidance about other benefits that are responsive to the needs of the work force. In the course of their survey of small businesses, the authors developed the Workforce Profile instrument (Spitzer, 1989) that helped them determine both *whether* employee assistance and other workplace services were needed and the *kind* of programs that would be most responsive to the needs of the work force. The Workforce Profile focuses on the demographics of the work force and workers' psychosocial needs, as well as the resources available in the community. Hence, it may provide a way for companies to exercise an active role in planning and operating EAPs that is congruent with social work's emphasis on self-determination. Such an approach makes it possible to decide which types of resources should be included in a benefits package. For example, it could be determined whether day care centers for children or elderly family members (or both) would be needed by a particular work population. For small companies that cannot afford to offer all types of services, occupational social workers can play an important role in establishing priorities among their needs and creatively developing programs that use the resources of external EAPs in collaboration with appropriate groups and associations in the community.

External EAPs serving a variety of work organizations and using a demographics-driven program-development orientation are indeed in an excellent position to assist the workplace in addressing the needs of the changing work force (Yandrick, 1991). It is projected that by the year 2000, 85 percent of new entrants into the work force will be ethnic minorities or women (Johnston, 1987); this change will inevitably affect employees' needs, attitudes, and relationships in the workplace.

Porter (1990, p. 7) presented the following vision of the potential of a demography-driven response to the changing composition of the work population by the year 2000: "Multicultural training can help co-workers of various cultures communicate and interact effectively. It also teaches supervisors how to motivate a diverse group of employees. Managers learn how to capitalize on the cultural differences and to develop organizational policies that are not culturally biased." In this construct, social workers are viewed as catalysts for developing a diversity-awareness program in the workplace that is built on an appreciation of each person's unique experience of his or her culture. Social workers may also provide training to managers and supervisors concerning effective communication techniques to utilize when dealing with workers of various ethnic backgrounds.

Consistent with this comprehensive approach to the dramatically changing nature of the workplace, many external EAPs are evolving into occupational service centers, providing not only employee assistance counseling but a comprehensive program, including wellness and health promotion, cultural diversity and sensitivity training, dependent care, and resources for retirees. Indeed, occupational service centers—staffed by occupational social workers and multidisciplinary human services professionals—appear to be the next step in the evolution of workplace programs as we move into the 21st century.

References

Anderson, M. D. (1989). The internal coordinator/external provider EAP model at General Dynamics. *The Almacan, 19*(5), 34–37.

Bernstein, J. (1989). Selling EAPs: Is the customer always right? *The Almacan, 19*(5), 31–33.

Blair, B. (1987). Internal and external models. In J. Spicer (Ed.), *The EAP solution: Current trends and future issues* (pp. 12–17). Center City, MN: Hazelden Educational Materials.

Blum, T. C., & Roman, P. M. (1987). Internal vs. external EAPs. In *Employee assistance programs: Benefits, problems, and prospects* (chap. 13). Washington, DC: Bureau of National Affairs.

Chiabotta, B. (1985). Evaluating EAP vendors: How to do it right the first time. *Personnel Administrator, 30*(8), 39–43.

Durkin, W. G. (1990). Our program structure, an internal program that uses external consultants, serves our needs best. *EAPA Exchange, 20*(3), 34–36.

Duvall, S. C. (1986). Comparing the three EAPs: External programs are easiest to use. *Occupational Health and Safety, 55*(12), 71–73.

Employee Assistance Society of North America. (1990). *EASNA Standards for Accreditation of Employee Assistance Programs Effective July 1, 1990.* Southfield, MI: Author.

Erfurt, J. C., Foote, A., & Heirich, M. A. (1990). *The core technology of megabrush: Employee assistance and wellness programs combined.* Ann Arbor: Institute of Labor and Industrial Relations, University of Michigan.

Freudenheim, M. (1989, November 13). More aid for addicts on the job. *New York Times*, Section D.

Getting down to brass tacks. (1989). *The Almacan, 19*(5), 26–30.

Googins, B. (1989). Problems integrating into the organizational structure. *The Almacan, 19*(5), 24–25.

Googins, B., & Godfrey, J. (1987). *Occupational social work.* Englewood Cliffs, NJ: Prentice Hall.

Harlow, K. C. (1987). A comparison of internal and external employee assistance programs. *New England Journal of Human Services, 7*(2), 16–21.

Hellan, R. T., & Campbell, W. J. (1981). Contracting for EAP services: A guide to making the right choice. *Personnel Administrator, 26*(9), 49–51.

Hofmann, J. J. (1988). Future EAPs: An internal vs. external debate. *The Almacan, 18*(7), 10–12.

Johnston, W. (1987). *Workforce 2000* (Report prepared by the Hudson Institute). Washington, DC: U.S. Department of Labor.

Keohane, R. G., & Newman, C. E. (1984). A family agency's approach to providing employee assistance programs in industry. *Social Work, 29,* 295–297.

Klarreich, S. H., DiGiuseppe, R., & DiMattia, D. J. (1987). EAPs: Mind over myth. *Personnel Administrator, 32,* 119–121.

Koca, G. (1986). Contracting services: The FAA experience. *EAP Digest, 6*(4), 57–62.

Leeman, C. P. (1974). Contracting for an employee counseling service. *Harvard Business Review, 52*(2), 20–22, 152–154.

McClellan, K., & Miller, R. E. (1988). EAPs in transition: Purpose and scope of services. *Employee Assistance Quarterly, 3*(3), 25–42.

Michigan Office of Substance Abuse Services. (1990). *Michigan directory of employee assistance programs (EAPs).* Lansing: Author.

Morrall, K. (1988). Assistance programs tackle employees' personal problems. *Savings Institutions, 109,* 70–72.

National Institute on Alcohol Abuse and Alcoholism. (1981). *Fourth special report to the U.S. Congress on alcohol and health.* Washington, DC: U.S. Government Printing Office.

Offield, J. (1988). Buyer beware. *Employee Assistance, 1*(4), 41–45.

Porter, G. (1990). Diversity awareness: Training for the multicultural workplace 2000. *Work and Social Work, 1*(1), 7.

Schneider, R., & Colan, N. B. (1990, October). *Supervisor training: A comparison of internal and external EAPs.* Paper presented at the 19th Annual Conference of the Employee Assistance Professionals Association, New Orleans, LA.

Spitzer, K. (1989). *The Workforce Profile: A needs assessment instrument for EAP providers.* Detroit: Wayne State University School of Social Work.

Straussner, S. L. A. (1988a). A comparative analysis of in-house and contractual employee assistance programs. In M. J. Holosko & M. D. Feit (Eds.), *Evaluation of Employee Assistance Programs* (pp. 43–56). New York: Haworth Press.

Straussner, S. L. A. (1988b). Comparison of in-house and contracted-out employee assistance programs. *Social Work, 33,* 53–55.

Sudduth, A. B. (1984). Assessing employee use of internal and external employee assistance programs for alcohol and control groups. In C. H. Grimes (Ed.), *EAP Research* (pp. 24–33). Troy, MI: Performance Resource Press.

U.S. Department of Labor, Bureau of Labor Statistics. (1989). *Survey of employer anti-drug programs* (Report 760). Washington, DC: U.S. Government Printing Office.

Vinton, P., & Brennan, K. (1988). How to tailor EAPs to reach small business. *The Almacan, 18*(10), 16–19.

What services does an employer want in an EAP? (1989). *The Almacan, 19*(7), 14–16.

Yandrick, R. M. (1991). New-generation workers line up at the company gate. *EAPA Exchange, 21*(1), 20–23.

CHAPTER 20

An International Perspective on the Development of Social Work in the Workplace

David Bargal

Who built the seven towers of Thebes? The books are
filled with the names of kings. Was it kings who hauled
the craggy blocks of stone?

—Bertolt Brecht
A Worker Reads History

Though known for almost a century under different titles, especially during the Industrial Revolution in Europe and toward the end of the 19th century in the United States, occupational social work has reemerged through the establishment of social services and social work roles in the workplace. Comparative analyses of social issues may contribute to a greater under-standing of the phenomenon under examination than may studying the issue in one context alone. This chapter seeks, by comparative analysis, to increase the understanding of occupational social work. It compares the academic and professional aspects of occupational social work in four countries—Austra-lia, Israel, Germany, and the Netherlands—in relation to these countries' economic, industrial, and social contexts. It also discusses the implications for the field of changes in the workplace and in the work forces in these countries and in the United States.

No Third-World country is included in this analysis because there has been little systematic writing about them. However, Balgopal's (1989) discussion of employee assistance programs (EAPs) in a cross-cultural perspective makes an important contribution to the subject and includes references to the unique attributes of occupational social work services in India.

The countries chosen for this comparative analysis have some unique features. Germany is a leading industrialized country that underwent an economic miracle when it reconstructed its ruined industries following its defeat in World War II. The Netherlands is a highly developed welfare state that provides comprehensive health and welfare services to its citizens (Kramer, 1981). Israel was established on collectivist principles and has a considerable number of industries and businesses that are owned by trade unions (Kramer, 1981; Neikrug & Katan, 1981). Australia has a history of labor–management relations that resemble those of Great Britain, where representatives of labor are involved in the welfare of the work force (Roman, 1983).

Furthermore, the economic, industrial, and social contexts of these four countries and the way occupational social work has been developing differ. Motives for the development of occupational social work in all countries seem to reflect management's interest in increased productivity and in the reduction of employees' problems, which affect their productivity. Under-lying universal motives can also be discerned. First, companies in each country feel responsible for the well-being of their employees. Second, occupational social work is established to foster the companies' compliance with laws to hire special groups of employees, such as minorities, women, and the disabled, and interest in integrating them into the companies. Third, the employment of occupational social workers may also be tied to political struggles between union and management for dominance over employees. Fourth, it may reflect a change in managerial philosophy to develop a work environment in which the self-fulfillment of employees, as well as their life-cycle tasks and career needs, are taken into account (Bargal, 1988a).

The analysis of the four countries and of occupational social work in them is based on three principal dimensions—societal characteristics, the profes-sional and academic characteristics of occupational social work, and the characteristics of occupational social work in workplaces—and nine subdimensions (see Figure 1).

Few systematic surveys or studies have been conducted in these countries, and those that have been are not available in English. Therefore, this chapter relies on the available up-to-date resources, which are not always compre-hensive enough to provide complete answers to coincide with the conceptual framework. The two major resources are Googins and Godfrey (1987) and the papers from the International Expert Meeting on Occupational Social Work, held in Wassenar, the Netherlands, November 10–13, 1987, that were published in *Eurosocial Reports* (see Bargal, 1988a, 1988b; Bobbink,

Figure 1
A Conceptual Framework for Analyzing the Characteristics of
Occupational Social Work

  I. Societal characteristics
     A. Economic and industrial culture
     B. Labor–management relations
     C. System of welfare and health services
  II. Academic and professional characteristics of occupational social work
     A. Academic specialization and scholarly disciplinary work:
        academic training and internships for students, research and
        the conceptualization of knowledge by academicians and
        practitioners
     B. Professional culture: networking, publications, conferences,
        involvement in policy issues, certification
 III. Characteristics of occupational social work in the workplace
     A. Defined professional domain
     B. Integration and resource building in the organization
     C. Formulation of service procedures
     D. Development of a generic repertoire of interventions in policy,
        administration, consultation, and counseling.

Mensinga, & Uri, 1988; Uri, 1988). Further cross-cultural comparative studies of occupational social work must gather information on the dimensions suggested here to create a full and balanced picture of their development in each country (United Nations, 1971).

Framework

A conceptual framework is a cognitive tool that identifies and maps certain areas of knowledge. It usually specifies the elements that are consistent in the realm of knowledge under consideration and points out the relationships among them. Ozawa's (1980) framework assumes that occupational social work in organizations develops progressively through four discernible stages. In the first stage, the occupational social worker's role is to provide counseling services to employees, whereas in the fourth and highest stage, his or her primary role is as an organizational developer who works side by side with management and labor to create a sociotechnical system that promotes high standards of work life. Because it is focused on occupational social work inside the organization, Ozawa's model disregards two factors—external professional and societal considerations; it also assumes cross-cultural validity.

Balgopal (1989) dealt with EAPs from a cross-cultural perspective and presented a useful conceptual framework that incorporates the importance of societal characteristics in understanding the development of these programs. His framework, however, does not include professional and organizational components of the occupational social work role.

The framework promoted here attempts to take all these factors into consideration and is based on a dynamic relationship among three interrelated principal dimensions:

1. The function of occupational social work is embedded in each country's social, economic, and labor–management conditions.

2. Occupational social work draws its body of knowledge and skills from an ongoing academic–professional specialization.

3. Occupational social work draws its practice resources and legitimacy from the implementation of its knowledge and skills in a certain business or industrial organization.

The author's principal proposition regarding the relationship of the three dimensions of the framework is: *The most effective occupational social work activity is possible when an academically and professionally based specialization encounters favorable societal conditions (mandatory welfare and health services) and operates from an influential position in the work organization.*

In other words, for a professional entity to be effective, three conditions are required. The first is systematic academic training, which is based on accumulating knowledge generated through research, and generalizations from practice. These practice and theoretical knowledge bases are fostered and disseminated through a professional culture (Sarfatti-Larson, 1977; Vollmer & Mills, 1966). However, two clusters of factors—the societal and the organizational—may either enable or constrain the optimal application of professional knowledge in the service of clients. In more concrete terms, *when business and industrial climates foster quality-of-life programs for employees and when unions have negotiating power to gain favorable conditions for members, occupational social work may find a fertile ground for its intervention.* Even more effective, from a professional point of view, is for occupational social work to develop within a society that has a system of nationalized health and welfare services. The referral of clients to these services and the role that these services may play during periods of layoffs or unemployment is invaluable. The third dimension emphasizes the importance of establishing a position of influence for occupational social work in the work organization through the formation of alliances with key administrators and labor representatives and by "proving" one's "expert knowledge" and, therefore, a defined domain for intervention. The more the repertoire of interventions encompasses a systemic approach that meets both the needs of individual employees and policy and advocacy issues in the workplace, the more effective the occupational social worker's role will be.

The Netherlands

Societal characteristics. The Netherlands is an advanced capitalist welfare state whose government is strongly involved in legislating business practices. The government also owns industrial and service firms, although there are pressures to privatize many of them. The economy's exposure to marketplace competition has forced the workplace to undergo social, organizational, and technological changes, and many industries are being forced to downsize their work forces considerably. The Netherlands provides health and welfare services through national legislation, as well as through voluntary organizations. Labor–management relations are marked by cooperation between unions and management. A considerable number of workers belong to unions.

Academic and professional characteristics of occupational social work. Students can specialize in occupational social work during their academic training. Furthermore, the professional social work association has a division of occupational social work that publishes a newsletter and is involved in policy issues, such as layoffs in industries, the consequences of automation and mergers, and the privatization of industries (Bobbink et al., 1988; Googins & Godfrey, 1987).

Characteristics of occupational social workers in the workplace. Occupational social work was established initially in government-owned companies. Its defined domain of intervention encompasses a full repertoire of interventions, from counseling individuals to consultation with management on reorganization and the development of personnel policy. The social worker's role is integrated into the work organization and is represented on the managerial level (Bobbink et al., 1988; Googins & Godfrey, 1987).

Germany

Societal characteristics. Germany is an advanced capitalist welfare state that emphasizes high production and productivity by its work force. Labor–management relations are cooperative, and a considerable number in the work force are affiliated with unions. Unions are represented in the workplace through workers' councils, which participate in the decision making of the corporation. The state provides health and welfare services through national legislation (Balgopal, 1989; Bilik, 1988).

Academic and professional characteristics of occupational social work. Social work in Germany is taught in institutions that are separate from the university in which there is no systematic or scholarly study of occupational social work. There is no supervised training in occupational social work during training, and no professional culture of occupational social work exists (Googins & Godfrey, 1987; Uri, 1988).

Characteristics of occupational social workers in the workplace. Occupational social workers play a peripheral role in work organizations, the majority of which do not recognize the importance of social workers' assistance in personnel matters. There is no resource-building orientation, and the social worker's position is marginal in the corporate structure, with interventions limited to counseling individual workers on personal problems (especially alcoholism) and helping solve problems that arise in the work teams. The small number of occupational social workers and of EAP programs in Germany may be attributed to cultural factors. There is a deep-rooted belief in Germany that all forms of health care are a basic human right and therefore should be provided by the state, not the workplace (Bilik, 1988).

Israel

Societal characteristics. Israel is a socialist welfare state. A considerable number of its industries are publicly owned, such as by the General Federation of Labor (Histadrut), and many are subsidized by the government. Because of the high rate of union affiliation, labor has considerable negotiating power and is an active party in all business decisions. Business and industry's culture emphasizes collectivistic values, and employees' rights are to be preserved. Labor–management relations are generally positive. Lately, pressure to introduce more privatization and to move toward a competitive economy has resulted in layoffs and the shutting down of companies, which have made the labor movement militant at times. Israel has a quasi-nationalized system of medicine—70 percent of it is run by the General Federation of Labor (Neikrug & Katan, 1981)—and everyone's health expenses, including hospitalization, are covered. It also has a system of welfare services, including personal services, that are provided by both national and municipal authorities.

Academic and professional characteristics of occupational social work. There is no specialization in occupational social work at the academic level, although several universities offer courses in the subject. Some scholarly work has been done—research, surveys of professionals and their work domains, and methods of intervention (Shamir & Bargal, 1983), and a textbook of occupational social work has been published (Bargal, 1984). The association of occupational social workers publishes a newsletter and maintains a close relationship with the labor union headquarters; there is also an ongoing training program for union personnel to help them understand occupational social work's knowledge base and methods.

Characteristics of occupational social workers in the workplace. All occupational social work programs have been established by the management of companies, not by unions. In most situations, occupational social workers have a defined domain for intervention that follows the job description established by the Israeli civil service (Bargal & Shamir, 1984) and are integrated into the work organization. Services are usually delivered in the workplace in a professional and organized manner, and social workers can rise to a considerable position of power, mainly as consultants to human resource departments or to management, especially during times of layoffs and downsizing (Uri, 1988). Because of the nationalized system of medical and personal services, it has been difficult to establish occupational social work services in companies that perceived them as overlapping with existing services.

Australia

Societal characteristics. Australia is a social democratic welfare state. Corporations and industries may be run jointly by the government, private owners, and the unions, and the emphasis is on improving the quality of life in the workplace through the continuous betterment of working conditions. A considerable portion of the work force is unionized, and there is a legal procedure to settle labor–management disputes through arbitration. The state provides health and welfare services to all citizens through a public system.

Academic and professional characteristics of occupational social work. A few universities provide courses in occupational social work, but they are just beginning to systematically codify knowledge and research in the field. There is no professional culture that promotes the dissemination and updating of knowledge about occupational social work. Some of the occupational social workers hold dual degrees in social work and psychology. They may belong to an industrial psychology association, from which they draw and update knowledge in the field (Uri, 1988).

Characteristics of occupational social workers in the workplace. Occupational social workers in work organizations mainly counsel employees and train supervisors in human relations skills. They usually are located in personnel departments and are not as a rule involved in the formulation of or decisions about policies. The work of the EAPs is performed mainly by non–social workers and focuses on treating alcohol and drug abuse problems (Roman, 1983; Uri, 1988).

Comparison of the Four Countries

When the four countries are compared across the three dimensions (see Figure 2), it is apparent that the Netherlands comes closest to having the ideal conditions for the effective performance of occupational social work. The societal conditions in the Netherlands support the fostering of a good quality of life in the workplace, the unions are strong, and the state provides welfare and health services. At the same time, the professional culture of occupational social work is relatively developed and the field's organizational function and position are well established and integrated in the work organization.

On the other end of the continuum are Germany and Australia. In Germany, even though unions participate in management through workers' councils, which are oriented toward improving work conditions, occupational social work plays a peripheral role in work organizations. In addition, there is little scholarly professional study, research, and systematic training in the field.

Australia has a tradition of labor-management relations that relies on bargaining and negotiations for worker's benefits. It also has almost a nationalized system of health and welfare services that, according to the thesis presented here, is an important ingredient in the development of advanced occupational social work services. However, the academic professional development of occupational social work in Australia is in its beginning stage. Occupational practice in Australian work organizations is limited and focuses mainly on counseling employees. Israel is a mixed case, but much closer to the Netherlands example, even though the professional academic position of occupational social work is not as advanced as it is in the Netherlands.

In this comparison of the development of occupational social work in the four countries, the interrelationship among societal factors and professional components is evident. Occupational social work cannot exercise an effective integrated role in Germany not because of the lack of socially provided health and welfare services, but because of the attitude against providing these services through the workplace. As a consequence of the development of a strong academic specialization in occupational social work, it may be possible to change this attitude with expert knowledge diffused through its professional authority. But the problem is that the social work profession has a low status in Germany, and its chances of reversing this situation there are not good.

The situation in Australia is different. The status of academic social work is not as low as it is in Germany, nor is there the deep resistance toward the establishment of social and human services that exists in Germany. The

Figure 2
The Characteristics of Occupational Social Work in Four Countries

CHARACTERISTICS	THE NETHERLANDS	GERMANY	ISRAEL	AUSTRALIA
Societal Characteristics				
Business and industry culture	Focus on the quality of life of employees	Focus on productivity and high standards of production	An emphasis on production and the provision of job security	Emphasis on production
Labor–management relations	Cooperation	Cooperation through worker–management councils	Cooperation	Cooperation
System of welfare and health services	A nationalized system mixed with a voluntary system	A nationalized system	Almost a nationalized system	Almost a nationalized system
Academic and Professional Characteristics				
Academic specialization and training, scholarly work	Academic specialization and some scholarly work	No academic specialization or scholarly work	No academic specialization but some scholarly work	No academic specialization; a few academic courses are offered
Professional culture	A partial professional culture	No professional culture	A partial professional culture	No professional culture
Characteristics of Occupational Social Work in the Workplace				
Defined professional domain	A defined domain	A partially defined domain	A defined domain	A partially defined domain
Integration and resource building	High degree of integration	Low degree of integration	Medium degree of integration	Low degree of integration
Service procedures	Formulation of procedures	Low degree of formulation of procedures	Formulation of procedures	Some formulation of procedures
Repertoire of interventions: counseling, policy administration, consultation	The full repertoire of interventions	Interventions focused mainly on counseling and consultation	The full repertoire of interventions	Interventions focused mainly on counseling and some consultation

relatively well established and institutionalized EAPs in Australia (Roman, 1983) promote occupational social work. Furthermore, there is a good chance that the development of solid academic specializations in occupational social work in Australian universities may advance its integration in that country's workplaces.

Implications of the Changing Workplace and Work Force

The implications of the new global economy for occupational social work have been discussed at length elsewhere (Bargal & Karger, 1991). In essence, it was argued that the significant economic and organizational transformations taking place worldwide are resulting in severe stress for millions of workers and their families. The consequences of these transformations for workplaces and the work force include the shutdown of plants, major industrial reorganization, and rapidly changing technology, causing workers' skills to become outdated quickly. Moreover, mergers and acquisitions of corporations have caused the loss of millions of jobs. Occupational dislocation and immeasurable human sorrow are the results, expressed through mounting social problems, including increased rates of mental illness and suicide (Feather & Davenport, 1981; Platt, 1984), a rise in the crime rate (Thornberry & Christensen, 1984), and the threat that the newly unemployed will become welfare clients (Briar, 1988).

The changes in the global economy affect the workplace and the work force not only in the United States, but in other industrialized countries, including those discussed in this chapter. In daily terms, they mean an emphasis on productivity, automation, and rationality. Industries require fewer workers, but each worker must have more sophisticated technological skills. The loss of job security, coupled with the pressure to learn new technological skills, may cause severe stress for workers. Those who are good candidates for retraining may find a place in the new industrial context, whereas those who are too old or who have scant human capital may lose their jobs or endure downward occupational mobility when they enter the lower-paid service sector of the secondary labor market.

In the United States, the attrition in the industrial labor force may also result in the continued decline in the power of unions as the number of workers continues to decrease with the reorganization of companies and the reduction of the unionized work force. On the other hand, a more productive industrial structure will require cooperation between labor and management. In the end, efforts to reindustrialize and economic changes in most advanced countries will require cooperation among governments, labor unions and corporations.

Mediating Change

Occupational social work may play an important role in mediating the impact of these significant changes. However, the traditional role of providing services to employees in the workplace that has been the concern of EAPs (Googins, 1975; Googins & Godfrey, 1987) may prove insufficient to deal with them. Therefore, occupational social workers may also need to emphasize advocacy and policy-initiation skills in addition to counseling employees and consulting with management (Akabas & Kurzman, 1982; Gould & Smith, 1988). Such an approach may be adopted more effectively in countries like the Netherlands and Israel that have strong welfare states than in the United States, where free-market forces are in effect.

Widespread reindustrialization, privatization, and the reorganization of industries, which will result in the layoff of many workers, will be encountered more smoothly in such countries as the Netherlands, Germany, Australia, and Israel, where long-term unemployment compensation and health insurance are provided by the state and mandated by law. Employees who will suffer the most from the economic–industrial fluctuations may benefit from representation by and the strong negotiating power of unions that can bargain to obtain retraining in appropriate educational or technological skills to enable laid-off employees to get new jobs. Again, in the Netherlands and Israel, as well as in Germany and Australia, the unions' central role as a counterforce to management may facilitate a smoother reindustrialization than in the United States.

Elsewhere (Bargal & Karger, 1991) this author presented a comprehensive framework and a repertoire of interventions for occupational social workers in the United States to deal with the rapid changes in the workplace and the work force that will accompany the new economic order. According to the framework, there are three targets of intervention by occupational social workers: the society (including federal and state authorities), the community, and the work organization. The modes of intervention for occupational social workers include advocacy and the initiation of policy, consultation, and counseling.

New Areas of Practice

In periods of rapid economic change, social workers should refocus their *counseling* efforts to help workers in three main areas: (1) working through the trauma of job loss and disengaging themselves from their lost occupational identities, (2) preparing for retraining, and (3) developing alternative life plans. They should also engage in *consultation*, contribute their knowledge and services at the federal or state level, working, for example, with an industrial-adjustment service (Batt, 1983), as well as at the community and the work-organization levels. At the community level, occupational social workers should consult with social service and mental health agencies to develop outreach programs and with unions and community leaders to create new forms of help for the unemployed. Within the work organization, they may consult representatives of unions and the management regarding the consequences of layoffs for individuals and families.

Advocacy and the initiation of policy are the most important roles that occupational social workers can play in confronting reindustrialization and similar inevitable changes in the work force. At the work-organization level these roles will involve helping to formulate criteria to be used in the layoff of industrial workers. At the community and societal levels, even more can be done. Communities can mobilize resources to revitalize areas that are struck by high unemployment. States can establish legislation and programs to mitigate the impact of plant closings that require management to notify employees in advance about such closings, as well as support for laid-off employees through the provision of counseling services and extended health benefits. Briar (1988) recommended that an organized professional lobby group be formed to pressure the U.S. government to deal with the issues of unemployment.

Need for Greater Professionalization

To perform effectively under new economic and industrial conditions, occupational social workers will have to be prepared in a much more thorough professional way and to gain power and influence in their work organizations. According to the professional-organizational framework presented here, students in all the countries discussed receive only partial training to prepare them for careers in occupational social work practice, and the professional cultures and scholarly work in the field are only in their beginning phases in most of the four countries discussed.

Furthermore, to serve in the capacities that were specified, especially consultation, advocacy, and the initiation of policy, occupational social workers must strengthen their position in work organizations so that it is central and well integrated. Such a situation is present only in the Netherlands, where there is a considerable degree of correspondence between societal commitments to the health and welfare needs of employees, strong labor unions, and a professionally prepared cohort of occupational social workers.

The situation in the United States is different. Even though the professionalization of occupational social work is more advanced than in other countries in the world, it is still in an initial stage of development, and few schools of social work offer a specialization in occupational social work. In addition, few articles on the subject appear in professional social work journals, and no journal that specializes in this field exists. Furthermore, there is no professional culture that sponsors research, conducts conferences, and promotes systematic scholarly work. The position of occupational social workers in work organizations is often peripheral to the main thrust of the organizations, and occupational social workers frequently are not integrated into the power structure of the workplace or able to build political and personal resources on which to draw (Googins & Godfrey, 1987).

Societal conditions in the United States do not make occupational social workers' activities easy. Under conditions of a highly competitive economic market and weak unions, occupational social workers may have a hard time adapting to the new economic order. However, the recent changes in the work force and in workplaces are an important opportunity for them to play a significant role in the reindustrialization of American industry. Occupational social workers worldwide are in an excellent position to effect change because of their proximity to both management and workers. For them to be able to shape the new industrial reality and to lower the human cost of economic change, they will have to improve their professional training, develop a more scholarly culture, and gain an integrated and influential position in new workplaces that are emerging in the postindustrial society.

References

Akabas S. H., & Kurzman, P. A. (Eds.). (1982). *Work, workers, and work organizations: A view from social work.* Englewood Cliffs, NJ: Prentice Hall.

Balgopal, P. R. (1989). Establishing employee assistance programs: A cross-cultural perspective. *Employee Assistance Quarterly, 5*(2), 1–20.

Bargal, D. (1984). *Social work in the world of work* [in Hebrew]. Jerusalem: Israeli Association of Schools of Social Work & Jewish Distribution Committee.

Bargal, D. (1988a). Occupational social work: Report based on participants' papers and group discussions. *Eurosocial Reports, 31*, 5–20.

Bargal, D. (1988b). A summary of discussion and implications for future development of occupational social work. *Eurosocial Newsletter, 49/50*, 9–16.

Bargal, D., & Karger, H. (1991). Occupational social work and the new global economy. *Administration in Social Work, 15*, 95–109.

Bargal, D., & Shamir, B. (1984). Job description of occupational welfare: A tool in role development. *Administration in Social Work, 8*, 59–71.

Batt, W. (1983). Canada's good example with displaced workers. *Harvard Business Review, 61*(4), 6–12, 20–22.

Bilik, S. (1988). EAPs in Germany: Options for transatlantic exchange. *Employee Assistance Quarterly, 3*(2), 83–97.

Bobbink, A., Mensinga, G., & Uri, J. (1988). Occupational social work in the Netherlands. *Eurosocial Reports, 31*, 49–60.

Briar, K. H. (1988). *Social work and the unemployed.* Silver Spring, MD: National Association of Social Workers.

Feather, N. T., & Davenport, P. R. (1981). Unemployment and depressive affect: A motivational and attributional analysis. *Journal of Personality and Social Psychology, 41,* 422–436.

Googins, B. (1975). Employee assistance programs. *Social Work, 20,* 464–475.

Googins, B., & Godfrey, J. (1987). *Occupational social work.* Englewood Cliffs, NJ: Prentice Hall.

Gould, G. M., & Smith, M. L. (Eds.). (1988). *Social work in the workplace: Practice and principles.* New York: Springer.

Kramer, R. (1981). *Voluntary agencies in the welfare state.* Berkeley: University of California Press.

Neikrug, S., & Katan, J. (1981). Social work in the world of work: Israel and the United States. *Journal of Applied Social Science, 5*(2), 47–65.

Ozawa, M. (1980). Development of social services in industry: Why and how? *Social Work, 25,* 464–470.

Platt, S. (1984). Unemployment and suicidal behavior: A review of the literature. *Social Science and Medicine, 19,* 93–115.

Roman, P. (1983). Employee assistance programs in Australia and the United States: Comparisons of origin, structure and the role of behavioral science research. *Journal of Applied Behavioral Science, 19,* 367–379.

Sarfatti-Larson, M. S. (1977). *The rise of professionalism: A sociological analysis.* Berkeley: University of California Press.

Shamir, B., & Bargal, D. (1983) Domains of work and methods of work of occupational welfare officers: An exploratory study of an emerging role. *Journal of Social Work Research, 5*(3–4), 51–70.

Thornberry, T. P., & Christensen, R. L. (1984). Unemployment and criminal involvement. *American Sociological Review, 49,* 398–411.

United Nations Department of Economic and Social Affairs. (1971). *Industrial social welfare.* New York: Author.

Uri, J. (1988). Similarities and differences in occupational social work: An analysis of the papers received from the participants. *Eurosocial Reports, 31,* 21–48.

Vollmer, H. M., & Mills, D. L., (Eds.). (1966). *Professionalization.* Englewood Cliffs, NJ: Prentice Hall.

Conclusions

A FUTURIST VIEW

Paul A. Kurzman

As the chapters in this book have noted in different ways, today's workplace does not resemble yesterday's workplace, either in clear or subtle ways. The changes have been both rapid and dramatic, and nothing that is known today suggests that such changes will cease or slacken in the decade ahead. Even the existence of a workplace per se can no longer be taken for granted. Not only have the factories, smokestack industries, and manufacturing plants of the 1980s been transformed (if not displaced) as prototypical work sites, but the nature of work itself barely resembles what Americans have known and taken for granted.

In this expanding information, communication, and service economy, workers today do not necessarily need to be assembled at sites to work together. Cellular mobile telephones, complete with call forwarding and teleconferencing, can link with supervisors' voice-mail systems to provide remote-access paging options. Workers at home or in transit can use palm-size personal computers to communicate by modem to their central offices. Building on the achievements of modern fiber optics, Bell Communications, moreover, now is using an eight-foot-high video window to conduct weekly staff meetings for colleagues who actually assemble at headquarters only twice a year. With a near life-size image and high-quality audio, the video window makes it seem like the staff are in the same room. Furthermore, wireless data systems are making it possible for employers to extend their internal computer systems to employees who may be on the road in distant cities. This linkage can be supported by connecting electronic mail services to mobile data networks through high-speed dedicated telephone lines. A reenactment of the *Wizard of Oz*? No, just the world of work in the 1990s.

Experts estimate that about 5 million people now work at home or in small satellite offices that are electronically linked with traditional work sites, and this number is expected to triple by the year 2005 (Perez-Peña, 1992, p. A-10). Hence, one now must talk not only of flextime, but of "flexplace" work. Supervisors may not always be physically present at an employee's workplace, and the camaraderie and informal social supports that are a latent function and benefit of the workplace may no longer exist.

As the workplace is changing, so, too, are workers and the work itself. Unlike 25 years ago, in more than 85 percent of American households today either *both* parents work or a *single* parent supports the family (Roberts, 1991). For the first time in history, moreover, the white male worker is in the minority—a trend that will accelerate in the years ahead. Indeed, only 35 years ago, the average worker was a white male breadwinner, motivated by job security, good benefits, and steady pay. The average current worker is just as likely to be a female person of color, working on a part-time or contingent-work basis, or a single-parent or working spouse, with low wages, little job security, and only a handful of legally mandated benefits. Downsizing, deregulation, a shift toward lower-paying industries, a weakened minimum wage, and the declining power of unions have had an impact on the jobs that are currently available to them. As an example, the U.S. Bureau of the Census recently reported that the proportion of full-time workers in the United States who are paid low wages (defined as less than $12,000 a year) nearly *doubled* during the decade of the 1980s ("Low-Wage Jobs," 1992).

Unfortunately, at a time when the workplace is presenting more uncertainty for its participants, the larger society has fewer systems of sustenance for working people. In many working families, for example, there may be no consistent systems of support, predictable (and symbiotic) roles and functions, or opportunities for self-sufficiency. Thus, these maxims of the past are no longer safe presumptions today. The family is an increasingly fragile unit. Today's nuclear families have replaced the informal support systems that existed before through extended family networks. Two parents often are working to bring home the wages and benefits that one brought home in the past. Union membership has become the *exception* (not present for 84 percent of the work force) (Kilborn, 1993). Underemployment and contingent employment have become common, and jobs, and even industries, have become less stable. Indeed, these have been the documented messages and realities described throughout this book.

A Social Work Function

Despite the changing workplace and the changing nature of work itself, individuals and families continue to depend on work and the workplace even more than before because other social systems—such as the church, school,

political club, ethnic organization, and local community—may be functioning less extensively or effectively than in the past. Therefore, the challenge
to occupational social work may be conceptualized as resulting from the need
to respond at the workplace to some of the unmet needs of workers and their
families. Providing social services, influencing policies on human resources,
and moving toward the individual (and collective) empowerment of workers
and work organizations are roles that are compatible with both the profession's
ideology and expertise.

Such goals seem harmonious as well with the needs of employing organizations. Bell (1973) noted that in this postindustrial society, economic enterprises,
if they are to flourish, will have to pay more attention to their "sociologizing"
(human welfare) functions than to their "economizing" (profit-making) functions. Occupational social workers are seen in this book as having a role in
performing many of these "sociologizing" functions, which may prove to be just
as critical to a managerial goal of "maximizing the market share" as are the tasks
that economists perform. In addition, organizational sanction to perform these
functions may give occupational social workers the opportunity to provide
services *and* to become proponents of progressive social change. This latent
component of occupational social workers' roles in work settings should be
made manifest and explicit. To wit, occupational social workers need to use
their presence as an occasion to advocate "subdominant values" that focus on
distributive justice (Patti, 1982; Rawls, 1971). The values that the social work
profession espouses—due process, pluralism, and social justice—tend not to
dominate in a capitalist economic system that esteems efficiency, cultural
homogeneity, and material success. This subdominant value set, however,
may inform employing organizations' decisions about human resources and
their allocation of material resources if occupational practitioners accept this
notion and seize the opportunity.

With the marked decline in union membership and the concomitant wane
of the contervailing power of the labor movement in the United States, few
forces are present to look at the workplace from a *worker's* viewpoint. As Mills
(1959, p. 264) noted in his study of labor leaders in 1948, and reaffirmed in
his later work, "the power of the business leader is likely to be more
continuous and more assured than that of the labor leader." Although great
captains of labor, such as Samuel Gompers and Sidney Hillman, may have
enjoyed political access to the highest levels of government and to power well
beyond the confines of their own constituencies, such is not the case today.
Trade union leaders, Mills concluded, "are pretty well set up as a dependent
variable in the main drift with no role in the power elite" (p. 265).

The ability of occupational social workers to be effective in the realm of
social service *and* social change, however, presumes their sophistication

about systems. In Lewin's (1951) terms, practitioners will need to be able to assess the field of forces in the world of work and to make astute forced-field analyses of the respective "driving" and "retraining" forces. By reducing or containing the restraining forces and strengthening the driving forces, they can generate a climate to permit change. As new human services functions and innovative programs are mounted, appropriate structures will be put in place once the initiatives are found to be of ongoing value to work organizations. For example, employers may establish progressive new human resource programs (which will become stable program functions) if there is (1) a shortage of skilled workers, (2) a need to match programs offered by their competitors, (3) a perceived community or consumer relations advantage, or (4) an obligation to comply with state and federal regulations. These driving forces often give birth to labor and managerial social programs that professional social workers will staff in the areas of substance abuse, stress management, relocation, dependent care, preretirement planning, affirmative action, corporate philanthropy, disability management, and employee assistance. Such benefits, or "new property," in Reich's (1966) terms, are the best (and often the only) family-protection plans available to Americans under conditions they can afford. These initiatives, as has been shown, are also "good business" in a competitive environment. Such is the contribution that this book has highlighted as being made every day by occupational social workers, here and abroad.

To the Future

If it is conceptualized broadly so as not to be tied to wages and salary—an understandable preoccupation in a society that focuses on the accumulation and distribution of capital—then work has a broader meaning. Work would include what we do when we volunteer (through a church or synagogue, a firehouse, the PTA, or a civic association) and what we do to maintain a family—those unpopular and unglamorous tasks we call "housework." These functions, after all, are *work*, the sole difference being that they do not precipitate pay directly by an employing organization. However, because the government has not provided non-means-tested programs, allowances, and benefits (universal health care, old age pensions, children's allowances, and day care) that are necessary to sustain strong and healthy family life, employment is a practical necessity for virtually all. Hence, this book has spoken not so much of the *glory* of work as of the *significance* of paid work in this country. Moreover, given the role of reciprocity that several authors have noted, the editors observe that the workplace is a community and that work itself performs nonmonetary functions. In the mixing and melding of work and family, one can, in fact, cite caregiving in the world of work and market values in the home.

In this spirit, this is not just a book on workplace services and EAPs; it is about the significance of work organizations in the lives of occupational social workers' clients. The notion is that occupational social workers can improve the human condition of workers and their families, at and beyond the workplace. Furthermore, the task of providing these services and promoting progressive change is not a lay job anymore. One cannot use the notion of "human resource programs" as a metaphor for compassion and goodwill in the workplace. The tasks to be performed require expert knowledge, skills, and professional values. This book claims that social work's ecological focus, sensitivity to systems, and work–family perspective are congruent with the ambience of the modern workplace, the needs of work organizations, and the expertise of the social work profession.

The decade of the 1980s may become known as a period when social workers "discovered" the workplace, when they came to realize that it is where so many of their clients are and, therefore, where they need to be. As we approach the year 2000, the profession now has the opportunity to demonstrate its occupational expertise and to make a permanent commitment to workers and to work organizations. A goal of this book is to move that agenda forward.

References

Bell, D. (1973). *The coming of post-industrial society: A venture in social forecasting.* New York: Basic Books.

Kilborn, P. T. (1993, February 15). Encouraged but still wary, union leaders gather. *New York Times*, p. B-1.

Lewin, K. (1951). *Field theory in social science.* New York: Harper & Row.

Low-wage jobs doubled in the 1980s. (1992, July 24–30). *Washington Report, 32*(18), 2.

Mills, C. W. (1959). *The power elite.* New York: Oxford University Press.

Patti, R. J. (1982). Applying business management strategies in social agencies: Prospects and limitations. In S. H. Akabas & P. A. Kurzman (Eds.), *Work, workers, and work organizations: A view from social work* (pp. 147–175). Englewood Cliffs, NJ: Prentice Hall.

Perez-Peña, R. (1992, January 7). For traffic weary workers, an office that's a long way from the office. *New York Times*, p. A-10.

Rawls, J. (1971). *A theory of justice.* Cambridge, MA: Harvard University Press.

Reich, J. (1966). The new property. *Public Interest, 3*, 57–89.

Roberts, M. W. (1991, August 30). What's Bush's problem with family leave? *New York Times*, p. A-10.

Index

The Editors

Paul A. Kurzman, PhD, ACSW, is professor, Hunter College School of Social Work, City University of New York, where he chairs the school's World of Work Field of Practice. He is the author of "Industrial–Occupational Social Work" in the 18th edition of the *Encyclopedia of Social Work* (1987) and numerous articles on occupational policy and practice in *Social Work, Social Casework,* and *Employee Assistance Quarterly*. He is also an editor or author of five books, including (with Sheila H. Akabas) *Labor and Industrial Settings: Sites for Social Work Practice* (1979) and *Work, Workers, and Work Organizations* (1982).

Sheila H. Akabas, PhD, is professor and chair of the World of Work Field of Practice, School of Social Work, and director, Center for Social Policy and Practice in the Workplace, Columbia University, New York. Principal investigator on numerous projects funded by the National Institute of Mental Health, National Institute of Disability and Rehabilitation Research, and other governmental agencies and several private foundations, she has also provided consultation to corporations; trade unions; social, rehabilitation, and mental health facilities; and educational institutions on the many issues involved in service delivery to workers.

The Contributors

Patricia Abelson, MSW, founded Corporate Health Systems/Employee Counseling Programs (CHS/ECP), a New York based external employee assistance and mental health managed care firm, in 1980 and has been the executive director since that time. Ms. Abelson is currently serving on the board of directors of the Employee Assistance Partnership of Greater New York, Inc. and is a member of its quality assurance committee.

Adrienne Asch, PhD, is associate professor, School of Social Work, Boston University, having earlier worked in the fields of civil rights and bioethics. In 1993, she was a member of the Working Group on Ethical Foundation of the New System of the Nation's Task Force on Health Care Reform.

Jerry Atkin, Dip.Ed., is a teacher and writer living in Portland, Oregon. He was one of the founding members of the Center for Working Life, Oakland, California, where he currently serves as director of materials development.

David Bargal, PhD, is associate professor at the School of Social Work at the Hebrew University of Jerusalem. He is the author of *Social Work in Industry* (in Hebrew) as well as many published articles and book chapters on occupational social work, intergroup relations, and the management of human resources in service organizations.

Frederica Barrow, MSW, ACSW, CEAP, is associate chief medical director for evaluation and development, Office of Disability, Social Security Administration, U.S. Department of Health and Human Services, Baltimore,

Maryland. She has an extensive background in mental health, family and addictive services, and management in the private and public sectors.

Maria DeOca Corwin, PhD, ACSW, is assistant professor, Graduate School of Social Work and Social Research, Bryn Mawr College, Bryn Mawr, Pennsylvania. She is on the editorial board of *Social Work*, has presented papers on time-limited intervention and cross-cultural practice, and has worked in the fields of family and children's services, employee assistance, and mental health.

Beth Grube Farrell, MSW, ACSW, is currently assistant dean of the Fordham University Graduate School of Social Service and director of its satellite campus in Tarrytown, New York. Prior to her appointment at Fordham, Ms. Grube Farrell was associate director of The Workplace Center at Columbia University School of Social Work, where she is pursuing doctoral studies. While at the Center she was involved in a variety of education, training, research, and consultation efforts to support workplace gender integration, disability management, and coalition building.

Alison Favorini, PhD, is associate professor, occupational concentration, Wayne State University School of Social Work, Detroit, Michigan. She has conducted research on substance use and abuse and organizational–occupational issues and has been a consultant and author of articles in the areas of substance abuse prevention, families and addiction, and employee assistance programs.

Lauren B. Gates, PhD, is director of research, Center for Social Policy and Practice in the Workplace, Columbia University School of Social Work, New York. She has been investigating issues related to job maintenance and advancement for the past seven years; her earlier work focused on neighborhood planning and the effect of perceptions of crime on the revitalization of neighborhoods.

Bradley K. Googins, PhD, is associate professor, School of Social Work, Boston University, and director of the university's Center on Work and Family. He is the author of several books and monographs, along with many articles on work–family issues, employee assistance, and workplace drug and alcohol programs.

Gary M. Gould, PhD, is president, Canadian Center for Social Justice (a think tank and social advocacy and change organization). He is on the faculty of Nipissing University, North Bay, Ontario, Canada and serves on behalf of the Trillium Foundation. He was chair of the NASW Employment and Economic Support Commission and has been director of several boards.

Muriel Gray, PhD, LCSW, is assistant professor, School of Social Work, University of Maryland at Baltimore, where she teaches courses in substance abuse and employee assistance programs. Her research interests include relapse prevention, differential treatment, and case management. She is also a certified alcohol and drug abuse counselor and a certified EAP professional.

Meredith Hanson, DSW, is assistant professor, School of Social Work, Columbia University, New York. He has been engaged in social work practice with substance abusers for over 20 years. His practice and scholarly interests include occupational social work, organizationally based social work, and work with dually diagnosed adults who experience substance abuse and mental disorders.

Jesse J. Harris, DSW, ACSW, is dean and professor, School of Social Work, University of Maryland at Baltimore. He served in the U.S. Army for 30 years and retired in the rank of colonel in the Medical Service Corps. His professional practice experience has included being social work consultant to the Army Surgeon General; chief of social work service, Walter Reed Army Medical Center; special consultant to the U.S. Ambassador to Mozambique; and commander of the U.S. Medical Research Unit, Fort Bragg, North Carolina.

Jacquelyn McCroskey, DSW, is associate professor, School of Social Work, University of Southern California, Los Angeles, and director of research, Los Angeles Roundtable for Children. She is the author of numerous articles and monographs on services for families and children and was coauthor of *Employer Supported Child Care: Investing in Human Resources.*

Daniel J. Molloy, DSW, is director, Social Service Department, National Maritime Union Pension and Welfare Plan, a national member assistance program with discrete social services, chemical dependence, and retiree components. Since 1989, he has been a senior legislative aide to the New York State Assembly Committee on Alcoholism and Drug Abuse.

Lawrence S. Root, PhD, is professor, School of Social Work, University of Michigan, Ann Arbor, and director, UAW-GM Educational Development Counseling Program. His area of specialization is the interplay between employment and social welfare. He has directed the National Older Worker Information System and was codirector of the University of Michigan's UAW-Ford Life/Education Planning Program.

Andrew E. Scharlach, PhD, is associate professor, School of Social Welfare, University of California, Berkeley, where he holds the Eugene and Rose Kleiner Chair in Aging and directs the gerontology specialization. He has published extensively on the needs of older adults and their families and is the author of *Elder Care and the Work Force: Blueprint for Action*. He is an expert on employee dependent care and consults widely on the development and evaluation of work and family programs. Dr. Scharlach also is a diplomate in clinical social work and a fellow of the Gerontological Society of America.

Lee Schore, MSW, LCSW, founded the Center for Working Life, a nonprofit organization in Oakland, California, that provides innovative education, training, and mental health services to workers and their families. She is a diplomate in clinical social work and has served on the NASW Commission for Employment and Economic Security.

Barbara Levy Simon, PhD, is associate professor, School of Social Work, Columbia University, New York. She is the author of *Never Married Women* (1987) and *The Empowerment Tradition in American Social Work: A History* (to be published in 1994). She specializes in issues involving caregiving, empowerment, and women and work.

Michael Lane Smith, PhD, is associate professor, Walter Richter Institute of Social Work, Southwest Texas University, San Marcos. A certified social worker and advanced clinical practitioner, he was formerly a social work officer in the U.S. Air Force. He is co-editor (with Gary M. Gould) of *Social Work in the Workplace: Practice and Principles*.

Kurt Spitzer, MSW, ACSW, professor emeritus, Wayne State University School of Social Work, Detroit, Michigan, developed the school's occupational social work curriculum. He is engaged in research on the scope of external employee assistance programs and the needs of work force populations in small businesses. He is co-author of publications on problem-focused practice, which integrates problem-solving and systemic practice approaches.

Cynthia Stuen, DSW, is vice president for education and training, The Lighthouse, and director of the Lighthouse's National Center for Vision and

Aging. She is a fellow of the Gerontological Society of America, a member of the editorial board of *The Gerontologist*, and a member of the board of the American Society on Aging.

Florence Wexler Vigilante, DSW, ACSW, is professor, Hunter College School of Social Work, City University of New York. She also is director of the Hunter College Employee Assistance Program, and co-editor of the *Journal of Teaching in Social Work.*

Barbara Drahus Worden, MSW, is director, Counseling Center for Families and Women, Fairfield, Connecticut, and is a doctoral candidate in social welfare at Columbia University. She has over 20 years of clinical experience in the field and is currently engaged in research on the utilization of knowledge in social work practice.